Freedom and Fulfillment

————————————————

Freedom and Fulfillment

PHILOSOPHICAL ESSAYS

Joel Feinberg

PRINCETON UNIVERSITY PRESS

PRINCETON, NEW JERSEY

Copyright © 1992 by Princeton University Press
Published by Princeton University Press, 41 William Street,
Princeton, New Jersey 08540
In the United Kingdom: Princeton University Press, Oxford

Library of Congress Cataloging-in-Publication Data

Feinberg, Joel, 1926–
Freedom and fulfillment : philosophical essays /
Joel Feinberg.
p. cm.
Includes index.
1. Ethics. 2. Social ethics. I. Title.
BJ1012.F42 1992 170—dc20 91-46753

ISBN 0-691-07412-7

This book has been composed in Linotron Galliard

Princeton University Press books are printed on acid-free paper,
and meet the guidelines for permanence and durability of the
Committee on Production Guidelines for Book Longevity of the
Council on Library Resources

Printed in the United States of America
1 3 5 7 9 10 8 6 4 2

CONTENTS

PREFACE

THIS IS THE THIRD COLLECTION of my essays to be published by Princeton University Press. In 1970 the Press published *Doing and Deserving*, eleven papers written during the 1960s. A decade later, in 1980, it published *Rights, Justice, and the Bounds of Liberty*, papers produced during the 1970s. Now, slightly more than another decade later, it is publishing this collection of articles written, more or less, in the decade of the 1980s. I have been greatly pleased by this collaboration, although I must confess that the policy of decennial republication, unlike the U.S. census, cannot continue indefinitely.

This volume may at first sight seem more motley than the other two, one of which concentrated on problems about responsibility, and the other on hard cases for the application of the concept of a right. But this volume continues its predecessor's concern with problems about rights, considering at least tangentially whether a fetus can have a right not to be born (as is claimed in "wrongful life" suits); whether a woman's reproductive rights imply in some circumstances a right to abort her fetus; whether a child has a right against its parents not to have its own professional options foreclosed by a restrictive education; whether a brain-dead body maintains its rights not to be experimented on so long as its arterial and respiratory systems keep working; what the limits are on a free adult citizen's right to express personal opinions; whether there are moral rights of the innocently imperiled to easy rescue by strangers, and of others citizens to make deliberate and conscientious protests against government policy, symbolically expressed by disobedience to the law. Finally, at the opposite end of the human life cycle from that at which we began, there are two recent essays on the problem of interpreting and evaluating the claim that suffering terminal patients and irrevocably comatose patients have a "right to die." These and similar problems induce in their several ways perplexity about the very concept of a moral right (as opposed to a legal or other conventional right). In three recent lectures, I have addressed three forms of skepticism about moral rights: doubts about their very existence, doubts about their value or importance, and doubts about their constitutional relevance. The final two essays included in this volume mark a transition to the quite different set of concepts that will be the object of my growing attention in the 1990s: absurdity, self-fulfillment, and "the literary criticism of cosmic attitudes."

I wrote "Wrongful Life and the Counterfactual Element in Harming" in a fit of despair over the inadequacies of my treatment of the problem of "prenatal harm" in my *Harm to Others* (New York: Oxford University Press, 1984), pp. 95–104. One can never rest completely satisfied with one's printed views on such difficult matters, but I am convinced that this long and complex paper is a big improvement over the earlier study. Fortunately, there are some advantages in writing a tetralogy (*Harm to Others* was volume 1 of a four-volume work published over a five-year period). In this case I was able to incorporate some of the improved material—not, of course, in the volume that had already been published—but in volume 4, then still in progress! (See *Harmless Wrongdoing* [New York: Oxford University Press, 1988], pp. 27–33, 325–28.)

The article on abortion is one of only two selections in this volume that were written originally for beginning students. Tom Regan asked me to write from scratch a new article on the subject to go in a collection of original articles he was editing to be entitled *Matters of Life and Death*. The anthology, now in its third edition, also includes articles (by others) on euthanasia, suicide, killing in war, capital punishment, infanticide, nonrelief of famine sufferers, and killing animals. Like all the other authors, I was free to express and defend my own views. I did not conceal my prochoice inclinations, but I did not flaunt them either, and in several places rejected arguments frequently used in the prochoice movement. (My position is that abortion should be legally permissible not because it is a kind of justified homicide, but rather because—and *only* because—it should be treated as no kind of homicide at all.) My pedagogic mission, as I saw it, was not to lead the student-reader about by the nose to the Truth as I see it, but to give structure to the debate by locating crucial but implicit presuppositions, centrally affected interests, critical distinctions, and so on. I wanted to line up the critical arguments and counterarguments on both sides, expose hidden difficulties, and align the strengths and weaknesses of opposed positions, thereby showing the student how sensible and useful philosophical discussions are, especially when compared with the shrill sloganeering and propagandistic rhetoric one encounters in the political forum and in "letters to the editor" columns of newspapers. My main regret over this article is that because I tried to penetrate deeply, I had no remaining space, so I was forced to leave unmentioned whole areas of controversy, including some vitally important ones.

The article on "The Child's Right to an Open Future" was also solicited by a philosopher (Hugh LaFollette) who was editing an anthology of original articles on a specific topic, in his case, "children's rights." I chose to write about a category of rights that children have "in trust," that is, until they are old enough, or competent enough, to exercise them. Frequently rights in this category come into conflict with the undeniable rights of adults to exercise their rights, typically but not universally their right to the free exercise of religion. Here I think of my position, giving priority to the rights in trust, as the radical, prochild stand. But to my astonishment, when I presented this paper orally to a Canadian conference on children's rights at Carleton University in Ottawa, my commentator, himself a crusading activist for children, accused me of being an "adultist," a term he modeled after "racist," "sexist," "speciesist," and "ageist" and applied to those who wrongfully discriminate against children. He reacted in that way apparently because of my view that a child's rights in trust must be held in reserve for exercise by "the adult he will one day become." In reply, I had occasion to tell of a similar epithet invented for application to my views by a commentator who was a crusading activist, in this case an ardent campaigner for environmentalism—a cause I surely share. He called me a "kingdomist" because in denying that the concept of a right can be meaningfully applied to vegetables, I was discriminating against a whole biological kingdom—a position more comprehensively perverse than mere speciesism. I am perhaps the only "adultistic kingdomist" in captivity!

The selection entitled "Sentiment and Sentimentality in Practical Ethics" was the presidential address at the 1982 convention of the Pacific Division of the American Philosophical Association in Sacramento, California. Its appearance too proved timely for my purposes in writing the tetralogy, and I included some of it in chapter 9 (pp. 72–85) of my *Offense to Others* (New York: Oxford University Press, 1985). Part of my thesis in this essay is that one must give sentiment a prominent role in one's understanding of what goes on in the discussions of such issues as abortion, capital punishment, organ banks, the treatment of animals, and the uses of dead bodies, but that sentiments, like beliefs, *are* subject to rational criticism. Some ethical positions are based not merely on sentiment, but on corrupted or ill-adopted sentiment, and those that give priority to such sentiment over the real interests of other people are guilty of "sentimentalism."

"Limits to the Free Expression of Opinion" is the other selection (along with "Abortion") that was intended primarily to be a guide for students. I wrote it with the intention that my students read it right after reading chapter 2 of John Stuart Mill's *On Liberty*—"Of the Liberty of Thought and Discussion." My purpose was to convince them that Mill's permissiveness is not as extreme as one might otherwise think, and to focus on certain specific areas in the law where it has been traditionally assumed that freedom of expression must have its limits—defamation, incitement, sedition, and so on. This article was first published in a textbook-anthology in the philosophy of law that I co-edited with Hyman Gross in 1975, and was no doubt actually composed several years before that, so the reader of the present volume must be warned that in the twenty-year interval, roughly speaking, there have been some important changes in the law, particularly in the American civil law of defamation. I do not think that these changes seriously affect the main philosophical arguments in my 1975 article, but they do affect the impression a reader might otherwise have of the law, and should be looked into by any serious student who further pursues the policy issues at the root of the law of defamation. In particular, there likely have been some subtle but relevant changes in the types of fault that can ground liability, the relative degrees to which public officials, and public and private figures can be defamed in the first place, limits on the kinds of expressions thought to be defamatory, the requirement of actual malice for some classes of defamers, reassignments of burdens of proof with respect to truth and defamatory effect, on the one hand, and negligence or recklessness of the publisher, on the other. On the whole, the tendency of these changes has been to make it more difficult for plaintiffs in libel suits, especially for those who are public figures or officials, to succeed in their suits against publishers. Traditionally, it was up to the publisher of a reputation-damaging story to prove its truth as an "affirmative defense." But in the United States now, when defamed plaintiffs are public figures or officials, *they* must prove a story's falsity, and more than that, must also shoulder the almost impossible task of proving that the report was published out of malice with "actual knowledge" of its falsity or at least with reckless indifference to the risk that it might be false.

"Civil Disobedience in the Modern World" was my contribution to a symposium sponsored by the graduate department of classics at the University of Southern California on the issue of civil disobedience. That somewhat unlikely topic had caught the interest of the USC's classicists through the work of the distinguished scholar on Hebrew, Greek, and Roman antiquity, David Daube of the University of California, Berkeley, Law School. Daube presented a paper at the morning session entitled "Civil Disobedience in the Ancient World," and I had been asked to speak in the afternoon on "Civil Disobedience in the Modern World"—the title suggested by my hosts. The whole symposium was published in *Humanities in Society*, a journal sponsored by the University of Southern California Center for the Humanities. That journal is now defunct.

My civil disobedience article, which according to a commentator at the USC symposium, "presents a startling, even shocking thesis," is probably the least original of the articles in this collection. Philosophers of law will recognize its primary thesis and the pattern of its supporting argument as basically similar to those of Rolf Sartorius, A. John Simmons, and especially M. B. E. Smith. My justification in borrowing their arguments in this way is that I believed I could present those arguments in a much clearer and more imaginative way, and make the insights I shared with these writers more accessible to students. As a teaching tool, the article has been a great success. I do not know how many student readers, however, have come to share "the startling, even shocking thesis" that the reason why we have a moral obligation to obey the law against murder is not that the statute has been validly enacted, but rather because murder is morally wrong.

I first presented "The Moral and Legal Responsibility of the Bad Samaritan" to the 11th World Congress on Philosophy of Law and Social Philosophy in Finlandia Hall in Helsinki. The distinguished French historian of philosophy who was one of my commentators apparently found my scholarship rather careless, or perhaps excessively imaginative, because he took the trouble of informing the audience that a careful perusal of the Gospel of St. Luke reveals that no so-called bad Samaritan is even mentioned there, but only the famous Good Samaritan of the parable. To a legal philosopher in the common law tradition my thesis will seem even more "startling and shocking" than that of the civil disobedience paper that precedes it, for it argues in favor of a legal "duty of easy rescue of unrelated parties" that has been so long rejected by Anglo-American criminal and tort law. I later expanded the article to more than three times its present length and included it as chapter 4—"Failures to Prevent Harm"—in my *Harm to Others*. My justification for including the earlier version here is that it is simpler, clearer, and more direct than the longer version and more likely therefore to be accessible to students.

All of the first seven chapters in this volume can be construed as efforts to solve puzzles involving some unusual moral rights. Chapters 8, 9, and 10 are efforts to defend the very idea of a moral right from various kinds of self-described skeptics, some of whom doubt that there are such things as moral rights; others of whom doubt the social value that moral rights are said to have or which they *would* have if they existed; others of whom doubt the constitutional relevance of appeals to "unenumerated" moral rights in the U.S. Constitution. All three chapters draw heavily on my 1990 Romanell Phi Beta Kappa Lectures at the University of Arizona, my 1991 David Ross Boyd Lectures at the University of Oklahoma, and my 1991 Herbert Hart Lecture on Jurisprudence and Moral Philosophy at University College, Oxford, all of which seemed to grow in distinct directions and large profusion, from their originally similar beginnings.

A word here may be well advised about my use of the jurisprudential theories of former judge Robert H. Bork, in chapter 10, on constitutional relevance. Like many other Americans, I first began to read Bork's writings (primarily his much earlier article on "Neutral Principles and Some First Amendment Problems" in the *Indiana Law Journal* [1971], and his Frances Boyer Lecture, "Tradition and Morality in Constitutional Law" [1984]) during the intense debate over Bork's nomination to the U.S. Supreme Court in 1987. Bork's chief work, containing the most finished statement of his jurisprudential theory and his passionate *apologia*, *The Tempting of America*, had not yet been published, and my own lecture was completed before I was able to see it. Some of the views that outraged his fiercest critics earlier have by now been withdrawn or toned down (though irenic moderation is not exactly the distinctive tone of what remains). But I should make it immediately clear that my concern with Bork's convictions and his career has nothing to do with determining his fitness for the Supreme Court. I am not interested here in determining the significance for his nomination of some of his wilder arguments in the earlier Indiana journal article, or in determining how thoroughly he has changed them. Bork is a fascinating specimen of a writer who rejects the whole idea of moral rights. This rejection and the larger moral skepticism that give it birth are central to Bork's whole approach to constitutional interpretation, and provide the whole justification for my interest in, and criticism of, some of his views. If my criticisms are right, then Bork's relativistic moral philosophy is his jurisprudential Achilles' heel.

Over the two academic years, 1989–1990 and 1990–1991, the department of criminal law of the University of Trento, Italy, sponsored a series of lectures and discussions under the general theme "Vivere: diritto o dovere?" (To go on living: A right or a duty?). I was invited to give a lecture under this heading in January 1991. My wife and I were treated with extraordinary warmth and kindness by the criminal law faculty in this new university in an old and beautiful town in North Italy. We are grateful especially to Alberto Cadoppi and Luigi Stortoni. I spoke on what I called "the argument from abusable discretion" against legalizing voluntary euthanasia. This argument, which I found a way to argue against, is especially interesting in that it permits its spokesperson to admit that in a given case euthanasia can be wholly justified morally when we treat that case only on its own merits, but at the same time it gives overriding strength to reasons extraneous to the case at hand, namely, the possibility of mistakes or abuses in other cases. I acknowledge that arguments of this general kind in practical ethics can be highly cogent, but I argue that euthanasia has special features that weaken the argument when applied to it. In chapter 12, I discover seven arguments of this general type (including the argument from abusable discretion) which are worthy of respect generally, but which fail nevertheless to make the case against legalized euthanasia.

"Absurd Self-Fulfillment" is an expanded version of an article published in 1980 in a festschrift for Richard Taylor. It was Taylor who first suggested to me a revision of the Sisyphus legend in which the gods "wax perversely merciful" by remaking Sisyphus's nature in such a way that his ridiculously absurd life nevertheless fulfills that nature. The expanded version of my paper printed here draws from an unfinished manuscript that, like Sisyphus's chores too, appears uncompletable. But it too promises considerably self-fulfilling labors throughout the 1990s. It is from this manuscript that I drew the concluding chapter in this volume: "The Absurd and the Comic: Why Does Some Incongruity Please?" The main reason why I selected *that* particular chapter of the manuscript to conclude *this* volume can be simply stated. I wanted to lighten up this collection which began after all with an examination of the view that some prospective lives may not be worth living, staggered through the labyrinths of the abortion debate, considered the plight of children whose fulfillment as adults has been squelched by their narrow education and upbringing, surveyed the varieties of harm that can be caused to others by irresponsible speech, and concluded by visiting the hospital wards of suffering and comatose terminal patients. By that point the reader deserves some laughter—or at least philosophical speculation about laughter, which may or may not itself be amusing.

J. F.
Tucson, Arizona
August 1991

ACKNOWLEDGMENTS

1. "Wrongful Life and the Counterfactual Element in Harming" was presented at the conference on Philosophy and Law held at the University of Michigan Law School in the spring of 1986. The conference was sponsored by the Social Philosophy and Policy Center of Bowling Green State University, Bowling Green, Ohio. The papers presented at the conference were all published in *Social Philosophy & Policy* 4/1 (Autumn 1986). This article was subsequently awarded the first biennial Fred Berger Memorial Prize for the best article in the philosophy of law in the preceding two-year period (December 1988). The article is reprinted here by permission of the editor of *Social Philosophy & Policy*.

2. "Abortion" is a very slightly revised version of my contribution to *Matters of Life and Death*, 2d ed., ed. Tom Regan (New York: Random House, 1986). It is reprinted here by permission of Random House, Inc. The third edition of *Matters of Life and Death*, now being prepared, contains a substantial expansion of the original article into problem areas not discussed originally. Writing on these new topics is the work of a newly appointed co-author, Barbara Levenbook.

3. "The Child's Right to an Open Future" was published in *Whose Child? Children's Rights, Parental Authority, and State Power*, ed. William Aiken and Hugh LaFollette (Totowa, N.J.: Rowman & Littlefield, 1980). It is reprinted by permission of Rowman & Littlefield, Inc.

4. "Sentiment and Sentimentality in Practical Ethics" was the presidential address given at the meetings of the Pacific Division of the American Philosophical Association at Sacramento, California, in 1982. It is reprinted by permission of the American Philosophical Association, Newark, Delaware.

5. "Limits to the Free Expression of Opinion" was first published in a textbook-anthology, *Philosophy of Law*, ed. Joel Feinberg and Hyman Gross (Belmont, Calif.: Wadsworth, 1975). It has also appeared in the second, third, and fourth editions. It is reprinted here by permission of the Wadsworth Publishing Company.

6. "Civil Disobedience in the Modern World" was published in *Humanities and Society* 2/1 (1979). The journal no longer exists, but the article is reprinted here by permission of the University of Southern California.

7. "The Moral and Legal Responsibility of the Bad Samaritan" was published in *Criminal Justice Ethics* 3/1 (1984). It is reprinted here by permission of the editor of *Criminal Justice Ethics*.

8. "In Defense of Moral Rights: Their Bare Existence" is scheduled to

appear under the title "In Defence of Moral Rights" in the *Oxford Journal of Legal Studies* (Spring 1992). It is reprinted here by permission of the general editor of the *Oxford Journal of Legal Studies*.

9. "In Defense of Moral Rights: Their Social Importance" is scheduled to appear under the title "The Social Importance of Moral Rights" in *Philosophical Perspectives*, volume 6, *Ethics*, ed. James E. Tomberlin (Spring 1992). The article is published here by agreement with James E. Tomberlin.

10. "In Defense of Moral Rights: Their Constitutional Relevance" has not been previously published.

11. "An Unpromising Approach to the 'Right to Die' " was published in *Ratio Juris* (July 1991). Permission to reprint it here was granted by the editor of *Ratio Juris* and Basil Blackwell, Publisher.

12. "Seven Modes of Reasoning That Can Justify Overlooking the Merits of the Individual Case—When the Facts Are Right" has not been previously published.

13. "Absurd Self-Fulfillment" appeared in *Time and Cause*, ed. Peter van Inwagen (Dordrecht: Reidel, 1980). It is reprinted here by permission of the Reidel Publishing Company (now Kluwer Academic Publishers).

14. "The Absurd and the Comic: Why Does Some Incongruity Please?" has not been previously published.

I would like to take this opportunity to thank Ann Himmelberger Wald of Princeton University Press for her enthusiastic support for the project, and Billie Comstock for efficient typing and help in assembling the manuscript.

For a variety of reasons it has become my custom to mention my former colleague, the late Josiah S. Carberry (1874–1988), in the acknowledgments for my books. As I reported at the time, Carberry died shortly before the publication of my *Harmless Wrongdoing* a few years ago. There would be no point in mentioning this matter again were it not for the fact that I have recently received a letter from Carberry in which he argues with his usual fanatic stubbornness that he is not dead! His argument, in my opinion, is weak and contrary to all the known evidence. It combines a misapplication of the Cartesian *cogito* with the kind of self-deception that characterized Carberry's long life. Some people simply cannot bear to accept the truth about themselves.

Freedom and Fulfillment

Chapter One

WRONGFUL LIFE AND THE COUNTERFACTUAL ELEMENT IN HARMING

I SHALL BE CONCERNED in this chapter with some philosophical puzzles raised by so-called wrongful life suits.[1] These legal actions are obviously of great interest to lawyers and physicians, but philosophers might have a kind of professional interest in them too, since in a remarkably large number of them, judges have complained that the issues are too abstruse for the courts and belong more properly to philosophers and theologians. The issues that elicit this judicial frustration are those that require the application to borderline cases of such philosophically interesting concepts as acting, causing, and, the one that especially interests me, harming.

I first became interested in the concept of harming in my work on the moral limits of the criminal law, where I had to come to terms with John Stuart Mill's famous "harm principle"—the principle that it is always a good reason in support of a criminal prohibition, indeed, the only legitimate reason, that it will prevent harm to persons other than the actor. I could not very well criticize that principle until I decided what the word "harm" must mean in its formulation. I gave what I took to be the requisite analysis of harm in my book *Harm to Others*.[2] Here I wish to improve that analysis, examine its implications for civil as well as criminal liability, and test it on conceptually hard cases, especially cases of prenatal harming, that is, cases in which the wrongful causative conduct occurs before the victim's birth, and the harmed state that is its upshot consists in being born in an impaired condition.

HARMING AND INTERESTS

For the purposes of the harm principle, we must think of harming as having two components: (1) it must lead to some kind of adverse effect, or create the danger of such an effect, on its victim's *interests*; and (2) it must

---

[1] Numerous paragraphs in this chapter have been taken with only small revisions from my "Comment: Wrongful Conception and the Right Not to Be Harmed," *Harvard Journal of Law and Public Policy* 8 (1985). This chapter can be considered an expansion and development of the earlier essay.

[2] Joel Feinberg, *Harm to Others* (New York: Oxford University Press, 1984).

be inflicted wrongfully in violation of the victim's *rights*. There is a broader, ordinary sense of "harm" in which that word refers to any state of adversely affected interest, whatever its cause. In that broader sense, people are often harmed by microbes, unforeseeable eruptions of nature, innocent actions of other persons, and actions of other persons to which they have freely consented. These are all examples of nonwrongful setbacks to interest, or "harms that are not wrongs" to those who suffer them. If the word "harm" as it occurs in Mill's harm principle had that broad sense, it would be quite implausible.

Similarly, just as one can be harmed (in the broad sense) without being wronged, so one can be wronged without being harmed, that is, without having one's interests adversely affected, although examples of this are harder to come by. Perhaps a wrongly broken promise that redounds by a fluke to the promisee's advantage is one kind of example. Again, I trust that no argument is needed to show that the harm principle for determining the limits of the criminal law would be implausible if its use of the word "harm" were broad enough to include such "harmless wrongs." What I concluded then was that for purposes of the harm principle, "harming" must mean adversely affecting another party's interest in a way that wrongs him or, alternatively, wronging him in a way that adversely affects his interest.

It is a necessary element in all harming, then, that it have an effect on someone's interests. The term "interests" is best left undefined here, except to say that interests are distinguishable components of a person's good or well-being. The language of interests is useful because it allows us to acknowledge the complexity of a person's good, how it contains various components, some of which may be flourishing while others languish at a given time, some of which might be advanced while others are set back by the same cause. Some interests are more basic or vital than others (I call these the "welfare interests") in the sense that when they are severely set back, no other interests in a person's interest-network can advance. Thus, the interest in having a certain minimum of food to eat, for example, is more basic or vital than the interest in being widely admired. Despite the diversity of component interests in any person's interest-network, and their different degrees of importance to one's overall good, our concepts seem to commit us to the view that interests can be summed up or integrated into one emergent personal interest. Suppose that Jones' act sets back one of Smith's interests thirty units but advances another of his interests twenty units. That would be a net loss of ten units. If interests can be related in such ways, then we can speak of offsetting benefits, and also net harms, or harms on balance, as opposed to component harms, or harms to component interests that can be offset by advancing other component interests. Thus, we speak not only of what promotes or sets back this or that particular interest of a person, but also of what promotes or sets back his self-interest as a whole, and we speak as if overall self-interest could in principle be plotted on a graph, like the profit-and-loss chart of a business corporation.

If we employ the "interest graph" as a kind of metaphorical model, it will be easy to see that there are various distinct ways of "adversely affecting" a person's self-interest:

> All of them involve a kind of directional metaphor [up or down on the interest chart]. To *set back* an interest is to reverse its course, turn it away, put it back toward the point from which it started. In terms of its associated goals, it is to reverse its progress, to put it in a worse condition than it was formerly in. To *defeat* an interest is to put it to utter rout, to set it back conclusively and irrevocably by destroying the conditions that are necessary for its advancement or fulfillment, as death for example can set back some interests once and for all. To *thwart* (or block or frustrate) an interest is to stop its progress without necessarily putting it in reverse; to successfully oppose it, and prevent it, at least for the time being, from making an advancement or improvement. To *impede* an interest is to slow its advancement without necessarily stopping or reversing it, to hinder or delay. Common to all these notions is the idea of a starting point or "baseline" from which the direction of advance or retreat is charted and measured.[3]

To complicate the picture further, the determination of harms and benefits is unavoidably affected by the prior locations, high or low, of interest states on the graph, their directions of movement at a given time, and their "momentum." If the current point of the interest curve is already near the top of the graph, then an event that has the effect of merely keeping it there has a protective or preservative influence and can be thought of as beneficial. If the point of the interest curve, however, is near the bottom of the chart, then the conduct of another that prevents it from improving can itself be harmful. When a person's situation is bad enough, simply to maintain it there when one could let it improve, may be to harm that person. Similarly, if another's conduct has the effect of only weakening upward momentum without actually stalling or reversing it, then I suppose its effect is harmful, though not seriously so, and correspondingly, to weaken an interest's downward momentum is to confer a benefit of a minor kind. What these examples show is that when we take prior condition, direction, and momentum of movement into account, an interest can be benefited without actually being advanced or promoted, and harmed without actually being thwarted or set back.

[3] Ibid., p. 53.

HARMING IN THE NORMAL POSTNATAL CASE

I shall mean by the phrase "harmful condition" a state in which a person is handicapped or impaired, a condition that has adverse effects on his whole network of interests. All states of harm, I think, are harmful conditions in this sense, but not all of them are "harmed conditions." I reserve the latter term for states of harm that are the product of a prior act of harming. In most moral-legal contexts, we are interested in states of harm only when they are also products of acts of harming. To be sure, there is a sense in which "state of harm" is the more fundamental concept, since there can be no act of harming unless a state of harm is its product, whereas we *can* have a state of harm without there being any prior act of harming as its cause. Still, more is required of an act, for most legal purposes, if it is to be considered an act of harming than that it had a state of harm as its product, else we would assimilate human acts of harming to natural events that incidentally produce harmful effects. I shall now present a rough analysis of harming in this legally relevant sense, and also, derivatively, of a special sense of "victim" that goes along with it, namely, that in which B is a victim of A when and only when A has harmed him in this full sense.

In the sense of the verb that is of interest and use to the law, A harms B if and only if:

1. A acts (in a sense wide enough to include omissions and extended sequences of activity).
2. A's action is defective or faulty with respect to the risks it creates to B, that is, it is done either with the intention of producing the consequences for B that follow, or similarly adverse ones, or with negligence or recklessness in respect to those consequences.
3. A's acting in that manner is indefensible, that is, neither excusable nor justifiable.
4. A's action is the cause of an adverse effect on B's self-interest (a "state of harm").
5. A's action is also a violation of B's right.[4]

There is in addition to these explicit requirements a further condition of great importance. This additional requirement might at first sight be thought to be implied by the terms "adverse effect" and "cause" as they are used in the fourth requirement, but we shall see that it is in truth an entirely

[4] This fifth condition might be redundant because it is implied by conditions 3 and 4. That seems plausible to me, but I make the condition explicit anyway because I cannot prove that it is implied by the others, and some might doubt that it is. I think it is implicit in the others in virtue of the principle that any adverse effect on a person's interest caused by another's unjustified and unexcused act is a violation of his right.

independent condition. We can call this requirement "the counterfactual test," for it is formulated as follows:

> 6. *B*'s personal interest is in a worse condition (usually but not always lower on the interest graph) than it would be in had *A* not acted as he did.

The subjunctive phrase—"had *A* not acted as he did"—is the counterfactual clause, for it means "*if*, contrary to fact, *A* had not acted as he did."

The counterfactual test should be distinguished from what might be called the "worsening test," which is not always required for an act of harming. The worsening test can be put as follows:

> 6X. *B*'s personal interest is in a worse condition (lower on the interest graph) than it was in before *A* acted.

The counterfactual requirement and the worsening requirement do not amount to the same thing, even though they are often satisfied together. There are numerous examples in which *B*'s condition is harmed by *A* even though it is not worsened. (We can think of worsening as putting an overall personal interest down at least one unit on the interest graph.) In these examples of harming, the counterfactual test is satisfied but the worsening test is not, for example, in cases of thwarting or impeding interest without actually setting it back, or in depriving someone of a gain without actually imposing a loss. Suppose a professional model (*B*) is wrongfully detained by *A* on the even of the Miss America contest, in which, let us suppose, she would otherwise have won a prize worth over a million dollars in subsequent engagements and opportunities. By the worsening criterion, she is not harmed because she is no worse off than before the detention, but she is much worse off than she *would have been if* she had not been detained. So by the counterfactual test, she is harmed, but judged by the worsening requirement, she is not.

Not only can one harm a person without worsening his condition; our analysis also implies that one can harm a person by behavior that actually improves his condition (on the overall interest graph). Suppose that doctor *A*, in giving patient *B* medical treatment, improves his condition but not to the extent that it would have been improved had the doctor performed up to a higher standard, as he should have. That aspect of *A*'s behavior that consists of his failure to perform up to a reasonably expected standard *did* adversely affect *B*'s interest. *A*'s subpar performance, however, was better than no performance at all, and *B*'s health is in a better condition than it would be in had *A* not acted at all. *A*'s negligence adversely affected *B*'s interest even though *B* is better off from what *A* did than he would be had *A* not been on the scene. The sixth condition in the analysis of harming supports the judgment that *A* harmed *B*, provided we interpret "as he did" to refer in part to the defective aspects of *A*'s actions. The example then shows that one can be harmed by an act that does not set back one's interest on balance, but also does not promote that interest as much as it could and should have done.[5]

CAUSAL OVERDETERMINATION
AND THE COUNTERFACTUAL CONDITION

The analysis of harming as it stands is vulnerable from another direction. In cases of causal overdetermination there can be harming that fails to satisfy the counterfactual test itself. In these cases, causing an adverse effect may not be to make a person worse off, on balance, than he would otherwise be. Suppose two schoolyard bullies both race after another child with the intention of inflicting a beating on him. One of the bullies gets to his victim a half-minute before the other, pummels him, thereby inflicting various bodily injuries, and leaves him bloodied and beaten on the ground before the other bully can arrive on the scene. But if, contrary to fact, the first bully had not acted as he did, the victim would have been no better off, at least not for long, for the second bully would then have inflicted at least as bad a beating. (Indeed, the victim may actually be better off if the first bully's beating was less severe than the beating the second bully was prepared to inflict.) According to our analysis of harming as it is thus far developed, the victim was not harmed by the first bully's beating because the bully's action fails to satisfy the counterfactual test. It is false that the "victim" (and the word must for the time being appear in quotes) is worse off than he would otherwise be, and yet common sense would attribute an act of harming to the first bully anyway. Something seems to have gone wrong.

Jurisprudential writers have long been familiar with such examples of the overdetermination of harm. Examples are legion in the literature of both torts and criminal law. A businessman in Sydney takes a taxicab to the airport with the intention of boarding a plane to Perth. On the way to the airport the reckless driving of the taxi driver causes a collision with a truck. The businessman, severely injured, is rushed in an ambulance to a hospital, and thus misses his plane. The plane, however, develops engine trouble and crashes shortly after takeoff, killing all the passengers. Questions of liability aside, did the cab driver *harm* the businessman by causing him to be injured? Common sense seems to say "yes," but our analysis of harming, with its counterfactual condition, seems to say "no," since the businessman's interest would not have been better off on balance had the cab driver driven more carefully. In fact, he would have been worse off, so

[5] So the counterfactual condition should perhaps be revised to read: *B*'s personal interest is in a worse state than it would be had *A* acted as he should have instead of as he did.

it seems, and not simply "not better off," suggesting that the cab driver's negligence actually benefited him on balance.

There is a short way with our problem. We could hold that neither the counterfactual condition nor the worsening condition is necessary for there to be an act of harming, since we can think of examples of harming that fail to satisfy one or the other of them, but that the two conditions should be combined into one disjunctive condition. Acts of harming, we might say, must satisfy conditions 1–5 and either the counterfactual condition or the worsening condition. That is a tempting solution since, while it is easy to think of harmings that do not satisfy the worsening condition (e.g., deprivations of gain), and easy to think of harmings that do not satisfy the counterfactual condition (e.g., cases of causal overdetermination), it is much more difficult to think of harmings that satisfy neither the counterfactual nor the worsening condition.

Difficult, but not impossible. Suppose that A's gang abducts B, the beauty queen, on the eve of the Miss America contest, as in the earlier example, but that if they had not done so then C's gang, in a quite independent conspiracy, would have abducted her only a few minutes later. In any case, B does not win the contest. It appears, according to the common-sense notion of harming (if there is such a thing), that A's gang harmed B, not by setting back her interest on the whole, but by having a different sort of "adverse effect," namely, preventing her from advancing her interest or depriving her of a gain. Yet neither the counterfactual nor the direct worsening test appears to be satisfied by this example. The potential Miss America is not worse off than she would have been had the abduction not occurred, for in that event she would have fallen into the clutches of C's equally resolute gang; and she is not worse off than she was before the abduction, at least not in her professional and financial interests, which in this artificial example we may suppose to be the only interests substantially affected. The abductors did not directly impose a loss on her in their effort to deprive her of a gain. If this story is a reasonably clear example of an act of harming, it shows that even our disjunctive test is not satisfied by every example of harming.

But that preliminary point leaves a great deal unsaid about the riddles of causal overdetermination. What remains inadequately explored is the possibility that the counterfactual condition is satisfied in cases of causal overdetermination, first appearances to the contrary. Let me begin a very brief probe in that direction by calling attention to three different measures of what might be called the "gravity" of an act of harming. The gravity varies, first, with the extent of the adverse effect, what we might call "the degree of adversity." Thus, two broken legs are more adverse than one, and both are less adverse than bodily paralysis or death; and deprivation of a large gain is more adverse than deprivation of a small one. Second, the gravity varies with the duration of its adverse effect on personal interest. Obviously, injuries that take six months to heal are more grave than those that take six weeks, and those with lingering aftereffects are more grave, ceteris paribus, than those that can heal completely. Third, the gravity of an act of harming varies with the extent of the period during which the interest is in a worse condition than it otherwise would be in.[6] In the playground bully example, the victim's interest is in a worse condition than it would be had the first bully not acted as he did for about a half-minute (the time it would have taken for the slower bully to get to the victim and begin *his* pummeling). The businessman's interest is in a worse condition than it would have been had the taxi driver not driven as he did, but only for about a half-hour, that is, until the plane crash. In each case, the counterfactual condition is satisfied (only in the limiting case of simultaneous causes would it not be satisfied for *any* duration), but the gravity of the act of harming in the circumstances must be discounted by the brevity of the period during which it is satisfied.

Most of our problem cases seem to have a common form. The first harmer, H_1, harms a victim, V, by putting him in a state worse than he would otherwise be in for a period t. After t, a second harmer, H_2, would have caused equal or greater harm. H_1 is V's harmer, partly in virtue of his satisfying the counterfactual condition for time t. But V's injuries linger on well beyond time t. Long after his plane has crashed the businessman is still hospitalized in a severely impaired condition, and aftereffects may linger for years. The problem is whether we should ascribe to H_1 full responsibility for the harms he initially caused even though the duration of V's harmful state extends well beyond the period during which he is worse off than he otherwise would be.

This issue is usually addressed in the civil process when the amount of damages is assessed, not at the earlier stage when the harmer's liability in the abstract is determined. That harmful effects linger beyond the period when the counterfactual condition is satisfied is not usually taken to be a serious difficulty. The law, I think, implicitly assumes a distinction between the harm actually caused to V by H_1 on balance (which is determined in part by the counterfactual test) and the harm that H_1 is justly answerable for. The harmful state that V remains in is a kind of "causal residue" directly

---

[6] Thus, when a small boy falls from a cliff toward a certain death on the rocks below, but is electrocuted instantly when his hand touches an uninsulated wire through which the electric company has negligently allowed current to run, the company's negligence has harmed the boy by causing his instant death (a very adverse effect on his interest), but there was only the tiniest interval, perhaps one second, during which the boy was "worse off than he otherwise would have been," and that severely discounts the gravity of the harming. As the court put it in a case of this sort, the victim was deprived of a life "too short to be given pecuniary allowance" (*Dillon* v. *Twin States Gas and Electric Co.*, 85 N.H. 449, 163 A. 111 [1932]).

resulting from the harm that H_1 *did* cause. It is unquestionably a *harmful* condition but strictly speaking after the passage of interval t, it is not a *harmed* condition, that is, not a net harm produced by H_1's act of harming. Nevertheless, it is perfectly just to hold H_1 liable for the full damages, including those beyond what he actually caused, because only an unforeseeable fluke of chance (e.g., a plane crash) accounts for the brevity of the period during which the counterfactual condition continued to be satisfied. In short, H_1 harmed V because there was some period, however brief, during which the counterfactual condition was satisfied, and he is justly answerable for the effects of the harm he originally caused, since it was only a fluke of chance, not anything he can claim credit for, that limited the scope of his harming. The harmful residue has to be paid for by someone, and it seems less unfair to charge it to the original wrongdoer than to the hapless victim.

Another possible way of reconciling the counterfactual test with cases of causal overdetermination is to reformulate that test itself. We could say that A harms B only if his wrongful act leaves B worse off then he would be otherwise *in the normal course of events insofar as they were reasonably foreseeable in the circumstances*. With that doubly counterfactual formulation we can say that the taxi driver harmed the passenger to the full extent of his injuries, for "in the normal course of events" the airplane would not have crashed, and had the taxi collision been avoided *in those circumstances*, this new passenger would have been much better off than he is now in his hospital bed. This is another way of normativizing the concept of harming for legal purposes, but it has the advantage of not suggesting a kind of strict liability in which wrongdoers are held liable for harms beyond those which they actually caused. Given this reformulation of the counterfactual test, the taxi driver's negligence harmed the passenger to the full extent of his injuries, and the subsequent plane crash does not get the driver off the hook. His responsibility is more than a fiction in the interest of justice; it is a logical consequence of the analysis of harming with its reformulated counterfactual condition.

CIVIL LIABILITY FOR PRENATAL HARMING

So much for background. We come now to our central concern, prenatal harming. I shall begin with relatively unproblematic types of tort suits for prenatal harms and work up gradually to the wrongful life cases that generate the most acute philosophical perplexities. Consider first, cases in which the harming action occurs between conception and birth, and the infant is born in a harmed condition. A negligent motorist, for example, runs over a pregnant woman, directly injuring the fetus and causing it to be born in a permanently handicapped condition. After birth, the infant sues in her own name for damages. She charges that the defendant caused her injuries directly, not just that he allowed her to be born given that there would be injuries. Traditionally, I believe,[7] it was held that there is no right in the fetus actually to be born, but a "contingent right," assuming that it will be born, to be born unharmed. Assuming that the child will be born, the law seemed to say, various interests that she will come to have after birth must be protected from damage they can incur before birth.

In a second class of cases, the harming act occurs before conception, and the infant is born in a harmed condition. There are various familiar legal examples. A pharmaceutical manufacturer who carelessly prepares medicine six months before an infant's conception will be answerable to that child fifteen months later if the medicine taken by the mother damages the embryo, and the fetus survives until birth. In another example, a blood transfusion gives a woman syphilis. One year later she conceives, and her child is born syphilitic. *He* will recover damages for negligence from the hospital. Finally, for a clincher, consider a fanciful hypothetical example from the criminal law. A wicked misanthrope desires to blow up a schoolhouse in order to kill or mutilate the pupils. He conceals a bomb in a closet in the kindergarten room and sets a timing device to go off in six years. It goes off on schedule, killing or mutilating dozens of five-year-old children. It was the evil action of the wicked criminal six years earlier, *before they were even conceived*, that harmed them. It set in train a causal sequence that led directly to the harm.

The only problem with these two relatively unproblematic categories of prenatal harming is that they seem to involve legal duties to not yet existent persons. I am not impressed by the difficulty. There are at least two possible responses. Both have some cogency, but I prefer the second. First, one can argue in the negligence cases (the negligent motorist, the prepregnancy medication, and the hospital blood transfusion) that the negligent party had a duty to the mother (or the woman who was to become a mother), and a breach of *that* duty led to a later derivative harm to another party, the child not yet born or conceived—a "third-party victim" on analogy with the "third-party beneficiary" in other branches of the law. The second response is to affirm that a person has a duty of care toward *anyone* who is likely to be harmed as a consequence of his conduct (a "foreseeable victim"), and in the case of some actions, that includes persons not yet born nor even conceived. I prefer this second response because it includes the first, but is more comprehensive and general. It would cover the school bomb example, for instance, whereas the third-party victim analysis would not. One of its implied consequences, incidentally, is that when you are

---

[7] See William Salmond, *Jurisprudence*, 5th ed., ed. P. J. Fitzgerald (London: Sweet & Maxwell, 1966), pp. 303–4.

dealing, medically or commercially, with a woman of a certain age, you have to think of her as potentially pregnant, and her merely potential future child as a "foreseeable victim" of your transaction with her now.

We come now to more philosophically puzzling categories of tort suits: wrongful birth, wrongful pregnancy, and, most puzzling of all, the so-called wrongful life suits that will be our main concern. Let me explain this terminology and give examples. First, *wrongful birth* actions are brought by parents, usually against medical providers, for compensation for their own costs and suffering, occasioned by the birth defects of their newly born infants. In a very typical kind of case, a woman contracts rubella in her second month of pregnancy. Her doctor says, "Don't worry, there is no danger of birth defects." Then her child is born defective. The doctor's negligence did not *cause* the defects (the rubella did that), but the parents might have chosen a legal abortion otherwise. They were in effect deprived of the opportunity to abort, and now they want compensation for the many years of heartbreak, expensive care, and suffering caused to them by their child's handicapped existence. In other cases, abortion is not involved. The doctor (say) fails to advise the parents of the likelihood of a harmful hereditary condition, depriving them not of the opportunity to abort but, rather, of *the opportunity not to conceive* in the first place.

Second, what are called *wrongful pregnancy* suits (also *wrongful conception* and *failed contraception*) are brought by parents against medical providers for negligence leading to contraceptive failure and unwanted pregnancy, *even when the emergent infant is fully normal and healthy*. Again there are familiar examples. Pharmacists are sued for negligence in filling prescriptions for oral contraceptives; physicians are sued for negligence in performing sterilizations or abortions. Wrongful birth and wrongful pregnancy are similar actions in that both are brought by the parents of the child, but they differ in that the damages for wrongful birth are typically much greater, and this for obvious reasons: the costs (economic and psychological) of a severely defective child are greater than the costs of a merely unwanted one.[8]

---

[8] Wrongful pregnancy suits may be "relatively unproblematic," but they are far from non-controversial. Many judges have argued that the "intangible benefits of having a child offset the expenses of raising a child" (*Rieck* v. *Medical Protective Company of Fort Wayne, Indiana*, 64 Wis. 2d 514, 219 N.W. 2d 242 [1974]). Others have claimed that an offsetting benefit is shown by the parents' retention of the child when there is the option of putting it up for adoption. Typically, the action is brought by parents who have acted in reliance on medical assurances that a vasectomy or tubal ligation has made pregnancy impossible, and then have had their new life plans dashed by the birth of an unexpected child. Normally they sue for the costs of rearing a child to the age of eighteen years. Compromise settlements in which plaintiffs are allowed to recover only the costs of the unsuccessful operation, "compensation" for pain and suffering, medical complications, the costs of delivery, and lost wages and consortium during pregnancy are now common. For a definitive survey of cases, see Anne C. Reich-

We come now to the most interesting and controversial category. A *wrongful life* suit is brought by the infant himself, usually against medical providers, but sometimes against the biological parent(s), for wrongfully allowing him to come into existence at all, given that it was known, or should have been known, that he would probably be born with severe afflictions. The 1980 California case of *Curlender* v. *Bio-Science Laboratories*[9] is one of the very few successful wrongful life suits to date. An infant was born severely impaired as a result of a medical testing laboratory's negligence in conducting genetic tests on the parents (Mr. and Mrs. Curlender). If properly done, the tests should have revealed a high probability of inherited Tay-Sachs disease.[10] The mother then would have had amniocentesis early in pregnancy in order to check, or the parents might have opted not to conceive at all. (Tay-Sachs disease, as I understand it, is carried by a recessive gene. Only when both parents are carriers is the probability of transmission high.) Little Shauna Curlender lived in intense pain for four years, severely retarded, with extensive loss of motor reactions, including the ability to feed orally. In addition, her attorney's list of harms included "deprivation of 72.6 years of her life," but that, I think, is a logical confusion.[11]

Misgivings over Wrongful Life Suits

Misgivings of at least five kinds have been expressed over wrongful life suits.[12] I think that reassuring replies can be given to at least four of them. It is said, first of all, that they are *unnecessary* given the possibility of wrongful birth suits by the parents, that there is a kind of wasteful redundancy in permitting either or both, child or parents, to sue for the same wrong and

---

man, "Damages in Tort for Wrongful Conception—Who Bears the Cost of Raising the Child?" *Sydney Law Review* 10 (March 1985).

[9] *Curlender* v. *Bio-Science Laboratories*, 106 Cal. App. 3d 811, 165 Cal. Rptr. 477 (1980).

[10] Bonnie Steinbock describes the usual course of the disease: "The child appears well at birth and develops normally for six to eight months when progressive psychomotor degeneration slowly begins. By eighteen months the child is likely to be paralyzed and blind, unable to take food by mouth, suffering from constipation and decubitus ulcers. There are increasingly frequent convulsions which cannot be controlled by medication. The last few years of the child's life are usually spent in a vegetative state." See her "Wrongful Life," *Hastings Center Report* 15 (April 1986): 17.

[11] The argument is based on there being a life expectancy of 76.6 years for white females. Shauna lived for only four years, so her disease deprived her of the other 72.6 years. But either the testing laboratory would be negligent, in which case she was destined to a life of only four years, or it would not be negligent, in which case she would not have been conceived and born at all. In neither case would she have lived 76.6 years!

[12] I am indebted to Nora K. Bell and Barry M. Loewer. See their valuable article "What Is Wrong with 'Wrongful Life' Cases?" *Journal of Medicine and Philosophy* 10 (May 1985): 127–46.

the same harm. In fact, the two kinds of action are usually brought together, so some commentators might well wonder whether "wrongful birth" might be sufficient for both. Surely there would be fewer philosophical problems that way. And in either case, the bills would get paid by the harming party.

One might give three different replies to this first kind of misgiving.[13] The first is to point out that the courts are sometimes very tough on the parents who bring the wrongful birth cases. Judges often find it hard to agree that the parents have themselves been harmed on balance by the birth of an impaired child. They often say that the birth of a child—any child— is a "blessed event" whose benefits to its parents far exceed its burdens.[14] In *Becker* v. *Schwartz*[15] the judge made a more modest claim that seems quite undeniable: "Parents may yet experience a love that even an abnormality cannot dampen." That kind of consideration is often meant to show that the parents, on balance, are unharmed. This attitude encourages, indeed requires, suit by the child plaintiff. *Her* injuries are plain and less controversial. In some cases there would be no recovery at all unless the infant sues in her own name.

The second reply is that sometimes the biological parents themselves, or one of them, are the defendants in wrongful life suits. Suppose that *B*, who is mentally defective, is raped by *A*, who is wealthy, or that *A* seduces her in reckless disregard of the chance of pregnancy. *B* becomes pregnant, and it is subsequently determined that the baby is likely to inherit genetic defects from the mother. Suppose, finally, that abortion is either illegal (as it still is in many countries) or considered morally beyond the pale. The child is born out of wedlock to a helpless and indigent mother and with very costly medical needs. If we add to the example that the mother dies in childbirth, it will become more clear that there is no one to bring suit against but the biological father, and no one to bring suit but the infant.

The third reply to the redundancy objection is the most important one, namely, that in any case there is a basic difference between the indirect harm to the parents and the direct harm to the child that is produced when medical negligence permits the birth of a severely damaged baby. These are distinct harms and different in kind and degree. As Nora K. Bell and Barry M. Loewer put it, "While it might be true in some cases that the benefits to the *parents* of having an afflicted child may outweigh the burdens ["Better an afflicted child than none at all" might be their attitude] that doesn't address the issue of whether in some cases the burden to the *child* of being

---

[13] I borrow heavily here from Bell and Loewer, ibid., p. 131. Bonnie Steinbock gives still additional replies to this first misgiving in "Wrongful Life."

[14] We have seen (note 8) that this sort of thing is commonly said in wrongful conception cases, but it is also said in wrongful birth cases where prima facie it is less plausible.

[15] *Becker* v. *Schwartz*, 46 N.Y. 2d 401, 413 N.Y.S. 2d 895, 386 N.E. 2d 807 (1978).

born so afflicted outweighs the benefits to *him*."[16] It is quite conceivable that *that* question has an affirmative answer, so that a wrongful life suit might be more plausible (and more lucrative) than a wrongful birth one, and nor merely a dispensable redundancy.

The second misgiving over wrongful life suits has been expressed as a conceptual objection to all alleged cases of prenatal harm. This is the claim that a legal duty to the not yet existent is impossible. We have already encountered it, and replied that a duty of care to any foreseeable victim, including the not yet existent, is a perfectly coherent notion.[17]

The third misgiving is an especially serious philosophical one. It is thought by many people that the counterfactual comparison normally used to determine whether *A* has harmed *B* is logically inapplicable in wrongful life cases because the question of whether *A*'s wrongful conduct made the emergent child worse off than he would otherwise have been reduces to the question of whether the child would have been "better off had he never been born." Since it is necessary to *be* if one is to *be better off*, it is a logical contradiction to say that someone could be better off though not in existence.[18] If *A* had prevented *B*'s birth by contraception, abstention, or abortion, *B* would not have been better off as a result, for *B* would not have *been* as a result. Nonexistence would not have been a better condition for *B* to be in, for it would have been no condition of *B* at all.

Obviously, the counterfactual test must be reformulated (yet again!) if it is to serve as an adequate test and measure of harming in wrongful life cases. I think this can be done. Instead of asking whether *B* would be better off if he had never been born, we could ask what most of us really mean when we use this idiomatic phrase intending it to convey sense instead of paradox. When a miserable adult claims that he would be "better off dead," for example, surely he is not making some subtle metaphysical claim implying that there is a realm of being in which even the nonexistent have a place. What he is saying is that he *prefers* to be dead, that is, not to *be* at all. Similarly, when we claim that some grossly deformed, impaired, and suffering infant would have been better off unborn, we are expressing, belatedly, our belief that that state of affairs is preferable. If we speak in the first person, we may be expressing the *wish* (not a desire) that we had never come into existence—"Would that I had never been born." When that wish is expressed in terms of being "better off not having come into existence," it is to be understood not simply as a wish, but as a claim that the prefer-

[16] Bell and Loewer, "What Is Wrong," p. 131.

[17] That is not to say that problems do not remain, especially in specifying the correlative right-holder. See my discussion of "birthrights" below.

[18] Improving the lot of the no longer existent may be an exception to this. See my *Harm to Others*, pp. 79–83; Aristotle, *Nicomachean Ethics* 1.10. Improving the lot of the not yet existent, though, does seen to be logically impossible.

ence implied in the wish is understandable and justifiable, rationally based on the nature of the speaker's present plight. When one party says that another would have been better off had he never been born, he is claiming that the preference for the one state of affairs over the other is a rational preference. Whether true or not, this is an intelligible claim without contradiction or paradox. What we must ask, then, in wrongful life cases is "whether nonexistence or nonlife is preferable to life attended by certain hardships."[19] If nonexistence in a given case would have been objectively preferable to existence, as judged for example by the law's convenient "reasonable person," then any wrongful act or omission that caused (permitted) the child to be born can be judged to have harmed the child.

That brings us to the fourth misgiving. The question now becomes this: Is nonexistence in fact ever rationally preferable to a severely encumbered existence? Surely, in most cases of suffering and impairment we think of death as even worse. This is shown by the widespread human tendency to "cling to life at all costs." And even for severe genetic handicaps and inherited maladies, most competent persons who suffer from them will not express regret that they were born in the first place. The persons who might be expected to have the contrary view in their own case are often so badly off that they are not even competent to form the opinion or express it, and it must be expressed on their behalf by others. In the most extreme cases, however, I think it is rational to prefer not to have come into existence at all, and while I cannot prove this judgment, I am confident that most people will agree that it is at least plausible. I have in mind some of the more severely victimized sufferers from brain malformation, spina bifida, Tay-Sachs disease, polycystic kidney disease, Lesch-Nyhan syndrome, and those who, from whatever cause, are born blind and deaf, permanently incontinent, severely retarded, and in chronic pain or near-total paralysis, with life expectancies of only a few years.

Even if we can judge that A's breach of duty was the cause of B's being born (although not the cause of B's impairment) and that B's nonexistence would have been preferable to him coming into existence so impaired, and hence that A harmed B, we might still reject wrongful life suits on the ground that there is no possible way of determining damages for the harmed party. This fifth misgiving makes the strongest objection to wrongful life suits.

I think it must be conceded that so long as we think of damages as representing compensation (in certain senses) for the harm, then it cannot make sense to order their payment to a victim of wrongful life, for the

---

[19] *Williams* v. *State*, 18 N.Y. 2d at 485, 276 N.Y.S. 2d at 888, 223 N.E. 2d at 345 (1966) (Keating, J. concurring). Judge Keating goes on to say that "it is impossible to make that choice," but surely he overstates the point. Experience as a bastard in contemporary America, a key harm in the case in question, clearly is preferable, ceteris paribus, to nonexistence.

simple reason that his harms are not (in those senses) compensable. Consider the various things that have been meant by "compensation."

1. *Bringing the plaintiff back to where he was* (repairing the damage). No money payment could do this for the person who is so extremely and irreparably harmed that his life is not worth living. Apparently only death itself—which is not one of the permitted tort remedies—could do that.

2. *Market compensation.* The required payment would be the amount of money the plaintiff would have freely agreed to in advance as his price for submitting to the harm. But the plaintiff in our examples did not even exist "in advance." Before the harmful act that assured his existence he had no values formed, and therefore no order of priorities is retroactively ascribable to him now. If we nonetheless ascribe "normal values" supposititiously to his preexistent self, then presumably we would judge that no conceivable amount of money would be a sufficient price for taking on a life not worth living.

3. *Diversionary displacement.* This is best illustrated by a story. George, a successful forty-year-old engineer, was badly burned in a car accident in which he was blameless. After countless skin grafts, he recovered his health and resumed his job, but now he was quite grotesque in appearance, his face a maze of wrinkled scar tissue. He was deeply depressed until he won a settlement of four million tax-free dollars. Some of this paid his ongoing medical bills, but most of it was pure "profit." The effect of this infusion of wealth was to divert George from his depression. He no longer looks in the mirror each morning; now he looks at stock market figures, thinks about investments (a fascinating game hitherto unknown to him), and cultivates his new interests in sports cars and gourmet restaurants. For people like George, life has its consolations (displacements of interest) if one has enough cash, even though no amount of cash would have seemed worth it in advance. We can contrast the extremely impaired and cognitively undeveloped spina bifida or Tay-Sachs baby. There is no way to make her feel better about things and no amount of money could divert her attention and console her. The cognitively unimpaired adult quadraplegic, however, might find playing the stock market or contributing to worthy causes sufficiently diverting to make his life worth continuing, even though he would not have agreed in advance to *any* price for his paralysis, and he would happily trade all his wealth, if he could, to recover his health. That would be an example of "compensation" rendering a life worth living that would not otherwise be so, but that is not the kind of example we find in the wrongful life cases.

4. *"Compensation for pain and suffering."* Often awards for pain and suffering have a disguised punitive role, functioning primarily as a way of getting back at the wrongdoer, but in what way do these damages "compensate" for suffering that has come and gone? They do not annul or oblit-

erate pain, or make it as if the pain or suffering never were, or make one mind the pain less in retrospect. In some cases they can divert competent persons from their depression, but they would hardly console the wretched Tay-Sachs child.

5. *Payment of maintenance costs* (hospital fees, medicine, food). This is the only sense of compensation that seems applicable to an infant whose life is so terrible it is not worth living. But even if the child sues in her own name, *she* is not the one who is in any primary way benefited. Rather, those who would otherwise have to pay are relieved of their burden. Their financial costs will now be paid by the defendant, thus compensating *them* for out-of-pocket costs, not the actual plaintiff whose costs would otherwise have been paid somehow by someone (in the last resort, the state). Perhaps, then, there should not be tort actions for wrongful life at all, but only maintenance suits, as, for example, in paternity suits. There could even be administrative tribunals assigning the costs of support to the most appropriate party. But *if* justice would make the assignment of those costs to the party most at fault (which is not necessarily true), that question is best settled by traditional procedures of tort litigation, and that would mean, in cases of this kind, wrongful life suits.

SOME SPECULATIVE CONSEQUENCES OF THESE REASONINGS

1. Applying the counterfactual test in wrongful life cases. In the special case of harming by bringing into existence, as we have seen, a reformulation of the counterfactual test is required. For these cases we should say that *B* is in a harmed state if, because of *A*'s breach of duty, *B* comes into existence in a condition such that *it would be rational to prefer nonexistence to that condition*. This test does require a comparison of the usual kind between *B*'s actual condition and a state of affairs alternative to it (that which would have obtained had *A* acted rightly), but that is not a comparison of two possible conditions of *B*. When we speak for *B*, we do not say, "I would rather be in that condition than in this one"; rather, we say, "I would rather not be at all than be in this condition."

It may seem objectionably ad hoc to revise the general account of harming to accommodate the one kind of case that it does not seem to fit. Revising a generalization to cover a recalcitrant special case, however, is only sometimes objectionably ad hoc. Consider a clearer example of an illicit ad hoc revision. Scientists in Melbourne conclude from an experiment that under certain circumstances, *C*, electrons behave in a certain way, *x*. The experiment is repeated in Bundoora and fails to yield the same result. Undaunted, the scientists amend their theory to say that electrons behave in way *x* under circumstances *C except in Bundoora*. This is unsatisfactory, of course, because of the well-founded expectation that if electrons do not behave *x*ly in Bundoora, then they do not elsewhere either. That is, we assume that there is nothing special about Bundoora that would uniquely affect the behavior of electrons there. There is, however, something very special about the context of "harmful conception" that might lead us to expect that its peculiarities will not be repeated elsewhere. It is the only example we can have of a person's being harmed by the very act that brings him into existence.

2. *How do we decide what is "rationally preferable"*? Further philosophical difficulties are raised by the phrase "It would be rational to prefer nonexistence to that condition." Two questions in particular require answers: Rational for whom? In which sense of "rational"—"dictated by reason" or merely "consistent with reason"?[20] I shall consider the former question first.

The phrase "It would be rational to prefer," as it stands, is vague and elliptical. Rational for *whom* to prefer? There are three possibilities. Perhaps we mean that it would be rational for the seriously impaired infant to prefer not to have been born. But if he is impaired to the point where it is plausible to suppose that his life is not worth living, then he may be incapable of having, now or ever, such a preference. He may never be capable of forming the concepts of existence and nonexistence. Hence, it seems to make no sense to say that he should prefer one or the other, or that it would be rational for *him* to have such a preference. Would it be rational for a jellyfish to prefer saline to fresh water, nonvoracious to voracious neighbors, a rising to a falling barometer, existence to nonexistence? If that makes no sense, what are we to say of similar statements about the hypothetical rationality of the preferences of a human neonate with (say) only half a brain? It is easy to tumble into a paradox here. The statement about the impaired infant is of even more doubtful intelligibility than that about the jellyfish. We can say that jellyfish are not rational beings, since they lack brains altogether, but if, contrary to fact, a jellyfish were a rational being, everything else the same, then it would be rational for it to have the preferences mentioned above (including the metaphysical one). It is also true that the seriously impaired infant is not a rational being, since it is both immature and possessed of only half a brain. But if, contrary to fact, he were older and possessed a full normal brain, then, everything else the same, it might *not* be true that it would be rational for him to prefer nonexistence to his present (not so impaired) condition. For if he were rational enough to make a choice at all, he might be sufficiently unimpaired for his life to be worth living after all. What can we mean, then, by the claim that it would be rational for *him* to prefer not to have been born?

---

[20] I am indebted to Thomas McKay of Syracuse University for reminding me of this distinction.

Suppose that the statement is interpreted in a different way. The second possible interpretation is that an infant is in a harmed state if he comes into existence in a condition such that it would be rational for some other person (you or me or any "reasonable person"?) to prefer his own nonexistence to his continued existence if he were in that condition. This interpretation leads into a thicket of metaphysical entanglements. It requires someone to say that *if I were he*, it would be rational for *me* to prefer nonexistence to the condition I would then be in. When I say "if I were he," I imagine that somehow he (as he is now) is mixed with me (as I am now). This can be a strong mixture (most of my present properties and only some of his) or a weak mixture (most of his present properties and only some of mine). It would be my rational capacities, values, and principles mixed with his pain, impairment, and dim prospects. If such a composite person were possible, then *he* would prefer nonexistence to his present condition. Perhaps, however, such a composite would be logically impossible, on the one hand having, let us suppose, only half a brain—that is the source of the painful impairment and the dim prospects—but also my full and normal brain. Thus, the first interpretation's paradox threatens to return.

Now consider the third and final categorical possibility. Suppose that the impaired product of a wrongful conception is not *rationally* impaired, but largely paralyzed and in constant pain. Suppose that he does not bring suit until he is (say) twenty years old. He then claims both that his life is and has never been worth living and that he himself is competent to make that judgment, being aware of his plight and understanding his options. Now to say that some medical provider or parent harmed him by permitting him to be born is to say that that person put him in a condition which is such that (1) he in fact prefers nonexistence to that condition, and (2) it is rational for him, or for anyone in his shoes, to have that preference. It is likely, however, that rational persons in that condition might reasonably differ in their preferences. We should therefore revise the claim of the competent twenty-year-old to say that it is *not irrational* (or not unreasonable) for him to have that preference, not that it would be irrational not to have it. The test of the rationality of the actual preferences of a competent person is the weak one of "consistency with reason."

For the competent subject, then, the paradoxes of the first two interpretations do not seem to arise. But that fact is itself paradoxical, for it is precisely the incompetent subjects who seem most clearly in a position to claim that their lives are not worth living. How can we make sense of this claim? The only interpretation that remains open to us is that it would be rational (now in a much stronger sense) for a proxy chooser, any representative of the best interests of an extremely impaired infant, to express on the infant's behalf the preference for nonexistence. The judgment, once more, is not that the infant would be better off dead, as if death were a possible condition for him to be in, but, rather, that the preference for death over impaired present condition would be, in a strong sense, rational if it were expressed by a party concerned not to promote the infant's future good so much as to bring to an end his present harm. There is no need for a hypothetical mixing of selves in the proxy chooser's imagination. He need only represent the interests of the incompetent party. To be sure, that party may not yet have any values, goals, ideals, or aspirations, the stuff of which interests are made. But the proxy chooser is not therefore required to substitute his own, ascribing them hypothetically to the infant. Rather, he exercises his judgment that *whatever* interests the impaired party might have, or come to have, they would already be doomed to defeat by his present incurable condition. Thus, it would be irrational—contrary to what reason decrees—for a representative and protector of those interests to prefer the continuance of that condition to nonexistence. The proxy might also express the retroactive preference, on the incompetent's behalf, not to have been born at all. Parents with dangerous genetic disorders express the preference not to have children beforehand, and exercise that preference for the sake of the impaired children they might otherwise produce. "It wouldn't be fair to bring a child into existence in such a condition," they might say. If parents can express this preference intelligibly beforehand, how is the same judgment, made on the same grounds after the fact, any less rational?

It is not possible to prove conclusively that a preference, prospective or retrospective, for oneself or for another, *can* be rational in the strong sense of "required by reason," but an experiment in the imagination may serve to make that proposition seem more plausible. Suppose that after the death of your body a deity appears to you and announces that, contrary to the simplistic teachings of many moral theologians, he has far more alternatives for the afterlife than heaven, hell, and purgatory. There are infinite subtle gradations in human character, he explains, not just unqualified good and evil. Corresponding to these are a range of complex rewards and punishments tailored to each individual's complex deserts. In your case, he continues, he proposes to give you an option. You can be born again after death (reincarnated), but only as a Tay-Sachs baby with a painful life expectancy of four years to be followed by permanent extinction, or you can opt for permanent extinction to begin immediately. I should think you would have to be crazy to select the first option. Self-interest clearly dictates that you leave well enough alone and quit while you are still ahead. Similarly, if the deity required you to make a choice between the same alternatives for a loved one, say your spouse or child, someone for whose good you truly cared, you would not hesitate, insofar as you are rational, to opt once more for immediate nonexistence.

In summary, the judgment that his nonexistence would be (or would have been) preferable to his existence in such and such condition, if made by a competent adult or mature older child, is correct provided (1) he does in fact have a free and informed preference, prospective or retrospective as the case may be, for nonexistence, and (2) that preference is rational in the weak sense, that is, not contrary to reason, even though other equally rational persons in his circumstances might not share it. A preference for nonexistence over continued existence with a cut finger is clearly contrary to reason; a preference for nonexistence to inescapable hideous tortures might be required by reason; but in between is a range of options about which reasonable persons might differ, for example, whether nonexistence is preferable to life as a permanently hospitalized quadraplegic.

On the other hand, the judgment that nonexistence would be (or would have been) preferable to existence in an extremely impaired condition, if made by a proxy on behalf of an incompetent infant, is correct if and only if it is rational in the strong sense, that is, "required by reason" of anyone who is concerned to protect the interests of the incompetent subject.

Finally, let us suppose that we agree, for the sake of the argument, that because of another party's negligence, a certain infant is in a condition such that nonexistence would have been preferable (in the appropriate sense) to being born in that incurably impaired condition. Would not the appropriate remedy by simply to give that infant a painless injection that would cause its death? Would not that solution make more sense than complex litigation over costs? (The harming party might still be civilly liable to pay all the infant's costs up to now—hospitalization, treatment, medication, legal fees, even the costs of the instruments of euthanasia.) Ideally, I think, euthanasia would be the most just and humane solution, but the conceptual riddles we are attempting to resolve here arise against a background of current legal practice, and for better or worse, we have an inflexible rule against homicide that is not likely to be relaxed in the foreseeable future. Moreover, a wise legislator would have to be assured that the substitute practice he is to vote upon is free of the possibility of mistake and abuse, an assurance that is not imminently forthcoming. Another complication is that it may not be inconsistent for a subject, either himself competent or else competently represented by proxy, to judge that not to have been born would have been preferable to being born but that, nevertheless, now that he does exist he prefers not to die. If that combination of rational preferences is possible,[21] then the ideal solution may after all be to make a wrongful harmer liable for the damages of a life that ought never to have been allowed to begin, while withholding the means to its abrupt termination.

---

[21] I find this to be a difficult question that requires an examination of the instinct of self-preservation, and the concepts of weakness of will and voluntariness and their relations to rationality. I am skeptical, but in the absence of detailed examination, I prefer to leave it an open question.

3. A new interpretation of a birthright. If the creation of a baby whose life is not worth living is to count as a *harming* of that baby, one more requirement in our analysis of "harming" must be satisfied: *A* must *wrong B* and not merely affect his interests adversely. The duty toward *B* that was breached must be a duty that was logically correlated with *B*'s right against *A*. The right in question, I suspect, is a very special kind of right indeed, since it seems in some sense to attach to a merely potential being, and to be violated only at the moment its possessor is allowed to come into existence. I shall try to show, however, that prospective rights of this kind are not as mysterious as they may first seem.

Before the fetus becomes a person, it is a potential person with the potential attributes, including possession of rights, of a person. If it should be the case that the potential person has an unalterable destiny of extreme impairment and suffering, and if it is true that one of the rights he will have at birth (at the presumed onset of personhood[22]) is the right to be free of these total impediments to development and fulfillment, that is, a right to *some* opportunity for a tolerable life, then the potential rights at the very moment they are actualized are violated. A grossly impaired infant comes into existence not simply with rights, but with rights already violated. From the moment such an infant is born he has a grievance—a claim that he has been wronged. There are rights that are affirmable from the moment of birth (or the onset of personhood, whenever that is), and some of these birthrights have been violated from the moment they are initially assertable. A new interpretation of the idea of a "birthright" is suggested by this point, namely that

> if you cannot have that to which you have a birthright then you are wronged
> if you are brought to birth. Thus, if the conditions for the eventual fulfillment
> of the child's future interests are destroyed before he is born, the child can
> claim, after he has been born, that his *rights* (his present rights) have been
> violated. Moreover, if before the child has been born, we *know* that that con-
> ditions for the fulfillment of his most basic interests have already been de-
> stroyed, and we permit him nevertheless to be born, we become a party to the
> violation of his rights. It bears repeating that not all interests of the newborn

---

[22] In the account I sketch in the text, I refer to birth as the "presumed onset of personhood," and the rights that become actual at that point as "birthrights." But if the reader believes that the onset of personhood is earlier than birth, he should substitute "personhood-inception rights" for my "birthrights," and locate their origin at whichever developmental stage he wishes. I use the point of birth as an example only. I do not mean to beg any controversial questions in the abortion debate. There is one acknowledged implication for that debate, however, in my account: If the only way to prevent a child from being born into a life not worth living, and thereby being severely harmed, is to abort, and if we can know this in advance (a big *if*), then it would seem to follow that the mother has a moral duty to submit to an abortion. See my "Wrongful Conception and the Right Not to Be Harmed."

child should or can qualify for prenatal protection, but only those very basic ones whose satisfaction is known to be indispensable to a [minimally] decent life.[23]

In those extreme cases, then, in which a child is negligently or deliberately permitted to be born into a life not worth living, the infant is both wronged and put into a state of harm, and therefore *harmed* in the full sense.[24]

4. Criminal liability for wrongful life? Up to now I have been discussing mostly the law of torts, even though my interest in questions about prenatal harming arose in the course of a book on the moral limits of the criminal law. But now, just for completeness, I shall consider whether it could ever be feasible to impose criminal liability for wrongful life. Civil suits for wrongful life, as we have seen, are in principle acceptable, though in fact perhaps of limited utility given the possibility of wrongful birth suits by parents, and the limited applicability of meaningful notions of compensation to incompetent infants. Statutes permitting criminal prosecutions for wrongful life could also be legitimate in principle, since they would be aimed at the prevention of genuine and serious harms. Wrongfully permitting or enabling an infant to be born into a life not worth living would not be a so-called victimless crime. There are numerous decisive reasons against such statutes, however, and no legislature has ever even considered passing such legislation. The fault in most wrongful life cases is negligence, and that is a rather problematic ground for severe criminal liability. Moreover, vulnerability to criminal prosecution would have a chilling effect, with diverse deleterious consequences, on the medical profession. Reckless and intentional causing of pregnancy in the face of known risks of abnormal birth is very often a crime under some other name, like rape or fraud, and new legislation is not needed to cope with it. Moreover, deliberate failures to undergo abortions are usually motivated by the conviction that abortion is morally wrong—hardly a suitable state of mind for criminal punishment. Even the question of whether a given handicapped life is worth living is one on which reasonable persons can and often do conscientiously disagree, creating further difficulties of an intractable kind.

Still, it is possible to conceive of instances of deliberate and wrongful life creation that would be plausible targets of criminal legislation, though at present we must resort to examples from philosophical science fiction. Imagine an evil scientist who does genetic research on fetuses and newborns in the hope of creating a super-race or slave-race. He creates test-tube embryos through in vitro fertilization from chemically altered sperm and ova. Then he reimplants them in a natural womb of a willing subject.

---

[23] Feinberg, *Harm to Others*, p. 99.
[24] I must therefore repudiate my position in *Harm to Others*, p. 102.

The emergent infants have horrible afflictions and no opportunity of ever having normal lives, but the scientist respects their "right to life" and keeps then under observation until their lives mercifully sputter out. Perhaps there is a crime with some familiar name that is already applicable to this sort of behavior, but if not, a bill carefully defining "criminal wrongful life" might well be in order. At present, fortunately, there seems to be no need for it.

WHEN THE NEWBORN IS NOT SO SEVERELY HANDICAPPED THAT HIS LIFE IS NOT WORTH LIVING

The class of examples I shall consider now are cases in which the wrong-doing is flagrant (in the most interesting cases deliberate or reckless, rather than merely negligent), and done by one or both of the biological parents, rather than by some medical provider. In an ingenious example of Derek Parfit's,[25] a woman is warned that if she gets pregnant while she suffers from some temporary illness, her baby will be born in a defective condition. Nonetheless, whether through intentional perversity or reckless impulsiveness, she heeds not her physician's warning, and gets pregnant at the dangerous time. If her emergent child is so defective that his life is not worth living, then he would have a strong case for wrongful life damages against the mother. He would surely have a *moral* grievance against her. "But for your wrongful conduct," he might say (or his lawyer might say for him), "I would never have been conceived much less born, and nonexistence would surely be preferable to my miserable state." By the counterfactual test, reformulated for wrongful life cases, this wretched infant has indeed been harmed: he is in a condition so bad that even nonexistence would have been preferable to it. Moreover, his birthright has been violated from the moment he came into existence, since the conditions for a minimally decent life had already been destroyed. His interests have been adversely affected and he has been wronged, so it follows that he has been harmed in the full sense, and his impaired state can be understood also as a harmed state, that is, a state of harm that is the product of a prior act of harming.

In Parfit's example, however, the inherited defect is not so severe as to render the child's life not worth living. The child never regrets that he was born, but only that he was born (say) with a withered arm—a serious handicap but surely not such that nonexistence would be preferable to it. Therefore, when we apply the counterfactual test as reformulated for wrongful life situations, it turns out that the mother did not harm her

---

[25] Derek Parfit, "On Doing the Best for Our Children," in *Ethics and Population*, ed. Michael D. Bayles (Cambridge, Mass.: Schenkman, 1976).

child. She had only two options with respect to his birth. One was to do what she did, which led to his being born with the withered arm. The other was to obey the doctor, which would have led to his never having existed at all, which even the child acknowledges was the worse fate. Hence, she picked the option that had the best total consequences for the child that eventually emerged. Hence, her act did not harm that child (at least by the revised counterfactual test). Thus, the child's impaired condition is not a harmed condition, that is, not a state of harm that is the product of a prior act of harming. It clearly is nevertheless a state of harm, however we characterize its causal antecedents, since it does have adverse effects on the child's interests. I prefer to call it, therefore, a *harmful* condition rather than a *harmed* condition.

Did the mother wrong the child by causing him to come into existence in a harmful (handicapped) condition? I do not think the child can establish a grievance against her so long as he concedes that his handicapped existence is far preferable to no existence at all. For if he were to claim that she wronged him by doing what she did, that would commit him to the judgment that her duty to him had been to refrain from doing what she did; but if she had refrained, that would have led to his never having been born, an even worse result from his point of view. There is no doubt that the mother did act wrongly, but it does not follow that her wrongdoing wronged any particular person, or had any particular victim. She must be blamed for wantonly introducing a certain evil into the world, not for harming, or for violating the rights of, a person.

If I am right about this, there may be a case against tort liability in this instance, since the wrongful act of the defendant did not harm (on balance) the plaintiff. To hold her liable anyway, would be (at least with respect to the harm element) something like holding a rescuer liable for injuries he caused an endangered person that were necessary to his saving that person's life. He may have caused the imperiled party's arm to be broken in the rescue effort, but the alternative, let us suppose, was to let him die. So the broken-armed plaintiff suffered a harmful condition with respect to his arm, but the rescuer-defendant did not cause a condition that was harmful on balance, offset as it was by the overriding benefit of rescue, and he cannot be said, therefore, to have *harmed* the plaintiff (in the relevant full sense) at all.[26] Similarly, a statute imposing criminal liability on the mother for her behavior in Parfit's example would not appear at first sight to be legitimate, at least not according to the liberal doctrine that there should be no criminal liability without a proper victim. Such a statute would cre-

---

[26] For all this to be true, we must assume that the rescuer was not himself responsible for the other party's peril. If he put that party in the precarious situation in the first place, he himself is responsible for the costs of rescuing him, including the costs of repairing the broken arm.

ate a victimless crime, and could be justified only on the grounds that wrongdoing deserves punishment even when it harms no one and violates no one's rights (the illiberal doctrine of "legal moralism").

Nevertheless, I shall investigate in the space that remains the possibility that criminal and/or tort liability for wrongful life might be justified even in cases where the harmful condition is not so severe as to make the wrongfully created life not worth living. And we shall have to ask what consequences these cases might have for the liberal condemnation of victimless crimes, and for the way in which we apply such terms as "harm," "wrong," and "victim" to the infants who are plaintiffs in civil suits for wrongful life.

CRIMES WITHOUT VICTIMS

If "negligent conception" (as we might call it) were more common, and impaired infants began to appear in increased numbers, it might not seem unjust even to a liberal's conscience to create a class of "victimless crimes." In an example of Gerald Dworkin's, we are asked to suppose that when the barometer falls to X, any baby conceived under those meteorological conditions will be born with some serious impairment, much worse than a cleft palate, club feet, or a withered arm, but not so severe that his life will not be worth living. Imagine that nearly every bedroom has a barometer on the night stand, and that all radio and television stations broadcast warnings when the barometric pressure reaches the dangerous point. A criminal statute forbidding unprotected intercourse at such times would seem, at least at first sight, to create a victimless crime, since babies born with these handicaps, severe as they are, would not be wronged/harmed by their negligent or self-indulgent parents. And yet, in the example a certain amount of avoidable misery might be introduced into the world if we do not pass the statute. Surely, one might argue (on grounds that *resemble* the liberal's), the prevention of unnecessary suffering is a legitimate reason for a criminal prohibition. Still, on the other side, we can imagine a child born with the handicap in question who feels positively lucky that his parents negligently conceived *him* (of all people) against huge odds. He does not rejoice in his handicaps, but since he does not regret having been born, handicaps notwithstanding, he does not *feel* like a "victim," and he might resent the injustice of treating his parents as criminals.

We can strengthen the case for the legitimacy in principle of criminal legislation by imagining hypothetical examples of "wrongful conception" that are not merely negligent, but deliberate, malicious, and sadistic. In conducting this experiment in the imagination, it is important to notice that there is a great conceptual, though perhaps not as great a moral, difference between the case in which a woman takes a drug *after* she is pregnant, causing her fetus to be born later in a harmed condition, and the case in which she takes drugs first and then, after she is herself in a condition that would be perilous for a fetus, she has intercourse and becomes pregnant. If a woman takes thalidomide while already pregnant, knowing its well-publicized effects, then the child that is born months later is her victim. The counterfactual test for harming yields a clear and unequivocal judgment in his case. He is much worse off than he would have been had his mother not taken the dangerous drug. This case is on all fours with that of the negligent motorist who runs over a pregnant woman, causing her child, months later, to be born in an impaired condition. Since it is criminal liability we are considering, however, let us imagine that the mother's fault is much more serious than mere negligence. Suppose she deliberately damages her fetus in this way because she wants the experience later of mothering a child that will be more completely dependent on her, and for a longer period, than a normal child would or, even worse, because she wishes to glory sadistically in a child's frustrations and sufferings. Now we have a picture of a parent who is morally indistinguishable from a serious criminal. Criminal liability for her, given her culpability and her real on-balance victim, does not seem illegitimate.

But now change the example in only one small respect. Suppose the mother has already been taking some dangerous drug for a long time when she chooses to become pregnant. Suppose she is, as a consequence, in a bodily condition such that any fetus conceived while she is in that condition will develop in the manner typical of thalidomide fetuses. Knowing full well the dangers, she deliberately chooses to become pregnant, precisely in order to have an overly dependent child whose sufferings she can enjoy. She is precisely as culpable morally as the woman in the other version of the story, but she does not harm her child since, had she behaved otherwise, her child would never have existed; and since the thalidomide-type impairments are preferable to nonexistence, the counterfactual test for harming is not satisfied, and there is no proper victim. The advocate of criminalization might argue that so trivial a difference between the two cases as the order in which the pill-taking and the act of conception took place cannot support so momentous a moral difference as that between criminal liability and no criminal liability. If criminal prohibition would be legitimate in the one case, he might conclude, then it must equally be legitimate in the other, whether there is a victim or not.

Of course, there are powerful reasons against criminalizing the behavior in the highly artificial examples we have been driven to in this section. Criminalization would not be necessary in the barometric pressure example because people can be presumed to have more than enough incentive to avoid producing impaired infants, quite without gratuitous threats from the state. And deliberate conception of foreseeably handicapped infants for selfish or sadistic reasons would be so rare and extraordinary that surely more economical means of dealing with it could be used than the cumbersome apparatus of the criminal justice system. But these rejoinders miss the point. The examples do not show that there are some imaginable circumstances in which criminal legislation would be justified as good public policy. Rather, these examples, contrived and unlikely though they be, are designed to show that there are conceivable circumstances in which criminalization even without a victim would be *legitimate in principle*, even if unjustifiable, for practical reasons, on balance.

It is beyond question that the severe handicaps of wrongfully conceived children (where the wrongful conceiving follows rather than precedes the event that causes the impairment) constitute a great evil. Moreover, that evil, unless so widespread as to be a public harm, is a "nongrievance evil," lacking determinate victims who can complain that their rights have been violated. As nongrievance evils go, however, this one carries a great deal of moral weight, enough to command even the liberal's respect. The evil is not the basis of any one's legitimate personal grievance but it is not an evil that is unassociated with human interests and well-being. A criminal statute designed to prevent such evils would be a departure from strict liberal legitimizing standards, but it would not be contrary to the animating humane spirit of the liberal's harm principle. The liberal can be expected to combat harmful conditions of other human beings even when they are not harmed conditions. Such conditions may be nongrievance evils but their connection to human suffering puts them in a special category of nongrievance evils, having much greater moral weight, for example, than consensual taboo infractions, unnatural matings, beetle squashings, defamations of the ancient dead, evil thoughts, even nonconsequential species extinctions.[27] They have as much weight, in fact, as it is possible for a nongrievance evil to bring to the legislative scales, and for some liberals that might even be enough, ceteris paribus, to warrant criminal legislation. I do not think that such liberals can be charged with making an ad hoc exception (in the illicit sense) to liberalism. The case is an exception, but on the other hand, the circumstances truly are special and not likely to recur indiscriminately. For those who suffer congenital defects, the evil of their condition does not "float free" of their interests, even though it has not set back those interests on balance nor violated their rights. I can concede, then, that nongrievance evils do have *some* weight, simply as evils, but no other nongrievance evil

[27] This is a partial list of "free-floating evils" from my "Legal Moralism and Free-Floating Evils," *Pacific Philosophical Quarterly* 61 (1980): 130–63. I have changed my usage, however. I prefer now to distinguish "grievance evils" from "nongrievance evils" as generic classes, and then to distinguish two species of nongrievance evils, the welfare-connected ones (like impairment stemming from wrongful conception) and the free-floating ones (like those listed above in the text). In the earlier article, I used "nongrievance evil" and "free-floating evil" as synonyms, but that was a mistake.

has as much weight as this one derived from avoidable, nonconsensual suffering. Liberalism must bend to permit an exception in this special kind of case. I think it can bend without breaking.

Torts Without Victims

Given our analysis of harming, the infant in the Parfit story has not been harmed by his parents in the sense of "harming" that involves a genuine grievance in the victim against the party whose conduct put him in a harmful condition. If, nevertheless, we wish to argue that tort actions in such cases, practical difficulties aside, would be legitimate in principle, we can attempt to do so in either of two ways. We can argue for enlarged conceptions of "harming," "grievance," and "victim," such that the woman in Parfit's example did, after all, harm the child, who is after all her victim, and has, after all, a legitimate grievance against her. Or we can hold fast to our analysis of harming, which does neatly fit the normal cases of postnatal harming, and abandon the view that liability can be legitimately imposed only when the harm principle is satisfied. The second course seems the wiser to me. A person can be justly held answerable for the harmful condition of another, in some circumstances, even when that condition, strictly speaking, is not his doing.

If we take the first course, however, and insist that there is some relevant sense in which the infant in Parfit's example has been *harmed* by his mother, that could have the unfortunate consequence of legitimizing wrongful life suits for such harmful states as illegitimacy, ugliness, below-average intelligence, and the like, all of which are "harmful conditions," but which, since all are rationally preferable to nonexistence, are not harms on balance. Therefore, if a writer were to advocate a special sense of "harming" just to permit wrongful life suits in cases life Parfit's to be legitimized by the harm principle, the proposal would founder on these other examples where the harms are relatively insignificant. Minor harms could be awarded relatively minor but appropriate compensation, and the courts would be flooded with plaintiffs airing fancied "grievances" against their parents for providing them with disadvantageous environments or poor genetic inheritances.[28]

It would be better in these exceptional cases that traditional tort rules

---

[28] Cf. the opinion in *Zepeda* v. *Zepeda*, 41 Ill.App. 2d 240, 190 N.E. 2d 849 (1963): "What does disturb us is the . . . related suits that would be encouraged. Encouragement would extend to all others born into the world under conditions they might regard as adverse. One might seek damages for being born of a certain color, another because of race; one for being born with a hereditary disease, another for inheriting unfortunate family characteristics; one for being born into a large and destitute family, another because a parent has an unsavory reputation."

requiring harming be suspended, as they have been elsewhere. Instead of requiring that the defendant violated the plaintiff's rights, we might require only that her conduct was indeed seriously wrongful, and instead of requiring that she harmed him, we could require that she was responsible for his coming into existence in a seriously harmful condition. There would be fault aplenty in these examples, and harm too, even though the fault does not give the plaintiff a personal grievance, and the harm is not the product of an act of harming. This would be a "victimless tort," that is, not a tort at all in the traditional sense, but perhaps justice would support it anyway, as it supports various kinds of strict and vicarious liability. It might not be fair to make a person pay damages to another whom she has not directly wronged, but it may be more unfair still to make the miserable impaired party pay, or do without the aid he needs. In that case, however, I would prefer changing our practices to changing our concepts, dropping the requirement that the defendant must have harmed the plaintiff to inventing a new sense of "harming" tailored to the case at hand.[29]

There would be no point, of course, in the child in Parfit's example suing his own mother, since her care and funding would probably be forthcoming anyway, and there would be no actual gain in support from a judicial award of damages (unless she were to put him up for adoption and wash her hands of him, but I put that possibility aside). Imagine, then, a twist on the Parfit story. Suppose that the woman's lover is none other than her gynecologist. In this version of the story, he knows that if the woman gets

[29] I have not revised this chapter to accommodate an important suggestion made by Wayne Sumner at the Ann Arbor conference at which the original paper was read. Sumner, accepting an invitation I made to the audience to help me "better preserve my liberal purity," suggests a way in which I might avoid, at least in Parfit-type cases, the view that liability without a properly harmed victim is morally legitimate after all. All that stands in the way of saying that the Parfit child has been harmed, he points out, is my counterfactual test for harming. Sumner therefore proposes that we modify that test (as I did, namely, in cases of overdetermination) by casting it in an *impersonal* form. In the Parfit case, Sumner writes, "the child is worse off than *the child the woman would (or might) otherwise have had* would have been, had she acted otherwise." This is an attractive suggestion to me because, in permitting me to be steadfast in support of the liberal doctrine of "no liability without a harmed and wronged victim," it contributes to the greater overall coherence of my political philosophy, and on Sumner's alternative account of harming, the Parfit baby *is* a "harmed and wronged victim." The disadvantage of Sumner's suggestion is that it seems to make a rather sharp departure from the concept of harming—wronging as it is normally and naturally employed. "How can I have wronged you when you admit that you are better off for what I did than you would otherwise be?" asks the Parfit mother. "Yes," Sumner would have her child reply, "but I am not better off than the child you would have had a month later if you had waited." This reply has the merit of establishing the child's grievance, if that is what we antecedently wish to do, but we might have some sympathy with the mother's further response if she questioned what relevance *that* counterfactual has to the question of whether she harmed (wronged) the child by bringing him into existence. Still, I think the Sumner suggestion deserves further serious exploration. As my argument now stands, I seem to prefer (relative) linguistic purity to the (relative) moral purity required by my initial liberal commitment.

pregnant now (instead of, say, next month), she will conceive a child with severe defects, though not so severe as to render his life not worth living. Instead of warning the woman, however, he conceals the information, seduces her, and recklessly runs the risk of pregnancy. Nine months later the severely impaired baby is born, much to his mother's distress. Somebody will have to pay the heavy costs of rearing this handicapped child. Why not the person at fault, the wealthy gynecologist, even though his fault did not consist in a violation of the child's rights, and the child, therefore, was not his "victim"?

Some readers will want more than this. They will not be content with civil liability created by useful and just public policies for the more extreme Parfit-type cases. They will also insist that there *is* a victim in these cases whose right has been violated and who therefore has a genuine moral grievance against the wrongdoer. I am willing to go part of the way to meet this objection. The impaired person (plaintiff) is indeed in a special moral relation to the wrongdoer that makes a certain kind of negative attitude toward him appropriate and understandable. I think the best word for that attitude is "resentment." The specific type of righteous moral indignation that stems from an awareness that one has been personally wronged by another is not quite the same thing as generic resentment, since it is closely linked with perceived right-infraction, and resentment need not be. Neither must resentment imply imputation of guilt, charges or claims, or other such legalistic postures. "Having a grievance" is a vague phrase that might conceal the difference between resentment and the feeling that one has been personally wronged. To be sure, there is something personal in the disapproving sort of ill-will we call "resentment." We do not resent everything that we disapprove of. But it is sufficient for resentment that the attitudes or behavior we disapprove of be directed at a class we feel part of, or can identify with, or somehow feel associated with.

The plaintiff in the hypothetical stories we are considering may come in time to resent his biological parent, not for violating his right by an act that made him worse off on balance than he would otherwise be but, rather, for being the sort of scoundrel he or she is, a person who has manifested an indifference to the possibility of human suffering and is prepared to bring people into existence with harmful impairments for no morally respectable reason. The plaintiff recognizes that he is a member of a class of possible persons, those that might have come into being through the defendant's wrong act, toward whom the defendant's hateful unconcern was directed. Only in that way is there anything "personal" in his resentment. He is in a position similar to that of a black in the presence of an honorable bigot who never violates the rights of blacks, but shows by his behavior that he is the sort of person who always prefers the well-being of whites to blacks, other things being equal. He always roots for the white boxer, for example, when watching televised contests between a white and a black, and he gives generously to worthy white charities but nothing at all to worthy black ones. (It is possible to have that sort of bigoted character while also being a resolute Kantian determined never to violate anyone's rights.) The white person's attitude does not by itself give the black person a personal grievance in the absence of any right-infractions, but the black person's resentment, as a member of a group whose welfare is valued less than others', is well grounded and understandable.

One final point. For that class of cases that are similar to Parfit's example in that the life wrongfully produced is worth living, but different in that the parties at fault are medical providers rather than biological parents, there is less obviously a need for radical departure from those traditional tort rules that require wrongful harming. If a physician negligently fails to diagnose a married woman's illness as Parfit's disease, so that without the warning that it was her right to receive from the physician she gets pregnant during the dangerous period and gives birth, to her surprise and distress, to a son with a withered arm, then she should have a cause of action against the physician for wrongful birth, even though her son, on traditional tort grounds, has no cause of action for wrongful life. In this kind of case the physician directly wrongs the parents and causes them to suffer the indirect harm of having a handicapped child. *They* would clearly have been better off had the physician not been negligent, for then they would have waited for the prescribed interval before conceiving a child—a different child to be sure—who would have been healthy. The parents in this example have been harmed in the full sense (adversely affected and wronged)[30] even though the child himself, the person who comes into existence in a directly impaired condition, has not been wronged or harmed by the physician, since the only alternative for him would be nonexistence, which he does not, and rationally could not, prefer. Moreover, allowing the parents to recover damages in this case would give them the wherewithal to care for their child's special needs (if they are the child's legal guardians), and thus fulfill *some* of the functions of a wrongful life suit in the child's own name.

CONCLUSION

This chapter has been concerned with both conceptual and policy questions. The chief problems of the former kind concern the application of the

---

[30] This is the judgment that would seem clear when made from a prospective vantage point at the time of the harming, even though *now*, years later in retrospect, it might be admitted that love of *this* particular child "offsets" the harm. I think it is the prospective judgment, however, which should control. After all, the parents, but for the negligence of others, could have had another child that they would have loved every bit as much as this one, but without the heartbreaking handicaps.

concept of harm employed in Mill's "harm principle" to cases of prenatal harming, and in particular to the most difficult of these, that in which the act said to cause an infant's impaired condition is the very same as that which brought him into existence. Because of the counterfactual condition that must be part of the analysis of harming, whether prenatal or postnatal, I concluded that an infant is harmed by a wrongful act responsible for his coming into existence only if that act causes him to be born in a condition so bad that he would have been "better off if he had never been born at all." The paradox implied in this wording is eliminated, I claimed, if we analyze it in terms of rational preferability, a notion that is not without its own difficulties, but which, I claimed, is coherent and actually applicable to the preference for nonexistence over some extremely severe impairments. More typically, however, infants are born with impairments that are *not* such that nonexistence would be rationally preferable to them. These unfortunate children suffer the continuing residual harms caused by the acts that produced their existence, but even when those acts were negligent or more seriously wrongful, the child cannot claim that he was wronged or harmed on balance by them, so long as he admits that he prefers his present impaired existence to the nonexistence that was its only alternative for him. I think that he has no grievance against those responsible for his existence, since they did not violate his rights, but that his resentment of them, in some circumstances, would be understandable and justified.

The policy questions in this chapter are largely derivative from the conceptual ones. How can we apply the liberal doctrine ("liberal" at least when applied to criminal law) that it is morally illegitimate to impose liability without a wronged/harmed victim to cases of wrongful life and their (largely hypothetical) analogues in criminal law? When the impairment of the infant is so severe that his life is not rationally preferable to nonexistence (or as we say, is "not worth living"), and it was produced by another party's negligence or deliberate wrongful conduct, then criminal liability would be legitimate in principle, since the harm principle would be satisfied, but I could illustrate such cases only with science fiction examples that are at present no threat. Wrongful life tort suits, where the life is worse than no life at all, are conceptually coherent, and legitimate in principle, but in most of the familiar senses of "compensation," there can be no compensation for a life that is so terrible that nonexistence would be preferable to it. Tort suits can only achieve a transfer of the costs of maintaining such a life to a more appropriate party.

When the infant's impairment is serious but not so bad that nonexistence would have been preferable to it, the liberal's policy problems are even more difficult. Here the liberal may have to concede grudgingly that criminal prohibitions of some wrongful acts are legitimate in principle (though rarely justified in fact) even though they do not have victims, that is, persons who are wronged and harmed on balance by them. These prohibitions would be legitimate only when an interest-connected nongrievance evil is extreme. This result appears to be a departure from the strict letter of the liberal's doctrine, but I have claimed that it accords with the animating humane spirit of that doctrine. Similarly, I concluded, wrongful life suits against a biological parent could conceivably be legitimate, even for harms that are not worse than nonexistence. That is partly because in the civil, as opposed to the criminal law, a party may be justly answerable for another's harmful condition, even though that condition is not, strictly speaking, his doing.

Chapter Two

ABORTION

ABORTION CAN BE DEFINED as the deliberate causing of the death of a fetus, either by directly killing it or (more commonly) by causing its expulsion from the womb before it is "viable," that is, before it is capable of surviving outside its mother's body. The word "fetus" in this definition refers to a human offspring at any stage of its prenatal development, from conception to birth. There is a narrower medical sense of the word "fetus" in which it refers to the unborn entity from roughly the eighth week of pregnancy (when brain waves can first be monitored) until birth, normally at nine months. In this technical sense the word "fetus" is used to contrast the relatively mature unborn being with its earlier stages when it is called a "zygote" (from conception to implantation a week later in the uterine wall) or an "embryo" (from implantation until the eighth week). I shall use the word "fetus" as a convenient general term for the unborn at all phases of its development except when the contrast between fetus and embryo or zygote becomes central in the argument.

The question of the moral permissibility of abortion demands that we answer two very hard philosophical questions. The first requires us to consider which traits of the developing fetus are relevant to deciding what morally may and may not be done to it. The general problem discussed in this regard is often called "the problem of the status of the fetus." In discussing problems under this heading, moral philosophers are especially concerned to determine at which stage, if any, and in virtue of which properties, the fetus becomes a human right-holder, capable of claiming such basic goods as life itself. If at some given stage a fetus has a right to life, then (it would seem to follow) it is culpable homicide (murder) deliberately to kill it at that or subsequent stages. If the fetus at a given point in its development does not have a right to life, then it is not homicide deliberately to kill it at that point, but it does not follow that it is *morally* permissible to do so, or that some lesser form of criminal prohibition might not be justified. These and related questions will be discussed in the first part of this chapter.

In "The Problem of the Conflict of Claims," we shall consider a quite different cluster of questions. Suppose, just for the sake of the argument, that the fetus, at some given stage, is a full moral person with a full panoply of rights including the right to life. In that case killing it at that stage would be homicide by definition, but if the woman carrying the fetus herself (or for that matter, some third party) has some moral claim or claims even stronger than, and incompatible with, those of the fetus, abortion in that case might be treated as a kind of "justified homicide," in the same innocent category as killing in self-defense or defense of others, the execution of valid death sentences by licensed executioners, and killing enemy soldiers in time of war. In this part of the chapter we consider what moral claims the pregnant woman (in particular) might have that could override even the acknowledged right to life of the fetus.

THE STATUS OF THE FETUS

The problem of the status of the fetus can be formulated as follows: At what stage, if any, in the development between conception and birth do fetuses acquire the characteristic (whatever it may be) that confers on them the appropriate status to be included in the scope of the moral rule against homicide—the rule "Thou shalt not kill"? Put more tersely: At what stage, if any, of their development do fetuses become people? A variety of familiar answers have been given—for example, that the fetus becomes a person "at the moment of conception," at "quickening" (that is, at the moment of the fetus's first self-initiated movement in the womb), at viability (that is, when the fetus is able to survive independently outside the mother's womb). Debates about when the fetus becomes a person, however, are premature unless we have first explored what a person is. Answers to the question "When does the fetus become a person?" attempt to draw a boundary line between prepersons and persons; even if correctly drawn, however, a boundary line is not the same thing as a criterion of personhood. Indeed, until we have a criterion, we cannot know for sure whether a given proposed boundary is correct. Let us mean by "a criterion of personhood" that characteristic (or set of characteristics) that is common and peculiar to all persons and in virtue of which they are persons. "A proposed criterion of personhood," as we shall understand the phrase, is some statement (true or false) of what the "person-making characteristic" is.

The statement of a mere boundary line of personhood, in contrast, may be correct and useful even though it mentions no person-making characteristic at all. Such a statement may specify only some theoretically superficial characteristic that happens to be invariably (or perhaps only usually and roughly) correlated with a person-making characteristic. For example, even if it is true that all persons can survive outside the mother's womb, it does not follow that being able to survive outside the mother's womb is what makes someone a person or that this is even partially constitutive of what it is to be a person. The "superficial characteristic," then, can be used as a clue, test, or indication of the presence of the basic personhood-conferring characteristic and therefore of personhood itself, even though it is in no sense a cause or a constituent of personhood. An analogy might make the point clearer. What makes any chemical compound an acid is a feature of its molecular structure, namely, that it contains hydrogen as a positive radical. But it also happens that acids "typically" are soluble in water, sour in taste, and turn blue litmus paper red. The latter three characteristics, then, while neither constitutive nor causative of acidity, can nevertheless be useful and reliable indexes to, or tests of, acidity. The litmus test in particular draws a "boundary" between acids and nonacids. The question now to be addressed is whether a reasonable criterion for personhood can be found, one that enables us to draw an accurate boundary line.

Human Beings and Persons

The first step in coming to terms with a concept of a person is to disentangle it from a concept with which it is thoroughly intertwined in most of our minds, that of a human being. Mary Anne Warren has pointed out that the term "human" has two "distinct but not often distinguished senses."[1] In what she calls the "moral sense," a being is human provided that it is a "full-fledged member of the moral community," a being possessed (as Jefferson wrote of all "men") of inalienable rights to life, liberty, and the pursuit of happiness. For beings to be humans in this sense is precisely for them to be people, and the problem of the "humanity" of the fetus in this sense is that of determining whether the fetus is the sort of being—a person—who has such moral rights as the right to life. On the other hand, a being is human in what Warren calls the "genetic sense" provided he or she is a member of the species *Homo sapiens*, and all we mean in describing someone as a human is the genetic sense is that he or she belongs to that animal species. In this sense, when we say that Jones is a human being, we are making a statement of the same type as when we say that Fido is a dog (a canine being). Any fetus conceived by human parents will of course be a human being in this sense, just as any fetus conceived by dogs will of course be canine in the analogous sense.

It is possible to hold, as no doubt many people do, that all human beings in the moral sense (persons) are human beings in the genetic sense (members of *Homo sapiens*) and vice versa, so that the two classes, while distinct in meaning, nevertheless coincide exactly in reality. In that case all genetically human beings, including fetuses from the moment of conception, have a right to life, the unjustified violation of which is homicide, and no beings who are genetically nonhuman are persons. But it is also possible

---

[1] Mary Anne Warren, "On the Moral and Legal Status of Abortion," *Monist* 57 (1973): 43–61. Reprinted in J. Feinberg and H. Gross, eds., *Liberty: Selected Readings* (Belmont, Calif.: Wadsworth, 1977), pp. 133–43. The quotation is from the latter source, p. 138.

to hold, as some philosophers do, that some genetically human beings (for example, zygotes and irreversibly comatose "human vegetables") are *not* human beings in the moral sense (persons), and/or that some persons (for example, God, angels, devils, higher animals, intelligent beings in outer space) are *not* members of *Homo sapiens*. Surely it is an open question to be settled, if at all, by argument or discovery, whether the two classes correspond exactly. It is not a question closed in advance by definition or appeals to word usage.

Normative versus Descriptive Personhood

Perhaps the best way to proceed from this point is to stick to the term "person" and avoid the term "human" except when we clearly intend the genetic sense, in that way avoiding the ever-present danger of being misunderstood. The term "person," however, is not without its own ambiguities. The one central ambiguity we should note is that between purely normative (moral or legal) uses of "person" and purely descriptive (conventional, commonsense) uses of the term.

When moralists or lawyers use the term "person" in a purely normative way they use it simply to ascribe moral or legal properties—usually rights or duties or both—to the beings so denominated. To be a person in the normative sense is to have rights, or rights and duties, or at least to be the sort of being who could have rights and duties without conceptual absurdity. Most writers think that it would be sheer nonsense to speak of the rights or duties of rocks, or blades of grass, or sunbeams, or historical events, or abstract ideas. These objects are thought to be conceptually inappropriate subjects for the attribution of rights or duties. Hence we speak of them as "impersonal entities," the types of beings that are contrasted with objects that can stand in personal relationships to us or make moral claims on us. The higher animals—our fellow mammalian species in particular—are borderline cases whose classification as persons or nonpersons has been a matter of controversy. Many of them are fit subjects of right-ascriptions but cannot plausibly be assigned duties or moral responsibilities. In any case, when we attribute personhood in a purely normative way to any kind of being, we are attributing such moral qualities as rights or duties but not (necessarily) any observable characteristics of any kind—for example, having flesh or blood or belonging to a particular species. Lawyers have attributed (legal) personhood even to states and corporations, and their purely normative judgments say nothing about the presence or absence of body, mind, consciousness, color, and the like.

In contrast to the purely normative use of the word "person" we can distinguish a purely empirical or descriptive use. There are certain characteristics that are fixed by a rather firm convention of our language such that the general term for any being who possesses them is "person." Thus, to say of some being that he is a person, in this sense, is to convey some information about what the being is like. Neither are attributions of personhood of this kind essentially controversial. If to be a person means to have characteristics *a*, *b*, and *c*, then to say of a being who is known to have *a, b,* and *c* that he or she is a person (in the descriptive sense) is no more controversial than to say of an animal known to be a young dog that it is a puppy, or of a person known to be an unmarried man that he is a bachelor. What makes these noncontroversial judgments true are conventions of language that determine what words mean. The conventions are often a bit vague around the edges but they apply clearly enough to central cases. It is in virtue of these reasonably precise linguistic conventions that the word "person" normally conveys the idea of a definite set of descriptive characteristics. I shall call the idea defined by these characteristics "the commonsense concept of personhood." When we use the word "person" in this wholly descriptive way we are not attributing rights, duties, eligibility for rights and duties, or any other normative characteristics to the being so described. At most we are attributing characteristics that may be a ground for ascribing rights and duties.

These purely normative and purely descriptive uses of the word "person" are probably unusual. In most of its uses, the word both describes or classifies someone in a conventionally understood way and ascribes rights and so forth to him. But there is enough looseness or flexibility in usage to leave open the question of whether the classes of moral and commonsense persons correspond in reality. Although some may think it obvious that all and only commonsense persons are moral persons, that identification of classes does not follow simply as a matter of word usage, and must, therefore, be supported independently by argument. Many learned writers, after all, have maintained that human zygotes and embryos are moral persons despite the fact that they are almost certainly not "commonsense persons." Others have spoken of wicked murderers as "monsters" or "fiends" who can rightly be destroyed like "wild beasts" or eliminated like "rotten apples." This seems to amount to holding that "moral monsters" are commonsense persons who are so wicked (only *persons* can be wicked) that they have lost their moral personhood, or membership in our moral community. Sir William Blackstone maintained that convicted murderers forfeit their right to life. If one went further and maintained that moral monsters forfeit all their human rights, then one would be rejecting the view that the classes of moral and commonsense persons exactly coincide, for wicked persons who are answerable for their foul deeds must first of all be persons in the descriptive sense; but as beings without rights, they would not be moral persons.

The Criterion of Commonsense Personhood

A criterion of personhood in the descriptive sense would be a specification of those characteristics that are common and peculiar to commonsense persons and in virtue of which they are such persons. They are necessary conditions for commonsense personhood in the sense that no being who lacks any one of them can be a person. They are sufficient conditions in the sense that any being who possesses all of them is a person, whatever he or she may be like in other respects. How shall we formulate this criterion? If this question simply raises a matter of fixed linguistic convention, one might expect it to be easy enough to state the defining characteristics of personhood straight off. Surprisingly, the question is not quite that simple, and no mere dictionary is likely to give us a wholly satisfactory answer. What we must do is to think of the characteristics that come at least implicitly to mind when we hear or use such words as "person," "people," and the personal pronouns. We might best proceed by considering three different classes of cases: clear examples of beings whose personhood cannot be doubted, clear examples of beings whose nonpersonhood cannot be doubted, and actual or hypothetical examples of beings whose status is not initially clear. We probably will not be able to come up with a definitive list of characteristics if only because the word "person" may be somewhat loose, but we should be able to achieve a criterion that is precise enough to permit a definite classification of fetuses.

UNDOUBTED COMMONSENSE PERSONS

Who are undoubted persons? Consider first your parents, siblings, or friends. What is it about them that makes you so certain that they are persons? "Well, they look like persons," you might say. "They have human faces and bodies." But so do irreversibly comatose human vegetables, and we are, to put it mildly, not so certain that they are persons. "Well then, they are males and females and thus appropriately referred to by our personal pronouns, all of which have gender. We cannot refer to any of them by use of the impersonal pronoun 'it,' because they have sex; so perhaps being gendered is the test of personhood." Such a reply has superficial plausibility, but is the idea of a "sexless person" logically contradictory? Perhaps any genetically human person will be predominantly one sex or the other, but must the same be true of "intelligent beings in outer space," or spirits, gods, and devils?

Let us start again. "What makes me certain that my parents, siblings, and friends are people is that they give evidence of being conscious of the world and of themselves; they have inner emotional lives, just like me; they can understand things and reason about them, make plans, and act; they can communicate with me, argue, negotiate, express themselves, make agreements, honor commitments, and stand in relationships of mutual trust; they have tastes and values of their own; they can be frustrated or fulfilled, pleased or hurt." Now we clearly have the beginnings, at least, of a definitive list of person-making characteristics. In the commonsense way of thinking, persons are those beings who, among other things, are conscious, have a concept and awareness of themselves, are capable of experiencing emotions, can reason and acquire understanding, can plan ahead, can act on their plans, and can feel pleasure and pain.

UNDOUBTED NONPERSONS

What of the objects that clearly are not persons? Rocks have none of the above characteristics; neither do flowers and trees; neither (presumably) do snails and earthworms. But perhaps we are wrong about that. Maybe rocks, plants, and lower animals are congeries of lower-level spirits with inner lives and experiences of their own, as primitive men and mystics have often maintained. Very well, that is possible. But if they do have these characteristics, contrary to all appearances, then it would seem natural to think of them as persons too, "contrary to all appearance." In raising the question of their possession of these characteristics at all, we seem to be raising by the same token the question of their commonsense personhood. Mere rocks are quite certainly not crowds of silent spirits, but if, contrary to fact, they are such spirits, then we must think of them as real people, quite peculiarly embodied.

HARD CASES

Now, what about the hard cases? Is God, as traditionally conceived, a kind of nonhuman—or better, superhuman—person? Theologians are divided about this, of course, but most ordinary believers think of Him (note the personal pronoun) as conscious of self and world, capable of love and anger, eminently rational, having plans for the world, acting (if only through His creation), capable of communicating with humans, of issuing commands and making covenants, and of being pleased or disappointed in the use to which humans put their free will. To the extent that one believes that God has these various attributes, to that extent does one believe in a *personal* God. If one believes only in a God who is an unknown and unknowable First Cause of the world, or an obscure but powerful force sustaining the world, or the ultimate energy in the cosmos, then, it seems fair to say, one believes in an *impersonal* deity.

Now we come to the ultimate thought experiment. Suppose that you are a space explorer whose rocket ship has landed on a planet in a distant galaxy. The planet is inhabited by some very strange objects, so unlike anything you have previously encountered that at first you do not even know whether to classify them as animal, vegetable, mineral, or "none of the above." They are composed of a gelatinous sort of substance much like mucus except that it is held together by no visible membranes or skin, and it continually changes its shape from one sort of amorphous glob to another, sometimes breaking into smaller globs and then coming together again. The objects have no appendages, no joints, no heads, no faces. They float mysteriously above the surface of the planet and move about in complex patterns while emitting eerie sounds resembling nothing so much as electronic music. The first thing you will wish to know about these strange objects is whether they are extraterrestrial *people*, to be respected, greeted, and traded and negotiated with, or mere things or inferior animals to be chopped up, boiled, and used for food and clothing.

Almost certainly the first thing you would do is try to communicate with them by making approaches, gesturing by hand, voice, or radio signals. You might also study the patterns in their movements and sound emissions to see whether they have any of the characteristics of a language. If the beings respond even in a primitive way to early gestures, one might suspect at least that they are beings who are capable of perception and who can be aware of movements and sounds. If some sort of actual communication then follows, you can attribute to them at least the mentality of chimpanzees. If negotiations then follow and agreements are reached, then you can be sure that they are rational beings; and if you learn to interpret signs of worry, distress, anger, alarm, or friendliness, then you can be quite confident that they are indeed people, no matter how inhuman they are in biological respects.

A WORKING CRITERION OF COMMONSENSE PERSONHOOD

Suppose then that we agree that our rough list captures well the traits that are generally characteristic of commonsense persons. Suppose further (what is not quite as evident) that each trait on the list is necessary for commonsense personhood, that no one trait is by itself sufficient, but that the whole *collection* of traits is sufficient to confer commonsense personhood on any being that possesses it. Suppose, that is, that consciousness is necessary (no permanently unconscious being can be a person), but that it is not enough. The conscious being must also have a concept of its self and a certain amount of self-awareness. But although each of these last traits is necessary, they are still not enough even in conjunction, since a self-aware, conscious being who is totally incapable of learning or reasoning would not be a person. Hence minimal rationality is also necessary, though not by itself sufficient. And so on through our complete list of person-making characteristics, each one of which, let us suppose, is a necessary condition, and all of which are jointly a sufficient condition of being a person in the commonsense, descriptive sense of "person." Let us call our set of characteristics C. Now at last we can pose the most important and controversial

the set of characteristics of a person

question about the status of the fetus: What is the relation, if any, between having C and being a person in the normative (moral) sense, that is, a being who possesses, among other things, a right to life?

Proposed Criteria of Moral Personhood

It bears repeating at the outset of our discussion of this most important question that formulating criteria of personhood in the purely moral sense is not a scientific question to be settled by empirical evidence, not simply a question of word usage, not simply a matter to be settled by commonsense thought experiments. It is instead an essentially controversial question about the possession of moral rights that cannot be answered in these ways. That is not to say that rational methods of investigation and discussion are not available to us, but only that the methods of reasoning about morals do not often provide conclusive proofs and demonstrations. What rational methods can achieve for us, even if they fall short of producing universal agreement, is to list the various options open to us and the strong and weak points of each of them. Every position has its embarrassments, that is, places where it appears to conflict with moral and commonsense convictions that even its proponents can be presumed to share. To point out these embarrassments for a given position is not necessarily to refute it but rather to measure the costs of holding it to the coherence of one's larger set of beliefs generally. Similarly, each position has its own peculiar advantages, respects in which it coheres uniquely well with deeply entrenched convictions that even its opponents might be expected to share. I shall try in the ensuing discussion to state and illustrate as vividly as I can the advantages and difficulties in all the major positions. Then I shall weigh the cases for and against the various alternatives. For those who disagree with my conclusion, the discussion will serve at least to locate the crucial issues in the controversy over the status of the fetus.

A proposed criterion for moral personhood is a statement of a characteristic (or set of characteristics) that its advocate deems both necessary and (jointly) sufficient for being a person in the moral sense. Such characteristics are not thought of as mere indexes, signs, or "litmus tests" of moral personhood but as more basic traits that actually confer moral personhood on whomever possesses them. All and only those beings having these characteristics have basic moral rights, in particular the right to full and equal protection against homicide. Thus, fetuses must be thought of as having this right if they satisfy a proposed criterion of personhood. The main types of criteria of moral personhood proposed by philosophers can be grouped under one or another of five different headings, which we shall examine in turn. Four of the five proposed criteria refer to possession of C (the traits we have listed as conferring commonsense personhood). One of these four specifies actual possession of *C*; the other three refer to either actual or potential possession of *C*. The remaining criterion, which we shall consider briefly first, makes no mention of *C* at all.

THE SPECIES CRITERION

"All and only members of the biological species *Homo sapiens*, 'whoever is conceived by human beings,' are moral persons and thus entitled to full and equal protection by the moral rule against homicide." The major advantage of this view (at least for some) is that it gives powerful support to those who would extend the protection of the rule against homicide to the fetus from the moment of conception. If this criterion is correct, it is not simply because of utilitarian reasons (such that it would usefully increase respect for life in the community) that we must not abort human zygotes and embryos, but rather because we owe it to these minute entities themselves not to kill them, for as members of the human species they are already possessed of a full right to life equal in strength to that of any adult person.

The species criterion soon encounters serious difficulties. Against the view that membership in the species *Homo sapiens* is a *necessary* condition of membership in the class of moral persons, we have the possibility of there being moral persons from other planets who belong to other biological species. Moreover, some human beings—in particular, those who are irreversibly comatose "vegetables"—*are* human beings but doubtfully qualify as moral persons, a fact that casts serious doubt on the view that membership in the species *Homo sapiens* is a *sufficient* condition of being a moral person.

The species criterion might be defended against these objections if some persuasive reason could be given why moral personhood is a unique feature of all and only human beings. Aside from an arbitrary claim that this is "just obvious," a position that Peter Singer argues amounts to a pernicious prejudice against nonhuman animals comparable to racism and sexism, the only possible way to defend this claim to uniqueness is by means of some theological argument: for example, that *all* human beings (including human fetuses) and *only* human beings (thereby excluding all nonhuman animals and possible beings from other planets) are moral persons *because God has made this so.*[2] Now, if one already believes on faith that God had made it true that all and only humans are moral persons, then of course one has quite conclusive reason for believing that all and only humans are moral persons. But if we leave faith aside and confine our attention to reasons, then we shall have to ask what grounds there are for supposing that

[2] See Paul Ramsey, "The Morality of Abortion," in *Life or Death: Ethics and Options*, ed. D. H. Labby (Seattle and London: University of Washington Press, 1968), pp. 60–93.

"God has made this so," and any reason we might have for doubting that it *is* so would count equally as a reason against supposing that God made it so. A good reason for doubting that $7 + 5 = 13$ is an equally good reason for doubting that God made it to be the case that $7 + 5 = 13$; a good reason for doubting that cruelty is morally right is, if anything, a better reason for denying that God made it to be the case that cruelty is right.

THE MODIFIED SPECIES CRITERION

"All and only members of species generally characterized by C, whether the species is *Homo sapiens* or another and whether or not the particular individual in question happens to possess C, are moral persons entitled to full and equal protection by the moral rule against homicide." This modification is designed to take the sting out of the first objection (above) to the unmodified species criterion. If there are other species or categories of moral persons in the universe, it concedes, then they too have moral rights. Indeed, if there are such, then *all* of their members are moral persons possessed of such rights, even those individuals who happen themselves to lack C, because they are not yet fully developed or because they have been irreparably damaged.

The major difficulty for the modified species criterion is that it requires further explanation why C should determine moral personhood when applied to classes of creatures rather than to individual cases. Why is a permanently unconscious but living body of a human or an extragalactic person (or, for that matter, a chimpanzee, if we should decide that that species as a whole is characterized by C) a moral person when it lacks as an individual the characteristics that determine moral personhood? Just because opposable thumbs are a characteristic of *Homo sapiens*, it does not follow that this or that particular *Homo sapiens* has opposable thumbs. There appears to be no reason for regarding right-possession any differently, in this regard, from thumb-possession.

THE STRICT POTENTIALITY CRITERION

"All and only those creatures who either actually or potentially possess C (that is, who either have C now or would come to have C in the natural course of events) are moral persons now, fully protected by the rule against homicide." This criterion also permits one to draw the line of moral personhood in the human species right at the moment of conception, which will be counted by some as an advantage. It also has the undeniable advantage of immunity from one charge of arbitrariness since it will extend moral personhood to all beings in *any* species or category who possess C, either actually or potentially. It may also cohere with our psychological attitudes, since it can explain why it is that many people, at least, think of unformed

Intuitive

or unpretty fetuses as precious. Zygotes and embryos in particular are treasured not for what they are but for what they are biologically "programmed" to become in the fullness of time: real people fully possessed of C.

The difficulties of this criterion are of two general kinds, those deriving from the obscurity of the concept of "potentiality," which perhaps can be overcome, and the more serious difficulties of answering the charge that merely potential possession of any set of qualifications for a moral status does not logically ensure actual possession of that status. Consider just one of the problems raised by the concept of potentiality itself.[3] How, it might be asked, can a mere zygote be a potential person, whereas a mere spermatozoon or a mere unfertilized ovum is not? If the spermatozoon and ovum we are talking about are precisely those that will combine in a few seconds to form a human zygote, why are they not potential zygotes, and thus potential people, *now*? The defender of the potentiality criterion will reply that it is only at the moment of conception that any being comes into existence with exactly the same chromosomal makeup as the human being that will later emerge form the womb, and it is *that* chromosomal combination that forms the potential person, not anything that exists before it comes together. The reply is probably a cogent one, but uncertainties about the concept of potentiality might make us hesitate, at first, to accept it, for we might be tempted to think of both the germ cell (spermatozoon or ovum) and the zygote as potentially a particular person, while holding that the differences between their potentials, though large and significant to be sure, are nevertheless differences in degree rather than kind. It would be well to resist that temptation, however, for it could lead us to the view that some of the entities and processes that combined still earlier to form a given spermatozoon were themselves potentially that spermatozoon and hence potentially the person that spermatozoon eventually became, and so on. At the end of that road is the proposition that everything is potentially everything else, and thus the destruction of all utility in the concept of potentiality. It is better to hold this particular line at the zygote.

The remaining difficulty for the strict potentiality criterion is much more serious. It is a logical error, some have charged, to deduce *actual* rights from merely *potential* (but not yet actual) qualification for those rights. What follows from potential qualification, it is said, is potential, not actual, rights; what entails actual rights is actual, not potential, qualification. As Stanley Benn put it, "A potential president of the United States is not on

---

[3] These problems are discussed in more detail in Joel Feinberg, "The Rights of Animals and Future Generations" (Appendix: The Paradoxes of Potentiality), in *Philosophy and Environmental Crisis*, ed. W. T. Blackstone (Athens, Ga.: University of Georgia Press, 1974), pp. 67–68.

that account Commander-in-Chief [of the U.S. Army and Navy]."[4] This simple point can be called "the logical point about potentiality." Taken on its own terms, I do not see how it can be answered as an objection to the strict potentiality criterion. It is still open to antiabortionists to argue that merely potential commonsense personhood is a ground for *duties* we may have toward the potential person. But they cannot argue that it is the ground for the potential person's *rights* without committing a logical error.

THE MODIFIED OR GRADUALIST POTENTIALITY CRITERION

"Potential possession of C confers not a right, but only a claim, to life, but that claim keeps growing stronger, requiring ever stronger reasons to override it, until the point when C is actually possessed, by which time it has become a full right to life." This modification of the potentiality criterion has one distinct and important advantage. It coheres with the widely shared feeling that the moral seriousness of abortion increases with the age of the fetus. It is extremely difficult to believe on other than very specific theological grounds that a zygote one day after conception is the sort of being that can have any rights at all, much less the whole armory of "human rights" including "the right to life." But it is equally difficult for a great many people to believe that a full-term fetus one day before birth does not have a right to life. Moreover, it is very difficult to find one point in the continuous development of the fetus before which it is utterly without rights and after which it has exactly the same rights as any adult human being. Some rights in postnatal human life can be acquired instantly or suddenly; the rights of citizenship, for example, come into existence at a precise moment in the naturalization proceedings after an oath has been administered and a judicial pronouncement formally produced and certified. Similarly, the rights of husbands and wives come into existence at just that moment when an authorized person utters the words "I hereby pronounce you husband and wife." But the rights of the fetus cannot possibly jump in this fashion from nonbeing to being at some precise moment in pregnancy. The alternative is to think of them as growing steadily and gradually throughout the entire nine-month period until they are virtually "mature" at parturition. There is, in short, a kind of growth in "moral weight" that proceeds in parallel fashion with the physical growth and development of the fetus.

An "immature right" on this view is not to be thought of simply as no right at all, as if in morals a miss were as good as a mile. A better characterization of the unfinished right would be a "weak right," a claim with some moral force proportional to its degree of development but not yet as

---

[4] Stanley I. Benn, "Abortion, Infacticide, and Respect for Persons," in *The Problem of Abortion*, ed. J. Feinberg (Belmont, Calif.: Wadsworth, 1973), p. 102.

much force as a fully matured right. The key word in this account is "claim." Elsewhere I have given an account of the difference between having a right (which I defined as a "valid claim") and having a claim that is not, or not quite, valid. What would the latter be like?

> One might accumulate just enough evidence to argue with relevance and cogency that one has a right . . . although one's case might not be overwhelmingly conclusive. The argument might be strong enough to entitle one to a hearing and fair consideration. When one is in this position, it might be said that one "has a claim" that deserves to be weighed carefully. Nevertheless the balance of reasons may turn out to militate against recognition of the claim, so that the claim is not a valid claim or right.[5]

Now there are various ways in which a claim can fail to be a right. There are many examples, particularly from the law, where *all* the claims to some property, including some that are relevantly made and worthy of respect, are rejected, simply because none of them is deemed strong enough to qualify as a right. In such cases, a miss truly is a good as a mile. But in other cases, an acknowledged claim of (say) medium strength will be strong enough to be right unless a stronger claim appears on the scene to override it. For these conflict situations, card games provide a useful analogy. In poker, three of a kind is good enough to win the pot unless one of the other players "makes claim" to the pot with a higher hand, say a flush or a full house. The player who claims the pot with three of a kind "has a claim" to the pot that is overridden by the stronger claim of the player with the full house. The strongest claim presented will, by that fact, constitute a right to take the money. The player who withdrew with a four flush had "no claim at all," but even that person's hand might have established a right to the pot if no stronger claim were in conflict with it.

The analogy applies to the abortion situation in the following way. The game has at least two players, the woman and the fetus, although more can play, and sometimes the responsible sex partner and/or the doctor are involved too. For the first weeks of its life, the fetus (zygote, embryo) has hardly any claim to life at all, and virtually any reason of the mother's for aborting it will be strong enough to override a claim made in the fetus's behalf. At any stage in the game, any reason the mother might have for aborting will constitute a claim, but as the fetus matures, its claims grow stronger, requiring ever-stronger claims to override them. After three months or so, the fact that an abortion would be "convenient" for the mother will not be a strong enough claim, and the fetus's claim to life will defeat it. In that case, the fetus can be said to have a valid claim or right to life in the same sense that the poker player's full house gives him a right to

[5] Joel Feinberg, *Social Philosophy* (Englewood Cliffs, N.J.: Prentice-Hall, 1973), p. 66.

the pot: it is a right in the sense that it is the strongest of the conflicting claims, not in the sense that it is stronger than any conflicting claim that could conceivably come up. By the time the fetus has become a neonate (a newborn child), however, it has a "right to life" of the same kind all people have, and no mere conflicting claim can override it. (Perhaps more accurately, only claims that other human persons make in self-defense to their own lives can ever have an equal strength.)

The modified potentiality criterion has the attractiveness characteristic of compromise theories when fierce ideological quarrels rage between partisans of more extreme views. It shares one fatal flaw, however, with the strict potentiality criterion. Despite its greater flexibility, it cannot evade "the logical point about potentiality." A highly developed fetus is much closer to being a commonsense person with all the developed traits that qualify it for moral personhood than is the mere zygote. But being almost qualified for rights is not the same thing as being partially qualified for rights; nor is it the same thing as being qualified for partial rights, quasi-rights, or weak rights. The advanced fetus is closer to being a person than is the zygote, just as a dog is closer to personhood than a jellyfish, but that is not the same thing as being "more of a person." In 1930, when he was six years old, Jimmy Carter did not know it, but he was a potential president of the United States. That gave him no claim *then*, not even a very weak claim, to give commands to the U.S. Army and Navy. Franklin D. Roosevelt in 1930 was only two years away from the presidency, so he was a potential president in a much stronger way (the potentiality was much less remote) than was young Jimmy. Nevertheless, he was not actually president, and he had no more of a claim to the prerogatives of the office than did Carter. The analogy to fetuses in different stages of development is of course imperfect. But in both cases it would seem to be invalid to infer the existence of a "weak version of a right" from an "almost qualification" for the full right. In summary, the modified potentiality criterion, insofar as it permits the potential possession of C to be a *sufficient condition* for the actual possession of claims, and in some cases of rights, is seriously flawed in the same manner as the strict potentiality criterion.

THE ACTUAL-POSSESSION CRITERION

"At any give time *t*, all and only those creatures who actually possess C are moral persons at *t*, whatever species or category they may happen to belong to." This simple and straightforward criterion has a number of conspicuous advantages. We should consider it with respect even before we examine its difficulties if only because the difficulties of its major rivals are so severe. Moreover, it has a certain tidy symmetry about it, since it makes the overlap between commonsense personhood and moral personhood complete—a total correspondence with no loose ends left over in either direction. There can be no actual commonsense persons who are not actual moral persons, nor can there be any actual moral persons who are not actual commonsense persons. Moral personhood is not established simply by species membership, associations, or potentialities. Instead, it is conferred by the same characteristics (C) that lead us to recognize personhood wherever we find it. It is no accident, no mere coincidence, that we use the moral term "person" for those beings, and only those beings, who have C. The characteristics that confer commonsense personhood are not arbitrary bases for rights and duties, such as race, sex, or species membership; rather they are the traits that make sense out of rights and duties and without which those moral attributes would have no point or function. It is because people are conscious; have a sense of their personal identities; have plans, goals, and projects; experience emotions; are liable to pains, anxieties, and frustrations; can reason and bargain, and so on—it is because of these attributes that people have values and interests, desires and expectations of their own, including a stake in their own futures, and a personal well-being of a sort we cannot ascribe to unconscious or nonrational beings. Because of their developed capacities they can assume duties and responsibilities and can have and make claims on one another. Only because of their sense of self, their life plans, their value hierarchies, and their stakes in their own futures can they be ascribed fundamental rights. There is nothing arbitrary about these linkages. For these reasons I am inclined to believe that the actual-possession criterion is the correct one.

Despite these impressive advantages, however, the actual-possession criterion must face a serious difficulty, namely, that it implies that small infants (neonates) are not moral persons. There is very little more reason, after all, to attribute C to neonates than to advanced fetuses still *in utero*. Perhaps during the first few days after birth the infant is conscious and able to feel pain, but it is unlikely that it has a concept of itself or of its future life, that it has plans and goals, that it can thing consecutively, and the like. In fact, the whole complex of traits that make up C is not obviously present until the second year of childhood. And that would seem to imply, according to the criterion we are considering, that the deliberate destruction of babies in their first year is no violation of their rights. And *that* might seem to entail that there is nothing wrong with infanticide (the deliberate killing of infants). But infanticide *is* wrong. Therefore, critics of the actual-possession criterion have argued that we ought to reject this criterion.

THE KILLING OF NORMAL INFANTS

Advocates of the actual-possession criterion have a reply to this objection. Even if infanticide is not the murder of a moral person, they believe, it may yet be wrong and properly forbidden on other grounds. To make this clearer, it is useful to distinguish between (1) the case of killing a normal healthy infant or an infant whose handicaps are not so serious as to make a worthwhile future life impossible and (2) the case of killing severely deformed or incurably diseased infants.

Most advocates of the actual-possession criterion take a strong stand against infanticide in the first (the normal) case. It would be seriously wrong for a mother to kill her physically normal infant, they contend, even though such a killing would not violate anyone's right to life. The same reasons that make infanticide in the normal case wrong also justify its prohibition by the criminal law. The moral rule that condemns these killings and the legal rule that renders them punishable are both supported by "utilitarian reasons," that is, considerations of what is called "social utility," "the common good," "the public interest," and the like. Nature has apparently implanted in us an instinctive tenderness toward infants that has proven extremely useful to the species, not only because it leads us to protect our young from death, and thus maintain our population, but also because infants usually grow into adults, and in Benn's words, "if as infants *they* are not treated with some minimal degree of tenderness and consideration, they will suffer for it later, as persons."[6] One might add that when they are adults, others will suffer for it too, at their hands. Spontaneous warmth and sympathy toward babies then clearly have a great deal of social utility, and insofar as infanticide would tend to weaken that socially valuable response, it is, on utilitarian grounds, morally wrong.

There are other examples of wrongful and properly prohibitable acts that violate no one's rights. It would be wrong, for example, to hack up Grandfather's body after he has died a natural death, and dispose of his remains in the trash can on a cold winter's morning. That would be wrong not because it violates *Grandfather's* rights; he is dead and no longer has the same sort of rights as the rest of us, and we can make it part of the example that he was not offended while alive at the thought of such posthumous treatment and indeed even consented to it in advance. Somehow acts of this kind if not forbidden would strike at our respect for living human persons (without which organized society would be impossible) in the most keenly threatening way. (It might also be unhygienic and shocking to trash collectors—less important but equally relevant utilitarian considerations.)

THE KILLING OF RADICALLY DEFORMED INFANTS

The general utilitarian reasons that support a rather rigid rule against infanticide in the case of the normal (and not too abnormal) infant might not be sufficiently strong to rule out infanticide (under very special and strict circumstances) when the infant is extremely deformed or diseased.

[6] Benn, "Abortion," p. 102.

Very likely, a purely ulitatian-based rule against homicide would have exceptive clauses for extremely abnormal neonates. In this respect such rules would differ sharply from rules against infanticide that derive from the ascription to the newborn infant of a full-fledged right to life. If the deformed neonate is a moral person, then he or she is as fully entitled to protection under the rule forbidding homicide as any reader of these words; if the neonate is not a moral person, then in extreme cases there may be a case on balance for killing him. The partisan of the actual-possession criterion of moral personhood actually takes this consequence of nonpersonhood to be an advantage of his view rather than an embarrassment for it. If his view is correct, then we can destroy hopelessly malformed infants *before* they grow into moral persons, thus saving them from a longer life that would be so horrible as to be "not worth living," and this can be done without violating their rights.

Indeed, *failure* to kill such infants before they reach moral personhood may itself be a violation of their rights, according to this view. For if we permit such children to grow into moral personhood knowing full well that the conditions for the fulfillment of their most basic future interests have already been destroyed, then we have wronged these persons before they even exist (as persons), and when they become persons, they can claim (or it can be claimed in their behalf) that they have been wronged. I have argued elsewhere that an extension of the idea of a birthright is suggested by this point. If we know that it will never be possible for a fetus or neonate to have that to which he has a birthright and we allow him nevertheless to be born or to survive into personhood, then that fetus or neonate is wronged, and we become a party to the violation of his rights.[7]

Not just any physical or mental handicaps, of course, can render a life "not worth living." Indeed, as the testimony of some thalidomide babies[8] now growing into adulthood shows, it is possible (given exceptional care) to live a valuable life even without arms and legs and full vision. But there may be some extreme cases where deformities are not merely "handicaps" in the pursuit of happiness but guarantees that the pursuit must fail. A brain-damaged, retarded child born deaf, blind, partially paralyzed, and doomed to constant pain might be such a case. Given the powerful general utilitarian case against infanticide, however, the defender of the "right to die" position must admit that in cases of doubt, the burden of showing that a worthwhile life is impossible rests on the person who would elect a

[7] Joel Feinberg, "Is There a Right to Be Born?" in *Understanding Moral Philosophy*, ed. James Rachels (Encino, Calif.: Dickenson, 1976), pp. 353–54. See also chapter 1 in this volume.

[8] Thalidomide is the trade name of a potent tranquilizer once manufactured in Europe but never permitted in the United States. In the late 1950s, thousands of deformed babies were born to European women who had taken thalidomide during pregnancy.

quick and painless death for the infant. And there is almost always some doubt.

IMPLICATIONS FOR THE PROBLEM OF ABORTION

The implications of the actual-possession criterion for the question of the status of the fetus as a moral person are straightforward. Since the fetus does not actually possess those characteristics (C) that we earlier listed as necessary and sufficient for possessing the right to life, the fetus does not possess that right. Given this criterion, therefore, abortion never involves violating a fetus's right to life, and permitting a fetus to be born is never anything *we owe* it, is never something that is *its due*.

It does not follow, however, that abortion is never wrong. As we saw earlier, despite the fact that infants fail to meet the actual-possession criterion and thus are not moral persons, reasons can be given, of a utilitarian kind, why it is wrong to kill them, at least if they are not radically deformed. It is possible, therefore, that similar reasons can be given in opposition to aborting fetuses at later stages in their development if they are likely not to be radically deformed when born.

Utilitarian reasons of the sort we have considered are so very important that they might suffice to rule out harsh or destructive treatment of *any* nonperson whose resemblance or similarity to real persons is very close: not only deceased ex-persons and small babies, but even adult primates and human fetuses in the final trimester of pregnancy. Justice Blackmun may have had such considerations in mind when in his majority opinion in *Roe v. Wade* he declared that even though no fetuses are legal persons protected by the law of homicide, nevertheless during the final trimester, "The State in promoting its interest in the potentiality of human life, may if it chooses, regulate, and even proscribe, abortion."[9] Whatever interest the state has in "the *potentiality* of human life" must be derivative from the plain interest it has in preserving and promoting respect for *actual* human life. It is not only potential persons who merit our derivative respect but all near-persons, including higher animals, dead people, infants, and well-developed fetuses, those beings whose similarity to real persons is close enough to render them sacred symbols of the real thing.

In the light of these considerations, it seems that a gradualist approach similar to that discussed earlier is a more plausible solution to the general problem of the moral justifiability of abortion than it is to the narrow problem of the criterion of moral personhood. Even if the fetus as a merely potential person lacks an actual right to life, and even if it would not be homicide therefore to kill it, its potential personhood may yet constitute a *reason* against killing it that requires an even stronger reason on the other

---

[9] From Justice Blackmun's opinion in *Roe* v. *Wade*, 410 U.S. 113 (1973).

side if abortion is to be justified. If that is so, it is not implausible to suppose that the more advanced the potential for personhood, the more stringent the case against killing. As we have seen, there are reasons relevant to our moral decisions other than considerations of rights, so that sometimes actions can be judged morally wrong even though they violate no one's rights. Killing a fetus, in that case, could be wrong in certain circumstances, even though it violated no rights of the fetus, even though the fetus was not a moral person, even though the act was in no sense a murder.

Summary and Conclusion

Killing human beings (homicide) is forbidden by both our criminal law and the moral rules that are accepted in all civilized communities. If the fetus at any point in its development is a human being, then to kill it at that point is homicide, and if done without excuse or mitigation, murder. But the term "human being" is subtly ambiguous. The fetus at all stages is obviously human in the genetic sense, but that is not the sense of the term intended in the moral rule against homicide. For a genetically human entity to have a right to life it must be a human being in the sense of a person. But the term "person" is also ambiguous. In the commonsense descriptive meaning of the term, it refers to any being of any species or category who has certain familiar characteristics, of which consciousness of the world, self-concepts, and the capacity to plan ahead are prominent. In the purely normative (moral or legal) sense, a person is any being who has certain rights and/or duties, whatever his other characteristics. Whether or not abortion is homicide depends on what the correct criterion of moral personhood is.

We considered five leading formulations of the criterion of moral personhood and found that they are all subject to various embarrassments. One formulation in terms of species membership seemed both too broad and too narrow, and in the end dependent on an arbitrary preference for our own species. A more careful formulation escaped the charge of being too restrictive and the charge of arbitrariness, but suffered from making the status of an individual derived from his membership in a group rather than from his own intrinsic characteristics. The two formulations in terms of potential possession of the characteristics definitive of commonsense personhood both stumbled on "the logical point about potentiality," that potential qualification for a right does not entail actual possession of the right. The modified or gradualist formulation of the potentiality criterion, however, does have some attractive features, and could be reformulated as a more plausible answer to another question, that about the moral permissibility of abortion. Even if the fetus is not a person and lacks a right to life, ever stronger reasons might be required to justify aborting it as it grows older and more similar to a person.

The weaknesses of the first four proposed criteria of moral personhood create a strong presumption in favor of the remaining one, the actual-possession criterion. It is clear that fetuses are not "people" in the ordinary commonsense meaning of that term. Hence, according to our final criterion, they are not moral persons either, since this criterion of moral personhood simply adopts the criteria of commonsense personhood. The very grave difficulty of this criterion is that it entails that infants are not people either, during the first few months or more of their lives. That is a genuine difficulty for the theory, but a far greater embarrassment can be avoided. Because there are powerful reasons against infanticide that apply even if the infant is not a moral person, the actual-possession criterion is not subject to the devastating objection that it would morally or legally justify infanticide on demand.

THE PROBLEM OF THE CONFLICT OF CLAIMS

The problem of the status of the fetus is the first and perhaps the most difficult of the questions that must be settled before we can come to a considered view about the moral justifiability of abortion, but its solution does not necessarily resolve all moral perplexities about abortion. Even if we were to grant that the fetus is a moral person and thus has a valid claim to life, it would not follow that abortion is always wrong. For there are other moral persons, in addition to the fetus, whose interests are involved. The woman in whose uterus the fetus abides, in particular, has needs and interests that may well conflict with bringing the fetus to term. Do any of these needs and interest of the woman provide grounds for her having a genuine claim to an abortion and, if they do, which of the two conflicting claims— the woman's claim to an abortion or the fetus's presumed claim to life— ought to be respected if they happen to conflict? This is the second major moral question that needs to be examined with all the care we can muster. To do this, one very important assumption must be made—namely, that the fetus is a moral person and so has a valid claim to life. As we have seen in the previous section, this assumption might very well be unfounded and is unfounded in fact if we accept what appears to be the most reasonable criterion for moral personhood—namely, the actual-possession criterion. For purposes of the present section, however, we shall assume that the fetus is a moral person; this will enable us to investigate whose claim, the fetus's or the woman's, ought to be honored if both have genuine but conflicting claims.

Formulation of the "Right to an Abortion"

The right to an abortion that is often claimed on behalf of all women is a *discretionary right* to be exercised or not, on a given occasion, as the woman sees fit. For that reason it is sometimes called a "right to choose." If a pregnant woman has such a right, then it is up to her, and her alone, whether to bear the child or to have it aborted. She is at liberty to bear it if she chooses and at liberty to have it aborted if she chooses. She has no duty to bear it, but neither can she have a duty, imposed from without, to abort it. In respect to the fetus, her choice is sovereign. Correlated with this liberty is a duty of others not to interfere with its exercise and not to withhold the necessary means for its exercise. These duties are owed to her if she has a discretionary right to abortion, and she can claim their discharge as her due.

As a discretionary right, a right to an abortion would resemble the "right to liberty," or the right to move about or travel as one wishes. One is under no obligation to leave or stay home or to go to one destination rather than another, so that it is one's own choice that determines one's movements. But the right to move about at will, like other discretionary rights, is subject to limits. One person's liberty of movement, for example, comes to an end at the boundary of another person's property. The discretionary right to an abortion may be limited in similar ways, so that the statement of a specific right of a particular woman in a definite set of concrete circumstances may need to be qualified by various exceptive clauses—for example, "may choose to have an abortion *except* when the fetus is viable." Which exceptive clauses, if any, must be appended to the formulation of the right to an abortion depends on what the basis of this discretionary right is thought to be. For example, if a woman is thought to have a right to an abortion because she has a right to property *and* because the fetus is said to be her property, then the only exceptions there could be to exercising the right to an abortion would be those that restrict the disposing of one's property. What we must realize, then, is that the alleged right to an abortion cannot be understood in a vacuum; it is a right that can be understood only by reference to the other, more fundamental rights from which it has often been claimed to be derived. Three of these rights and their possible association with the right to an abortion deserve our closest scrutiny: (1) the previously mentioned property rights, (2) the right to self-defense, and (3) the right to bodily autonomy. We shall consider each in its turn.

Possible Grounds for the Woman's Right

PROPERTY RIGHTS OVER ONE'S BODY

Within very wide limits any person has a right to control the uses of his or her own body. With only rare exceptions, surgeons are required to secure the consent of the patient before operating because the body to be cut open, after all, is the patient's own, and he or she has the chief interest in it, and should therefore have the chief "say" over what is done to it. If we think of a fetus as literally a "part" of a woman's body in the same sense as, say, an organ, or as a mere growth attached to a part of the body on the model of a tumor or a wart, then it would seem to follow that the woman may choose to have it removed if she wishes just as she may refuse to have it removed if she prefers. It is highly implausible, however, to think of a human fetus, even if it does fall short of moral personhood, as no more than a temporary organ or parasitic growth. A fetus is not a constituent organ of the mother, like her vermiform appendix, but rather a potentially independent entity temporarily growing inside the mother.

It would be still less plausible to derive a maternal right to an abortion from a characterization of the fetus as the *property* of its mother and thus in the same category as the mother's wristwatch, clothing, or jewelry. One may abandon or destroy one's personal property if one wishes; one's entitlement to do those things is one of the "property rights" that define ownership. But one would think that the father would have equal or near-equal rights of disposal if the fetus were "property." It is not in his body, to be sure, but he contributed as much genetically to its existence as did the mother and might therefore make just as strong (or just as weak) a claim to ownership over it. But neither claim would make very good conceptual sense. If fetuses were property, we would find nothing odd in the notion that they can be bought and sold, rented out, leased, used as collateral on loans, and so on. But no one has ever seriously entertained such suggestions. Finally, we must remember the methodological assumption that we shall make throughout this section, at least for the sake of the argument, that the fetus is a full moral person, with a right to life like yours and mine. On this assumption it would probably be contradictory to think of the fetus as *anyone's* property, especially if property rights included what we might call "the right of disposal"—to abandon or destroy as one chooses.

It is more plausible at first sight to claim that the pregnant woman owns not the fetus but the body in which she shelters the fetus. On this analogy, she owns her body (and particularly her womb) in roughly the way an innkeeper owns a hotel or a homeowner a house and garden. These analogies, however, are also defective. To begin with, it is somewhat paradoxical to think of the relation between a person and her body as similar to that of ownership. Is it possible to sell or rent or lease one's body without selling, renting, or leasing oneself? If one's body were one's property the answer would be affirmative, but in fact one's relationship to one's own body is much more intimate than the ownership model suggests. More important for our present purposes, the legal analogies to the rights of innkeepers and householders will not bear scrutiny. One cannot conceive of what it would be like for a fetus to enter into a contract with a woman for the use of her womb for nine months or to fall in arrears in its payments and thus forfeit its right of occupancy. Surely that cannot be the most apt analogy on which to base the woman's abortion rights! Besides, whatever this, that, or the other legal statute may say about the matter, one is not *morally* entitled, in virtue of one's property rights, to expel a weak and helpless person from one's shelter when that is tantamount to consigning the person to a certain death, and surely one is not entitled to shoot and kill a trespasser who will not, or cannot, leave one's property. In no department of human life does the vindication of property rights justify homicide. The maternal right to an abortion, therefore, cannot be founded on the more basic right to property.

SELF-DEFENSE AND PROPORTIONALITY

Except for the most extreme pacifists, moralists agree that killing can be justified if done in self-defense. If, for example, one man (*A*) is attacked with a lethal weapon by another (*B*), we think that *A* has a right to defend himself against *B*'s attack. Sometimes, in fact, we think that *A* would be justified in killing *B* if this were the only way for *A* to defend himself. Now, some of those who urge the maternal right to an abortion believe that this right is associated with the more basic right to self-defense. There are many difficulties standing in the way of rational acceptance of this view. In particular, the innocence and the nonaggressive nature of the fetus need our special attention. We shall turn to these matters shortly. First, though, it is important to realize what reasons would not count as morally good reasons for an abortion if the right to an abortion were supposed to be founded on the more basic right of self-defense.

All parties to the abortion dispute must agree that many women can be harmed if they are required to bring an unwanted fetus to term. Unwanted sexual intercourse imposed on a woman by a rapist can inflict on its victim severe psychological trauma of a sort deemed so serious by the law that a woman is entitled under some rules to use deadly force if necessary to prevent it. Similarly, an unwanted pregnancy in some circumstances can inflict equally severe psychological injury on a woman who is forced to carry her child to birth. There are various familiar examples of such harm. To borrow an example from Judith Thomson, a terrified fourteen-year-old high-school girl whose pregnancy has been caused by rape has already suffered one severe trauma. If she is now required, over her protests, to carry the child to full term despite her fear, anguish, deep depression, and fancied public mortification, the harmful ramifications may be multiplied a hundredfold. The forty-year-old housewife who has exhausted herself rearing a large family in unfavorable economic circumstances while dependent upon an unreliable and unsympathetic husband may find herself, to her horror, pregnant again and rightly feel that if she is forced to give birth to another child, she will forfeit her last opportunity to escape the intolerably squalid conditions of her life. A man must be morally blind not to acknowledge the severe harms that enforced continuance of unwanted pregnancies can inflict on women. An unwanted child need not literally cost the woman her life, but it can effectively ruin her life from her point of view, and it is a useful moral exercise for men to put themselves imaginatively in the woman's place to share that point of view.

At this stage in the argument the antiabortionist has a ready rejoinder. A woman need not keep her child, assume the responsibilities of rearing it to adulthood, and forfeit her opportunities for self-fulfillment, he might reply, simply because she foregoes an abortion. She can always put the child up for adoption and be assured in the process that it will find loving parents who will give it a good upbringing. All she really has to suffer, the rejoinder concludes, is nine months of minor physical inconvenience. This is an argument that comes easily to the lips of men, but it betrays the grossest sort of masculine insensitivity. In the first place, it is not always true that a woman can have her baby adopted. If she is married, that transaction may require the consent of her husband, and the consent might not be forthcoming. But waiving that point, the possibility of adoption does not give much comfort to the unhappily pregnant woman, for it imposes on her a cruel dilemma and an anguish that far surpass "minor inconvenience." In effect, she has two choices, both of which are intolerable to her. She can carry the child to term and keep it, thus incurring the very consequences that make her unwilling to remain pregnant, or she can nourish the fetus to full size, go into labor, give birth to her baby, and then have it rudely wrenched away, never to be seen by her again. Let moralistic males imagine what an emotional jolt that must be!

Still, on the scale of harms, mere traumas and frustrations are not exactly equal to death. Few women would choose their own deaths in preference to the harms that may come from producing children. According to a common interpretation of the self-defense rule, however, the harm to be averted by a violent act in self-defense need not be identical in severity to that which is inflicted upon one's assailant but only somehow "proportional" to it. Both our prevailing morality and our legal traditions permit the use of lethal force to prevent harms that are less serious than death, so it is plausible to assume that the rule of "proportionality" can be satisfied by something less than equality of harms. But how much less? Jane English offers an answer that, although vague, is in accordance with the moral sentiments of most people when they think of situations other than that involving abortion:

> How severe an injury may you inflict in self-defense? In part this depends upon
> the severity of the injury to be avoided: you may not shoot someone merely

to avoid having your clothes torn. This might lead one to the mistaken conclusion that the defense may only equal the threatened injury in severity; that to avoid death you may kill, but to avoid a black eye you may only inflict a black eye or the equivalent. Rather our laws and customs seem to say that you may create an injury *somewhat but not enormously greater* than the injury to be avoided. To fend off an attack whose outcome would be as serious as rape, a severe beating, or the loss of a finger, you may shoot; to avoid having your clothes torn, you may blacken an eye.[10]

Applying English's answer to the abortion case, and assuming that both the fetus and the woman have legitimate claims, we derive the conclusion that killing the presumed "fetal person" would not be justified when it is done merely to prevent lesser harms to the mother's interests. Not *all* cases of abortion, therefore, can morally be justified, even if there is a maternal right to abortion derived from the more basic right to self-defense.

SELF-DEFENSE: THE PROBLEM OF THE INNOCENT AGGRESSOR

Suppose, however, that the harms that will probably be caused to the mother if the fetus is brought to term are not trivial but serious. Here we have a case where the mother's right to have her important interests respected clashes with the assumed right to life of the fetus. In these circumstances, do not the mother's claims outweigh the fetus's? Does not self-defense in these circumstances justify abortion?

There is a serious, previously undiscussed difficulty that calls out for attention. Consider a case where someone aggressively attacks another. The reason we think that, to use English's expression, we may in self-defense create a "somewhat but not enormously greater injury" than would have been caused by the aggressor is that we think of the aggressor as the party who is morally at fault. If he had not launched the aggression in the first place, there should have been no occasion for the use of force. Since the whole episode was the aggressor's fault, his interests should not count for as much as those of the innocent victim. It is a shame that anybody has to be seriously hurt, but if it comes down to an inescapable choice between the innocent party suffering a serious harm or the culpable party suffering a still more serious harm, then the latter is the lesser of the two evils. Aggressors of course, for all their guilt, remain human beings, and consequently they do not forfeit all their human rights in launching an attack. We still may not kill them to prevent them from stealing ten dollars. But their culpability does cost them their right to equal consideration; we may kill them to prevent them from causing serious harm.

But now suppose that the party who threatens us, even though he is the

[10] Jane English, "Abortion and the Concept of a Person," *Canadian Journal of Philosophy* 5 (1975): 242; emphasis added.

aggressor who initiates the whole episode, is not morally at fault. Suppose the person cannot act otherwise in the circumstances and thus cannot justly be held morally responsible. For example, he was temporarily (or permanently) insane, or it was a case of mistaken identity (he mistook you for a former Gestapo agent to whom you bear a striking resemblance), or someone had drugged the person's breakfast cereal and his behavior was influenced by the drug. George Fletcher, a Columbia law professor, provides a vivid illustration of the problem in what he calls "the case of the psychotic aggressor":

> Imagine that your companion in an elevator goes berserk and attacks you with a knife. There is no escape: the only way to avoid serious bodily harm or even death is to kill him. The assailant acts purposively in the sense that his means further his aggressive end . . . [but] he does act in a frenzy or a fit . . . [and] it is clear that his conduct is non-responsible. If he were brought to trial for his attack, he would have a valid defense of insanity.[11]

The general problem, as lawyers would put it, is "whether self-defense applies against an excused but unjustified aggression."[12] To *justify* an act is to show that it was the right thing to do in the circumstances; to *excuse* an act is to show that although it was unjustified, the actor did not mean it or could not help it, that it was not, properly speaking, his doing at all. In the "excused but unjustified aggression" we have a more plausible model for the application of self-defense to the problem of abortion, for *the fetus is surely innocent* (not because of insanity but because of immaturity, and because *it* did not choose to threaten its mother—it did not "ask to be born").

Upon reflection, most of us would agree, I think, that one would be justified in killing even an innocent aggressor if that seemed necessary to save one's own life or to prevent one from suffering serious bodily injury. Surely we would not judge harshly the slightly built lady who shoots the armed stranger who goes berserk in the elevator. If we were in her shoes, we too would protect ourselves at all costs to the assailant, just as we would against wild animals, runaway trucks, or impersonal forces of nature. But while the berserk assailant, as well as those persons mentioned in the last paragraph, all are innocent—are not *morally* responsible for what they do—they all *are* assailants, and in this respect they differ in a quite fundamental respect from the fetus. For the fetus is not only innocent but also not an aggressor. *It* did not start the trouble in any fashion. Thus, it would seem that while we are justified in killing an innocent assailant if this is the only way to prevent him from killing us, it does not follow that we are

---

[11] George Fletcher, "Proportionality and the Psychotic Aggressor: A Vignette in the Comparative Criminal Law Theory," *Israel Law Review* 8 (1973): 376.

[12] Ibid.

similarly justified in killing a fetal person, since, unlike the innocent aggressor, the fetus is not an aggressor at all.

Thomson has challenged this argument. She presents the following far-fetched but coherent hypothetical example:

> Aggressor is driving his tank at you. But he has taken care to arrange that a baby is strapped to the front of the tank so that if you use your anti-tank gun, you will not only kill Aggressor, you will kill the baby. Now Aggressor, admittedly, is in the process of trying to kill you; but that baby isn't. Yet you can presumably go ahead and use the gun, even though this involves killing the baby as well as Aggressor.[13]

The baby in this example is not only "innocent" but also the "innocent shield of a threat."[14] Still it is hard to quarrel with Thomson's judgment that you *may* (not that you *should*) take the baby's life if necessary to save your own, that it is morally permissible, even if it is not morally obligatory, to do so. After all, you are (by hypothesis) perfectly innocent too. This example makes a better analogy to the abortion situation than any we have considered thus far, but there are still significant dissimilarities. Unless the fetus is the product of rape, it cannot conceivably be the shield of some third-party aggressor. There is simply no interpersonal "aggression" involved at all in the normal pregnancy. There may nevertheless be a genuine *threat* to the well-being of the mother, and if that threat is to her very life, then perhaps she does have a right to kill it, if necessary, in self-defense. At any rate, if the threatened victim in Thomson's tank example is justified in killing the innocent shield, then the pregnant woman threatened with similar harm is similarly entitled. But all that this would establish is that abortion is justified only if it is probably required to save the pregnant woman's life. So not only could we not use the self-defense argument to justify abortion for trivial reasons, as we argued earlier; it appears that the only reason that authorizes its use is the one that cites the fact that the mother will probably die if the fetus is not aborted.

BODILY AUTONOMY: THE EXAMPLE OF THE PLUGGED-IN VIOLINIST

The trouble with the use of self-defense as a model for abortion rights is that none of the examples of self-defense makes an *exact* analogy to the abortion situation. The examples that come closest to providing models for justified abortion are the "innocent aggressor cases" and these would apply, as we have seen, only to abortions that are necessary to prevent death to the mother. Even these examples do not fit the abortion case ex-

[13] Judith Jarvis Thomson, "Self-Defense and Rights," The Lindley Lecture, 1976 (Lawrence, Kans.: University of Kansas Philosophy Department, 1977).

[14] The term comes from Robert Nozick, *Anarchy, State, and Utopia* (New York: Basic Books, 1974), p. 35.

actly, since the fetus is in no way itself an aggressor, culpable or innocent, but is at most a "nonaggressive, nonculpable threat," in some respects like an innocent shield.[15] And the more we change the examples to bring them closer to the situation of the fetus, the less clear is their resemblance to the central models of self-defense. Once we are allowed to protect ourselves (and especially to protect interests less weighty than self-preservation) at the expense of nonaggressive innocents, it become difficult to distinguish the latter from innocent bystanders whom we kill as means to our own good, and that, in turn, begins to look like unvarnished murder. The killing of an innocent person simply because his continued existence in the circumstances would make the killer's life miserable is a homicide that cannot be justified. It is not self-defense to kill your boss because he makes your work life intolerable and you are unable to find another job, or to kill your spouse because he or she nags you to the point of extreme misery and will not agree to divorce,[16] or (closer to the point) to kill your shipwrecked fellow passenger in the lifeboat because there are provisions sufficient for only one to survive and he claims half of them, or to kill your innocent rival for a position or a prize because you can win only if he is out of the running. In all these cases the victim is either innocent or relatively innocent and in no way a direct aggressor.

Partly because of deficiencies in the hypothetical examples of self-defense, Thomson invented a different sort of example intended at once to be a much closer analogy to the abortion situation and also such that the killing can be seen to be morally justified for reasons less compelling than defense of the killer's very life:

> You wake up in the morning and find yourself back to back in bed with an unconscious violinist. A famous unconscious violinist. He has been found to have a fatal kidney ailment, and the Society of Music Lovers has canvassed all the available medical records and found that you alone have the right blood type to help. They have therefore kidnapped you, and last night the violinist's circulatory system was plugged into yours, so that your kidneys can be used to extract poisons from his blood as well as your own. The director of the hos-

---

[15] Even when self-defense is acceptable as a defense to homicide in the case of forced killings of nonaggressive innocents, that may be because it is understood in those cases to be an excuse or a mitigation rather than a justification. If a criminal terrorist from a fortified position throws a bomb at my feet and I can escape its explosion only by quickly throwing it in the direction of a baby buggy whose infant occupant is enjoying a nap, perhaps I can be *excused* for saving my life by taking the baby's, perhaps the duress under which I acted mitigates my guilt, perhaps the law ought not to be too severe with me. But it is not convincing to argue that I was entirely justified in what I did because I was acting in self-defense. But the problem is a difficult one, and the case may be borderline.

[16] See Ludwig Lewisohn's remarkable novel, *The Case of Mr. Crump* (New York: Farrar, Straus, 1947).

pital now tells you, "Look, we're sorry the Society of Music Lovers did this to you—we would never have permitted it if we had known. But still they did it, and the violinist now is plugged into you. To unplug you would be to kill him. But never mind, it's only for nine months. By then he will have recovered from his ailment, and can safely be unplugged from you." Is it morally incumbent on you to accede to this situation? No doubt it would be very nice of you if you did, a great kindness. But do you have to accede to it? . . . What if the director . . . says . . . "Granted you have a right to decide what happens in and to your body, but a person's right to life outweighs your right to decide what happens in and to your body. So you cannot . . . be unplugged from him." I imagine you would regard this as outrageous.[17]

Suppose that you defy the director on your own, and exercise your control over your own body by unplugging the unconscious violinist, thereby causing his death. This would be to kill in defense of an interest far less important than self-preservation or the prevention of serious injury to oneself. And it would be to kill an innocent nonaggressor, indeed a victim who remains unconscious throughout the entire period during which he is a threat. We have, therefore, an example that—if it works—offers far more encouragement to the proabortion position than the model of self-defense does. We must now pose two questions: Would you in fact be morally justified in unplugging the violinist? How close an analogy does this bizarre example make to the abortion situation?

There is no way to argue conclusively that unplugging the violinist would be morally justified. Thomson can only make the picture as vividly persuasive as possible and then appeal to her reader's intuitions. It is not an easy case, and neither an affirmative nor a negative judgment will seem self-evident to everyone. Still the verdict for justification seems as strong as in some of the other examples of killing innocent threats, and some additional considerations can be brought to bear in its support. There is, after all, a clear "intuition" in support of a basic right "to decide what happens in and to one's own body," even though the limits of that right are lost in the fog of controversy. So unless there is some stronger competing claim, anyone has a right to refuse to consent to surgery or to enforced attachment to a machine. Or indeed to an unconscious violinist. But what of the competing claim in this example, the violinist's right to life? That is another basic right that is vague around the edges.

In its noncontroversial core, the right to life is a right not to be killed directly (except under very special circumstances) and to be rescued from impending death whenever this can be done without unreasonable sacrifice. But as Warren has pointed out, one person's right to life does not

---

[17] Judith Jarvis Thomson, "A Defense of Abortion," *Philosophy and Public Affairs* 1 (1971): 48–49.

impose a correlative duty on another person to do "whatever is necessary to keep him alive."[18] And although we all have general duties to come to the assistance of strangers in peril, we cannot be forced to make enormous sacrifices or to run unreasonably high risks to keep people alive when we stand in no special relationship to them, like "father" or "lifeguard." The wife of the violinist perhaps would have a duty to stay plugged to him (if that would help) for nine months; but the random stranger has no such duty at all. So there is good reason to grant Thomson her claim that a stranger would have a right to unplug the violinist from herself.

But how close an analogy after all is this to the normal case of pregnancy? Several differences come immediately to mind. In the normal case of pregnancy, the woman is not confined to her bed for nine months but can continue to work and function efficiently in the world until the final trimester at least. This difference, however, is of doubtful significance, since Thomson's argument is not based on a right to the protection of one's interest in efficient mobility but rather on a right to *decide* on the uses of one's own body, which is quite another thing. Another difference is that the mother and her fetus are not exactly "random strangers" in the same sense that the woman and the violinist are. Again the relationship between mother and fetus seems to be in a class by itself. If the person who needs to use the woman's body for nine months in order to survive is her mother, father, sister, brother, son, daughter, or close friend, then the relationship would seem close enough to establish a special obligation in the woman to permit that use. If the needy person is a total stranger, then that obligation is missing. The fetus no doubt stands somewhere between these two extremes, but it is at least as close to the "special relationship" end of the spectrum as to the "total stranger" end.

The most important difference, however, between the violinist case and the normal pregnancy is that in the former woman had absolutely nothing to do with creating the situation from which she wishes to escape. She bears no responsibility whatever for being in a state of "plugged-in-ness" with the violinist. As many commentators have pointed out, this makes Thomson's analogy fit at most one very special class of pregnancies, namely, those imposed upon a woman entirely against her will, as in rape. In the "normal case" of pregnancy, the voluntary action of the woman herself (knowingly consenting to sexual intercourse) has something to do with her becoming pregnant. So once again, we find that a proabortion argument fails to establish an *unrestricted* moral right to abortion. Just as self-defense justifies abortion at most in the case where it is necessary to save the mother's life, the Thomson defense justifies abortion only when the

---

[18] Warren, "Abortion," p. 135.

woman shares no responsibility for her pregnancy, as, for example, when it has been caused by rape (force or fraud).

If we continue the line of reasoning suggested by our criticism of the violinist example, we will soon reach a general principle, namely, that whether or not a woman has a duty to continue her pregnancy depends, at least in part, on how responsible she is for being pregnant in the first place, that is, on the extent to which her pregnancy is the consequence of her own voluntary actions. This formula, in turn, seems to be an application of a still more general moral principle, one that imposes duties on one party to rescue or support another, even a stranger and even when that requires great personal sacrifice or risk, to the degree that the first party, through his own voluntary actions or omissions, was responsible for the second party's dependence on him. A late-arriving bystander at the seaside has no duty to risk life or limb to save a drowning swimmer. If however, the swimmer is in danger only because the bystander erroneously informed him that there was no danger, then the bystander has a duty to make some effort at rescue (although not a suicidal one), dangerous as it may be. If the swimmer is in the water only because the "bystander" has pushed him out of a boat, however, then the bystander has a duty to attempt rescue at any cost to personal safety,[19] since the bystander's own voluntary action was the whole cause of the swimmer's plight.

Since the voluntariness of an action or omission is a matter of degree, so is the responsibility that stems from it, as is the stringency of the duty that derives from that responsibility. The duty to continue a pregnancy, then, will be stronger (other things being equal) in the case where the pregnancy was entered into in a fully voluntary way than it will be in the case that fits the violinist model, where the pregnancy is totally involuntary. But in between these two extremes is a whole range of cases where moral judgments are more difficult to make. We can sketch the whole spectrum as follows:

1. Pregnancy caused by rape (totally involuntary).
2. Pregnancy caused by contraceptive failure, where the fault is entirely that of the manufacturer or pharmaceutical company.
3. Pregnancy caused by contraceptive failure within the advertised one percent margin of error (no one's fault).
4. Pregnancy caused by the negligence of the woman (or the man, or both). They are careless in the use of the contraceptive or else fail to use it at all, being unaware of a large risk that they *ought* to have been aware of.
5. Pregnancy caused by the recklessness of the woman (or the man, or both).

[19] The examples are Sissela Bok's. See her article "Ethical Problems of Abortion," *Hastings Center Studies* 2 (1974): 35.

They think of the risk but get swept along by passions and consciously disregard it.

6. Pregnancy caused by intercourse between partners who are genuinely indifferent at the time whether or not pregnancy results.

7. Pregnancy caused by the deliberate decision of the parties to produce it (completely voluntary).

There would be a somewhat hollow ring to the claim in case 7 that one has no obligation to continue one's bodily support for a moral person whose dependence on that support one has deliberately caused. That would be like denying that one has a duty to save the drowning swimmer that one has just pushed out of the boat. The case for cessation of bodily support is hardly any stronger in 6 and 5 than in 7. Perhaps it is misleading to say of the negligence case (4) that the pregnancy is only partially involuntary, or involuntary "to a degree," since the parents did not *intentionally* produce or run the risk or producing a fetus. But there is no need to haggle over that terminological question. Whether wholly or partially involuntary, the actions of the parents in the circumstances were faulty and the pregnancy resulted from the fault (negligence), so they are to a substantial degree responsible (to blame) for it. It was within their power to be more careful or knowledgeable, and yet they were careless or avoidably ignorant. So they cannot plead, in the manner of the lady plugged to the violinist, that they had no control over their condition whatever. In failing to exercise due care, they were doing something else and doing *it* "to a degree voluntarily." In these cases—4, 5, 6, and 7—the woman and her partner are therefore responsible for the pregnancy, and on the analogy with the case of the drowning swimmer who was pushed from the boat, they have a duty not to kill the fetus or permit it to die.

Cases 2 and 3 are more preplexing. In case 2, where the fault was entirely that of the manufacturer, the woman is no more responsible for being pregnant than in case 1, where she is the unwilling victim of a rape. In neither case did she choose to become pregnant. In neither case was she reckless or negligent in respect to the possibility of becoming pregnant. So if she has no duty to continue to provide bodily support for the dependent fetus in the rape case, then equally she has no duty in the other case. To be sure, there is always *some* risk of pregnancy whenever there is intercourse, no matter how careful the partners are. There may be only one chance in ten thousand that a contraceptive pill has an undetectable flaw, but there is no chance whatever of pregnancy without intercourse. The woman in case 2, then, would seem to have *some* responsibility, even if vanishingly small, for her pregnancy. She could have been even more careful by abstaining from sex altogether. But notice that much the same sort of thing could be said of the rape victim. By staying home in a locked building patrolled round the clock by armed guards, she could have reduced the chances of bodily assault from, say, one in fifty thousand to effectively nil. By staying off the dangerous streets, she would have been much more careful than she was in respect to the risk of rape. But surely that does not entitle us to say that she was "partially responsible" for the rape that made her pregnant. When a person takes all the precautions that she can *reasonably* be expected to take against a certain outcome, then that outcome cannot fairly be described as her responsibility. So in case 2, where the negligence of the manufacturer of the contraceptive is the cause of the pregnancy, the woman cannot be held responsible for her condition, and that ground for ascribing to her a duty not to abort is not present.

Case 3 brings us very close to the borderline. The couple in this example do not choose to have a baby and, indeed, they take strong precautions against pregnancy. Still they know that there is a one percent danger and they deliberately choose to run that risk anyway. As a result, a woman becomes pregnant against her will. Does she then have a right to abandon to a certain death a newly formed moral person (remember that personhood is presumed here only "for the sake of the argument") who is even less responsible for his dependence on her than she is? When one looks at the problem in this way from the perspective of the fetus to whom we have suppositively ascribed full moral rights, it becomes doubtful that the pregnant woman's very minimal responsibility for her plight can permit her to abandon a being who has no responsibility for it whatever. She ran a very small risk, but the fetus ran no risk at all. Nevertheless, this is a borderline case for the following reason. If we extend to this case the rule we applied to case 2, then we might be entitled to say that the woman is no more responsible than the fetus for the pregnancy. To reach that conclusion we have to judge the one percent chance of pregnancy to be a *reasonable* risk for a woman to run in the circumstances. That appraisal itself is a disguised moral judgment of pivotal importance, and yet it is very difficult to know how to go about establishing it. Nevertheless, *if* it is correct, then the woman is, for all practical purposes, relieved of her responsibility for the pregnancy just as she is in cases 1 and 2, and in that event the fetus's "right to life" does not entail a duty on her part to make extreme sacrifices.

Summary and Conclusion

Assuming that the fetus is a moral person, under what conditions, if any, is abortion justifiable homicide? If the woman's right to an abortion is derived from her right to own property in her body (which is not very plausible), then abortion is never justifiable homicide. Property rights simply cannot support that much moral weight. If the right is derived from self-defense, then it justifies abortion at most when necessary to save the woman from death. That is because the fetus, while sometimes a threat to the interests of the woman, is an innocent and (in a sense) nonaggressive threat. The doctrine of proportionality, which permits a person to use a degree of force in self-defense that is likely to cause the assailant harm greater (within reasonable limits) than the harm the assailant would otherwise cause the victim, has application only to the case where the assailant is culpable. One can kill an "innocent threat" in order to save one's life but not to save one's pocketbook. The right of bodily autonomy (to decide what is to be done in and to one's own body) is a much more solid base for the right to abortion than either the right to property or the right to self-defense, since it permits one to kill innocent persons by depriving them of one's "life-support system," even when they are threats to interests substantially less important than self-preservation. But this justification is probably available at most to victims of rape, or contraceptive failure caused by the negligence of other parties, to the risk of which the woman has not consented. That narrow restriction on the use of this defense stems from the requirement, internal to it, that the woman be in no way responsible for her pregnancy.

It does not follow automatically that because the victim of a homicide was "innocent," the killing cannot have been justified. But abortion can plausibly be construed as justifiable homicide only on the basis of inexact analogies, and then only (1) to save the woman from the most extreme harm or else (2) to save the woman from a lesser harm when the pregnancy was the result of the wrongful acts of others for which the woman had no responsibility. Another possibility that was only suggested here is (3) when it can be claimed for a defective or diseased fetus that it has a right *not* to be born. These narrow restrictions on the right of the woman to an abortion will not satisfy many people in the proabortion camp. But if the assumption of the moral personhood of the fetus is false, as was argued in the first part of this chapter, then the woman's right to bodily autonomy will normally prevail, and abortions at all but the later stages, at least, and for the most common reasons, at least, are morally permissible.

POSTSCRIPT

The assumption behind the arguments presented immediately above is that a fetus at every stage between conception and parturition is a full moral being, in that respect like every postnatal human person, unconditionally in possession of the basic human rights, including the right to life. We made that working assumption only for methodological reasons: to see what positions about the moral permissibility of abortion follow from it. Our results are not encouraging to the liberal proabortion position. If we assume that abortion is homicide (another way of putting the "methodological assumption") then it seems very unlikely that most abortions are justifiable homicides. But in fact I have argued in the first part of this chapter against the position "assumed" in the second part—that the moral status of the fetus is that of a full moral person with a right to life. If the argument of the first part is correct then it follows that killing a fetus is not homicide at all, and for *that* reason not "justified homicide." And that result, tentative though it may be, is not encouraging to the conservative antiabortionist.

In addition to the argumentative support for the right-to-choose position, one can cite some evidence supporting the suspicion that hardly any of the antiabortionists *really believe* that a fetus has the full moral status of a typical postnatal person. If the fetus really has that status, then startling things follow from the law of homicide. Abortion would be first-degree murder, since it consists in directly and deliberately causing the death of a fellow human being. Not only would the physician who performed the abortion be guilty of murder; so would the pregnant woman, as a full-fledged principal in the crime. A whole network of accomplices, including the doctor's receptionist, would be guilty of serious though lesser complicity, and would have to be punished accordingly. The punishment for the convicted criminals would be as severe as that for any crime on the books; in thirty-five states, it could well be the death penalty. In contrast the recent antiabortion legislation in Louisiana (1991), passed into law over the governor's veto, holds only the physician, not the pregnant woman, liable as principal, and prescribes only ten years as the punishment—lenient treatment indeed for what is held to be, in principle, no less than first-degree murder!

Similar reluctance to draw out the full logical consequences of one's theory is illustrated in a variety of other ways, and seems to apply even to those antiabortionists who otherwise seem most strident and uncompromising. Since I wrote the original article on which this chapter is based, there have been numerous legislative attempts to undermine the constitutional right to an abortion declared by the U.S. Supreme Court in *Roe* v. *Wade* (1973). Perhaps the most prominent of these efforts was the bill, S. 158, introduced in the Senate in 1982 by Senator Jesse Helms, which resolves that "human life shall be deemed to exist from conception." The Congress, had it passed this bill, would have created a legal status for human fetuses and embryos that presumably would imply their possession of various constitutional rights, including "the right to life." Among the other intended legal consequences of this new status is that the killing of a fetus at any stage of its development would be a kind of criminal homicide.

Whatever difficulties might attend a legislative or constitutional rule endorsing some particular point in mid- or late pregnancy as the starting point of moral personhood (and they, too, would be considerable), the consequences of the criterion endorsed by S. 158, or any other rule dating personhood from "the moment of conception," are intolerably paradoxical. Consider how this chapter has treated the question: Is the single-cell zygote a moment after conception already a full-fledged human being? Depending on how we interpret the question, Helms' affirmative answer is either self-evidently, but trivially and irrelevantly, true, or else absurd. The one-celled conceptus, the product of a human spermatozoon and a human ovum, is, of course, itself human. No scientist who counted its chromosomes could possibly classify it as feline, canine, or equine. The species to which it belongs is obviously the human species. Moreover, unless or until it aborts along the way, it is clearly a living thing as opposed to an inert piece of dead tissue. Therefore, the newly conceived "zygote" (the word for the fertilized egg before it becomes a hollow sphere of cells or "blastocyst" on the sixth day) is—in the most trivial and obvious sense—a form of "human life." There would appear to be nothing to quarrel about in this innocent claim—except, of course, whether the zygote is already "human life" in the sense that is morally significant, namely, that of a person with rights, the legal status Helms wishes to establish.

To show that living human zygotes have rights, it is not enough to point out that they are living things associated with the human species. One must also show that they are *people*, in all morally relevant respects like you and me. Fertilized human eggs, of course, are *potential* people. That is to say, that they will develop into actual people if all goes well in the normal course of pregnancy. But that obvious truth is not sufficient to establish their present rights. To be a potential human person, as we have seen, is to be only a potential bearer of human rights; actual rights must await actual personhood. To infer actual possession of rights from future qualification is a mistake that seems peculiar to the abortion controversy; we are rarely tempted to make it in other contexts. A twelve-year-old American child, for example, is a potential voter in American elections in the sense that he will have an actual right to vote six years from now if all goes well in the natural course of his adolescence. But we are not tempted to admit him to the voting booths now simply on the grounds that he is a "potential voter" who will be qualified later.

The relevant question, then, is whether human zygotes, a few minutes after conception, are already *actual* people. Helms' affirmative answer to this question conflicts violently with common sense. The only people who are likely to agree with it are those who are prepared to abandon common sense or those who confuse this question with the obvious but irrelevant questions about life and species membership that we have already dismissed. The one-celled speck of protoplasm, or small cluster of cells, of which we speak has none of the characteristics we normally have in mind when we speak of persons. No one, not even Helms himself, believes that this tiny entity is *already* conscious of itself and the world, capable of sensation and emotion, able to understand and reason, remember and anticipate, make plans and act, be pleased or frustrated or hurt. Nor do we, or he, take seriously the logical consequences of "deeming" human embryos in their earliest stages to be people. In particular our attitudes toward spontaneous miscarriage ("natural abortion") show that we do not regard embryos as full-fledged moral persons. We may be disappointed when a pregnancy miscarries because our desire to produce a child has been at least temporarily frustrated, but we do not grieve for the embryo's sake. Funeral rites are not performed for tiny clusters of cells; baptism and extreme unction are not given upon the arrival of a tardy menstrual period over menses that may have contained an embryo; names and "conception dates" are not recorded; death certificates are not required. Why would we be so casually negligent if we believed with Helms that a real person has died?

More important, if zygotes and embryos are actual people, why do we not make a monumental effort to "rescue" the millions who are bound to perish each year from natural causes? If there are a dozen trapped coal miners in a caved-in mine or a million persons threatened by starvation in a famine, we are prepared to spend millions of dollars to save them because they are, after all, undeniably fellow human beings. Why then do we not budget millions more for research toward the discovery of a drug that would prevent spontaneous abortions? Embryologists have estimated that only 58 percent of fertilized ova survive until implantation (seven days after conception) and that the spontaneous abortion rate after that stage is from 10 to 15 percent. If we left that many miners and farmers to die each year without rescue efforts, we would be very callous indeed. But if we did save all the fetuses with some wonder drug, then, according to one embryologist, instead of a population in which approximately 2 percent suffer from relatively minor congenital defects, we would have a population in which 10 to 20 percent would be abnormal "and most of the defects would be gross and incapacitating."[20] Does Helms intend to prepare us to face this consequence, or is he content to let millions of salvageable "human lives" perish?

Other absurd consequences of the redefinition in the "human life statute" have been more widely publicized. Women who use contraceptives that make the uterine wall unreceptive to implantation, for example, would themselves be murderers since they deliberately cause the death of fertilized human ova. The government could take vigilant steps to protect "unborn persons," and many of these would involve intrusions into women's private affairs—requiring monthly pregnancy tests, for example, to determine

[20] Malcolm Potts, "The Problem of Abortion," in *Biology and Ethics*, ed. E. J. Ebling (New York: Academic, 1969), pp. 76, 78.

whether any unborn persons exist in their wombs, or requiring registration of all suspected pregnancies. If we really took seriously the view that fertilized eggs are people with the full panoply of human rights, these absurd practices would not seem implausible.

It seems to me that a case can be made for taking a human life statute that dates the origin of personhood at conception to be an "establishment" of religious doctrine. The argument runs as follows. For reasons given above, it is quite contrary to common sense to claim that a newly fertilized human ovum is already an actual person. Employing the term "person" in the normal fashion, no one thinks of a fertilized egg in that way. The only arguments that have been advanced to the conclusion that fertilized eggs *are* people, common sense notwithstanding, are arguments with theological premises. These premises are part of large theological and philosophical systems that are very much worthy of respect indeed, but they can neither be established nor refuted without critical discussion of the whole systems of which they form a part. In fact, many conscientious persons reject them, often in favor of doctrines stemming from rival theological systems; so for the state to endorse the personhood of newly fertilized ova would be for the state to embrace one set of controversial theological tenets rather than others, in effect to enforce the teaching of some churches against those of other churches (and nonchurches), and to back up this enforcement with severe criminal penalties. The state plays this constitutionally prohibited role when it officially affirms a doctrine that is opposed to common sense and understanding and whose only proposed arguments proceed from theological premises. This case, it seems to me, is a good one even if there is reason, as there could be—for all I have been able to argue to the contrary here—for affirming the personhood of fetuses in the second or third trimester of pregnancy.

Chapter Three

THE CHILD'S RIGHT TO AN OPEN FUTURE

RIGHTS IN TRUST

How do children's rights raise special philosophical problems? Not all rights of children, of course, have a distinctive character. Whole classes of rights are common to adults and children; many are exclusive possessions of adults; perhaps none at all are necessarily peculiar to children. In the common category are rights not to be mistreated directly, for example, the right not to be punched in the nose or to be robbed. When a stranger slaps a child and forcibly takes away his candy in order to eat it himself, he has interfered wrongfully with the child's bodily and property interests and violated his rights just as surely as if the aggressor had punched an adult and forcibly helped himself to her purse. Rights that are common to adults and children in this way we can call "*A-C* rights."

Among the rights thought to belong only to adults ("*A* rights") are the legal rights to vote, to imbibe, to stay out all night, and so on. An interesting subspecies of these are those autonomy rights (protected liberties of choice) that could hardly apply to small children, such as the free exercise of one's religion, which presupposes that one has religious convictions or preferences in the first place. When parents choose to take their child to religious observances and to enroll her in a Sunday school, they are exercising *their* religious rights, not (or not yet) those of the child.

The rights that I shall call "*C* rights," while not strictly peculiar to children, are generally characteristic of them, and possessed by adults only in unusual or abnormal circumstances. Two subclasses can be distinguished, and I mention the first only to dismiss it as not part of the subject matter of this chapter, namely, those rights that derive from the child's dependence upon others for the basic instrumental goods of life—food, shelter, protection. Dependency rights are common to all children, but not exclusive to them, of course, since some of them belong also to handicapped adults who are incapable of supporting themselves and must therefore be "treated as children" in this respect for the whole of their lives.

Another class of *C* rights, those I shall call "rights-in-trust," look like adult autonomy rights of class *A*, except that the child cannot very well exercise his free choice until later when he is more fully formed and capable. When sophisticated autonomy rights are attributed to children who are clearly not yet capable of exercising them, their names refer to rights that are to be *saved* for the child until he is an adult, but which can be violated "in advance," so to speak, before the child is even in a position to exercise them. The violating conduct guarantees *now* that when the child is an autonomous adult, certain key options will already be closed to him. His right while he is still a child is to have these future options kept open until he is a fully formed, self-determining adult capable of deciding among them. These "anticipatory autonomy rights" in class *C* are the children's rights in which I am most interested, since they raise the most interesting philosophical questions. They are, in effect, autonomy rights in the shape they must assume when held "prematurely" by children.

Put very generally, rights-in-trust can be summed up as the single "right to an open future," but of course that vague formula simply describes the form of the particular rights in question and not their specific content. It is plausible to ascribe to children a right to an open future only in some, not all respects, and the simple formula leaves those respects unspecified. The advantage of the general formula, however, is that it removes temptation to refer to certain rights of children by names that also apply to rights of adults that are quite different animals.[1] The adult's right to exercise his religious beliefs, for example, is a class *A* right, but the right of the same name when applied to a small child is a right-in-trust, squarely in class *C*. One can avoid confusing the two by referring to the latter simply as part of the child's right to an open future (in respect to religious affiliation). In that general category it sits side by side with the right to walk freely down the public sidewalk as held by an infant of two months, still incapable of self-locomotion. One would violate that right in trust *now*, before it can even be exercised, by cutting off the child's legs.

Some rights with general names are rather more difficult to classify, especially when attributed to older, only partly grown, children. Some of these appear to have one foot in class *A* and the other in the rights-in-trust subclass of the *C* category. For example, the right of free speech, inter-

---

[1] John Locke preferred the more uniform usage according to which all human rights are *A-C* rights. In his usage, from which I here depart, we are all born with certain rights that we possess throughout our lives, from infancy through senectitude. Some of these rights, however, children cannot exercise, although they continue to possess them until they acquire the requisite capability. "Thus we are born free as we are born rational; not that we have actually the exercise of either; age that brings one, brings with it the other too" (*Second Treatise of Government*, section 61). It would be a mistake to elevate this terminological difference into a philosophical quarrel. Obviously Locke can say everything in his terminology that I can in mine and vice versa. He was concerned to emphasize the similarity in the moral status of children and adults, whereas this chapter focuses on the differences. I have no objection if people talk about *A* rights as if they are actually possessed by small infants (e.g., the right to vote as one pleases) provided it is clearly understood that they are "possessed" in the sense that they are held in trust for the autonomous adults the children will (probably) become one day, and they are subject to violation now in a way that is sui generis.

preted as the freedom to express political opinions, when ascribed to a ten-year-old is perhaps mainly an actual *A* right, but it is still partly a *C* right-in-trust, at least in respect to those opinions that the child might one day come to form but are presently beyond his ken.

People often speak of a child's "welfare" or his "interests." The interests protected by a child's *A-C* rights are those interests the child actually has *now*. Their advancement is, in a manner of speaking, a constituent of the child's good qua child right now. On the other hand the interests he might come to have as he grows up are the ones protected by his rights-in-trust of class *C*. While he is still a child these "future interests" include those that he will in fact come to have in the future and also those he will never acquire, depending on the directions of his growth.

It is a truism among philosophers that interests are not the same things as present desires with which they can, and often do, clash. Thus if the violation of a child's autonomy right-in-trust cannot always be established by checking the child's present interests, a fortiori it cannot be established by determining the child's present desires or preferences.[2] It is the adult he is to become who must exercise the choice, more exactly, the adult he will become if his basic options are kept open and his growth kept "natural" or unforced. In any case, that adult does not exist yet, and perhaps he never will. But the child is *potentially* that adult, and it is that adult who is the person whose autonomy must be protected now (in advance).

When a mature adult has a conflict between getting what he wants now and having his options left open in the future, we are bound by our respect for his autonomy not to force his present choice in order to protect his future "liberty." His present autonomy takes precedence even over his probable future good, and he may use it as he will, even at the expense of the future self he will one day become. Children are different. Respect for the child's future autonomy, as an adult, often requires preventing his free choice now. Thus the future self does not have as much moral weight in our treatment of adults as it does with children. Perhaps it should weigh as much with adults pondering their *own* decisions as it does with adults governing their own children. In the self-regarding case, the future self exerts its weight in the form of a claim to prudence, but prudence cannot rightly be imposed from the outside on an autonomous adult.

FORMS OF CONFLICT

Moral perplexity about children's *C* rights-in-trust is most likely to arise when those rights appear to conflict with certain *A* rights of their parents, and the courts must adjudicate the conflict. Typically the conflict is be-

---

[2] See William O. Douglas's dissenting opinion in *Wisconsin* v. *Yoder*, 406 U.S. 205 (1972).

tween the child's protected personal interests in growth and development (rather than his immediate health or welfare) and the parents' right to control their child's upbringing, or to determine their own general style of life, or to practice their own religion free of outside interference. Very often the interests of the general community as represented by the state are involved too (for example, the concern that children not be a source of infection to others, that they grow up well enough informed to be responsible voting citizens, or that they not become criminal or hopeless dependents on state welfare support). Thus custody hearings, neglect proceedings against parents, and criminal trials for violating compulsory school attendance laws and child labor statutes often become three-cornered contests among the rights of children, parents, and the state as representative of the collective interests of the community.[3] Sometimes, however, the community's interests are only marginally involved in the case, and the stark conflict between parent and child comes most clearly to the fore. Among the more difficult cases of this kind are those that pose a conflict between the religious rights of parents and their children's rights to an open future.

Children are not legally capable of defending their own future interests against present infringement by their parents, so that task must be performed for them, usually by the state in its role of *parens patriae*. American courts have long held that the state has a "sovereign power of guardianship" over minors and other legally incompetent persons, which confers upon it the right, or perhaps even the duty, to look after the interests of those who are incapable of protecting themselves. Mentally disordered adults, for example, who are so deranged as to be unable to seek treatment for themselves, are entitled, under the doctrine of *parens patriae*, to psychiatric care under the auspices of the state. Many "mentally ill" persons, however, are not cognitively deranged, and some of these do not wish to be confined and treated in mental hospitals. The government has no right to impose treatment on these persons, for the doctrine of *parens patriae* extends only to those unfortunates who are rendered literally incapable of deciding whether to seek medical treatment themselves; and even in these cases, the doctrine as liberally interpreted grants power to the state only to "decide for a man as we assume he would decide for himself if he were of sound mind."[4] When the courts must decide for children, however, as they presume the children themselves would (or will) when they are adults, their problems are vastly more difficult. As a general rule, the courts will not be so presumptuous as to speak now in the name of the future adult;

---

[3] For an illuminating analysis of these three-sided conflicts, see Stuart J. Baskin, "State Intrusion into Family Affairs: Justifications and Limitations," *Stanford Law Review* 26 (1974): 1383.

[4] Note on "Civil Restraint, Mental Illness, and the Right to Treatment," *Yale Law Journal* 77 (1967): 87.

but, on the other hand, there are sometimes ways of interfering with parents so as to postpone the making of serious and final commitments until the child grows to maturity and is legally capable of making them himself.

In 1944 in the case of *Prince* v. *Massachusetts*[5] the U.S. Supreme Court upheld a Massachusetts statute that had been applied to prevent Jehovah's Witnesses' children from distributing religious pamphlets on the public streets in what their parents claimed was the free exercise of their religion. The decision in this case has been severely criticized (and I think rightly) as a misapplication of the *parens patriae* doctrine,[6] but the court's statement of that doctrine is unusually clear and trenchant. The state is concerned, said the Court, not only with the immediate health and welfare of children but also with

> the healthy, well-rounded growth of young people into full maturity as citizens with all that implies [in a democracy]. . . . Parents may be free to become martyrs themselves. But it does not follow that they are free in identical circumstance to make martyrs of their children before they have reached the age of full and legal discretion when they can make that decision for themselves.[7]

It was no doubt an overstatement to describe the exposure of children to the apathy or scorn of the passersby in the streets as "martyrdom," but the Court's well-stated but misapplied principle suggests other cases where religious liberty must retreat before the claims of children that they be permitted to reach maturity with as many open options, opportunities, and advantages as possible.

Twenty years later, in a quite different sort of case, the religious rights of parents were upheld in a Long Island court at the expense of their three small children. The twenty-four-year-old mother, injured in an automobile collision, was allowed to die when her husband refused on religious grounds to permit doctors to give her a blood transfusion. The husband, like his wife a member of Jehovah's Witnesses, remained adamant despite the pleadings of doctors. Finally the hospital administrator appealed to State Supreme Court Judge William Sullivan, who refused to order the transfusion.

It is too easy to criticize a judge who was forced to make a life or death decision in a legally difficult case on only a moment's notice, and I have no intention of doing so. On balance his decision might well have been justified even though the case for reading the balancing scales in the children's favor in this instance was strong indeed. The three children whose interests

---

[5] *Prince* v. *Massachusetts*, 321 U.S. 158 (1944).

[6] See Justice Frank Murphy's dissenting opinion in *Prince*; and Donald Giannella, "Religious Liberty, Nonestablishment, and Doctrinal Development," part 1, "The Religious Liberty Guarantee," *Harvard Law Review* 81 (1967): 1395.

[7] *Prince* v. *Massachusetts*, at 168, 170.

in present welfare and future development were directly involved could not, of course, make the momentous decision for themselves, and both natural parents were determined to decide against the children's interests. Only the state in its capacity as protector of those who cannot help themselves (*parens patriae*) had the legal power to overrule the parents' decision. The religious beliefs of the parents were sincere and important; their contravention, according to the tenets of the parents' sect, would be serious sin, perhaps something akin to both cannibalism and adultery.[8] On the other balance pan was the diminished prospect of three children for a "healthy, well-rounded growth into full maturity," and their immediate and continuous need of maternal care and affection. The parents' "sin" would certainly be mitigated by the fact that it was "committed" involuntarily under governmental duress; whereas the children's deprivation, while perhaps being something short of "martyrdom," would be a permanent and possibly irreplaceable loss. On the other hand, some fathers might be able to replace their deceased wives quite effectively, either on their own or through prompt remarriage, so it is not perfectly clear that the case for applying the *parens patriae* doctrine in this instance ought to have been decisive.

Another close case, I think, but one where the interests of children do seem prior to the religious interests of their parents, was that in which the Kansas courts refused to permit an exemption for Amish communities from the requirement that all children be sent to state-accredited schools.[9] The Amish are descended from eighteenth-century immigrants of strong Protestant conviction who settled in this country in order to organize self-sufficient farming communities along religious principles, free of interference from unsympathetic outsiders. There is perhaps no purer example of religious faith expressed in a whole way of life, of social organization infused and saturated with religious principle. The aim of Amish education is to prepare the young for a life of industry and piety by transmitting to them the unchanged farming and household methods of their ancestors and a thorough distrust of modern techniques and styles that can only make life more complicated, soften character, and corrupt with "worldliness." Accordingly, the Amish have always tried their best to insulate their communities from external influences, including the influence of state-operated schools. Their own schools teach only enough reading to make a lifetime of Bible study possible, only enough arithmetic to permit the keeping of budget books and records of simple commercial transactions. Four or five years of this, plus exercises in sociality, devotional instruction, in-

---

[8] " 'If I allow blood to be given into her and if she lived, she wouldn't be considered my wife,' the police said Mr. Jackson had told the doctors" (*New York Times*, November 13, 1968).

[9] *State* v. *Garber*, 197 Kan. 567 (1966).

culcation of traditional virtues, and on-the-job training in simple crafts of
field, shop, or kitchen are all that is required, in a formal way, to prepare
children for the traditional Amish way of life to which their parents are
bound by the most solemn commitments.

More than this, however, was required by law of any accredited private
school in the state of Kansas. Education is compulsory until the age of
sixteen, and must meet minimal curricular standards, including courses in
history, civics, literature, art, science, and mathematics more advanced
than elementary arithmetic. Why not permit a limited exemption from
these requirements out of respect for the constitutional right of the Amish
to the free exercise of their religion and to the self-contained way of life
that is inseparable from that exercise? The case for the exemption was a
strong one. The Amish "sincerity" is beyond any question. The simple "un-
worldly" life that is part of their religion is prima facie inconsistent with
modern education; and the virtues of simplicity and withdrawal are "important," that is, more than merely incidental or peripheral to the Amish
religion. Moreover, the small size of the Amish sect would minimize the
effect of an exemption on the general educational level in Kansas. Indeed,
insofar as there is a *public* interest involved in this problem (in addition to
the clash of private interests) it seems to weigh more heavily on the Amish
side of the scale, for as John Stuart Mill pointed out in *On Liberty*,[10] we all
profit from the example of others' "experiments in living." They permit us
to choose our own way of life more aware of the various alternatives, thus
facilitating our own reasoning about such choices and reducing the possibility of error in our selection. Living examples of radically different ways
of life constantly before our eyes cannot help but benefit all of us, if only
by suggesting different directions in case our majority ways lead to dead
ends.

The case against the exemption for the Amish must rest entirely on the
rights of Amish *children*, which the state as *parens patriae* is sworn to protect. An education that renders a child fit for only one way of life forecloses
irrevocably his other options. He may become a pious Amish farmer, but
it will be difficult to the point of practical impossibility for him to become
an engineer, a physician, a research scientist, a lawyer, or a business executive. The chances are good that inherited propensities will be stymied in a
large number of cases, and in nearly all cases, critical life decisions will have
been made irreversibly for a person well before he reaches the age of full
discretion when he should be expected, in a free society, to make them
himself. To be prepared for anything, including the worst, in this complex
and uncertain world would seem to require as much knowledge as a child
can absorb throughout his minority. These considerations have led many

[10] *On Liberty*, chapter 3, paragraphs 2–3.

to speak of the American child's birthright to as much education as may be available to him, a right no more "valid" than the religious rights of parents, but one that must be given reluctant priority in cases of unavoidable conflict.

Refusal to grant the exemption requested by the Amish only puts them in the same kind of position vis-à-vis their children as all other parents. They are permitted and indeed expected to make every reasonable effort to transmit by example and precept their own values to their children. This is in fact a privileged position for parents, given their special relations of intimacy and affection with their children, even when compared to the rival influences of neighbors and schools; but still, in the interest of eventual full maturity, self-fulfillment, and natural many-sided development of the children themselves, parents must take their chances with outside influences.

The legal setback to the Amish at the hands of the Kansas Supreme Court was only temporary, however, and six years later in the case of *Wisconsin* v. *Yoder*[11] they won a resounding victory in the Supreme Court of the United States. The Amish litigants in that case had been convicted of violating Wisconsin's compulsory school attendance law (which requires attendance until the age of sixteen) by refusing to send their children to public or accredited private school after they had graduated from the eighth grade. The U.S. Supreme Court upheld the Wisconsin Supreme Court's ruling that application of the compulsory school attendance law to the Amish violated their rights under the Free Exercise of Religion Clause of the First Amendment.[12] The Court acknowledged that the case required a balancing of legitimate interests but concluded that the interest of the parents in determining the religious upbringing of their children outweighed the claim of the state in its role as *parens patriae* "to extend the benefit of secondary education to children regardless of the wishes of their parents."

Chief Justice Burger delivered the opinion of the Court, which showed a commendable sensitivity to the parental interests and the ways they are threatened by secular public education:

> The concept of a life aloof from the world and its values is central to their faith. . . . High school attendance with teachers who are not of the Amish faith, and may even be hostile to it, interposes a serious barrier to integration of the Amish child into the Amish religious community. . . . Compulsory school attendance to the age of sixteen for Amish children carries with it a very real threat of undermining Amish community and religious practice as they

---

[11] *Wisconsin* v. *Yoder, et al.*, 406 U.S. 205 (1972).
[12] As made applicable to the states by the Fourteenth Amendment.

exist today; they must either abandon belief and be assimilated into society at large, or be forced to migrate to some other and more tolerant region.[13]

Burger shows very little sensitivity, however, to the interests of the Amish child in choosing his own vocation in life. At one point he begs the question against anyone who suggests that some Amish children might freely and even wisely decide to enter the modern world if given the choice:

> The value of all education must be assessed in terms of its capacity to prepare the child for life. It is one thing to say that compulsory education for a year or two beyond the eighth grade may be necessary when its goal is the preparation of the child for life in modern society as the majority live, but it is quite another if the goal of education be viewed as the preparation of the child for life in the separated agrarian community that is the keystone of the Amish faith.[14]

But how is the "goal of education" to be viewed? That is the question that must be left open if the Court is to issue a truly neutral decision. To *assume* that the "goal" is preparation for modern commercial-industrial life is to beg the question in favor of the state, but equally, to assume that the "goal" is preparation for a "life aloof from the world" is to beg the question in favor of the parents. An impartial decision would assume only that education should equip the child with the knowledge and skills that will help him choose whichever sort of life best fits his native endowment and matured disposition. It should send him out into the adult world with as many open opportunities as possible, thus maximizing his chances for self-fulfillment.

More than 80 percent of the way through his opinion, Burger finally addresses the main issue:

> The state's case . . . appears to rest on the potential that exemption of Amish parents from the requirements of the compulsory education law might allow some parents to act contrary to the best interests of their children by foreclosing their opportunity to make an intelligent choice between the Amish way of life and that of the outside world.[15]

That is indeed the argument that Burger must rebut, and his attempt to do so is quite extraordinary:

> The same argument could, of course, be made with respect to all church schools short of college. [Burger forgets that church schools must satisfy certain minimal curricular standards if they are to be accredited by the state. The state of Wisconsin has not prohibited the Amish from establishing parochial schools that meet the same standards that other church schools do.] Indeed it

[13] *Wisconsin* v. *Yoder* at 209, 216.
[14] Ibid., at 213.
[15] Ibid., at 230.

seems clear that if the State is empowered, as *parens patriae*, to "save" a child from himself or his Amish parents by requiring an additional two years of compulsory formal high school education, the State will in large measure influence if not determine, the religious future of the child. Even more markedly than in *Prince*, therefore, this case involves the fundamental interest of parents, as contrasted with that of the State, to guide the religious future and education of their children.[16]

Burger seems to employ here a version of the familiar argument that to prevent one party from determining an outcome is necessarily to determine a different outcome, or to exercise undue "influence" on the final outcome. So it has been argued in similar terms that to prevent one party's coercion of a second party's decision is itself to influence that decision coercively.[17] Often this sort of argument is directed at inactions as well as actions so that the would-be guarantor of impartiality is beaten from the start. Thus it is sometimes said that to abstain from coercion is to permit an outcome that could have been prevented and thus to exercise undue influence, or (in other contexts) that not to punish is to "condone." The upshot of these modes of reasoning is the conclusion that state neutrality is not merely difficult but impossible in principle, that by doing nothing, or permitting no other parties to do anything that will close a child's options before he is grown, the state in many cases itself closes some options.

There are two ways of replying to this argument of Burger's. The first is to claim that there is some reasonable conception of neutrality that is immune to his blanket dismissal, so that while there are severe practical difficulties that stand in the way, they are not insolvable in principle, and that in any event, even if perfect neutrality is unachievable in an imperfect world, there is hope that it can be approached or approximated to some degree. Ideally, the neutral state (in this "reasonable conception") would act to let *all* influences, or the largest and most random possible assortment of influences, work equally on the child, to open up all possibilities to him, without itself influencing him toward one or another of these. In that way, it can be hoped that the chief determining factor in the grown child's choice of a vocation and life style will be his own governing values, talents, and propensities. The second reply to Burger is to ask, on the supposition that neutrality *is* impossible, why the Court should automatically favor the interests of the parents when they conflict with those of their children.

---

[16] Ibid.

[17] Consider also the commonly heard argument that state policies that keep religious observances and practices out of the public schools have the effect of "estabishing" one religion in preference to all others, namely, the "religion of secular humanism." The conclusion then presented is not that the state should try nevertheless to be as neutral as it can, but rather that since neutrality is absolutely impossible whichever policy is adopted, the state might as well permit Christian observances.

Despite these animadversions on Burger's reasoning, I do not wish to contend that the decision in *Yoder* was mistaken. The difference between a mere eight years of elementary education and a mere ten years of mostly elementary education seems so trivial in the technologically complex modern world, that it is hard to maintain that a child who has only the former is barred from many possible careers while the child who has only the latter is not. It is plausible therefore to argue that what is gained for the educable fourteen-year-old Amish child by guaranteeing him another two years of school is more than counterbalanced by the corrosive effect on the religious bonds of the Amish community. From the philosophical standpoint, however, even the sixteen-year-old educable youth whose parents legally withdraw him from school has suffered an invasion of his rights-in-trust.

I am more sympathetic to the separate concurring opinion in the *Yoder* case, written by Justice White and endorsed by Justices Brennan and Stuart, than to the official majority opinion written by the Chief Justice, and I should like to underline its emphasis. These justices join the majority only because the difference between eight and ten years is minor in terms of the children's interests but possibly crucial for the very survival of the Amish sect. (Secular influences on the children had been minimal during the first eight years since they attended a "nearby rural schoolhouse," with an overwhelming proportion of students of the Amish faith, none of whom played rock records, watched television, or the like.) Nevertheless, even though the facts of this case are not favorable for the state's position, the case is still a close one, and had the facts been somewhat different, these justices would have upheld the *C* rights represented by the state whatever the cost to the Amish sect. "This would be a very different case for me," White wrote, "if respondents' claim were that their religion forbade their children from attending any school at any time and from complying in any way with the educational standards set by the State."[18] In that hypothetical case, as in various intermediate ones where we can imagine that the respondents withdrew their children after two or four years of schooling, no amount of harm to the parents' interest in the religious upbringing of their children could overturn the children's rights-in-trust to an open future.

White gives eloquent answer to Burger's claim that compulsory education of Amish youth in large modern high schools is in effect a kind of indoctrination in secular values. Education can be compulsory, he argues, only because, or only when, it is neutral:

> the State is not concerned with the maintenance of an educational system as an end in itself; it is rather attempting to nurture and develop the human potential of its children, whether Amish or non-Amish: to expand their knowledge, broaden their sensibilities, kindle their imagination, foster a spirit of free

[18] *Wisconsin* v. *Yoder*, at 236.

inquiry, and increase their human understanding and tolerance. It is possible that most Amish children will wish to continue living the rural life of their parents, in which case their training at home will adequately equip them for their future role. Others, however, may wish to become nuclear physicists, ballet dancers, computer programmers, or historians, and for these occupations, formal training will be necessary. . . . A State has a legitimate interest not only in seeking to develop the latent talents of its children but also in seeking to prepare them for the life style that they may later choose, or at least to provide them with an option other than the life they have led in the past.[19]

The corrective emphasis of the White concurring opinion then is on the danger of using *Yoder* uncritically as a precedent for finding against children's *C* rights when they are clearly in conflict with the supervisory rights of their parents. A quite different case, involving a child custody decision, will illustrate the equal and opposite danger, of overruling parental rights for the supposititious future interests of a child interpreted in a flagrantly "non-neutral" manner. This horror story is an example of a court taking far too seriously its right under *parens patriae* by enforcing on a child its own special and partisan conception of the way of life that is truly best for it. I refer to the case of six-year-old Mark Painter of Ames, Iowa.[20] An automobile accident took the lives of his mother and sister. His father then left Mark temporarily with his prosperous maternal grandparents on a large Iowa farm, and went to a suburb of San Francisco to begin a new career. A year later, having remarried, he went back to Iowa to pick up his son and return with him to his new home. The grandparents refused to give up the boy, however, and the case went to court. A lower court decision returning the boy to the custody of his natural father was eventually overturned by a state Supreme Court decision favoring the grandparents. The U.S. Supreme Court refused to review that decision, and thus a father was legally deprived of the custody of his own son.

The opinion of the Iowa Supreme Court is a melancholy document. Mr. Painter's new home, it concluded, would not satisfy the child's right to well-rounded growth into full maturity:

Our conclusion as to the type of home Mr. Painter would offer is based upon his Bohemian approach to finances and life in general. . . . He is either an agnostic or an atheist and has no concern for formal religious training. . . . He has read a lot of Zen Buddhism . . . [his new wife] Mrs. Painter is Roman Catholic. . . . He is a political liberal and got into difficulty in a job at the

---

[19] Ibid., at 237–38.
[20] See the book about the case by his father: Hal Painter, *Mark, I Love You* (New York: Simon & Schuster, 1968). The citations in notes 21 and 22 below are from Justice William C. Stuart's decision in the Iowa Supreme Court, reprinted as an appendix in the paperback edition of *Mark, I Love You* (New York: Ballantine Books, 1969).

University of Washington for his support of the activities of the American
Civil Liberties Union. . . . We believe the Painter household would be unstable, unconventional, arty, Bohemian, and probably intellectually stimulat-
ing.[21]

The home of Mark's Protestant Sunday school-teaching grandparents, on
the other hand, was spacious and commodious, and sure to provide him
"with a stable, dependable, conventional, middle-class, Middle West background."[22]

If a parent, as such, has a legally recognized right to the custody of his
own child (and surely this must be the case) then we should expect courts
to infringe that right only with the greatest reluctance and only for the
most compelling reasons. One such reason would be conflict with an even
more important right of the child himself. Parents who beat, torture, or
mutilate their children, or who willfully refuse to permit them to be educated, can expect the state as *parens patriae* to intervene and assign the children to the custody of court-appointed trustees. Given satisfaction of reasonable moral standards of care and education, however, no court has the
right to impose its own conception of the good life on a child over its
natural parents' objections. The state cannot properly select the influences
that are best for a child; it can only insist that all public influences be kept
open, that all children through accredited schools become acquainted with
a great variety of facts and diversified accounts and evaluations of the myr-
iad human arrangements in the world and in history. This is what it means
for parents to "take their chances" with external influences. But apart from
that, every parent is free to provide any kind of religious upbringing he
chooses, or none at all; to send his child to public or accredited private
schools, sectarian or nonsectarian; to attempt to transmit his own ideals,
moral and political, whatever they may be, to his child; in short, to create
whatever environment of influence he can for his child, subject to the
state's important but minimal standards of humanity, health, and education. For a child to be exposed mainly and directly to unconventional values is still, after all, a long way from "martyrdom."

As to the content of the values of any particular parents, there the liberal
state is and must be neutral. Indeed, the state must be as neutral between
atheism and the theism in the private households of citizens as it is between
Protestantism and Catholicism. The wretched decision in the Painter case,
therefore, can be construed in part as a violation of a citizen's right to the
free "nonexercise" of religion, for reasons that include no weighable interest or right of his child. It sounds innocuous enough to say that a child's
welfare has priority even over a parent's right of custody; but this is no

[21] Ibid., pp. 226f.
[22] Ibid., p. 225.

more than an empty platitude when the child's welfare is not objectively and unarguably at issue.

THE PARADOXES OF AUTONOMY AND SELF-FULFILLMENT

The coherence of the above account of the child's right to an open future is threatened by a number of philosophical riddles. The existence of such a right, as we have seen, sets limits to the ways in which parents may rear their own children, and even imposes duties on the state, in its role as *parens patriae*, to enforce those limits. The full statement of the grounds for these protective duties will invoke the interrelated ideals of autonomy (or self-determination) and self-fulfillment, and these concepts are notoriously likely to generate philosophical confusion. Moreover, both friends and enemies of the child's right to an open future are likely to use the obscure and emotionally charged epithet "paternalism," the one side accusingly, the other apologetically, a practice that can only detract further from conceptual clarity.

The pejorative term "paternalism" is commonly applied to acts of authorities or rule-makers that are thought to treat adults as if they were children—for example, orders prohibiting some sort of predominantly self-regarding behavior, when they are issued for the subject's "own good" quite apart from his own considered preferences in the matter, or actions that deliberately impose some pattern on the subject's life without his consent or even against his wishes, but once more, like bitter medicine, "for his own good." How is it possible then for parents to be "paternalistic" in a similarly derogatory sense, toward their own children? The term can be applied pejoratively in this way only because there is a series of stages in a child's growth between total helplessness and incapacity at the beginning and near self-sufficiency at the threshold of adulthood. Blameable "paternalism" must consist in treating the child at a given stage as if he were at some earlier, less developed stage. But "paternalism" in the upbringing of children, in some sense, is inevitable and therefore wholly proper, whether imposed by the state in the child's interest or by the parents themselves, and that is because there will be some respects at least in which even an older child cannot know his own interest, some respects in which he must be protected from his own immature and uninformed judgment. Moreover, since children are not born with a precisely determined character structure, they must be socialized by measures of discipline if they are to become fit members of the adult community, and this must be done even if it is against the wishes of the presocialized children themselves. As Kenneth Henley puts it, "We cannot always await their consent to the sometimes painful steps of growing up."[23]

---

[23] Kenneth Henley, "The Authority to Educate," in *Having Children: Philosophical and Le-*

It is characteristic of parents, of course, not only to protect children from their own folly, but also to protect them from external dangers generally, including the dangers posed by other persons. This is a task in which the state joins parents as a cooperative partner in defining crimes against children and enforcing criminal laws by its police powers and the threat of punishment. Since the state shares this safeguarding function with willing parents, its protective policies are "paternalistic" in an innocent, nonpejorative sense, namely, that of "protective in a manner characteristic of parents." In the cases we have considered in this chapter, however, the state exercises its tutelary powers for the sake of children *against their own parents*. These state policies are "paternalistic" in the general sense of "characteristically parental," but the question of their justification in all but extreme cases is genuinely controversial. Insofar as the word "paternalism" has acquired a fixed derogatory overtone it can be applied to these difficult cases only at the risk of equivocation between pejorative and neutral senses and consequent question-begging against the defender of state intervention.

Typically the state must shoulder a greater burden of justification for its interferences with parents for the sake of their children than that which is borne by parents in justification of *their* interferences with children for the children's own sake. That is because state action by its very nature tends to be cumbersome and heavy-handed, and because it constitutes a threat to such well-established parental rights as the right to supervise the upbringing of one's own children and the right to the free exercise of one's own religion (which unavoidably influences the developing attitudes and convictions of the children). But although the burden on the state is characteristically heavier than that shouldered by parents for their own interventions, it is essentially of the same general kind, requiring the same sorts of reasons. In either case, the justification appeals (to speak roughly at first) to the eventual *autonomy* and to *the good* of the child.

The word "autonomy," which plays such an essential role in the discussion of children's rights, has at least two relevant senses. It can refer either to the *capacity* to govern oneself, which of course is a matter of degree, or (on the analogy to a political state) to the *sovereign authority* to govern oneself, which is absolute within one's own moral boundaries (one's "territory," "realm," "sphere," or "business"). Note that there are two parallel senses of the term "independent," the first of which refers to self-sufficiency, the de facto capacity to support oneself, direct one's own life, and be finally responsible for one's own decisions, and the second of which, applied mainly to political states, refers to de jure sovereignty and the right

---

gal Reflections on Parenthood, ed. Onora O'Neill and William Ruddick (New York: Oxford University Press, 1978), p. 255. Henley's excellent article is strongly recommended.

of self-determination. In a nutshell, one sense of "autonomy" (and also of "independence") refers to the capacity and the other to the right of self-determination. When the state justifies its interference with parental liberty by reference to the eventual autonomy of the protected child, it argues that the mature adult that the child will become, like all free citizens, has a right of self-determination, and that that right is violated in advance if certain crucial and irrevocable decisions determining the course of his life are made by anyone else before he has the capacity of self-determination himself.

The child's own good is not necessarily promoted by the policy of protecting his budding right of self-determination. There is no unanimity among philosophers, of course, about that in which a human being's own good consists, but a majority view that seems to me highly plausible would identify a person's good ultimately with his self-fulfillment—a notion that is not identical with that of autonomy or the right of self-determination. Self-fulfillment is variously interpreted, but it surely involves as necessary elements the development of one's chief aptitude into genuine talents in a life that gives them scope, an unfolding of all basic tendencies and inclinations, both those that are common to the species and those that are peculiar to the individual, and an active realization of the universal human propensities to plan, design, and make order.[24] Self-fulfillment, so construed, is not the same as achievement and not to be confused with pleasure or contentment, though achievement is often highly fulfilling and fulfillment is usually highly gratifying.

One standard way of deriving the right of self-determination is to base it solidly on the good of self-fulfillment. A given normal adult is much more likely to know his own interests, talents, and natural dispositions (the stuff of which his good is composed) than is any other party, and much more capable therefore of directing his own affairs to the end of his own good than is a government official, or a parent at an earlier stage who might preempt his choices for him. The individual's advantages in this regard are so great that for all practical purposes we can hold that recognition and enforcement of the right of self-determination (autonomy) are causally necessary conditions for the achievement of self-fulfillment (the individual's own good). This is the view of John Stuart Mill who argues in *On Liberty* that the attempt even of a genuinely benevolent state to impose upon an adult an external conception of his own good is almost certain to be self-defeating, and that an adult's own good is "best provided for by allowing him to take his own means of pursuing it."[25] Promotion of human well-being and the prevention of harms are primary in Mill's system,

[24] For a further analysis of self-fulfillment, see my "Absurd Self-fulfillment: An Essay on the Merciful Perversity of the Gods," in *Time and Cause, Essays Presented to Richard Taylor*, ed. Peter van Inwagen (Dortrecht: Reidel, 1979).

[25] John Stuart Mill, *On Liberty*, chapter 5, paragraph 11.

so that even so basic a right as that of self-determination must be derived from its conducibility to them. In those rare cases where we can know that free exercise of a person's autonomy will be against his own interests, as, for example, when he freely negotiates his own slavery in exchange for some other good, there we are justified in interfering with his liberty in order to protect him from harm.

The second standard interpretation of the right of self-determination holds that it is entirely underivative, as morally basic as the good of self-fulfillment itself. There is no necessity, on this view, that free exercise of a person's autonomy will promote his own good, but even where self-determination is likely, on objective evidence, to lead to the person's own harm, others do not have a right to intervene coercively "for his own good." By and large, a person will be better able to achieve his own good by making his own decisions, but even where the opposite is true, others may not intervene, for autonomy is even more important a thing than personal well-being. The life that a person threatens by his own rashness is after all his life; it belongs to him and to no one else. For that reason alone, he must be the one to decide—for better or worse—what is to be done with it in that private realm where the interests of others are not directly involved.[26]

A compromising way of regarding the adult's right of autonomy is to think of it as neither derivative from nor more basic than its possessor's own good (self-fulfillment), but rather as coordinate with it. In the more plausible versions of this third view,[27] a person's own good in the vast majority of cases will be most reliably furthered if he is allowed to make his own choices in self-regarding matters, but where that coincidence of values does not hold, one must simply do one's best to balance autonomy against personal well-being, and decide between them intuitively, since neither has automatic priority over the other. In any case, the two distinct ideals of sovereign autonomy (self-determination) and personal well-being (self-fulfillment) are both likely to enter, indeed to dominate, the discussion of the grounding of the child's right to an open future. That right (or class of rights) must be held in trust either out of respect for the sovereign independence of the emerging adult (and derivatively in large part for his own good) or for the sake of the lifelong well-being of the person who is still a child (a well-being from which the need of self-government "by and large" can be derived), or from both. In such ways the good (self-fulfillment) and

---

[26] This second interpretation of autonomy rights is defended in my essay "Legal Paternalism," *Canadian Journal of Philosophy* 1 (1971): 105–24; and also in my "Freedom and Behavioral Control," in *The Enclyclopedia of Bioethics,* ed. Warren T. Reich (New York: Free Press, 1978).

[27] See, for example, Johnathan Glover, *Causing Death and Saving Lives* (New York: Penguin Books, 1977), pp. 74–85.

the right (self-determination) of the child enter the justificatory discussion. And both can breed paradox from the start, unless handled with care.

The paradoxes I have in mind both have the form, prima facie, of vicious circles. Consider first the self-determination circle. If we have any coherent conception of the fully self-determined adult, he is a person who has determined both his own life circumstances and his own character. The former consists of his career (doctor, lawyer, merchant, chief), his life style (swinger, hermit, jogger, scholar), and his religious affiliation and attitude (piety, hypocrisy, indifference, total absorption), among other things. The latter is that set of habitual traits that we create by our own actions and cultivated feelings in given types of circumstances, our characteristic habits of response to life's basic kinds of situations. Aristotle analyzed these as deeply rooted dispositions to act or feel in certain ways in certain kinds of circumstances, and since his time it has become a philosophical truism that we are, in large part, the products of our own making, since each time we act or feel in a given way in a given kind of circumstance, we strengthen the disposition to act or feel in that (brave or cowardly, kind or cruel, warm or cold) way in similar circumstances in the future. Now, whatever policy is adopted by a child's parents, and whatever laws are passed and enforced by the state, the child's options in respect to life circumstances and character will be substantially narrowed well before he is an adult. He will have to be socialized and educated, and these processes will inevitably influence the development of his own values, tastes, and standards, which will in turn determine in part how he acts, feels, and chooses. That in turn will reinforce his tendencies to act, feel, and choose in similar ways in the future, until his character is set. If the parents and the state try to evade the responsibility for character and career formation by an early policy of drift, that will have consequences on the child too, for which they will have to answer. And in any case, simply by living their own lives as they choose, the parents will be forming an environment around the child that will tend to shape his budding loyalties and habits, and they will be providing in their own selves ready models for emulation.[28] This inevitable narrowing of options can yet be done without violation of the child's C right of self-determination provided it is somehow in accordance with the child's actual

---

[28] Henley makes this point especially well in his discussion of the parents' religious rights: "In the early years of the child's socialization, he will be surrounded by the religious life of his parents; since the parents have a right to live such religious lives, and on the assumption that children will normally be raised by their parents, parental influence on the child's religious life is both legitimate and unavoidable. But at such an early stage it can hardly be said that coercion is involved; the child simply lives in the midst of a religious way of life and comes to share in it. But surely the assertion that the child is born with religious liberty must entail that parents are under at least moral constraints not to *force* their religious beliefs upon the child once he is capable of forming his own views" ("Authority to Educate," pp. 260–61).

or presumptive, explicit or tacit consent. But we can hardly ask the child's actual explicit consent to our formative decisions because at the point when these processes start—where the "twig begins to be bent"—he is not developed enough to give his consent. But neither has he values and preferences of his own for the parents to consult and treat as clues to what his disposition to give or withhold consent would be. At the early stage the parents cannot even ask in any helpful way what the child *will* be like, apart from the parental policies under consideration, when he *does* have relevant preferences, values, and the capacity to consent. That outcome will depend on the character the child will have then, which in part depends, in turn, on how his parents rear him now. They are now shaping the him who is to decide later and whose presumptive later decision cannot be divined. As Henley puts it: "Whether a certain sort of life would please a child often depends on how he has been socialized, and so we cannot decide to socialize him for that life by asking whether that kind of life would please him."[29]

The paradox of self-determination can be put even more forcefully as an infinite regress. If the grown-up offspring is to determine his own life, and be at least in large part the product of his own "self-determination," he must already have a self fully formed and capable of doing the determining. But he cannot very well have determined *that* self on his own, because he would have to have been already a formed self to do that, and so on, ad infinitum. The vicious circle is avoided only by positing an infinite series of prior selves, each the product of an earlier self.[30]

The paradoxes of self-fulfillment present much the same sort of appearance as the paradoxes of self-determination and can be expressed in quite parallel language. These arise, however, not when we ask what a child will come to prefer, choose, or consent to later in the exercise of his matured autonomy, but rather, simply, what would be good for him, his presumptive choice notwithstanding. To answer this question we must seek to learn his governing propensities, his skills and aptitudes, his highest "potential." We must gauge how his nature is "wound up" and in what direction he is faced, in order to determine what would fulfill his most basic tendencies. We stumble into the vicious circle when we note that if a person's own good is to be understood as self-fulfillment, we cannot fully know the small child's long-term future good until its "nature" is fully formed, but equally we cannot determine how best to shape its nature until we know what will be for its own good. We cannot just leave the child's entire future open for him to decide later according to his settled adult values, because he must begin to acquire those values now in childhood, and he will in fact acquire

---

[29] Ibid., p. 256.

[30] Cf. John Wisdom's not altogether playful argument that moral responsibility presupposes that we have *always* existed, in his *Problems of Mind and Matter* (Cambridge: Cambridge University Press, 1934), pp. 110–34.

his governing dispositions now, whatever we do. And in closing his future options in some ways now by our educating, our socializing, our choice of influential environments, we cannot be guided entirely by what accords with the child's own future character, because that character will in large part be a product of the self we are molding now. In a nutshell: the parents help create some of the interests whose fulfillment will constitute the child's own good. They cannot aim at an independent conception of the child's own good in deciding how to do this, because to some extent, the child's own good (self-fulfillment) depends on which interests the parents decide to create. The circle is thus closed.

THE PARADOXES RESOLVED

Closed, but not closed tight. The plausible-sounding propositions that seem to lock us into paradox in reality are only approximate generalizations, merely partial truths whose soft spots make viable escape-hatches. The "paradoxes" stem from a failure to appreciate how various judgments used in their formulation are only partly true, and how certain central distinctions are matters of degree. It is an overstatement, for example, that there is any early stage at which a child's character is *wholly* unformed and his talents and temperament *entirely* plastic, without latent bias or limit, and another that there can be *no* "self-determination" unless the self that does the determining is already *fully* formed. Moreover, it is a distortion to represent the distinction between child and adult in the rigid manner presupposed by the "paradoxes."

There is no sharp line between the two stages of human life; they are really only useful abstractions from a continuous process of development, every phase of which differs only in degree from that preceding it. Many or most of a child's C rights-in-trust have already become A rights by the time he is ten or twelve. Any "mere child" beyond the stage of infancy is only a child in some respects, and already an adult in others. Such dividing lines as the eighteenth or twenty-first birthday are simply approximations (plausible guesses) for the point where *all* the natural rights-in-trust have become actual A rights. In the continuous development of the relative-adult out of the relative-child there is no point before which the child himself has no part in his own shaping, and after which he is the sole responsible maker of his own character and life plan. The extent of the child's role in his own shaping is again a process of constant and continuous growth already begun at birth, as indeed is the "size" of his self, that is, the degree to which it is already formed and fixed.

Right from the beginning the newborn infant has a kind of rudimentary character consisting of temperamental proclivities and a genetically fixed potential for the acquisition of various talents and skills. The standard sort of loving upbringing and a human social environment in the earliest years will be like water added to dehydrated food, filling it out and actualizing its stored-in tendencies. Then the child's earliest models for imitation will make an ineluctable mark on him. He will learn one language rather than another, for instance, and learn it with a particular accent and inflection. His own adult linguistic style will be in the making virtually from the beginning. For the first year or two he will have no settled dispositions of action and feeling of the kind Aristotle called virtues and vices (excellences and defects of character), but as Aristotle said, he is born with the capacity to acquire such dispositions, and the process is underway very early as his basic habits of response are formed and reinforced.

At a time so early that the questions of how to socialize and educate the child have not even arisen yet, the twig will be bent in a certain definite direction. From then on, the parents in promoting the child's eventual autonomy and well-being will have to respect that initial bias from heredity and early environment. Thus from the beginning the child must—inevitably *will*—have some "input" in its own shaping, the extent of which will grow continuously even as the child's character itself does. I think that we can avoid, or at least weaken, the paradoxes if we remember that the child can contribute toward the making of his own self and circumstances in ever-increasing degree. Always the self that contributes to the making of the new self is itself the product of both outside influences and an earlier self that was not quite as fully formed. That earlier self, in turn, was the product of both outside influences and a still earlier self that was still less fully formed and fixed, and so on, all the way back to infancy. At every subsequent stage the immature child plays an ever-greater role in the creation of his own life, until at the arbitrarily fixed point of full maturity or adulthood, he is at last fully and properly in charge of himself, sovereign within his terrain, his more or less finished character the product of a complicated interaction of external influences and ever-increasing contributions from his own earlier self. At least that is how growth proceeds when parents and other authorities rear a child with maximal regard for the autonomy of the adult he will one day be. That is the most sense that we can make of the ideal of the "self-made person," but it is an intelligible idea, I think, with no paradox in it.

Similarly, the parents who rear their child in such a way as to promote his self-fulfillment most effectively will at every stage try to strengthen the basic tendencies of the child as manifested at that stage. They will give him opportunities to develop his strongest talents, for instance, after having enjoyed opportunities to discover by various experiments just what those talents are. And they will steer the child toward the type of career that requires the kind of temperament the child already has rather than a temperament that is alien to him by his very nature. There can be no self-fulfillment for a child prone to sedentary activity by his native body type and endowed with fine motor control over his sensitive fingers if he is inescapably led into a job calling for a large-muscled, energetic person with high gross motor control but no patience for small painstaking tasks, or vice versa. The child will even have very basic tendencies toward various kinds of attitudes from an early stage, at least insofar as they grow naturally out of his inherited temperamental propensities. He may be the naturally gregarious, outgoing sort, or the kind of person who will naturally come to treasure his privacy and to keep his own counsels; he may appreciate order and structure more or less than spontaneity and freedom; he may be inclined, ceteris paribus, to respect or to challenge authority. Such attitudes grow from basic dispositions of temperament and are the germ in turn of fundamental convictions and styles of life that the child will still be working out and trying to understand and justify when he is an adult. The discerning parent will see all of these things ever more clearly as the child grows older, and insofar as he steers the child at all, it will be in the child's own preferred directions. At the very least he will not try to turn him upstream and make him struggle against his own deepest currents. Then if the child's future is left open as much as possible for his own finished self to determine, the fortunate adult that emerges will already have achieved, without paradox, a certain amount of self-fulfillment, a consequence in large part of his own already autonomous choices in promotion of his own natural preferences.

Chapter Four

SENTIMENT AND SENTIMENTALITY IN
PRACTICAL ETHICS

THE ROLE OF SENTIMENT

What relevance, if any, do appeals to sentiment have for issues in practical ethics? The abrupt way to answer this question is to respond, "None. Sentiment is one thing and argument is another, and nothing fogs the mind so thoroughly as emotion." Yet in discussions of every basic question in practical ethics appeals to sentiment are commonly made, sometimes to be sure by demagogues, but also by respectable scholars who presumably know what they are doing and proceed unashamedly. Probably no "argument" against abortion, for example, has been so effective as photographs of the tender little faces and chubby paws of "sleeping" ten-week-old fetuses. "Can you deny," ask the antibortion partisans, "that this cute little thing with its human face and hands is a person with a person's right to life?" Well, of course one can deny its right to life because having recognizably human features and the capacity to evoke tender responses from observers are not plausible criteria of personhood, but it may be harder to reject in toto the relevance of the feelings induced in nearly everyone by the pictures, especially if we concede that they are natural feelings, "honest and true."

Roger Wertheimer bids us imagine a universal mutation that renders the membranous shields of pregnant women transparent so that developing fetuses can be in full public view.[1] He is unsure of the relevance of this *Gedankenexperiment*, but he suspects that if the facts were as supposed fewer of us would be liberals about abortion. I for one remain convinced that fetuses are not persons in the sense pertinent to the possession of rights, but Wertheimer's imaginative surmise raises another possibility for me. There may be morally relevant properties of fetuses other than rights and personhood that have a bearing on how we ought to treat them. In virtue of their recognizably human features, ten-week-old fetuses are natural symbols, themselves only prepersons yet as such sacred emblems of the real thing. As symbols they become transferred objects of tender sentiments, and their destruction might shock in the manner of a violent desecration of any cherished icon.

[1] Roger Wertheimer, "Understanding the Abortion Argument," in *The Problem of Abortion*, ed. Joel Feinberg (Belmont, Calif.: Wadsworth, 1973), p. 50.

Appeals to sentiment are made in similar ways in discussions of other ethical issues. When the subject is our treatment of animals, vegetarians are often charged with being sentimentalists and they reply by inviting their opponents to witness commercial slaughterings, and note what that does for their appetites. In respect to capital punishment, Hugo Bedau notes with approval that "many abolitionists rest their case on the . . . fact that this method of punishment consists in deliberately killing human beings, and that the better one gets to know them as persons, the quicker one loses one's stomach for executing them."[2] Similar appeals to sentiment are made on the opposite side of this issue by writers who dwell on the gory details of crimes committed on innocent victims, thus evoking our vengeful anger as surely as the other side stimulates our feelings of horrified repugnance and mercy. James Fitzjames Stephen appeals to outraged sentiments in a more general argumentative way, claiming that the "gratification" of indignant feelings produced by crimes is itself a major justification of punishment.[3] Vengeance is a sentiment of great power at least partly because it is a response to maliciously produced injury. What is surprising, however, is that indignation can achieve red hot intensity when there is no harm produced at all, but only disrespect shown to some precious symbol, like a flag or a cross. The "gratification" of patriotic outrage alone has produced some of the more savage penalties in our criminal codes.[4]

The question of the relevance of outraged sentiment arises even more clearly in a relatively neglected class of issues involving the treatment of

---

[2] Hugo Bedau, ed., *The Death Penalty in America* (Garden City: Doubleday Anchor Books, 1964), p. 488.

[3] James Fitzjames Stephen, *A History of the Criminal Law of England* (London, 1883), 1:478. Stephen continues: "the feeling of indignation and desire for revenge, which is excited in the minds of decent people is . . . deserving of legitimate satisfaction," hence murderers and rapists "should be destroyed . . . in order to gratify the indignation such crimes produce."

[4] Montana was one of numerous states to pass its own sedition laws during the First World War, and the wording of its statute was quite typical:

Thus Montana imposed a penalty of twenty years in prison for various insults to the Constitution, the uniform, and the flag, which were considered too trivial to be federal crimes, until Congress in 1918 inserted the whole Montana law into the middle of the Espionage Act. Nothing could show better the way state war legislation works than the fate of Starr of Montana, as described by a United States judge. "He was in the hands of one of those too common mobs, bent upon vindicating its peculiar standard of patriotism and its odd concept of respect for the flag by compelling him to kiss the latter." In the excitement of resisting their efforts, Starr said: "What is this thing anyway? Nothing but a piece of cotton with a little paint on it and some other marks in the corner there. I will not kiss that thing. It might be covered with microbes." The state authorities did nothing to the mob, but they had Starr convicted under the Montana Sedition Act for using language "calculated to bring the flag into contempt and disrepute," and sentenced him to the penitentiary for not less than ten nor more than twenty years at hard labor.

See Zechariah Chafee, *Free Speech in the United States* (Cambridge, Mass.: Harvard University Press, 1941), p. 286.

corpses. A newly dead human body is even more natural a symbol of a human person than is a developing fetus. Both postpersons and prepersons are naturally associated with actual persons, and thus become natural repositories for the sentiments real persons evoke in us, but our sentiments are even more sharply focused on the neomort because it is not only a symbol of human beings generally, but unlike the fetus, it is the symbolic remains of a particular person and his specific traits and history. Moreover, we are not even tempted in rhetoric to ascribe rights and interests to the neomort (with the possible exception of those stemming from testimonial directions he left before he died), and surely not "the right to life." One cannot murder a corpse, or commit assault or battery or rape on it; but one can violate it symbolically, and few societies are prepared to tolerate its public mutilation. Hacking it up and throwing its limbs about would be, as we say, a shock to decent human sentiment.

Before proceeding further, I should stipulate, if only vaguely, what I mean by the word "sentiment." I can begin by ruling out one sense quite emphatically, namely, that of "an attitude, thought, or judgment prompted by feeling." "We ought to take action to alleviate the sufferings of the poor" is a worthy or noble sentiment in this sense, as its denial is a harsh one. What I have in mind, in contrast, is an affective state without the explicit attitude of judgment. A sentiment, in my sense, nevertheless has some cognitive mediation. It is a response to some object (property, occurrence, etc.) and is experienced in virtue of what is perceived in, or believed about, that object. It does not come out of the blue like some moods, nor is it aimless or objectless like some emotions. In short, there is an irreducible "aboutness" to it. Sentiments are also to some degree dispositional—not mere singular occurrences but states of mind likely to recur in similar circumstances involving similar objects. Sentiments, in my sense, also have a certain passivity to them; for the most part they happen to us, or get pulled out of us by external stimuli. We are subject to them in virtue of our prior receptivity, which is often called our "sensibility." They are more like emotions than attitudes, although they may have some features of both.[5] Like emotions they are all "in some degree agitating or disturbing," and while they can in some sense conflict on occasion, they are not illogical or contradictory when they do. In these and other respects they differ from attitudes toward things, which are dispositions to be favorable or unfavorable, for or against.[6] Unlike some emotions, sentiments are not mere objectless

[5] See Mary Warnock, "The Justification of Emotions," *Proceedings of the Aristotelian Society*, supplementary volume 21 (1957): 43–51.

[6] That construction of eighteenth-century moralists, the "sentiment of approbation," would be a contradiction in terms if it employed my sense of "sentiment." Approbation is more like an attitude than a sentiment, although as George Pitcher has shown, it is still more

perturbations with subtle but neutral affective colorings. They too have an essential polarity to them (pleasant-unpleasant, friendly-unfriendly, positive-negative), although unlike attitudes, the positive or negative character of sentiments is not simply a "pro" or "con," "for" or "against" posture.

The negative sentiments are the ones more directly or immediately involved in ethical controversies. They include revulsion, disgust, shock, horror, and vengeful anger. Very often the negative sentiment arises, however, from a perceived affront to a positive sentiment like piety, reverence, affection, pity, and tender protectiveness. Some of the terms we apply to the objects of positive or negative sentiments are themselves definable not in terms of the inherent properties of those objects but rather in terms of the sentiments they are thought naturally or properly to awaken. Thus a sacred object is one to which the proper response is awed veneration, and in calling an object "obscene" we endorse shocked repugnance as the appropriate response to it. Inappropriate responses—failures to feel or express the appropriate sentiment—themselves evoke negative sentiments. Thus, disrespectful gestures toward what is regarded as sacred (beyond contempt or ridicule) are themselves shocking or repugnant, and another party's enthusiastic enjoyment of what is thought to be obscene is itself doubly obscene.[7]

When we turn from practical to theoretical ethics we find that various moral philosophers, in a variety of different ways, have found a place for appeals to sentiment in the discussion of practical issues. I can run through some of their theories quickly. The first of them argues that people deserve protection from some of their own unpleasant negative sentiments when these are induced in them predictably by the behavior of others. Actions can be wrong on a number of grounds, the argument goes, because they harm others, break faith with others, or for other reasons, but one independent way of going wrong is to place others in such states of mind as shock, repugnance, or disgust. This is the moral analogue of the "offense principle" in the philosophy of law, which holds that the criminal law can legitimately prohibit certain classes of action on the ground that they tend to cause offense to others. The objectionable offenses are called nuisances when they cannot be avoided without one's suffering unreasonable inconvenience or harm, so one is, in effect, trapped by them, and forced to endure states of mind that are acutely unpleasant even though ultimately harmless. While nuisances may be the legitimate concern of the law, however, they can hardly be a welcome model to the moralist who wishes to ground his outrage at what he takes to be moral desecrations. The relevant

---

like a judgment than a mere attitude. See Pitcher's "On Approval," *Philosophical Review* 67, (1958).

[7] See my "The Idea of the Obscene" (The Lindley Lecture, 1979, Department of Philosophy, University of Kansas) for a development of this point.

moral sentiments for him are not mere irritations; they are more properly called "profound offenses," affronts to positive sentiments that are among "the highest feelings of civilized persons," inherently worthy of respect, and socially useful to the point of indispensability. Nevertheless, despite all that highblown rhetoric, the offending actions, on the present theory, are wrong for no reason other than their effects on the feelings of observers, and not just any observers at that, but only those who are in "captive audiences" and cannot reasonably turn their backs without inconvenience. Moralists might object then to the public display of dead bodies (hung, let us suppose, on lamp posts) or to their disposal in garbage pails, or to public mistreatments of them, hacking and dismembering them in savage fury say, but if one wishes to mistreat a corpse in the privacy of one's own room, then no harm is done to *it*, since only living persons can be harmed, and no offense is caused to the feelings of observers since there are no observers. The matter would seem then to be beyond the scope of moral concern.

This result has been disquieting to a number of writers even when the example is used in the philosophy of law where only legal prohibition, not moral judgment, is at issue.[8] In legal contexts the issue is sometimes called "the bare knowledge problem." If it is prevention of offense that justifies a given criminal prohibition then *whose* offense is at issue? That of all observers? That only of "captive observers"? That also of nonobservers who have "bare knowledge" that the offending acts are taking place beyond their observations? Or that of anyone with the very bare knowledge that since such acts are legal they *might* be going on somewhere for all one knows? Clearly a distinction must be drawn between acts whose offensiveness is entirely or primarily in the perception, for example, those, like the marital intercourse of others, the sight of which would be profoundly embarrassing but the idea of which evokes no particular sentiment, and those acts the bare knowledge of which evokes shocked outrage. My former view was that anyone who needs protection from his own "bare knowledge" that others are behaving in voluntary and harmless (though revolting) ways

---

[8] Louis B. Schwartz, the co-author of the *Model Penal Code*, descries the debates that occurred at American Law Institute discussions of the proposed section on mistreatment of corpses. See his "Morals Offenses and the Model Penal Code," *Columbia Law Review* 63 (1963): 774:

As I search for the principle of discrimination between the moral offenses made punishable only when committed openly and those punishable even when committed in secrecy, I find nothing but differences in the intensity of the aversion with which the different kinds of behavior are regarded. It was the intuition of the draftsman and his fellow lawmakers in the Institute that disrespectful behavior to a corpse and cruelty to animals were more intolerable affronts to ordinary feelings than disrespectful behavior to a flag. Therefore, in the former cases, but not the latter, we overcame our general reluctance to extend penal controls of immorality to private behavior that disquiets people solely because they learn that things of this sort are going on.

behind locked doors and drawn blinds is suffering from abnormal susceptibility to offense, and can no more demand legal prohibition of the behavior whose bare idea revolts him than the person who is allergic to table salt
can demand its criminal prohibition to protect his abnormal vulnerability
to harm. I no longer think that this view is adequate as it stands. It is
plausible enough to say of the heterosexual who is oppressed beyond tolerance by his bare knowledge that a homosexual couple lives discreetly
down his block that his susceptibility to offense is excessive and pathological, though we would respect his offended reaction to "open lewdness,"
and even protect him from it. The antiabortionist, on the other hand, does
not think of his own sentiments as the ground for either the wrongness or
the prohibitability of abortion. He is not placated by the principle "out of
sight, out of mind." His offended state of mind is more typical of profound
offense than mere aversion to gross, irritating, or embarrassing sights. Perhaps we should say that his moral sensibility and not merely his delicacy is
affronted.

Adapting (with apologies) an example from Kurt Baier,[9] suppose that
we encounter one day a sign on a storefront advertising:

> Mistreatments of corpses, room 209. See dismemberments, mutilations, nec-
> rophilia, cannibalism. $15. Active participation $25.

One could be haunted by the bare knowledge that such things go on in
room 209 to the point of severe distress, even though mercifully one is
never forced to witness them. Perhaps then the law should forbid the com-
mercialization (and in particular the advertising) of such activities while
permitting them when discreetly performed in private residences. That
way no one would even have specific knowledge of them to be distressed
by, and the only complaints would be from those who claim to be acutely
offended at the bare thought that somewhere or other, at some time or
other, such activities, being legal, might for all one can know be occurring.
That offense might be deemed too remote, and its susceptibility too extreme, to qualify for legal protection. But even if tolerance is required as a
solution to the problem of legal policy, it surely will not do as a solution
to the moral question. There might still be something wrong with the act
of mutilating a corpse, even though the wrongness is not such as to justify
interference or punishment. Those whose moral sensibilities are offended
by the very idea of such conduct are just those who will argue that the
wrongness of the actions is what causes their distress, not the other way
round.

It is not very plausible then to formulate a criterion of moral wrongness

[9] Kurt Baier, "The Liberal Approach to Pornography," *University of Pittsburgh Law Review*
40 (1979): 622.

in terms of the effects of actions on human sentiments. What makes wrong acts wrong according to such a theory, is that they would evoke a negative sentiment of some appropriate kind in some appropriate class of people— perhaps all people with "normal susceptibilities," or the average person in our culture. Because other things besides evoked sentiment make acts wrong on occasion, the theory to be even remotely plausible would have to maintain that the capacity to evoke negative sentiment is only one of several distinct kinds of "wrong-making characteristic." This would make the capacity to evoke sentiment into what C. D. Broad calls a "wrong-tending" (as opposed to wrong-making) characteristic.[10] The disposition to cause annoyance, of course, *is* a "wrong-tending characteristic," but the mere nuisance and unpleasantness it produces are only "moral misdemeanors," not the moral crimes that abortion and corpse abuse are commonly charged to be. So, even as watered down, the theory when applied to the problem cases is implausible. Those very persons who take moral sentiment more seriously will think of *this* theory as putting the cart before the horse, for in many cases, they think of their shocked moral sentiments as the effects of their apprehensions of wrongness, not as themselves causative or constitutive of that wrongness.

A more credible version of the theory dilutes it still further. The capacity to evoke sentiments of the appropriate kind in the appropriate class of people, on this view, is not what makes (or tends) wrong acts to be wrong, so much as our way of telling when an act is wrong. Just as the capacity to affect litmus paper in a certain way is a sign of acidity (rather than a cause or analysis of acidity) so is the capacity to produce appropriate sentiment a test of the presence of moral wrongness. The trouble with this theory is that it is not skeptical enough. For most of the familiar negative moral sentiments invoked in practical ethical controversies we have hundreds of examples of their unreliability. Shock, repugnance, and abhorrence have led to the condemnation of innocent acts as diverse as alleged witchcraft and unmarried cohabitation. Surely some of these sentiments are at least sometimes suspect. At the very least the litmus theory would have to describe very precisely the sorts of sentiments that would qualify as reliable indexes, and the theoretical burden would shift from the original problem—distinguishing right from wrong acts—to the derivative problem—distinguishing reliable from unreliable sentiments. It is as if, before we could use the litmus test to distinguish acids from nonacids, we had to construct a much more complicated noncircular test to distinguish reliable from unreliable litmus paper.

[10] C. D. Broad, "Some of the Main Problems of Ethics," in *Readings in Philosophical Analysis*, ed. Herbert Feigl and Wilfred Sellars (New York: Appleton, Century, Crofts, 1949), pp. 551–52.

A third theory of the role of sentiment is more dilute still. This is the contention that sentiment, while neither a ground nor a test of wrongness, nevertheless has the power, in the appropriate circumstances, to cause people to change their pro or con attitudes and thus revise their judgments of rightness or wrongness. On this view, sentiments can be "reasons" for moral judgments in the only sense of "reason" Stevensonian emotivists are able to accommodate. I think it less misleading to say that if ethical agreements are produced in this way, then reasons are simply not necessary, even though sufficient reasons of a nonemotivist kind may be available. There are many encouraging examples of how this causal process works. Imagine a calloused bomber pilot who never witnesses the damage produced by the bombs he drops. Show him films of the carnage caused by air raids and you may induce in him humanitarian sentiments of such power that they change his attitudes toward his own conduct from approval to disapproval.[11] On the other side, however, there are familiar examples in everyone's experience of rabble-rousing demagogues pandering to the most primitive emotions of their audiences, and often with great success. Perhaps our final verdict about the role of appeals to sentiment must depend on the quality and nature of the sentiment induced. That possibility leads us to a consideration of how sentiments and their uses can be criticized and appraised.

THE CRITIQUE OF SENTIMENT

When partisans appeal argumentatively to sentiment they often commend the feeling they invoke by characterizing it as "true," "honest," "natural," or "human" sentiment, thus contrasting it implicitly with contrived, artificial, false, or inhuman sentiment, or with corruptions, distortions, diseases, or counterfeits of genuine sentiment. Evaluation of a sentiment in such terms may be addressed to its inherent character or mode of origin, or to its appropriateness to its object, or to the quality of the action engendered by or expressive of it. When the appraisal is unfavorable, it is often voiced by one of the standard terms we employ for forms of flawed feeling, for example, "sentimentality," "squeamishness," and "romanticism."[12] Sentimentality can serve here as our primary example of corrupted sentiment.

[11] Note that the sentiment is one thing, and the pro or con attitude is another, and the relation between the two is a causal one. Similarly, the pro or con attitude and the judgment of approval or disapproval are distinct, although closely (causally?) related, things. Similar examples abound: letting a racist read *Black Like Me* by J. H. Griffin (Boston: Houghton Mifflin, 1960)—an account of a white man who disguised himself as a black man and lived for several months in the deep South—or seeing the film *One Flew over the Cuckoo's Nest* with Jack Nicholson and experiencing sentiments that change one's attitude toward psychosurgery. (The latter was my own experience.)

[12] Aristotle's doctrine of virtue as a golden mean between excess and deficiency applies at

A sentiment is criticized in its own right when it is condemned either for the manner in which it originates or, less frequently and more problematically, for its own inherent quality quite apart from its manner of origin or fitness to its object. The latter mode of criticism is a favorite of music critics who sometimes condemn music as excessively sentimental even though as music it has no object to be sentimental about. I confess that I do not understand how this is possible, although I do recognize that some music is syrupy sweet, angry, heroic, melancholy, or even erotic. To condemn such music because the expressed sentiment is judged independently to be defective, must be to think of that emotion as inappropriate to *any* conceivable real-life object, a judgment that seems too sweeping, unless the emotion discovered in the music is laden with specific attitudes and judgments toward real-life experiences. Michael Tanner, in some of his examples of what he takes to be "intrinsically sentimental feelings" expressed by instrumental music, seems to take the latter tack. The "shocking" emotion (as he calls it) expressed by César Franck's piano quintet, for example, he identifies (I do not know how) as curbed eroticism in which "part of the enjoyment comes precisely from the curbing, which means that it can continue more or less indefinitely."[13] One can understand how indefinitely curbed eroticism might be condemned in its own character as "rancidly sentimental"[14] and inappropriate as a response to real life, but it is harder, at least for a musical amateur, to understand how the musical emotion can be so precisely characterized as that.

When the criticism of a sentiment points to its manner of origin, the feeling is often judged to be contrived (as opposed to "natural"), or dishonest (as opposed to "true"), or cheap (as opposed to "earned"). Sentimentalists, notoriously, are persons who deliberately cultivate their sentiments. A "sentimental journey," for example, is one undertaken for the purpose of re-creating sentiments associated with past experiences and absorbing oneself in them. There need be nothing discreditable about such projects, of course, within limits. Visits to the grave of a loved one often have the same point, as do alumni reunions. The phrase "communing with one's thoughts" is often a polite way of referring to absorption in one's self-induced emotions. But when the practice becomes excessive and habit-

---

least as tidily to virtuous sentiment as to virtuous action (as Aristotle himself suggested). Thus, being sensitive is a mean between the extremes of sentimentality and unfeeling coldness; realism is a mean between the extremes of romanticism and cynicism; and businesslike tough-mindedness is a mean between the extremes of squeamishness and cruelty.

[13] Michael Tanner, "Sentimentality," *Proceedings of the Aristotelian Society* 77 (1976/77): 136.

[14] Ibid. Tanner applies these terms not to Franck's indefinitely curbed eroticism but to "innumerable would be *Tristan Preludes* [excepting the original] in which passion is unleashed but the whole thing is rotten, rancidly sentimental."

ual dependence is created, then the techniques of autogeneration become more demanding and the detachment from real-life stimuli more marked. At that point the sentiments, being patently strained and artificial, are properly condemned as mere sentimentality, and the energetic efforts to remain absorbed in them, disconnected as they are from real-life purposes, are described as "wallowing." Moreover, emotions that would normally weaken and vanish tend to turn rancid when kept alive artificially, like the anger of Burns' "sulky sullen dame."

> Gathering her brows like gathering storm,
> Nursing her wrath to keep it warm.[15]

We do not accuse this woman of "sentimentality" only because her artificial feeling is not sweetly flavored, but it shares its contrived character with a whole range of defective feelings—sweet, sour, and bitter. Even painful feelings are sometimes nourished for "sentimental reasons" when they can only do mischief all around. "The feelings associated with unrequited love," Tanner reminds us, "are hideously painful, yet it is part of the syndrome that one goes on turning them over, inflicting ever greater degrees of torture on oneself, in no way enjoying it at all."[16] Perfectly natural feelings, entirely appropriate to their objects in the first instance, become morbid when artificially kept alive.

Autogeneration renders a sentiment contrived; settling for the appearance in the absence even of a memory of real feeling renders it dishonest. The mouthing of pious clichés in the absence of conviction is rendered only slightly better than a lie by the occurrence of an automatic pang of sentiment, a stock response to a triggering stimulus without conscious monitoring or control. It is sentimental to cultivate this sort of false piety, stock feeling and all. Feigned sentiment, originally meant to deceive others,

---

[15] Robert Burns, "Tam O'Shanter" (1793).

[16] Tanner, "Sentimentality," p. 132. Despite the active efforts at "autogeneration" involved in many instances of sentimentality, Tanner argues persuasively for the essential "passivity of the mind" in all sentimentality. "The only activity which the sentimentalist manifests naturally is . . . that of rendering himself more passive . . . inhibiting those checking devises for interrogating one's experiences." Tanner shrewdly distinguishes two types of sentimentalist, the first of which corresponds to one of the things historically called "romanticism." This first kind, typified by the German *Stürmer und Dranger*, "energetically courted emotions that then took over, got out of control, and were therefore attributable to the workings of destiny" . . . seizing "every opportunity for 'drinking life to the dregs,' etc." The second group of sentimentalists, in contrast, are those who "let life do what it will with them and languish in more or less exquisite torment." "In the end," Tanner concludes, "both court the same emotions, and it is simply a question of whether they think they can indulge them most satisfactorily by adopting a preliminary active or passive role . . . the aim of both being that variety of passivity sometimes called 'being carried away' " (p. 134).

has a tendency in the end to deceive the deceiver, in which case it is false through and through, and dishonest on a double ground.

Reflex emotions are not only inauthentic; they are also tarnished parodies of the real thing and offensive on that ground too. The person whose emotional life is largely a response to greeting card verses, time-tested illustrations of smiling children, puppies, kittens, and Christmas lights in snow-covered villages, gets his emotions on the cheap, but they are worth no more than he pays for them. Faced with real-life emotion-inducing experiences he may well respond in the same stereotyped way. Indeed, knowing no better, he may come to take his own affective knee-jerks as models for the whole emotional life of man. No wonder that the sentimentalist, as Oscar Wilde says, "is always a cynic at heart."[17]

The cynicism of sentimentality is often revealed by gestures that would not be made if a feigned sentiment were genuine. A legal commentator speaks of the "unsavoriness" of the practice of sales by next of kin of the bodily organs of their relatives after sudden accidental deaths. The unsavoriness, I suspect, stems from the suggestion that the next of kin's grief lacks a certain wholeheartedness, even if in other respects he goes through all the motions of mourning. The authenticity of other of his sentiments is also called into question—his friendship, love, or respect, for his departed parent, spouse, or child. It is offensive that something held to be precious has been degraded by the symbolism of "cashing in." But why do we third parties object? Perhaps we sense that we have a stake in preserving the integrity of honest sentiments from the circulation of hypocritical counterfeits, or perhaps simply because the hypocrisy is offensive to *our* "honest sentiments." In a similar way we might object to parents "cashing in" for the tragic loss of a child by lodging a wrongful death suit against a negligent defendant for the millions of dollars officially labeled as "compensation" for their loss. If their grief is mere sentimentality then it is a shallow emotion indeed; if it is authentic then their action symbolically cheapens it.

Sentiment is more commonly criticized as ill-fitted to its object. The inappropriateness can be either qualitative, as when one is filled with radiant joy at the perception of another's misfortunes, or quantitative, when the sentiment is of the right kind but is either excessive or deficient in the circumstances. In either case what is often labeled "sentimentality" is either a sentiment rooted in false belief, or a false belief (sometimes called a "sentimental belief") itself the product of a distorting sentiment. In the former case the sentiment comes into existence or grows to a certain intensity precisely because of an unreasonable belief about its object. If the belief were to change, then the sentiment would change in intensity or vanish altogether. One leading example is the distressed compassion human beings

---

[17] *The Letters of Oscar Wilde*, ed. Rupert Hart-Davis, p. 501, as quoted by ibid., p. 127.

have felt toward dead persons because they must lie in the cold ground and suffer the depredations of worms and snails. The sentiment of compassion for cold and suffering persons is a natural and honest one; if it amounts to sentimentality in the present case it is only because it is misdirected through unreasonable belief. When we sympathize with the dead, writes Adam Smith, "the idea of that dreary and endless melancholy which the fancy naturally ascribes to their condition, arises altogether . . . from our lodging . . . our own living souls in their inanimated bodies, and thence conceiving what would be our emotions in this case."[18] In short, the false beliefs about the dead arise through an unconscious projection of self, and that factual distortion produces the inappropriate sentiment.

Quite commonly the causal process works in the reverse direction. An inappropriate (or otherwise defective) sentiment blinds one to the facts, producing a false belief itself drenched in the sentimental culture from which it grows. Examples abound. Tanner mentions how "people who spend unspeakable years of misery in the war emerge remembering the wonders of comradeship, and nothing else."[19] In this example a sentiment appropriate to one element only in a larger complex spreads over the whole, attaching itself to the others only by distorting memories and thus creating "sentimental beliefs." Sentimentality about small children, by a similar mechanism, produces the conviction that all tots and urchins are perfect little angels, a sentimental belief that can blind one forever to the evidence of experience. The death scenes of children in Victorian novels could be moving enough in a natural way, but when the dying child is endowed with preternatural nobility, amazingly adult dignity, wisdom, and every moral virtue, the scenes notoriously become so sentimental that only the deluded can be moved at all. Sentimental beliefs about the newly dead are often created by "funeral homes," working on the preexisting materials of their customers' sentiments and transforming them into comforting convictions about the improved happiness of the departed. The mechanism is no less crude than that opposite process described by Adam Smith.

Another example is the deluded sentimental attitude toward another that is sometimes called "romantic." The mistaken beliefs produced by this phenomenon are self-deceptive, often produced without outside help by the romantic's own sentiments. The romantic

invests ordinary people or objects or occurrences with an extraordinary interest. . . . He reads attributes into them which they don't possess, or exaggerates

---

[18] Adam Smith, *The Theory of Moral Sentiments*, 6th ed. (1790). Reprinted in L. A. Selby-Bigge, *British Moralists* (New York: Bobbs-Merrill, 1964), 1:262–63.

[19] The works are Tanner's, "Sentimentality," p. 129, but he credits the example to I. A. Richards' *Practical Criticism* (New York: Harcourt Brace, 1930), p. 261.

those which they do possess. . . . He looks at a person and can't help thinking
that there is nobody on earth quite like her.[20]

The great trouble with romantic beliefs, of course, is that they get worn
down eventually by hard experience, and the disillusionment can be bitter.

Sometimes the causal interplay between false belief and flawed sentiment
runs in both directions, producing a mutual reinforcement. No doubt an
element of reciprocity is in all the examples I have cited thus far, but another example may provide the clearest illustration. A newspaper column
denouncing abortion quotes with approval a passage from a book by
Magda Denes in which the author, examining the body of an aborted fetus,
projects her own natural feelings into it. She describes the face as showing
"the agonized tautness of one forced to die too soon,"[21] as if the fetus were
capable of forming the concept of its own death and agonizing over it.
That unreasonable belief in turn reinforces the sentiment, which in its new
intensity generates stronger conviction in the belief.

Finally, the pejorative term "sentimental" is sometimes applied not to
sentiments directly but to actions based on sentiments or to the use of
sentiments as reasons for action. Actions can be subject to such criticism
even when the sentiment they express is itself natural, honest, and appropriate, and thus beyond reproach. Suppose I develop a "sentimental attachment" to an old shirt. The fondness for the shirt may properly be called
"sentimental" in a familiar nonpejorative sense. It seems harmless enough,
and while not dictated by reason, it is not contrary to reason either. Perhaps the shirt has become a symbol through its association in my mind
with good times. Perhaps, on the contrary, I have worn it through good
times and bad, and grown fond of it through years of habitual dependence
on it. Naturally I am reluctant to throw it away even though it is worn.
Provided my sentiment is just that and no more—not a fetish, not a dominant passion, not a "sentimental (and unreasonable) belief"—I think it is
innocent enough to escape stricture. But if my sentiment leads me to wear
it to a formal dinner party where it makes me look ridiculous, or in frigid
gales where protection requires a shirt of heavier material, then it leads me
to act against my interest for quite insufficient reason. Innocent sentiment,
in this example, when it becomes a reason for inappropriate action, becomes blamable sentimentality.

Sentimental actions very often are excessive responses to mere symbols
at great cost to genuine interests, one's own or others'. In the more egregious cases, the cherished symbol is an emblem of the very class of interests
that are harmed, so that there is a kind of hypocritical inconsistency in the

[20] Norman Douglas, *South Wind* (New York: Heritage, 1939), p. 86.
[21] As quoted by George Will, "Fetal Pain at Death," *Washington Post*, November 6, 1981,
from Denes' *In Necessity and Sorrow: Life and Death in an Abortion Hospital*.

sentimental behavior. William James' famous example of the Russian lady who weeps over the fictitious characters in a play while her coachman is freezing to death on his seat outside the theater is an instance of sentimentality of this kind. The error consists of attaching a value to a symbol, and then absorbing oneself in the sentiments evoked by the symbol at the expense of real interests, including the very interests the symbol represents. The process is not consciously fraudulent, for the devotion to sentiment may be sincere enough. Nor does it consist simply in a conflict between avowal and practice. Rather the faulty practice is partly caused by the nature of one's commitment to the ideal. Sentimental absorption in symbols distracts one from the interests that are symbolized.[22] Sentimental patriotism, for example, is bad enough when through its devotion to symbols it produces actions contrary to legitimate interests, including those of people in other nations. It acquires an additional, paradoxically self-defeating character when the patriot's devotion to symbols leads him to act against the welfare of his own country. Many a manipulated patriot has thrilled to the very sound of a name, flag, or anthem, while remaining quite indifferent to the well-being of those designated by the symbols, if only because he is so enchanted by the symbols that he cannot attend to the condition of their referents.

Even neutral and good sentiments then can fail as decisive reasons for action when the actions they support invade legitimate interests of self or others. If acting out of sentiment against interest is one of the things called "sentimentality" in the pejorative sense, then many of the appeals to sentiment in practical ethics are in fact appeals to sentimentality. A fetus is a natural symbol of a human being and as such should be respected, but to respect it by forbidding abortion to the twelve-year-old-girl who becomes pregnant and contracts a life-threatening veneral disease because of a gang rape is to protect the symbol of humanity at the expense of the vital human interests of a real person. Similarly, a newly dead human body is a sacred symbol of a real person, but to respect the symbol by banning autopsies and research on cadavers is to deprive living human beings of the benefits of medical knowledge and condemn unknown thousands to illnesses and deaths that might have been prevented. That is a poor sort of "respect" to show a sacred symbol.

The primary thesis of this chapter is that appeals to interest have greater weight and cogency than appeals to sentiment, and should take precedence when conflict between the two is unavoidable. The point applies more ob-

---

[22] The sentiment may remain fullblown and powerful throughout this process, but as the sentimentality becomes more and more habitual, the nourishing sentiment may dwindle as in those

> Who sigh for wretchedness, yet shun the wretched, Nursing in some delicious solitude their slothful loves and dainty sympathies.

viously when the sentiment is itself flawed in one of the ways that I have discussed, but it applies in any case, no matter how noble or pure the sentiment. Justice Cardozo once wrote, in a civil case involving the reburial of a body, that "sentiments and usages devoutly held as sacred, may not be flouted for caprice."[23] I would agree but qualify the judgment in the obvious way: life-saving, medical research, criminal detection, and the like are not capricious. My conclusion may seem obvious to many but it is currently controverted by writers who discuss problems about the uses of dead bodies, a subject to which I now turn. I reject the Benthamite preference for "social utility" over rights of individuals, but I join the Benthamites here in their appeals to social utility over the cherished sentiments of the offended when the latter are contrary to utility. This is one area in which utilitarianism deserves support.

DEAD BODIES

In their characteristic modern form, ethical controversies about the treatment of corpses began when scientists discovered how useful the careful study of dead bodies could be. A Benthamite member of Parliament in 1828 introduced what became known as the Dead Body Bill to permit the use of corpses for scientific purposes when the death occurred in a poor house, hospital, or charitable institution maintained at public expense, and the body was not claimed within a specified time by next of kin. This bill was eventually passed but not before it was emphatically denounced by its opponents as unfair to poor people. So powerful was the dread of posthumous dissection it was predicted that the aged poor would be led by this bill to "avoid the hospitals and die unattended in the streets"![24]

Similar political battles, with similar results, occurred later in the nineteenth century over proposals to make autopsies mandatory when needed for crime detection or public health. These controversies died down until the recent spurt in medical technology but now they are coming back. One recent example was the controversy in 1978 between a California congressman and the Department of Transportation. The government had contracted with several university laboratories to test designs for automobile air-bags in actual crashes of cars at varying velocities. Dummies had proved unsatisfactory for measurements of the degree of protection for living passengers, so some researchers had substituted, with the consent of next of kin, human cadavers. Congressman Moss addressed an angry letter to the

---

[23] *Yome* v. *Gorman*, 242 N.Y. 395 (N.Y. Court of Appeals, 1926). For reference to this case and all the other materials mentioned in this section on dead body problems, I am indebted to Thomas C. Grey and his excellent new anthology, *The Legal Enforcement of Morality* (New York: Random House, 1983).

[24] M. J. Durey, "Bodysnatchers and Benthamites," *London Journal* 22 (1976).

Secretary of Transportation charging that "the use of human cadavers for vehicle safety research violates fundamental notions of morality and human dignity, and must therefore permanently be stopped."[25] And stopped it was, despite the Department's feeble protest that prohibition of the use of cadavers would "set back progress" on safety protection for "many years."[26]

The most widespread and enduring controversies, however, are those concerning procedures for the transplantation of organs from the newly dead to ailing patients who desperately need them. We are familiar, from the ingenious work of Philippa Foot among others, with the hypothetical moral problems raised by the new possibility of taking organs for transplant from *living* persons, thus setting back their interests or taking their lives with or without their consent. But the problems to which I call attention here involve possible conflicts not between interest and interest, or life and life, but between interest or life on one side and symbolism and sentiment on the other.

Should a dying person or his next of kin have the legal right to deny another the use of his organs after he has died a natural death? Few writers, even among those of marked utilitarian bent, would make the salvaging of organs compulsory over the protests of dying patients or their next of kin. In many cases this would override deep religious convictions, and in this country, probably violate the freedom of religion guaranteed by the First Amendment. A more frequently joined issue is whether organs should be taken from the newly dead only if they have previously registered their consent, or whether organs should be salvaged routinely unless the deceased had registered his objection while alive or his next of kin objects after his death. The routine method would produce more organs for transplant and experimentation, thus leading both directly and indirectly to a greater saving of lives in the long run. On the other side, writers have objected that since a person's body is essential to his identity while alive, it becomes a "sacred possession" whose fate after his death he must actively control, and that these facts are properly recognized only by a system that renders a body's transfer to others into a freely given gift. Failing to make objection to the posthumous use of one's organs is not the same thing, the argument continues, as "real giving." "The routine taking of organs," Paul Ramsey protests, "would deprive individuals of the exercise of the virtue of generosity."[27] On the one side of the scale is the saving of human lives;

---

[25] "The Quick, the Dead, and the Cadaver Population," *Science* (March 31, 1978): 1420.

[26] Ibid. Philosophers might well ponder the question of why the use of cadavers for trauma research would seem more violative of "morality" and "decency" than their use in pathological examinations and autopsies. The answer probably has something to do with the perceived symbolism of these different uses.

[27] Paul Ramsey, *The Patient as a Person* (New Haven: Yale University Press, 1970), p. 210.

on the other is the right of a person—not simply to grant or withhold his consent to the uses of his body after his death (that right is protected under either scheme)—but his power by the use of a symbolic ritual to convert his consent into a genuine "gift." Even in this extreme confrontation of interest with symbol, Ramsey gives the symbol more weight. If the subject were not itself so grim I might be tempted to charge him with sentimentality.

The most dramatic confrontation between interest and sentiment in connection with newly dead bodies, however, lies in the future. It has been clearly anticipated in Willard Gaylin's remarkable article "Harvesting the Dead."[28] Gaylin has us imagine some consequences of the new medical technology combined with new definitions of death as irrevocable loss of brain function or higher cortical function. Under these new definitions a body may be pronounced dead even though its heart continues to beat, its lungs breathe, and all other visceral functions are maintained. If there is total brain death then these physiological functions depend on the external support of respirators, but if only the cortex is dead, then the irrevocably comatose bodies might function on their own. As Gaylin puts it "they would be warm, respiring, pulsating, evacuating, and excreting bodies requiring nursing, dietary, and general grooming attention, and could probably be maintained so for a period of years."[29]

Gaylin then has us imagine institutions of the future—he calls them "bioemporiums"—where brain-dead bodies, now euphemistically called "neomorts," are maintained and put to various important medical uses. The bioemporiums would resemble a cross between a pharmaceutical laboratory and a hospital ward. Perhaps there will be hospital beds lined up in neat rows, each with a freshly scrubbed neomort under clean white sheets. The neomorts will have the same recognizably human faces they had before they died, the same features, even the same complexions. Each would be a perfect natural symbol not only of humanity in general but of the particular person who once animated the body and had his life in it. One might not even notice at first that the person was dead, his body lives on so efficiently.

But now along comes a team of medical students being taught the techniques of rectal or vaginal examination without fear of disturbing or embarrassing real patients with their amateur clumsiness. Later an experiment is scheduled to test the efficacy or toxicity of certain drugs in a perfectly reliable way—by judging their effects on real human bodies without endangering anyone's health or life. Elsewhere in the ward other neomorts are proving much better experimental subjects than live animals like dogs

[28] Willard Gaylin, "Harvesting the Dead," *Harper's Magazine* (September 1974).
[29] Ibid., p. 26.

and mice would be, and they feel no pain, unlike living animals who would be tortured if treated in the same way. Other neomorts serve as living organ banks or living storage receptacles for blood antigens and platelets that cannot survive freezing. From others are harvested at regular intervals blood, bone marrow, corneas, and cartilage, as needed for transfusion or transplant by patients in an adjacent hospital. Still others are used to manufacture hormones, antitoxins, and antibodies to be marketed commercially for the prevention or cure of other medical ailments.

Even if we use the whole-brain death criterion, Gaylin estimates that our population could produce at least seventy thousand suitable neomorts a year from cerebrovascular attacks, accidents, homicides, and suicides. Some of the uses of these bodies would be commercially profitable, thereby supporting the uses that were not, and the net benefit in the struggle against pain, sickness, and death would be incalculable. Yet when I asked my class of philosophy and third-year law students for a show of hands, at least half of them voted that the whole scheme, despite its benefits, was too repugnant to take seriously. Gaylin himself poses my question eloquently. After describing all the benefits of bioemporiums, he writes,

> And yet, after all the benefits are outlined, with life-saving potential clear, the humanitarian purposes obvious, the technology ready, the motives pure, the material costs justified—how are we to reconcile our emotions? Where in this debit-credit ledger of limbs and livers and kidneys and costs are we to weigh and enter the repugnance generated by the entire philanthropic endeavor?[30]

RECONCILING OUR EMOTIONS

The Benthamite utilitarian rests his case for social innovations on the expected benefits. As reasons they count decisively in favor of the innovation whatever the character of the "mere sentiment" that may seem to support the other side. Nevertheless, since Dukeminier's articles on routine salvaging of organs and Gaylin's essay on harvesting the dead, scandalized philosophers have rushed to cast their votes for sentiment and against "mere utility." William May's sensitive study of "Attitudes Toward the Newly Dead"[31] contains a fair sample of the forms of argument and rhetoric commonly used to support our natural repugnance toward automatic organ-salvaging. I shall now attempt to reconstruct and criticize three of these arguments.

[30] Ibid., p. 30.
[31] William May, "Attitudes Toward the Newly Dead," *Hastings Center Studies* 1/1 (1972): 3–13.

The Argument That the Offended Sentiment Is Essential to Our Humanity

May recalls the Grimm brothers' folk tale about the young man who was incapable of experiencing horror.

> He does not shrink back from the dead—neither a hanged man he encounters nor a corpse with which he attempts to play. From one point of view, his behavior seems pleasantly childish, but from another angle, inhuman. His father is ashamed of him, and so the young man is sent away "to learn how to shudder." Not until he learns how to shudder will he be brought out of his nameless, undifferentiated state and become human.[32]

May plausibly suggests that this story testifies to "our deep-going sense of the connection between human dignity and a capacity for horror."[33] The practice of routinely salvaging the reusable organs of the newly dead, he contends, is to be rejected for its "refusal to acknowledge the fact of human horror." "There is a tinge of the inhuman," he writes, "in the humanitarianism of those who believe that the perception of social need easily overrides all other considerations and reduces the acts of implementation to the everyday, routine, and casual."[34] We can acknowledge the second-level horror, implied in May's remarks, that consists of the perception that the primary horror has been rubbed off a practice to which it naturally belongs, so that what was formerly a morally shocking occurrence now becomes routine and normal. Recall the daily television news during the Vietnam War, when deliberate shootings, mangled babies, and regular "body counts" became mere routine occurrences portrayed in a humdrum fashion as if they were commonplace sporting events.

We can reconstruct May's argument so that it fits what can be called "one standard form of the argument from sentiment." The argument runs as follows:

1. Whatever leads to the weakening or vanishing of a natural, honest, human sentiment is a bad thing.
2. There are natural, honest, human sentiments toward dead human bodies.
3. Routine salvaging of organs would lead to the weakening and eventual vanishing of these sentiments.
4. Therefore, the practice would be a bad thing.

I have several comments about this argument. First, it is to be distinguished from the moral use of the offense principle, with which it might otherwise be confused. The offense principle argument takes as its major

---

[32] Ibid., p. 5.
[33] Ibid.
[34] Ibid.

premise the proposition that whatever causes most people, or normal people, deep revulsion is for that reason a bad thing. (It is unpleasant to experience revulsion, and wrong to cause others unpleasantness.) May's argument, in contrast, is that whatever weakens the tendency of most people, or normal people, to experience revulsion in certain circumstances is a bad thing. He is less concerned to protect people from revulsion than to protect their "humanity" to which the capacity for spontaneous revulsion is essential.

Similarly May's argument should be contrasted with the "causal substitute" argument that assumes natural causal connections between watching and shrinking from, and between shrinking from and judgments of disapproval. The latter, if thought of as an argument, would be a kind of *argumentum ad hominem*. The person in whom the appropriate sort of repugnance is naturally induced needs no further argument; one can simply appeal to the disapproval he feels already. Obviously that tactic will not do for May since the thought of routine salvaging and the like does not cause his opponents to shrink away and disapprove, and May does not want to impugn *their* humanity (although he does discern a "tinge of the inhuman" in their proposals).

My first objection to the above argument is that it proceeds in a kind of vacuum, abstracted from the practical world to which it is directed. There is no qualifying clause in premise or conclusions to acknowledge even the bare relevance of benefits gained and harms prevented, as if "the promise of cures for leukemia and other diseases, the reduction of suffering, and the maintenance of life"[35] were of no account at all. Indeed both May and Ramsey, whose earlier argument against routine salvaging rested on a subtle preference for symbolic gift-giving and guaranteed consciousness of generosity, approach these urgent questions more in the manner of literary critics debating the appropriateness of symbols than as moralists. One wants to remind them forcibly that while they distinguish between symbols and sentiments, there are people out there suffering and dying. William James' sentimental Russian countess too may have been experiencing genuine human feelings toward the characters on the stage, but the point of the story is not *that*, but the death of her coachman.

To be properly appreciated May's argument should be recast. At most the data from which he draws his premises show that insofar as a practice weakens natural human sentiment, it is a bad thing, so that unless there is some countervailing consideration on the other side, that practice is bad on balance and should not be implemented. Very well, one can accept that proposition, while pointing to the prevention of deaths and suffering as a

[35] Jesse Dukeminier, "Supplying Organs for Transplantation," *Michigan Law Review* 68 (1968): 811.

countervailing reason to weigh against the preference for untarnished symbols.

Why do May and like-minded writers seem so dismissive of appeals to the reduction of suffering and the saving of lives? I suspect it is because they assimilate all such consequentialist considerations to the most vulnerable kind of utilitarianism, as if weighting life-saving over sentiment were a moral misjudgment of the same category as sacrificing an unwilling individual to use his organs to save the lives of others. It simply will not bear rational scrutiny to claim that there is a right not to be horrified, or not to have one's capacity to be horrified weakened, of the same order of priority as a right not to be killed and "disorganized."[36] May speaks dismissively of those who let mere "social needs" override all other considerations, as if a desperate patient's need for an organ transplant were a mere social need like a city's call for an additional public library or improved public transportation. In another place he uses in a similar way the phrase "the social order," adding the suggestion of disreputable ideology. There he writes of the routine salvaging scheme that "One's very vitals must be inventoried, extracted, and distributed by the state on behalf of the social order."[37] The moral conflict as May sees it, is between honest human sentiment and an inferior kind of value, often called "merely utilitarian." What is overlooked is that the so-called social utility amassed on one side of the controversy is itself partly composed of individual rights to be rescued or cured. If, opposed to these, there are rights derived from sentiment, one would think that they are less weighty than the right to life and to the relief of suffering. Jesse Dukeminier makes the point well. He objects to labeling one of the conflicting interests "the need of society of organs." "Organs," he protests, "are not transplanted into society; organs are transplanted into people!"[38]

[36] This word for having one's organs taken for transplant without one's consent was introduced by John Harris in his "The Survival Lottery," *Philosophy* 50 (1975).

[37] May, "Attitudes," p. 6.

[38] Dukeminier, "Supplying Organs." Fleshing out this point, consider the following scenarios: Patient *A* dies in his hospital room, not having said anything, one way or the other, about the disposition of his cadaver. *B*, in the next room, needs his organ immediately to survive. *A*'s next of kin refuses to grant permission for the transplantation of his dead kin's organ, so *B* dies. Were *B*'s rights violated? Was an injustice done or was mere "social utility" withheld? Perhaps we would call this not merely an inutility but an injustice because *B* is a specific known person, a victim, and not a mere unknown possibility or abstraction. But consider a second scenario. Patient *C* dies in his hospital room not having said anything, one way or the other, about the disposition of his cadaver. *D*, at just that moment, is in an automobile crash. Five minutes later he arrives in an ambulance at the hospital in desperate need, as it turns out, of one of *C*'s organs to survive. At the time of *C*'s death no one knew anything about *D* who was a total stranger to all involved parties. At that moment *C*'s next of kin gives his blanket refusal to let anyone use *C*'s organs, so *D*, ten minutes later, dies. Were *D*'s rights violated or mere social utility diminished? To argue for the latter, it would not be relevant to point out that no one knew who *D* was; no one knew his name; no one had any personal

Even in its recast form with its more tentative conclusion, May's first argument causes misgivings. I have no problem with premise 2, that there are natural human sentiments toward newly dead bodies that are in no way flawed when considered in their own right. But I have reservations about the other two premises. Premise 1 needs qualifying. It states that whatever leads to the weakening or vanishing of such a sentiment is a bad thing. What is important, I think, is not only our capacity to have such sentiments but our ability to monitor and control them. To be sure persons sometimes need to "learn how to shudder," but it is even more commonly the case that people have to learn how *not* to shudder. Newly dead bodies cannot be made alive again, nor can they be made to vanish forever in a puff of smoke. Some of us can shudder and avert our eyes, but others must dispose of them. Pathologists often must examine and test them, physicians performing autopsies skin them open like game, cutting, slicing, and mutilating them; undertakers embalm them; cremators burn them. These professionals cannot afford to shudder. If they cultivate rather than repress their natural feelings in order to "preserve their humanness," then their actions will suffer and useful work will be undone. There is an opposite danger, of course, that these persons' work will be done at the expense of their own humanity and the extinction of their capacity for essential feeling. What is needed is neither repression nor artificial cultivation, the one leading to inhumanity, the other to sentimentality. Instead what is called for is a careful rational superintendency of the sentiments, an "education and discipline of the feelings."[39]

I must take stronger exception to the partially empirical premise 3, that routine salvaging of organs (and a fortiori "harvesting the dead") would lead to the general weakening or vanishing of essential human sentiments. These medically useful practices need not be done crudely, indiscreetly, or disrespectfully. They are the work of professionals and can be done with dignity. As for the professionals themselves, their work is no more dehumanizing than that of pathologists and embalmers today. Other professionals must steel their feelings to work on the bodies of *living* persons. I wonder if May would characterize surgeons as "inhuman," as various writers in the nineteenth century did? Does their attitude of the everyday, routine, casual acceptance of blood, gore, and pain lead them inevitably to beat

---

intention in respect to him. That would be to treat him as if he had no name, no identity, and no rights, as if his unknown and indeterminate status at the time of C's death deprived him of personhood, converting him into a mere impersonal component of "social utility."

[39] Tanner, "Sentimentality," p. 135. Tanner speaks elsewhere (p. 134) of sentimentality inhibiting "those checking devices which are available, though hard to handle, for interrogating one's experiences, for asking whether one's feelings are primarily controlled by their object, if they have one, and what *kind* of communication they are maintaining with it."

their wives, kick their dogs, and respond with dry-eyed indifference to the loss of their dear ones? That of course *would* render them inhuman.

This is the point where I should concede to May that complete loss of the capacity for revulsion *is* dehumanizing. To be incapable of revulsion is as bad a thing as the paralysis of succumbing to it, and for the same kind of reason. The perfect virtue is to have the sensibility but have it under control, as an Aristotelian man of courage has natural fear in situations of danger (otherwise *he* would be "inhuman") but acts appropriately anyway.

The Argument from Institutional Symbolism

Hospitals traditionally have been places where the sick and wounded are healed and nursed. The modern hospital mixes this therapeutic function with a variety of ancillary ones, leading in the public mind to a conflict of images and an obscuring of symbolism. Hospitals now are training facilities, places of medical research and experiment, warehouses for the terminally incapacitated, and so on. Now, May warns us, "The development of a system of routine salvaging of organs would tend to fix on the hospital a second association with death . . . the hospital itself becomes the arch-symbol of a world that devours."[40] Perhaps it is fair to say that all institutions are in their distinctive ways symbols, and that the mixing of functions within the institution obscures the symbolism, but it is hard for me to see how this is necessarily a bad thing, much less an evil great enough to counterbalance such benefits as life-saving and relief of suffering. Schools are traditionally places of book-learning. Now they host such diverse activities as driver-training and football teams. Prisons are traditionally places of punishment and penitence; now they also are manufacturing units and occupational therapy centers. Churches, which are essentially places of worship, now host dances and bingo games. One might regret the addition of new functions on the ground that they interfere with the older more important ones, but that is not the nub of May's argument. He does not suggest that the healing function of the hospital will be hurt somehow by the introduction of routine organ-salvaging. Rather his concern is focused sharply on the institutional symbolism itself. Like a skilled and subtle literary critic, he argues for the superiority of one kind of symbolism to another, just as if such benefits as life-saving were not involved at all.

Of course May's fear for the hospital's benign image is not for a symbol valued as an end in itself. With the change he fears, hospitals will come to be regarded in new ways by the patients. The prospect of an eventual death in a hospital is bad enough; now the patient has to think also of the hospital as a place where dead bodies are "devoured." It is just as if we landscaped hospital grounds with cemeteries and interspersed "crematorium

[40] May, "Attitudes," p. 6.

wards" among the therapeutic ones. That would be rubbing it in, and as prospective hospital patients we might all register our protest. These examples show that May does have a point. But the disanalogies are striking. It is not necessary that burial and cremation be added to the functions of a hospital. There would be hardly any gain, and probably a net loss, in efficiency, and a very powerful change for the worse in ambience. Organ-transplanting, however, *requires* hospital facilities; its beneficiaries are sick people already hospitalized and its procedures are surgical, requiring apparatus peculiar to hospitals. The most we can say for the argument is that if the change in symbolism is for the worse, that is a reason against the new function, so that if the change is capricious—not required for some tangible benefit—then it ought not to be allowed. But greater life-saving effectiveness is not a capricious purpose.

May's ultimate concern in this argument, however, may not be so much with symbolic ambience as with the morale of patients who are depressed by the bare knowledge that organ-salvaging occurs routinely in their hospital, even though it will not occur in their case because they have registered their refusal to permit it. But it is difficult to understand how the thought of bodies having their organs removed before burial can be more depressing than the thought of them festering in the cold ground or going up in flames. Only the morale of a patient with a bizarre "sentimental belief," or an independently superstitious belief similar to the one diagnosed by Adam Smith, would be hurt by such knowledge.

The Argument That the Threatened Sensibility Has Great Social Utility

The argument I have in mind is the familiar "rule-utilitarian" one. It is only suggested in May's article but it has been spelled out in detail by other writers discussing other topics in practical ethics, notably abortion and infanticide. The argument I have in mind differs from May's first argument from sentiment in that it appeals in its major premise not to the intrinsic value of a threatened sentiment, its status as the "best" or "most human" feeling, but to the high social utility of this sentiment being widespread. Formulated in a way that brings out a structure parallel to May's first argument, it goes as follows:

1. Whatever leads to the weakening or vanishing of a socially beneficial human sentiment is a bad thing.
2. There are sentiments toward dead bodies that when applied to things other than dead bodies promote actions that have highly beneficial consequences.
3. Routine salvaging of organs (or harvesting of brain-dead bodies) would lead to the weakening or vanishing of these sentiments.
4. Therefore, the practice would be a bad thing.

Stanley Benn has a similar but more plausible argument about infanticide and abortion.[41] Benn concedes that fetuses and even newborn infants may not be actual persons with a right to life, but points out that their physical resemblance to the undoubted human persons in our everyday experience evokes from us a natural sentiment of tenderness that is highly useful to the species. If we had a system of "infanticide on demand," that natural tenderness toward the infants we do preserve and rear to adulthood would be weakened, and the consequences for both them and the persons they later come in contact with will be highly destructive. As infants they will be emotionally stunted, and as adults they will be, in consequence, both unhappy and dangerous to others. The argument, in short, is an appeal to the social disadvantages of a practice that allegedly coarsens or brutalizes those who engage in it and even those who passively acquiesce in it. Benn cites the analogy to the similar argument often used against hunting animals for sport. Overcoming the sentiment of tenderness toward animals, according to this argument, may or may not be harmful on balance to the animals; but the sentiment's disappearance would be indirectly threatening to other human beings who have in the past been transferred beneficiaries of it. The advantage of this kind of argument is that it permits rational discussion among those who disagree, in which careful comparisons are made between the alleged disadvantages of a proposed new practice and the acknowledged benefits of its introduction.

The weakness of the argument consists in the difficulty of showing that the alleged coarsening effects really do transfer from primary to secondary objects. So far as I know, doctors who perform abortions do not tend to be cruel to their own children; the millions of people who kill animals for sport are not markedly more brutal even to their own pets than others are; and transplant surgeons are not notably inclined to emulate Jack the Ripper in their off hours. I think that the factual premise in arguments of this form usually underestimates human emotional flexibility. We can deliberately inhibit a sentiment toward one class of objects when we believe it might otherwise motivate inappropriate conduct, yet give it free rein toward another class of objects where there is no such danger.[42] That is precisely what it means to monitor the intensity of one's sentiments and ren-

[41] Stanley I. Benn, "Abortion, Infanticide, and Respect for Persons," in *The Problem of Abortion*, ed. Joel Feinberg (Belmont, Calif.: Wadsworth, 1973), pp. 92–104.

[42] Where there is little perceived difference between the two classes, however, the strain on emotional flexibility may be intolerable. It is hard not to sympathize, for example, with the nurses mentioned by Jane English ("Abortion and the Concept of a Person," *Canadian Journal of Philosophy* 5 [1975]) who were "expected to alternate between caring for six-week premature infants and disposing of viable 24-week aborted fetuses" (p. 242). The danger here, however, is not that the nurses will be brutalized, but that they will be severely distressed or even psychologically damaged.

der them more discriminating motives for conduct. Those who have not educated their sentiments in these respects tend to give in to them by acting in ways that are inadvisable on independent grounds, and then cite the "humanness," "honesty," or "naturalness" of the sentiment as a reason for their action. This pattern, as we have seen, is one of the things meant by "sentimentality" in the pejorative sense. Fortunately, it does not seem to be as widespread as some have feared, and in any event, the way to counter it is to promote the education of the feelings, not to abandon the fruits of life-saving technology.

In summary, I find no unmanageable conflict between effective humanitarianism and the maintenance, under flexible control, of the essential human sentiments. I hope that conclusion is not too optimistic.

Chapter Five

LIMITS TO THE FREE EXPRESSION OF OPINION

THE PURPOSE OF THIS CHAPTER is to determine how the liberal principles that support free expression of opinion generally also define the limits to what the law can permit to be said. The liberal principle in question, put vaguely, is that state coercion is justified only to prevent personal or public harm. That more harm than good can be expected to come from suppression of dissenting opinions in politics and religion has been amply documented by experience and argument, but concentration on this important truth, despite its salutary practical effects, is likely to mislead us into thinking that the liberal "harm principle" is simple in its meaning and easy in its application. For that reason, this chapter will only summarize (part 1) the impressive case for total freedom of expression of opinions of certain kinds in normal contexts, and concentrate instead (part 2) on the types of expressions excluded by the harm principle: defamation and "malicious truth," invasions of privacy, and expressions that cause others to do harm (those that cause panics, provoke retaliatory violence, or incite others to crime or insurrection). In the third part of the chapter we will examine the traditional crime of "sedition," and conclude that it is not properly among the categories of expressions excluded by the harm principle. Among the other lessons that will emerge from these exercises, I hope, is that the harm principle is a largely empty formula in urgent need of supplementation by tests for determining the relative importance of conflicting interests and by measures of the degree to which interests are endangered by free expressions.

THE CASE FOR FREEDOM

The classic case for free expression of opinion is made by John Stuart Mill.[1] Mill's purpose in his famous chapter "Of the Liberty of Thought and Discussion" is to consider, as a beginning, just one class of actions and how his "harm principle" applies to them. The actions in question are instances of expressing orally or in print opinions about matters of fact, and about historical, scientific, theological, philosophical, political, and moral questions. Mill's conclusion is that suppressing such expressions is always more harmful than the expressions themselves would be and therefore is never

[1] In chapter 2 of *On Liberty*. First published in 1859.

justified. But do expressions of opinion *ever* harm others? Of course they do, and it would be silly to ascribe to Mill the absurd contrary view. Expressions of opinion harm others when they are defamatory (libelous or slanderous), seditious, incitive to violence, malicious publications of damaging or embarrassing truths, or invasions of privacy. In fact, in classifying an expression under one of these headings, we are ipso facto declaring that it is harmful. Mill is not radical about this. Putting these obviously harmful expressions to one side (he is best understood as asking) is there any [further] ground for suppressing mere "opinions"? To this question Mill's answer is radical and absolutist: If an expression cannot be subsumed under one of these standard headings for harmfulness, then it can never be sufficiently injurious to be justifiably suppressed. Apart from direct harm to assignable persons, no other ground is ever a sufficient reason for overriding the presumption in favor of liberty. One may never properly suppress an expression on the grounds, for example, that it is immoral, shocking to sensibilities, annoying, heretical, unorthodox, or "dangerous," and especially not on the ground simply that it is false.

Expressions of opinion thus occupy a very privileged position in Mill's view. That is because their suppression, he contends, is not only a private injury to the coerced party but also and inevitably a very serious harm to the public in general. The argument has two distinct branches. The first has us consider the possibility that the suppressed opinion is wholly or partially true. On this assumption, of course, repression will have the harmful social consequence of loss of truth.

The crucial contention in this wing of the argument, however, is much stronger than that. Mill contends that there is always a chance, for all we can know, that the suppressed opinion is at least partially true, so that the act of repression itself necessarily involves some risk. Moreover, the risk is always an unreasonable one, never worth taking, since the risk of its alternative—permitting free expression generally—to our interest in acquiring knowledge and avoiding error, is negligible. By letting every opinion, no matter how "certainly true," be challenged, we minimize the risk of permanent commitment to falsehood. In the process, of course, we allow some falsehoods to be expressed, but since the truth is not denied its champions either, there is very little risk that the tolerated falsehood will become permanently enthroned. The balance of favorable risks then is on the side of absolute freedom of expression.

This argument is especially convincing in the world of science, where no hypothesis bears its evidence on its face, and old errors are continually exposed by new and easily duplicable evidence and by more careful and refined experimental techniques. Even totalitarian regimes have learned that it is in their own interest to permit physicists and plant geneticists to go their theoretical ways unencumbered by ideological restrictions. Sometimes, to be sure, the truth of a scientific theory is so apparent that it is well worth acting on even though it strains governmental priorities to do so and requires large investment of funds; but this very confidence, Mill argues, is justified only when every interested party has had an opportunity to refute the theory. In respect at least to scientific theories, the more open to attack an opinion is, the more confident we can eventually be of its truth. That "no one has disproved it yet" is a convincing reason for accepting a theory only when everyone has been free to try.

To deny that it is possible for a given opinion to be true, Mill maintains, is to assume one's own infallibility. This is no doubt an overstatement, but what does seem clear is that to deny that a given proposition can possibly be true is to assume one's own infallibility with respect to *it*, although of course not one's infallibility generally. To say that one cannot possibly be wrong in holding a given belief is to say that one knows that one's knowledge of its truth is authentic. We claim to know infallibly when we claim to know that we know. It is also clear, I think, that we are sometimes justified in making such claims. I know that I know that $2 + 3 = 5$, that I am seated at my desk writing, and that New York is in the United States. In the face of challenges from the relentless epistemological skeptic, I may have to admit that I do not know *how* I know these things, but it does not follow from that that I do not know them. It seems then that there is no risk, after all, in suppressing some opinions, namely, the denials of such truisms.

Yet what could ever be the point of forbidding persons from denying that $2 + 3 = 5$ or that New York is in the United States? There is surely no danger that general confidence in these true propositions would be undermined. There is no risk of loss of truth, I suppose, in suppressing their denials, but also no risk in allowing them free circulation. Conceding that we can know truisms infallibly, therefore, can hardly commit us to approve of the suppression of their denials, at least so long as we adhere, with Mill, exclusively to the harm principle. More important, there are serious risks involved in granting any mere man or group of men the power to draw the line between those opinions that are known infallibly to be true and those not so known, in order to ban expression of the former. Surely, if there is one thing that is *not* infallibly known, it is how to draw *that* line.

In any case, when we leave tautologies and truisms behind and consider only those larger questions of substance, doctrines about which have in fact been banned by rulers in the past as certainly false (for example, the shape of the earth, the cause of disease, the wisdom of certain wars or economic policies, and the morality of certain kinds of conduct), human fallibility is amply documented by history. The sad fact is that at every previous stage of history including the recent past there have been questions of the highest importance about which nearly everyone, including the wisest and most powerful, has been dead wrong. The more important the doctrines, then, the greater the risk we run in forbidding expressions of disagreement.

Mill's account, in this first wing of his argument, of the public interest in the discovery and effective dissemination of truth has many important practical implications. Mill himself thought that we should seek out our ideological enemies and offer them public forums in which to present and defend their views, or failing that, hire "devil's advocates" to defend unpopular positions in schools and in popular debates. Mill's reasons for these proposals also provide the grounding for the so-called adversary theory of politics. The argument is that "Truth can be sifted out from falsehood only if the government is vigorously and constantly cross-examined. . . . Legal proceedings prove that an opponent makes the best cross-examiner."[2] This states the rationale of the two-party system exactly. The role of the out-party is like that of the prosecutor in a criminal trial, or the plaintiff in a civil action. It is a vitally important role too. Numerous historical instances suggest that we are in grave danger when both parties agree. Witness, for example, the Vietnam debacle, which was the outcome of a twenty-year "bipartisan foreign policy." Foreign policy decisions are as difficult as they are important; hence the need for constant reexamination, probing for difficulties and soft spots, bringing to light new and relevant facts, and subjecting to doubt hitherto unquestioned first premises. Without these aids, we tend to drift quite complacently into dead ends and quagmires.[3]

The second branch of the argument has us assume that the unorthodox opinion we are tempted to suppress really is false anyway. Even in this case, Mill insists, we will all be the losers, in the end, for banning it. When people are not forced by the stimulus of dissent to rethink the grounds of their convictions, then their beliefs tend to wither and decay. The rationales of the tenets are forgotten, their vital direction and value lost, their very meaning altered, until at last they are held in the manner of dead dogmas rather than living truths.

No part of Mill's argument in *On Liberty* is more impressive than his case for totally free expression of opinion. It is especially ingenious in that it rests entirely on social advantages and foregoes all help that might come from appeals to "the inalienable right to say what one pleases whether it's good for society or not." But that very utilitarian ingenuity may be its Achilles' heel; for if liberty of expression is justified only because it is so-

---

[2] Zechariah Chafee, Jr., *Free Speech in the United States* (Cambridge, Mass.: Harvard University Press, 1941), p. 33.

[3] This point applies especially to discussions of moral, social, political, legal, and economic questions, as well as matters of governmental policy, domestic and foreign. "Cross-examination" in science and philosophy is perhaps less important.

cially useful, then some might think that it is justified only *when* it is socially useful. The possibility of special circumstances in which repression is still *more* useful is real enough to disturb allies of Mill who love liberty fully as much as he and would seek therefore a still more solid foundation for it. But even if the case for absolute liberty of opinion must rest ultimately on some theory of natural rights, Mill has given that case powerful utilitarian reinforcement.

LIMITS TO FREEDOM

Despite the impressive case for complete liberty of expression, there are obvious instances where permitting a person to speak his mind freely will cause more harm than good all around. These instances have been lumped together in various distinct legal categories whose names have come to stand for torts or crimes and to suggest, by a powerful linguistic convention, unpermitted wrongdoing. Thus, there can be no more right to defame or to incite to riot than there can be a right way, in Aristotle's example,[4] to commit adultery. Underlying these linguistic conventions, however, is a settled residue of interest weightings as well as actual and hypothetical applications of the harm principle, often filled in or mediated in various ways by principles of other kinds. The various categories of excluded expressions are worth examining not only for the light they throw on the harm principle, but also for the conceptual and normative problems each raises on its own for political theory.

Defamation and "Malicious Truth"

Defamatory statements are those that damage a person's reputation by their expression to third parties in a manner that "tends to diminish the esteem in which the plaintiff is held, or to excite adverse feelings or opinions against him."[5] The primary mode of discouraging defamers in countries adhering to the common law has been the threat of civil liability to a court-enforced order to pay cash to the injured party in compensation for the harm done his reputation. In cases of especially malicious defamation, the defendant may be ordered to pay a stiff fine ("punitive damages") to the plaintiff as well. Only in the most egregious cases (and rarely even then) has criminal liability been imposed for defamation, but nevertheless the threat of civil suit is sufficient to entitle us to say that our law does not

---

[4] Aristotle, *Nicomachean Ethics*, book 2, chapter 6, 1107a: "When a man commits adultery, there is no point in asking whether it was with the right woman or at the right time or in the right way, for to do anything like that is simply wrong."

[5] William L. Prosser, *Handbook of the Law of Torts*, 2d ed. (St. Paul: West, 1955), p. 584.

leave citizens (generally) free to defame one another. Here then is one clear limit to our freedom of expression.

Not all expressions that harm another's reputation, of course, are legally forbidden. Even when damaging defamation has been proved by the plaintiff, the defendant may yet escape liability by establishing one of two kinds of defense. He may argue that his utterance or publication was "privileged," or simply that it is true. The former defense is established by showing either that the defendant, in virtue of his public office or his special relation to the plaintiff, has been granted an absolute immunity from liability for defamation (for example, he spoke in a judicial or legislative proceeding, or he had the prior consent of the plaintiff), or that he had a prior immunity contingent on the reasonableness of his conduct. Examples of this category of privilege are the immunity of a person protecting himself or another by a warning that someone is of poor character, or of a drama, literary, or political critic making "fair comment" of an extremely unfavorable kind about a performance, book, or policy. These immunities are still other examples of public policies that protect an interest (in this case, the interest in reputation) just to the point where the protection interferes with interests deemed more important—either to the public in general or to other private individuals. These policies imply that a person's reputation is a precious thing that deserves legal protection just as his life, health, and property do, but on the other hand, a certain amount of rough handling of reputations is to be expected in courtrooms, in the heated spontaneous debates of legislative chambers, in reviews of works presented to the public for critical comment, and in the rough-and-tumble competition among eminent persons for power or public acclaim. To withhold immunities in these special contexts would be to allow nervous inhibitions to keep hard truths out of law courts to the detriment of justice, or out of legislatures to the detriment of the laws themselves; or to make critics overly cautious, to the detriment of those who rely on their judgments; or to make political commentators overly deferential to power and authority, to the detriment of reform.

There is, however, no public interest in keeping those who are not in these special contexts uninhibited when they speak or write about others. Indeed, we should all be nervous when we make unfavorable comments, perhaps not on the ground that feelings and reputations will simply be damaged (there may be both justice and social gain in such damage), but at least on the ground that the unfavorable comment may be false. In a way, the rationale for the defamation action at law is the opposite of Mill's case for the free expression of opinion. The great public interest in possessing the truth in science, philosophy, politics, and so on, is best served by keeping everyone uninhibited in the expression of his views; but there are areas where there is a greater interest in avoiding falsehood than in acquiring truth, and here we are best served by keeping people very nervous indeed when they are tempted to speak their minds.

Once the plaintiff has proved that the defendant has published a defamatory statement about him, the defendant may avoid liability in another way, namely, by showing that the statement in question is true. "Out of a tender regard for reputations," writes William L. Prosser, "the law presumes in the first instance that all defamation is false, and the defendant has the burden of pleading and proving its truth."[6] In the large majority of American jurisdictions, truth is a "complete defense" that will relieve the defendant of liability even when he published his defamation merely out of spite, in the absence of any reasonable social purpose. One wonders why this should be. Is the public interest in "the truth" so great that it should always override a private person's interest in his own reputation? An affirmative answer, I should think, would require considerable argument.

Most of the historical rationales for the truth defense worked out in courts and legal treatises will not stand scrutiny. They all founder, I think, on the following kind of case. A New York girl supports her drug addiction by working as a prostitute in a seedy environment of crime and corruption. After a brief jail sentence, she decides to reform, and travels to the Far West to begin her life anew. She marries a respectable young man, becomes a leader in civic and church affairs, and rears a large and happy family. Then twenty years after her arrival in town, her neurotically jealous neighbor learns of her past, and publishes a lurid but accurate account of it for the eyes of the whole community. As a consequence, her "friends" and associates snub her; she is asked to resign her post as church leader; gossipmongers prattle ceaselessly about her; and obscene inscriptions appear on her property and in her mail. She dare not sue her neighbor for defamation since the defamatory report is wholly true. She has been wronged, but she has no legal remedy.

Applied to this case the leading rationales for the truth defense are altogether unconvincing. One argument claims that the true gravamen of the wrong in defamation is the deception practiced on the public in misrepresenting the truth, so that where there is no misrepresentation there is no injury—as if the injury to the reformed sinner is of no account. A variant of this argument holds the reformed sinner to be deserving of exposure on the ground that in covering up her past she deceives the public, thereby compounding the earlier delinquency. If this sort of "deception" is morally blameworthy, then so is every form of "covering up the truth," from cosmetics to window blinds! Others have argued that a delinquent plaintiff should not be allowed any standing in court because of his established bad character. A related contention is that "a person is in no position to com-

---

[6] Ibid., p. 631.

plain of a reputation which is consistent with his actual character and be-havior."[7] Both of these rationales apply well enough to the unrepentant sinner, but work nothing but injustice and suffering on the reformed per-son, on the plaintiff defamed in some way that does not reflect upon his character, or on the person whose "immoralities" have been wholly private and scrupulously kept from the public eye. It does not follow from the fact that a person's reputation is consistent with the truth that it is "deserved."

The most plausible kind of argument for the truth defense is that it serves some kind of overriding public interest. Some have argued that fear of eventual exposure can serve as effectively as the threat of punishment to deter wrongdoing. This argument justifies a kind of endless social penalty and is therefore more cruel than a system of criminal law, which usually permits a wrongdoer to wipe his slate clean. Others have claimed that ex-posure of character flaws and past sins protects the community by warning it of dangerous or untrustworthy persons. That argument is well put (but without endorsement) by Fowler V. Harper and Fleming James when they refer to "the social desirability as a general matter, of leaving individuals free to warn the public of antisocial members of the community, provided only that the person furnishing the information take the risk of its being false."[8] (William Blackstone went so far as to assert that the defendant who can show the truth of his defamatory remarks has rendered a public service in exposing the plaintiff and deserves the public's gratitude.[9]) This line of argument is convincing enough when restricted to public-spirited defam-ers and socially dangerous plaintiffs; but it lacks all plausibility when ap-plied to the malicious and useless exposure of past misdeeds, or to non-moral failings and "moral" flaws of a wholly private and well-concealed kind.

How precious a thing, after all, is this thing denoted by the glittering abstract noun, the "Truth"? The truth in general is a great and noble cause, a kind of public treasury more important than any particular person's feel-ings; but the truth about a particular person may be of no great value at all except to that person. When the personal interest in reputation outweighs the dilute public interest in truth (and there is no doubt that this is some-times the case) then it must be protected even at some cost to our general knowledge of the truth. The truth, like any other commodity, is not so valuable that it is a bargain at *any* cost. A growing number of American states have now modified the truth defense so that it applies only when the defamatory statement has been published with good motives, or is neces-

---

[7] Fowler V. Harper and Fleming James, Jr., *The Law of Torts* (Boston: Little, Brown, 1956), 1:416. The authors do not endorse this view.

[8] Ibid.

[9] William Blackstone, *Commentaries on the Laws of England* (1765, repr. Boston: Beacon, 1962), 3:125.

sary for some reasonable public purpose, or (in some cases) both. The change is welcome.

In summary, the harm principle would permit all harmless statements about others whether true or false (harmless statements by definition are not defamatory), but it would impose liability for all defamatory false statements and all seriously defamatory true statements except those that serve (or seem likely to serve) some beneficial social purpose.

Invasions of Privacy

Still other expressions are neither defamatory nor false, and yet they can unjustly wound the persons they describe all the same. These do not invade the interest in a good reputation so much as a special kind of interest in peace of mind, sometimes called a sense of dignity, sometimes the enjoyment of solitude, but most commonly termed the interest in personal privacy. As the legal "right to privacy" is now understood, it embraces a miscellany of things, protecting the right-holder not only from "physical intrusions upon his solitude" and "publicity given to his name or likeness or to private information about him" without his permission, but also from being placed "in a false light [but without defamation] in the public eye" and from the "commercial appropriation of elements of his personality."[10] (Some of these are really invasions of one's property rights through unpermitted commercial exploitation of one's name, image, personality, and so on. For that reason it has been urged that the invaded right in these cases be called "the right to publicity.") What concerns us here are statements conveying true and nondefamatory information about the plaintiff, of a very intimate and properly private kind, gathered and published without his consent, often to his shame and mortification. Business advantage and journalistic profit have become ever stronger motives for such statements, and the invention of tiny, very sensitive snooping devices has made the data easier than ever to come by.

Since the "invasion of privacy" tort has been recognized, plaintiffs have recovered damages from defendants who have shadowed them, looked into their windows, investigated their bank accounts, and tapped their telephone wires. In many of these cases, the court's judgment protected the plaintiff's interest in "being let alone," but in other cases the interest protected was not merely this, or not this at all, but rather the interest in *not being known about*. If there is a right not to be known about in some respects by anyone, than a fortiori there is a right not to be known about, in those respects, by nearly everyone. Privacy law has also protected the interests of those who do not want details of their lives called to the public's

---

[10] Prosser, *Handbook*, p. 644.

attention and made the subject of public wonder, amusement, discussion, analysis, or debate. Hence some plaintiffs have recovered from defendants who have published embarrassing details of their illness or physical deformity; their personal letters or unpublished notes, or inventories of their possessions; their photographs in a "good looks" popularity contest, or in a "before and after" advertisement for baldness or obesity cures, or on the labels of tomato cans; and from defendants who have published descriptions of the plaintiffs' sexual relations, hygienic habits, and other very personal matters. No life, of course, can be kept wholly private or immune from public inspection, even in some of its most personal aspects. "No one enjoys being stared at," Harper and James remind us, yet if a person "goes out on the street he [can have] no legal objection to people looking at him."[11] On the other hand, life would be hardly tolerable if there were no secrets we could keep (away from "the street"), no preserve of dignity, no guaranteed solitude.

There would probably be very little controversy over the existence of a right to privacy were it not the case that the interest in being let alone is frequently in conflict with other interests that seem at least equally deserving of protection. Even where the right is recognized by law, it is qualified by the recognition of very large classes of privileged expressions. First of all, like most other torts and crimes, the charge of invasion of privacy is completely defeated by proof that the plaintiff gave his consent to the defendant's conduct. Second, and more interesting, the right of privacy can conflict with the constitutionally guaranteed freedom of the press, which, according to Prosser, "justifies the publication of news and all other matters of legitimate public interest and concern."[12] For a court to adjudicate between a paper's right to publish and an individual's right to privacy, it must employ some standard for determining what is of legitimate public concern or, what amounts to the same thing, which news about a person is "fit to print." Such legal standards are always in the making, never finished, but the standard of "legitimate interest" has begun to take on a definite shape. American courts have decided, first of all, that "the person who intentionally puts himself in the public eye . . . has no right to complain of any publicity which reasonably bears on his activity."[13] The rationale for this judgment invokes the maxim that a person is not wronged by that to which he consents, or by that the risk of which he has freely assumed. The person who steps into the public spotlight ought to know what he is letting himself in for; hence the law presumes that he *does* know, and therefore that he is asking for it. Much the same kind of presumption lies behind the

[11] Harper and James, *Law of Torts*, p. 680.
[12] Prosser, *Handbook*, p. 642.
[13] Ibid.

"fair comment" defense in defamation cases: The man who voluntarily publishes his own work is presumed to be inviting criticism and is therefore not entitled to complain when the criticism is adverse or harsh, providing only that it is relevant and not personally abusive. One can put oneself voluntarily into the public eye by running for or occupying public office; by becoming an actor, musician, entertainer, poet, or novelist; by inventing an interesting device or making a geographical or scientific discovery; or even by becoming wealthy. Once a person has become a public figure, he has sacrificed much of his right of privacy to the public's legitimate curiosity. Of course, one never forfeits *all* rights of privacy; even the public figure has a right to the privacy of his very most intimate affairs. (This may, however, be very small consolation to him.)

One cannot always escape the privilege of the press to invade one's privacy simply by avoiding public roles and offices, for the public spotlight can catch up with anyone. "Reluctant public characters" are nonetheless public and therefore, according to the courts, as legitimate objects of public curiosity as the voluntary public figures. Those unfortunates who attract attention unwillingly by becoming involved, even as victims, in accidents, or by being accused of crimes, or even as innocent bystanders to interesting events, have become "news," and therefore subject to the public's right to know. They maintain this unhappy status "until they have reverted to the lawful and unexciting life led by the great bulk of the community," but until then, "they are subject to the privileges which publishers have to satisfy the curiosity of the public as to their leaders, heroes, villains, and victims."[14] Again, the privilege to publish is not unlimited so that "the courts must somehow draw the distinction between conduct which outrages the common decencies and goes beyond what the public mores will tolerate, and that which the plaintiff must be expected in the circumstances to endure."[15]

When interests of quite different kinds head toward collisions, how can one determine which has the right of way? This problem, which lies behind the most puzzling questions about the grounds for liberty and coercion, tends to be concealed by broadly stated principles. The conflict between the personal interest in privacy and the public curiosity is one of the best illustrations of the problem, but it is hardly unique. In defamation cases, as we have seen, there is often a conflict between the public interest in truth and the plaintiff's interest in his own good name. In nuisance law, there is a conflict between the plaintiff's interest in the peaceful enjoyment of his land and the defendant's interest in keeping a hogpen, or a howling dog,

---

[14] American Law Institute, *Restatement of the Law of Torts* (St. Paul: West, 1934), section 867, comment c.

[15] Prosser, *Handbook*, p. 644.

or a small boiler factory. In suburban neighborhoods, the residents' interest in quiet often conflicts with motorcyclists' interest in cheap and speedy transportation. In buses and trains, one passenger's interest in privacy[16] can conflict with another's interest in listening to rock and roll music on a portable radio, or for that matter, with the interests of two nearby passengers in making unavoidably audible, but avoidably inane, conversation. The principle of "the more freedom the better" does not tell us whose freedom must give way in these competitive situations.

The invasion of privacy cases are among the very clearest examples of the inevitable clash of interests in populous modern communities. They are, moreover, examples that show that solving the problem is not just a matter of minimizing harm all around. Harm is the invasion of an interest, and invasions do differ in degree, but when interests of radically different kinds are invaded to the same degree, where is the greater harm? Perhaps we should say that some interests are more important than others in the sense that harm to them is likely to lead to greater damage to the whole economy of personal (or as the case may be, community) interests than harm to the lesser interest, just as harm to one's heart or brain will do more damage to one's bodily health than an "equal degree" of harm to less vital organs. Determining which interests are more "vital" in an analogous sense would be no easy task, but even if we could settle this matter, there would remain serious difficulties. In the first place, interests pile up and reinforce one another. My interest in peace and quiet may be more vital in my system than the motorcyclist's interests in speed, excitement, and economy are in his, but there is also the interest of the cyclist's employer in having workers efficiently transported to his factory, and the economic interest of the community in general (including me) in the flourishing of the factory owner's business; the interest of the motorcycle manufacturers in their own profits; the interest of the police and others (perhaps including me) in providing a relatively harmless outlet for adolescent exuberance, and in not having a difficult rule to enforce. There may be nowhere near so great a buildup of reinforcing interests, personal and public, in the quietude of my neighborhood.

There is still another kind of consideration that complicates the delicate task of interest-balancing. Interests differ not only in the extent to which they are thwarted, in their importance or "vitality," and the degree to which they are backed up by other interests, but also in their inherent moral quality. Some interests, simply by reason of their very natures, we

---

[16] "There are two aspects of the interest in seclusion. First, the interest in preventing others from seeing and hearing what one does and says. Second, *the interest in avoiding seeing and hearing what other people do and say.* . . . It may be as distasteful to suffer the intrusions of a garrulous and unwelcome guest as to discover an eavesdropper or peeper" (Harper and James, *Law of Torts*, p. 681; emphasis added).

might think better worth protecting than others. The interest in knowing
the intimate details of Brigitte Bardot's married sex life (the subject of a
sensational law suit in France) is a morally repugnant peeping tom's interest. The sadist's interest in having others suffer pain is a morbid interest.
The interest in divulging a celebrity's private conversations is a busybody's
interest. It is probably not conducive to the public good to encourage development of the character flaws from which these interests spring, but
even if there were social advantage in the individual vices, there would be
a case against protecting their spawned interests, based upon their inherent
unworthiness. The interests in understanding, diagnosing, and simply being apprised of newsworthy events might well outbalance a given individual's reluctance to be known about, but photographs and descriptions
with no plausible appeal except to the morbid and sensational can have
very little weight in the scales.

Causing Panic

Defamatory statements, "malicious truths," and statements that wrongfully
invade privacy do harm to the persons they are about by conveying information or falsehood to third parties. Their publication tends to instill certain beliefs in others, and the very existence of those beliefs constitutes a
harm to the person spoken or written about. Other classes of injurious
expressions do harm in a rather different way, namely, by causing those
who listen to them (or more rarely, those who read them) to act in violent
or otherwise harmful ways. In these cases, the expressions need not be
about any specifiable persons, or if they are about persons, those individuals are not necessarily the victims of the subsequent harm. When spoken
words cause panic, breach the peace, or incite to crime or revolt, a variety
of important interests, personal and social, will be seriously harmed. Such
expressions, therefore, are typically proscribed by the criminal, and not
merely the civil, law.

"The most stringent protection of free speech," wrote Holmes in his
most celebrated opinion, "would not protect a man in falsely shouting fire
in a theatre and causing a panic."[17] In some circumstances a person can
cause even more harm by *truthfully* shouting "Fire!" in a crowded theater,
for the flames and smoke might reinforce the tendency of his words to
cause panic, and the fire itself might block exits, leading the hysterical
crowds to push and trample. But we do not, and cannot fairly, hold the
excited alarm-sounder criminally responsible for his warning when it was
in fact true and shouted with good intentions. We can hardly demand on
pain of punishment that persons pick their words carefully in emergencies,

[17] *Schenck* v. *United States*, 249 U.S. 47 (1919).

when emotions naturally run high and there is no time for judicious deliberation. A person's warning shout in such circumstances is hardly to be
treated as a full-fledged voluntary act at all. Perhaps it can be condemned
as negligent, but given the mitigating circumstances, such negligence
hardly amounts to the gross and wanton kind that can be a basis of criminal
liability. The law, then, can only punish harmful words of this class when
they are spoken or written with the intention of causing the harm that in
fact ensues, or when they are spoken or written in conscious disregard of a
high and unreasonable risk that the harm will ensue. The practical joker in
a crowded auditorium who whispers to his comrade, "Watch me start a
panic," and then shouts, "Fire!" could be convicted for using words intentionally to cause a panic. The prankster who is willing to risk a general
panic just for the fun of alarming one particular person in the audience
could fairly be convicted for the grossly reckless use of dangerous words.
Indeed, his recklessness is akin to that of the motorist who drives at an
excessive speed just to frighten a timorous passenger.

Suppose, however, that the theater is virtually empty, and as the lights
come on at the end of the film, our perverse or dim-witted jokester shouts,
"Fire! Fire!" just for the sake of confusing the three or four other patrons
and alarming the ushers. The ushers quickly see through the ruse and suffer
only a few moments of anxiety, and the patrons walk quickly to the exits
and depart. No harm to speak of has been done; nor could any have reasonably been anticipated. This example shows how very important are the
surrounding circumstances of an utterance to the question of its permissibility. Given the presumptive case for liberty in general, and especially the
powerful social interest in leaving persons free to use words as they see fit,
there can be a countervailing case for suppression on the grounds of the
words' dangerous tendency only when the danger in fact is great and the
tendency immediate. These matters are determined not only by the particular words used, but by the objective character of the surrounding circumstances—what lawyers call "the time, place, and manner" of utterance.

The question of legal permissibility should not be confused with that of
moral blameworthiness or even with civil liability. The practical joker, even
in relatively harmless circumstances, is no moral paragon. But then neither
are the liar, the vulgarian, the rude man, and the scandalmonger, most of
whose faults are not fit subjects for penal legislation. We cannot make every
instance of mendacity, rudeness, and malicious gossip criminal, but we can
protect people from the serious injury that comes from fraud, battery, or
defamation. Similarly, practical jokers should be blamed but not punished,
unless their tricks reach the threshold of serious danger to others. On the
other hand, almost all lies, bad tales, jokes, and tricks create some risk, and
there is no injustice in making the perpetrator compensate (as opposed to
being punished) even his unlikely victim. Thus, if a patron in the nearly

empty theater described above sprains an ankle in hurrying toward an exit, there is no injustice in requiring the jokester to pay the medical expenses.

It is established in our law that when words did not in fact cause harm the speaker may nevertheless be punished for having uttered them only if there was high danger when they were spoken that serious harm would result. This condition of course could be satisfied even though the harm in fact was averted: Not everything probable becomes actual. Similarly, for a person rightly to be punished even for harm in fact caused by his words, the harm in its resultant magnitude must have been an objectively probable consequence of the spoken words in the circumstances; otherwise the speaker will be punished for an unforeseeable fluke. In either case, then, the clear and present danger that serious harm will follow a speaker's words is necessary if he is rightly to be punished.

As we have seen, punishment for the harm caused by words is proper only if the speaker caused the harm either *intentionally* or *recklessly*. Both of these "mental conditions" of guilt require the satisfaction of the clear and present danger formula, or something like it. Consider recklessness first. For there to be recklessness there must really be a substantial risk consciously and unreasonably run. A speaker is not being reckless if he utters words that have only a remote and speculative tendency to cause panics or riots.

Intentional harm-causing by words raises more complications. Suppose an evil-minded person wishes to cause a panic and believes what is false and wholly unsupported by any real evidence, namely, that his words will have that effect. Imagine that he attends a meeting of the Policemen's Benevolent Association and, at what he takes to be the strategic moment, he stands up and shrieks, "There's a mouse under my chair!" Perhaps these words would cause a panic at a meeting of boy scouts but it merely produces a round of contemptuous laughter here. Wanting a panic and sincerely believing that one is causing a panic by one's words, then, are not sufficient. Suppose, however, we complicate the story so that by some wholly unforeseeable fluke the spoken words do precipitate a panic. The story is hard to invent at this point, but let us imagine that one patrol officer laughs so hard that he tips over his chair causing another to drop his pipe, starting a fire, igniting live bullets, and so on. Now, in addition to evil desire and conscious belief in causal efficacy, we have a third important element: The words actually do initiate a causal process resulting in the desired panic. But these conditions still are not sufficient to permit us to say that the speaker *intentionally caused* a panic. Without the antecedent objective probability that a panic would follow these words in these circumstances, we have only a bizarre but tragic coincidence.

We would say much the same thing of a superstitious lady who "attempts" to start a riot by magical means. In an inconspicuous corner of a darkened theater, she sticks pins into a doll and mutters under her breath a magic incantation designed to produce a panic. Of course this does not work in the way intended, but a nearsighted and neurotic passerby observes her, takes the doll to be a real baby, and screams. The hoped-for panic then really follows. The evil lady cannot be found guilty of intentionally causing a panic, even though she intended to cause one and really did cause (or at least initiate a causal process that resulted in) one. She can be condemned for having very evil motives. But if people are sufficiently ignorant and impotent, the law, applying the harm principle, allows them to be as evil as they wish.

Provoking Retaliatory Violence

Suppose a person utters words that have as their unhappy effects violence directed *at him* by his angry audience, counterviolence by his friends and protectors, and escalation into a riotous breach of the peace. This is still another way of causing harm by words. Should the speaker be punished? In almost every conceivable case, the answer should be No. There is a sense, of course, in which the speaker did not start the physical violence. He used only words, and while words can sting and infuriate, they are not instruments of violence in the same sense that fists, knives, guns, and clubs are. If the law suppresses public speech, either by withholding permits in advance or punishing afterwards, simply on the ground that the expressed views are so unpopular that some auditors can be expected to start fighting, then the law punishes some for the criminal proclivities of others. "A man does not become a criminal because someone else assaults him," writes Zechariah Chafee. Moreover, he continues, on any such theory, "a small number of intolerant men . . . can prevent *any kind* of meeting. . . . A gathering which expressed the sentiment of a majority of law-abiding citizens would become illegal because a small gang of hoodlums threatened to invade the hall."[18] When violent response to speech threatens, the obvious remedy is not suppression but rather increased police protection.

So much seems evident, but there may be some exceptions. Some words uttered in public places in the presence of many unwilling auditors may be so abusive or otherwise offensive as to be "reasonably considered a direct provocation to violence."[19] The captive auditor, after all, is not looking for trouble as he walks the public streets intent on his private errands. If he is forced to listen, as he walks past a street meeting, to speakers denouncing and ridiculing his religion, and forced to notice a banner with a large and abusive caricature of the pope,[20] his blood might reasonably be expected

[18] Chafee, *Free Speech*, pp. 152, 161, 426. Cf. *Terminiello* v. *Chicago*, 337 U.S. 1 (1949).
[19] Chafee, *Free Speech*, p. 426.
[20] Ibid., p. 161.

to boil. Antireligious and anticlerical opinions, of course, no matter how unpopular, are entitled to the full protection of the law. Even abusive, virulent, and mocking expressions of such views are entitled to full protection if uttered to private gatherings, in private or privately reserved places. Such expressions become provocative only when made in public places to captive auditors.

What makes an expression "provocative"? Surely, if words are to be suppressed on the ground that they are provocative of violence, they must be more than merely "provoking," else all unpopular opinions will be suppressed, to the great public loss. As far as I know, the concept of provocation has received thorough legal elaboration only in the law of homicide, where provocation reduces a charge of murder to that of manslaughter, thus functioning as a kind of mitigating consideration rather than as a justification or complete excuse. In the common law, for there to be sufficient provocation to mitigate: (1) The behavior of the victim must have been so aggravating that it would have produced "such excitement and passion as would obscure the reason of an ordinary man and induce him . . . to strike the blow."[21] (2) There must not have elapsed so much time between the provocation and the violence that a reasonable man's blood would have cooled. (3) But for the victim's provocation the violence would not have occurred. In short, provocation mitigates only when it in fact produces a reason-numbing rage in the attacker and is such that it could be expected to produce such a rage in any normal person in his circumstances. Nazi emblems might be expected to have this effect on a former inmate of a Nazi death camp, but the Democratic party line cannot be sufficiently provocative to excuse a violent Republican, and similarly the other way round. Indeed, in the law of homicide, *no mere words alone*, no matter how abusive or scurrilous, can be adequate provocation to justify or totally excuse killing as a response.

There would seem to be equally good reason not to consider mere words either as justifying or totally excusing nonlethal acts of violence. The "reasonable man" in a democracy must be presumed to have enough self-control to refrain from violent responses to odious words and doctrines. If he is followed, insulted, taunted, and challenged, he can get injunctive relief, or bring charges against his tormentor as a nuisance; if there is no time for this and he is backed to the wall he may be justified in using "reasonable force" in self-defense; or if he is followed to his own home, he can use the police to remove the nuisance. But if he is not personally harassed in these ways, he can turn on his heels and leave the provocation behind, and this is what the law, perhaps, should require of him.

Only when public speech satisfies stringent tests qualifying it as "direct

---

[21] *Toler* v. *State*, 152 Tenn. 1, 13, 260 S.W. 134 (1923).

provocation to violence" (if that is possible at all) will the harm principle justify its suppression. But there are many possible modes of suppression, and some are far more restrictive of liberty than others. Orders to cease and desist on pain of arrest are most economical, for they permit the speaker to continue to air his views in a nonprovocative way or else retire with his audience to a less public place. Lawful removal of the provocation (as a public nuisance) may be more satisfactory than permitting violent response to it, and is infinitely preferable to punishing the speaker. Nowhere in the law where provocation is considered as a defense do the rules deem the proven provoker (the victim) a criminal himself! At best his conduct mitigates the crime of his attacker, who is the only criminal.

One final point. While it is conceivable that some public speech can satisfy the common law test for provocation by being so aggravating that even a reasonable man could be expected to lose control of his reason when exposed to it, this can never be true of books. One can always escape the provocation of the printed word simply by declining to read it, and where escape from provocation is that easy, no "reasonable man" will succumb to it.

Incitement to Crime or Insurrection

In the criminal law, anyone who "counsels, commands, or encourages another to commit a crime" is himself guilty of the resultant crime as an "accessory before the fact." Counseling, commanding, and encouraging, however, must consist in more than merely uttering certain words in the presence of others. Surely there must also be serious (as opposed to playful) intent and some possibility at least of the words having their desired effect. It is not possible that these conditions can be satisfied if I tell my secretary that she should overthrow the U.S. government, or if a speaker tells an audience of bank presidents that they should practice embezzlement whenever they can. These situations are analogous to the efforts to start a panic by magical means or to panic police officers with words about mice.

The problem of interpreting the meaning of a rule making the counseling of crime itself a crime is similar, I should think, to that raised by a statute forbidding the planting of a certain kind of plant. One does not violate such a statute if he scatters the appropriate kind of seeds on asphalt pavement or in barren desert, even with evil intent. (Again, if you are stupid enough, the law—insofar as it derives from the harm principle—can allow you to be as evil as you wish.) To violate the statute, either one would have to dig a little hole in the appropriate sort of soil, deposit the appropriate seeds, cultivate, fertilize, allow for sufficient water, protect against winds, worms, and dogs; or one would have to find suitable conditions ready-made, where the soil is already receptive and merely dropping the seeds will create a substantial likelihood that plants will grow and thrive. By analogy, even words of advice, if they are to count as incitements to crime, must fall on reasonably receptive ears. The harm principle provides a ready rationale for this requirement. If we permit coercive repression of nondangerous words we will confer such abundant powers on the repressive organs of the state that they are certain to be abused. Moreover, we will so inhibit persons in their employment of language as to discourage both spontaneity and serious moral discussion, thus doing a great deal of harm and virtually no good at all. (The only "gain," if it is that, to be expected from looser standards of interpretation would be that nondangerous persons with evil motives could be scooped up in the state's tighter nets and punished.)

Counseling others to crime is not the only use of speech that can be described as incitement. We must also come to terms with instigating, egging on, and inflaming others to violence. Even Mill concedes that the opinion that "corn dealers are starvers of the poor," which deserves protection when published in the press, may nevertheless "justly incur punishment when delivered orally to an excited mob assembled before the house of a corn dealer."[22] The metaphor of planting seeds in receptive soil is perhaps less apt for this situation than the commonly employed "spark and tinder" analogy. Words that merely express legitimate though unpopular opinion in one context become "incendiary" when addressed to an already inflammable mob. As Chafee puts it: "Smoking is all right, but not in a powder magazine."[23] Of course the man who carries a cigar into a powder magazine may not know that the cigar he is carrying is lighted, or he may not know that he has entered a powder magazine. He may plead his lack of intention afterward (if he is still alive) as a defense. Similarly, the man who speaks his opinion to what he takes to be a calm audience, or an excited audience with different axes all ground fine, may plead his ignorance in good faith as a defense. But "the law" (as judges are fond of saying) "presumes that a person intends the natural and probable consequences of his actions," so that a defendant who denies that he intended to cause a riot may have the burden of proving his innocent intention to the jury.

In summary, there are two points to emphasize in connection with the punishment of inflammatory incitements. First, the audience must really be tinder, that is to say, not merely sullen, but angry to the point of frenzy, and so predisposed to violence. A left-wing radical should be permitted to deliver a revolutionary tirade before the ladies of the Daughters of the American Revolution, even if his final words are "to the barricades!" for

[22] Mill, *On Liberty*, pp. 67–68.
[23] Chafee, *Free Speech*, p. 397.

that would be to light a match not in a powder magazine but in a Turkish steam bath. Second, no one should be punished for inciting others to violence unless he used words intentionally, or at least recklessly, with respect to that consequence. Otherwise at best a speaker will be punished for his mere negligence, and at worst he will be punished though perfectly innocent.

There is one further problem raised by the concept of incitement as a crime. It might well be asked how one person—the inciter—can be held criminally responsible for the free and deliberate actions of another person—the one who is incited by his words. This problem is common to both kinds of incitement, counseling and inflaming or egging on, but it seems especially puzzling in the case of advising and persuading; for the deliberate, thoughtful, unforced, and undeceived acceptance of the advice of another person is without question itself a voluntary act. Yet there may well be cases that are such that had not the advice been given, the crime would never have been perpetrated, so that the advisor can truly be said to have "got" the advisee to do something he might otherwise never have done. In this case, the initiative was the advisor's, and his advice was the crucial causal factor that led to the criminal act, so that it would be no abuse of usage to call it "the cause." And yet, for all of that, no one *forced* the advisee to act; he could have rejected the advice, but he did not.

If there is the appearance of paradox in this account, or in the very idea of one person's causing another to act voluntarily, it is no doubt the result of an unduly restrictive conception of what a cause is. There are, of course, a great many ways of causing another person to behave in a given way by the use of words. If we sneak up behind him and shout, "Boo!" we may startle him so that he jumps and shrieks. In this case our word functioned as a cause not in virtue of its meaning or the mediation of the other person's understanding, but simply as a noise, and the person's startled reaction to this physical stimulus was an involuntary as an eye-twitch or a knee-jerk. Some philosophers would restrict the notion of causing behavior to cases of this kind, but there is no good reason for such a restriction, and a strong case can be built against it based on both its capacity to breed paradox and common sense and usage. I can "get" an acquaintance to say "Good morning" by putting myself directly in his line of vision, smiling, and saying, "Good morning" to him. If I do these things and he predictably responds in the way I intended, I can surely say that my behavior was the cause, in those circumstances, of his behavior; for my conduct is not only a circumstance but for which his action would not have occurred, it is also a circumstance that, when added to those already present, made the difference between his speaking and remaining silent. Yet I did not force him to speak; I did not deceive him; I did not trick him. Rather I exploited those of his known policies and dispositions that made him antecedently "receptive" to my words. To deny that I caused him to act voluntarily, in short, is either to confuse causation with compulsion (an ancient philosophical mistake) or to regard one person's initiative as incompatible with another person's responsibility.[24]

In any case, where one person causes another to act voluntarily either by giving him advice or information or by otherwise capitalizing on his carefully studied dispositions and policies, there is no reason why *both* persons should not be held responsible for the act if it should be criminal. It is just as if the law made it criminal to contribute to a human explosion either by being human dynamite or by being a human spark: either by being predisposed by one's character to crime or by one's passions to violence, or else by providing the words or materials that could fully be anticipated to incite the violent or criminal conduct of others. It is surely no reasonable defense of the spark to say that but for the dynamite there would have been no explosion. Nor is it any more reasonable to defend the dynamite by arguing that but for the spark it should have remained forever quiescent.

There is probably even less reason for excluding from responsibility the speaker haranguing an inflammable mob on the grounds that the individuals in the throng are free adults capable of refraining from violence in the circumstances. A mob might well be understood as a kind of fictitious collective person whose passions are much more easily manipulated and whose actions more easily maneuvered than those of individual persons. If one looks at it this way, the caused behavior of an inflamed mob may be a good deal less than fully voluntary, even though the component individuals in it, being free adults, are all acting voluntarily on their own responsibility.

SEDITION

Causing panic, provoking violence, and inciting to crime or insurrection are all made punishable by what Chafee calls "the normal criminal law of words."[25] The relevant common law categories are riot, breach of the peace, solicitation, and incitement. All these crimes, as we have seen, require either intentionally harmful or reckless conduct, and all of them require, in addition—and for reasons partly derived from and explicable by the harm principle—that there be some objective likelihood that the relevant sort of harm will be produced by the words uttered in the circumstances. In addition to these traditional common law crimes, many governments have considered it necessary to create statutes making sedition a crime. It will be useful to consider the question of sedition against the

---

[24] For a more detailed exposition of this view, see my "Causing Voluntary Actions," in *Doing and Deserving* (Princeton, N.J.: Princeton University Press, 1970), p. 152.

[25] Chafee, *Free Speech*, p. 149.

background of the normal criminal law of words, for this will lead us quickly to two conclusions. The first is that sedition laws are wholly unnecessary to avert the harm they are ostensibly aimed at. The second is that if we must nevertheless put up with sedition laws, they must be applied by the courts in accordance with the same standards of objective likelihood and immediate danger that govern the application of the laws against provoking and inciting violence. Otherwise sedition statutes are likely to do far more social harm than good. Such laws when properly interpreted by enforcers and courts are at best legal redundancies. At worst they are corrosive of the values normally protected by freedom of expression.

The word "sedition," which in its oldest, prelegal sense meant simply divisiveness and strife, has never been the name of a crime in the English common law. Rather the adjective "seditious" forms part of the name of the common law crimes of "seditious words," "seditious libel," and "seditious conspiracy." Apparently the common ingredient in these offenses was so-called seditious intent. The legal definition of "seditious intent" has changed over the centuries. In the beginning any spoken or written words that in fact had a tendency, however remote, to cause dissension or to weaken the grip of governmental authorities, and were spoken or published intentionally (with or without the further purpose of weakening the government or causing dissension) were held to manifest the requisite intent. In the fifteenth and sixteenth centuries, for example, publicly to call the king a fool, even in jest, was to risk capital punishment. There was to be less danger somewhat later for authors of printed words; for all books and printed papers had to be submitted in advance to the censorship (a practice denounced in Milton's eloquent *Areopagitica*), so that authors of politically dangerous words risked not punishment but only prior restraint. There is little evidence, however, that many of them felt more free as a consequence of this development.

The abandonment of the censorship in 1695 was widely hailed as a triumph for freedom of the press, but it was soon replaced by an equally repressive and far more cruel series of criminal trials for "seditious libel." Juries were permitted to decide only narrow factual questions, whereas the matter of "seditious intent" was left up to very conservative judges who knew well where their own personal interests lay. Moreover, truth was not permitted as a defense[26]—a legal restriction that in effect destroyed all right

---

[26] In the words of the great common law judge, William Murray, First Earl of Mansfield, "The Greater the Truth, the Greater the Libel," hence Robert Burns' playful lines in his poem, "The Reproof":

> Dost not know that old Mansfield
> Who writes like the Bible,
> Says the more 'tis a truth, sir,
> The more 'tis a libel?

of adverse political criticism. Chafee[27] has argued convincingly that the First Amendment to the U.S. Constitution was proposed and adopted by men who were consciously reacting against the common law of seditious libel, and in particular against the applications of that law in the English trials of the time. "Reform" (of sorts) came in England through Fox's Libel Act of 1792, which allowed juries to decide the question of seditious intent and permitted the truth defense if the opinions were published with good motives. (The ill-advised and short-lived American Sedition Act of 1798 was modeled after this act.) In the hysterical reaction to the French Revolution and the Napoleonic Wars, however, juries proved to be even more savage than judges, and hundreds were punished for even the mildest political unorthodoxy.

Throughout most of the nineteenth century, the prevailing definition of seditious intent in English law derived from a statute passed during the repressive heyday of the Fox Act sedition trials. Citizens were punished for publishing any words with

> the intention of (1) exciting disaffection, hatred, or contempt against the sovereign, or the government and constitution of the kingdom, or either house of parliament, or the administration of justice, *or* (2) exciting his majesty's subjects to attempt, otherwise than by lawful means, the alteration of any matter in church or state by law established, *or* (3) to promote feelings of ill will and hostility between different classes.[28]

In short, the three possible modes of seditious libel were defamation of the institutions or officers of the government, incitement to unlawful acts, and a use of language that tends toward the breach of the peace "between classes." The normal criminal law of words sufficiently covers the last two modes; and the civil law of defamation would apply to the first. The criminal law, as we have seen, employs a clear and present danger test for incitement and breach of peace, and does so for good reasons derived from the harm principle and the analysis of "intentional causing." For other good reasons, also derived from the harm principle, the law of defamation privileges fair comment on public officials, and gives no protection at all to institutions. So there would seem to be no further need—at least none demonstrated by the harm principle—for a criminal law of sedition.[29]

Still, many have thought that the harm principle requires sedition laws, and some still do. The issue boils down to the question of whether the

[27] Chafee, *Free Speech*, pp. 18–22.

[28] Ibid., p. 506.

[29] Such things, however, as patriotic sensibilities are capable of being highly offended by certain kinds of language. The rationale of sedition laws, therefore, may very well derive from the "offense principle," which warrants prohibition of offensive behavior even when it is (otherwise) harmless.

normal law of words with its strict standard of immediate danger is too lax to prevent serious harms, and whether, therefore, it needs supplementing by sedition laws employing the looser standards of "bad tendency" and "presumptive intent." By the standard of bad tendency, words can be punished for their dangerous propensity "long before there is any probability that they will break out into unlawful acts,"[30] and by the test of presumptive intent, it is necessary only that the defendant intended to publish his words, not that he intended further harm by them. It is clear that most authors of sedition statutes have meant them to be interpreted by the courts in accordance with the tests of bad tendency and presumptive intent (although the U.S. Supreme Court has in recent decades declared that such interpretations are contrary to the First Amendment of the Constitution). Part of the rationale for the older tests was that if words make a definite contribution to a situation that is on its way to being dangerous, it is folly not to punish them well before that situation reaches the threshold of actual harm. There may seem to be no harm in piling up twigs as such, but if this is done with the purpose (or even the likely outcome) of starting a fire eventually, why not stop it now before it is too late? Those who favor this argument have often employed the harm principle also to defend laws against institutional defamation. The reason why it should be unlawful to bring the Constitution or the courts (or even the flag) into disrepute by one's words, they argue, is not simply that such words are offensive, but rather that they tend to undermine respect and loyalty and thereby contribute to more serious harm in the long run.

The focus of the disagreement over sedition laws is the status of advocacy. The normal law of words quite clearly outlaws counseling, urging, or demanding (under certain conditions) that others resort to crime or engage in riots, assassinations, or insurrections. But what if a person uses language not directly to counsel or call for violence but rather (where this is different) to *advocate* it? In the wake of the Russian Revolution, many working-class parties in America and Europe adopted some variant of an ideology that declared that the propertied classes derived their wealth from the systematic exploitation of the poor; capitalists controlled the major media of news and opinion as well as parliaments and legislators; the grievances of the workers therefore could not be remedied through normal political channels but required instead direct pressure through such means as general strikes, boycotts, and mass demonstrations; and that the working class would inevitably be triumphant in its struggle, expropriate the exploiters, and itself run industry. Spokesmen for this ideology were known for their flamboyant rhetoric, which invariably contained such terms as "arise," "struggle," "victory," and "revolution." Such persons were com-

---

[30] Chafee, *Free Speech*, p. 24.

monly charged with violations of the Federal Espionage Act during and after World War I, of state sedition laws during the 1920s, and, after World War II, of the Smith Act. Often the key charge in the indictment was "teaching or advocating" riot, assassination, or the violent overthrow of the government.

Trials of Marxists for advocacy of revolution tended to be extremely difficult and problematic partly because it was never clear whether revolution in any usual sense was something taught and approved by them, and partly because it was unclear whether the form of reference to revolution in the Marxist ideology amounted to "advocacy" of it. Marxists disagreed among themselves over the first point. Many thought that forms of group pressure well short of open violence would be sufficient to overturn the capitalists; others thought that "eventually" (when is that?), when conditions were at last ripe, a brief violent seizure of power might be necessary. Does this, in any case, amount to the advocacy of revolution? If it is criminal advocacy to teach that there are conceivable circumstances under which revolution would be justified, then almost everyone, including this author, "advocates" revolution. Suppose one holds further that the "conceivable justifying conditions" may one day become actual, or that it is even probable that they will be actual at some indeterminate future time. Is this to count as criminal advocacy?

Not according to Justice Holmes in his famous opinion in *U.S.* v. *Schenk*. Schenk and others had encouraged draft resistance in 1917 by mailing circulars denouncing conscription as unconstitutional and urging in very emotional prose that draft-eligible men "assert their rights." The lower court found this to be advocacy of unlawful conduct, a violation, in particular, of the Espionage Act of 1917. The Supreme Court upheld the conviction but nevertheless laid down in the words of O. W. Holmes the test that was to be applied, in a more generous spirit, in later cases: "The question in every case is whether the words . . . are used in such circumstances and are of such a nature as to create a clear and present danger that they will bring about the substantive evils that Congress has a right to prevent." Since Congress has the right to raise armies, any efforts to interfere by words or action with the exercise of that right are punishable. But the clear and present danger standard brings advocacy under the same kind of test as that used for incitement in the normal law of words. One can "advocate" draft resistance over one's breakfast table to one's daughter (though perhaps not to one's son), but not to a sullen group waiting to be sworn in at the induction center.

There is, on the other hand, never any real danger in this country in permitting the open advocacy of revolution, except, perhaps, as Chafee puts it, "in extraordinary times of great tension." He continues:

The chances of success are so infinitesimal that the probability of any serious attempt following the utterances seems too slight to make them punishable. . . . This is especially true if the speaker urges revolution at some future day, so that no immediate check is needed to save the country.[31]

Advocacy of assassination, on the other hand, is less easily tolerated. In the first place, the soil is always more receptive to that seed. It is not that potential assassins are more numerous than potential revolutionaries, although at most times that is true. Potential assassins include among their number persons who are contorted beyond reason by hate, mentally unstable persons, and unpredictable crackpots. Further, a successful assassination requires only one good shot. Since it is more likely to be tried and easier to achieve, its danger is always more "clear and present." There will be many circumstances, therefore, in which Holmes' test would permit advocacy of revolution but punish advocacy of assassination. Still in most contexts of utterance it would punish neither. It should no doubt be criminal for a prominent politician to advocate assassination of the president in a talk over national television or in a letter to the *New York Times*,[32] but when a patron of a neighborhood tavern heatedly announces to his fellow drinkers that "the bum ought to be shot," the president's life will not be significantly endangered. There are times and places where it does not matter in the slightest how carelessly one chooses one's words, and others where one's choice of words can be a matter of life and death.

I shall, in conclusion, sketch a rationale for the clear and present danger test, as a kind of mediating standard for the application of the harm principle in the area of political expression. The natural challenge to the use of that test has been adumbrated above. It is true, one might concede, that the teaching of communist ideology here and now will not create a clear and present danger of violent revolution. Every one knows that, including the communists. Every trip, however, begins with some first steps, and that includes trips to forbidden destinations. The beginning steps are meant to increase numbers, add strength, and pick up momentum at later stages. To switch the metaphor to one used previously, the communists are not just casting seeds on barren ground; their words are also meant to cultivate the ground and irrigate it. If the law prohibits planting a certain kind of shrub and we see people storing the forbidden seeds, garden tools, and fertilizer, and actually digging trenches for irrigation pipes, why wait until they are ready to plant the seed before stopping them? Even at these early stages of preparation, they are clearly attempting to achieve what is forbidden. So the argument goes.

---

[31] Ibid., p. 175.

[32] In which case the newspaper too would be criminally responsible for publishing the letter.

The metaphor employed by the argument, however, is not very favorable to its cause. There is a world of difference between making plans and preparations for a future crime and actually launching an attempt, and this distinction has long been recognized by the ordinary criminal law. Mere preparations without actual steps in the direction of perpetration are not sufficient for the crime of attempt (though if preparation involves talking with collaborators, it may constitute the crime of conspiracy). Not even preliminary "steps" are sufficient; for "the act must reach far enough toward the accomplishment of the desired result to amount to the commencement of the consummation."[33] So the first faltering steps of a surpassingly difficult fifty-year trip toward an illegal goal can hardly qualify as an "attempt" in either the legal or the everyday sense.

If the journey is a collective enterprise, the participants could be charged with conspiracy without any violation of usage. The question is whether it would be sound public policy to suppress dissenting voices in this manner so long before they reach the threshold of public danger. The argument to the contrary has been given very clear statement in our time by Chafee. Consider what interests are involved when the state employs some coercive technique to prevent a private individual or group from expressing an opinion on some issue of public policy, or from teaching or advocating some political ideology. Chafee would have us put these various interests in the balance to determine their relative weights. In the one pan of the scale, there are the private interests of the suppressed individual or group in having their opinions heard and shared, and in winning support and eventual acceptance for them. These interests will be effectively squelched by state suppression. In the other pan is the public interest in peace and order, and the preservation of democratic institutions. These interests may be endangered to some degree by the advocacy of radical ideologies. Now if these are the only interests involved, there is no question that the public interest (which after all includes all or most private interests) sits heavier in the pan. There is, however, another public interest involved of very considerable weight. That is the public interest in the discovery and dissemination of all information that can have any bearing on public policy, and of all opinions about what public policy should be. The dangers that come from neglecting *that* interest are enormous at all times. And the more dangerous the times—the more serious the questions before the country's decision-makers (and especially when these are questions of war and peace)—the more important it is to keep open all the possible avenues to truth and wisdom.

Only the interest in national safety can outweigh the public interest in

---

[33] *Lee* v. *Commonwealth*, 144 Va. 594, 599, 131 S.E. 212, 214 (1926), as cited by Rollin M. Perkins and Ronald N. Boyce, *Criminal Law* (Mineola, N.Y.: Foundation, 1982), p. 617.

open discussion, but *it sits in the scale only to the degree that it is actually imperiled*. From the point of view of the public interest alone, with no consideration whatever of individual rights, it would be folly to sacrifice the social benefits of free speech for the bare possibility that the public safety may be somewhat affected. The greater the certainty and imminence of danger, however, the more the interest in public safety moves on to the scale, until at the point of clear and present danger it is heavy enough to tip the scales its way.

The scales analogy, of course, is only an elaborate metaphor for the sorts of deliberations that must go on among enforcers and interpreters of the law when distinct public interests come into conflict. These clashes of interest are most likely to occur in times of excitement and stress, when interest-"balancing" calls for a clear eye, a sensitive scale, and a steady hand. At such times the clear and present danger rule is a difficult one to apply, but other guides to decision have invariably gone wrong, while the clear and present danger test has hardly ever been seriously tried. Perhaps that helps account, to some degree, for the sorry human record of cruelty, injustice, and war.

Chapter Six

CIVIL DISOBEDIENCE IN THE MODERN WORLD

THE COMMON ELEMENT among the various kinds of actions that have been called "civilly disobedient" is, as David Daube puts it, "an offense against human authority, committed openly in a higher cause, or a cause thought to be higher."[1] The focus of the modern discussion of civil disobedience, however, is somewhat narrower, since it is restricted to disobedience of political authority, usually by acts that violate the law of the state and thereby incur criminal sanctions. In Western countries in the nineteenth and twentieth centuries the focus is narrower still. Civilly disobedient acts do not aim to overthrow whole regimes thought to be illegitimate; nor do they reject an accepted principle of legitimacy itself, like that of "the divine right of kings" or "the consent of the governed." They occur in post-revolutionary countries against a background of acknowledged just constitutions, democratic parliaments, and valid laws; and their purpose is not to undermine authority but to protest its misuse.

Closely related to civil disobedience but properly distinguishable from it are rule departures by state officials, those of police officers who do not arrest law-breakers, prosecutors who do not prosecute them, jurors who acquit obviously guilty defendants, judges who depart from judicial rules—in general, deliberate failures, often for conscientious reasons, to discharge the duties of one's office. Such official derelictions resemble civil disobedience in important ways, but they do not normally render officials liable to criminal punishment, so I shall not consider them to be civilly disobedient, even though when their intended beneficiary is himself an avowed civil disobedient, refusal to arrest, prosecute, or convict him form part of the complete treatment of our subject. In this chapter I shall not discuss the official's problem but shall concentrate on civil disobedience as a moral problem for the private citizen. My question will be, When, if ever, is there a moral right to commit civil disobedience? and not the closely related derivative question, What are the moral duties of legal officials toward civilly disobedient law-breakers?

Civil disobedience, however, is not just *any* kind of deliberate infraction of valid penal law; so it will be useful, at the outset, to distinguish it from other sorts of law-breaking with which it can be confused. First of all, the

[1] David Daube, *Civil Disobedience in Antiquity* (Edinburgh: Edinburgh University Press, 1972), p. 1.

common crimes of robbers, muggers, burglars, killers, rapists, and con artists, although they are instances of deliberate law-breaking, have no other resemblance to the acts with which we are concerned. Civil disobedience is law-breaking from certain motives only and in certain circumstances only. The common crimes are committed from such familiar motives as personal gain, malice, and hate; their specific intent is to harm the interests of others; and they are accompanied either by a desire to escape apprehension or an emotionally induced indifference to the risk of apprehension. In all of these ways they differ from civil disobedience. In other respects civil disobedience contrasts with acts of "warfare against the state"—assassination, sabotage, terrorism, riot, insurrection, avowed revolution—since civil disobedience is a kind of resistance within the accepted political structure, a violation of the law without loss of respect for law and the other basic political institutions, which are acknowledged to be, by and large, fair.

When the only alternative in the circumstances to the evil of law-breaking is to permit an evil that is greater still, a desperate choice of the illegal "lesser evil" may often look like civil disobedience, but since most modern legal systems accept the defense of "necessity" as a complete justification, it is not really "disobedience" at all. I have in mind such examples as borrowing a stranger's car without his permission in order to get a heart attack victim quickly to the hospital, destroying another's property to prevent the spread of a raging fire, violating the speed limit in pursuit of an escaping criminal, and so on. The traditional attitude of the Anglo-American law toward such actions is well expressed in the words of the judge in a sixteenth-century criminal case: "An act may break the words of the law and yet not break the law itself." The defense of necessity is a generalized justification based on two judgments: first, when the evil produced by breaking a rule is likely to be substantially less than the evil that would result in a given case from complying with it, then it is reasonable to breach it; second, it is unfair to impose criminal liability on objectively reasonable conduct. Rule departures resulting from such forced choices of a lesser evil, then, are not examples of civil disobedience. But if our legal system did not recognize the defense of necessity and remained rigidly and stupidly literalistic, then exceeding the speed limit to get a wife in labor to the maternity ward might well count as civilly disobedient, dissimilar though it may be to the acts of disinterested political protest that are the most familiar examples, in our time, of that broad genre.

Even closer to civil disobedience, but probably still worth distinguishing from it, are deliberately created test cases for statutes of doubtful validity. These phenomena are a peculiar feature of the American system, in which private citizens can get constitutionally suspect laws overthrown by the tactic of getting themselves convicted for disobeying them and then

launching an appeal upward through the courts. "You pays your money
and you takes your chances," as carnival barkers used to say. You violate
the explicit prohibitions of the suspect law; you are found guilty; you get
an expensive constitutional lawyer, and proceed through the appellate system perhaps even to the Supreme Court, arguing always that the reason
why you are innocent is not that you did not do what the prosecution
alleges that you did, but rather that the statute you violated was not a valid
law in the first place. If you win, then you are a public benefactor, for you
have effectively employed what is virtually the only way in our system to
get rid of popular but unconstitutional pseudolaws, and you have paid a
price in money, time, and anxiety in order to do that public service. But if
you lose, and the Supreme Court does not accept your arguments, you are
as unlucky as any losing gambler, and the law may treat you no differently
from any common criminal. In addition to all the previously mentioned
personal costs, you may be sent to prison for a while as a reward for your
public service. Such test cases raise moral issues, similar to those we shall
be considering, but I still wish to distinguish them from genuine civil disobedience because the "law-breaker" is not intentionally violating a law.
He thinks that what he is doing is entirely within his legal rights, an opinion that happens to disagree with that of the local police, the prosecutor,
and the courts. He wants the appellate courts to settle the disagreement,
and "disobedience" is the only way he can get them to do so, since he must
have "standing" if he is to use the courts for that purpose, and one cannot
acquire standing by complying with the law in question. Of course, he may
want to repeat his behavior even after the Supreme Court has declared it
illegal once and for all, as an act of public protest against an unfair law, and
that would begin to look like civil disobedience proper.

Three types of law-breaking remain to be discussed: conscientious evasion, conscientious refusal, and disobedience as moral protest. Many writers, following John Rawls, speak of the third of these (moral protests) as
civil disobedience proper and contrast it with acts of conscientious evasion
and refusal. There are differences, of course, among these three forms of
disobedience, and clarity is always served by a recognition of dissimilarities
among classes otherwise easily confused. But since the three types of conduct raise importantly similar moral questions, we can lump them together, along with forced choices of the lesser evil in a system that does not
recognize the necessity defense, under the generic label "civil disobedience
in the wide sense" and reserve the label "civil disobedience in the strict and
narrow sense" for moral protests, those acts of law-breaking that Rawls
thinks of as "civil disobedience proper." Our concern in the second half of
this chapter will be with the moral justification of civil disobedience in the
broad sense.

Acts of conscientious evasion might be thought of as borderline cases of civil disobedience since they share with covert crimes the hope of escaping apprehension and arrest. Their impelling motives, however, are strikingly different from those of most ordinary crimes. The conscientious evader genuinely believes that the law he violates is morally wrong, even though validly enacted, and personal gain is not a large element—if it is present at all—in his motivation for violating it. He thinks that he can do more good for the cause of justice by remaining free to violate the iniquitous law some more than by making a martyr of himself. The clearest historical examples of what I have in mind were the covert infractions by white Northerners of the fugitive slave laws before the Civil War.

"Conscientious refusal" is the term Rawls used to describe deliberate "noncompliance with a more or less direct legal injunction or administrative order,"[2] where one's action is assumed to be known to the authorities, however much one might wish, in some cases, to conceal it. Among the examples cited by Rawls are the refusal of Jehovah's Witnesses to salute the flag, the refusal of pacifists to serve in the armed forces, and Thoreau's famous refusal to pay his taxes during the Mexican War on the ground that payment would make him a participant in a great evil. Conscientious refusal resembles civil disobedience in the narrow sense in that its motives are conscientious. It is not done from the desire for personal gain, and there is little hope of escaping apprehension. But neither is it impelled by a desire to act as a form of public protest. Rather one acts either to avert an evil close at hand or else simply to keep one's own hands, morally speaking, clean. (Thoreau had no hope of stopping the Mexican War, but at least he could avoid having guilt on *his* hands.)

Civil disobedience (in what I call the "narrow sense") is defined by Rawls as "a public, nonviolent, conscientious yet political act contrary to law usually done with the aim of bringing about a change in the law or policies of the government."[3] Rawls here describes a kind of conduct that was frequently engaged in by moral protestors in the 1960s, first against racial discrimination and then against the Vietnam War. Let us briefly consider the defining elements of this form of protest, one by one.

Civil disobedience is *public*—engaged in openly, often even with prior notice, since the protestor wants as much publicity and attention as possible for his tactical purposes. Civil disobedience is *nonviolent* for the simple tactical reason that injury to others, harm to property, and extreme inconvenience to others are likely to be self-defeating, since they can obscure one's message, cause bitter resentment, and distract public attention from what is vital. The main reason, in short, why the civil disobedient wants

---

[2] John Rawls, *A Theory of Justice* (Cambridge, Mass.: Harvard University Press, 1971), p. 368.
[3] Ibid., p. 364.

his act to be nonviolent is the same as his reason for wanting it to be public—so that he can convince the majority of his fellow citizens that the act is indeed conscientious and sincere and intended to address the public's sense of justice. Indeed it is absolutely essential to civil disobedience as Rawls conceives it that it is a form of address, a symbolic way of making a statement, in his words "an expression of profound and conscientious political conviction . . . in the public forum."[4] As such it can be valued on the one hand as an end in itself, either a kind of "bearing witness" to a moral truth for its own sake, or a disavowal of responsibility, or on the other hand (what is more likely) as a tactic. When it is meant to be a method for producing reform, it must be distinguished from intimidation. It is in essential contrast to such tactics as disruption of traffic, strikes, boycotts, and political pressure. It does not say, "Give us our way or else." That sort of threat often backfires. The only pressure involved is "moral pressure"— dramatically sincere appeal to the public's sense of justice.

The third defining characteristic in Rawls' account is *deliberate unlawfulness*. Under his heading two types of civil disobedience must be distinguished. Direct civil disobedience violates the very law that is the target of the protest, whereas indirect civil disobedience violates some other law whose reasonableness is not in question. As Rawls points out, civil disobedience cannot always be direct: "If the government enacts a vague and harsh statute against treason, it would not be appropriate to commit treason as a way of objecting to it."[5] Similarly, it has been observed that one does not protest capital punishment for rape by committing rape. In fact it is surprisingly difficult to protest the most likely sorts of unjust laws and policies by direct civil disobedience. White people sitting in the black sections of segregated buses in the 1950s and war protestors burning their draft cards are good examples. But more characteristically, acts of civil disobedience in recent years have been indirect, the most familiar being those that violate local trespass ordinances, for example, "sitting in" at an atomic energy site until one must be forcibly carried away by the police in order to protest, not trespass laws, but rather the policy of building atomic power plants.

Finally, civilly disobedient acts in Rawls' conception must be *conscientious*. The main point of this part of the definition presumably is to rule out the motives of private or personal gain or malicious emotion as primary and immediate. Insofar as those motives, which are characteristic of ordinary crimes, are present at all, we should hesitate to classify an infraction as "civil disobedience." Rawls reminds us that the civil disobedient suffers inconvenience, expense, taunts, threats, real danger, and eventually punish-

---

[4] Ibid., p. 366.
[5] Ibid., p. 365.

ment. His willingness, in the typical case, to suffer these consequences helps to demonstrate that his purpose is to protest an injustice or a wrong—not to achieve some immediate gain for himself. He suffers for a cause, some larger goal or principle for whose sake he breaks the law publicly and thereby sacrifices at least his short-run interests. While all of this is true, the word "conscientious," as we shall see, may be a misleading way of expressing it.

What does it mean to act conscientiously? I shall want to qualify the following answer shortly, but let me begin by giving what might be called "the strongest account of conscientiousness," namely, that to act conscientiously is to act because of one's honest and sincere conviction that what one is doing is right, not merely in the sense of "all right," but rather in the sense of "morally mandatory"—the uniquely correct thing to do, whatever the cost. "Here I stand; I can do no other," said Luther. "Here I sit; I can do no other" might have been said during the Southern sit-ins of the early 1960s. There are two important, though obvious, things to say about conscientiousness so construed: (1) people can be wrong in their conscientious convictions as in any other ones; but (2) insofar as convictions are genuinely conscientious, in this strong sense, they deserve respect from everyone and respectful treatment, insofar as that is consistent with other goals, from the law. Conscientious motives have a very special kind of moral value.

There is no denying that the motives of many acts of civil disobedience fit the above description, but if the strong account of conscientiousness is included in our definition, then many apparent examples of civil disobedience are not civil disobedience at all, because they are not "conscientious." I have in mind not acts done from a sense of duty, but rather acts done because the actor wishes to stand on his rights—to affirm them, vindicate them, and demand their recognition and enforcement. These are acts done *in* clear conscience, but not *from* conscientiousness (in the strong sense). Publicly drinking beer during Prohibition and attending a marijuana smoke-in are examples. The drinker may well have been affirming thereby his moral right to drink beer, but he was not doing what he did because his conscience required beer-drinking. One can hardly compare him with Luther! When one is prepared to sacrifice one's short-run interests in order to secure one's rights and acts out of genuine conviction that a moral principle does indeed confer those rights, then there is a sense in which one's action is disinterested, at least more so than actions that demand, in the absence of moral deliberation or conviction, of any kind, that others simply "gimme, gimme, gimme, gimme, what I cry for." We can even call them "conscientious" in a weaker sense of that term. It is important, however, to understand that civil disobedience (in the wide sense that includes principled protest, evasion, and refusal) need not be conscientious in the usual strong sense. To persist in the contrary view may be to fall into a serious muddle about the very concept of a conscience. It is essential to the idea of a person's conscience that it is a faculty of self-address concerned only with the duties of its possessor. My conscience tells me what it is right for me to do, what I must do, what it is my duty to do, and not merely what I may do if I wish. If we say, on the contrary, that my conscience tells me what my rights are, then we are committed logically to the view that one person's conscience can tell him what other people's duties are, which is not only conceptually odd, but politically dangerous as well.

The modern discussion among philosophers of the justifiability of civil disobedience has at least a dual source, partly in democratic political theory and partly in philosophical jurisprudence. On the one hand, the problem civil disobedience raises for our moral judgments derives from the almost universal belief that every citizen in a constitutional democracy with at least approximately just institutions has a general obligation to obey the valid laws and lawful commands of his government. Civil disobedience by definition is a violation of those laws or commands. How then can it be justified? Duties of course can be overridden in particular cases by a "higher duty" or in a "higher cause." What then must these higher principles be like, and when are they strong enough to override the general moral obligation to be law-abiding? That in turn depends, at least in part, on the grounds, strength, and limits of the latter obligation. In this way the question of civil disobedience draws philosophers into the traditional problem of the nature of political obligation.

There is also a path through the philosophy of law to the same destination. The period during which civil disobedience began to challenge modern thinkers largely corresponded with the rise of the doctrine called "legal positivism" and the decline of the traditional doctrines of natural law. According to the natural law theory, the validity of humanly made coercive laws depends in part on their content, that is, on what they require or prohibit. If they are, in the appropriate way, arbitrary, unjust, cruel, pointless, or immoral, then they have no authority or force of law whatever, in which case there is no more moral obligation to obey them than there is to comply with any pseudolaw or mere masquerade as law. To the legal positivists that view was intolerably paradoxical. The validity of law, they insisted, is one thing; its injustice or morality is another; so there can be no contradiction in characterizing a statute as an unjust valid law. The validity of law, on their view, stems from its proper enactment. All valid law is enacted law. So-called laws of nature may be standards for distinguishing good from bad law, but law is law, whether good or bad. It is the pedigree of a law (where it comes from) rather than its content (what it commands) that determines its validity.

The positivist account of legal validity obviously gains much support from common sense, but historically the legal positivists have often held another doctrine that is hard to reconcile with the first, namely, that valid law as such, no matter what its content, deserves our respect and our general fidelity. Even if valid law is bad law, we have some obligation to obey it simply because it is law. But how can this be so if a law's validity has nothing to do with its content? Why ashould I have any respect or duty of fidelity toward a statute with a wicked or stupid content just because it was passed into law by a bunch of men (possibly very wicked men like the Nazi legislators) according to the accepted recipes for making law? Thus Lon Fuller, the leading American critic of legal positivism, triumphantly springs his trap: the positivist cannot explain how "laws, even bad laws, have a claim to our respect."[6] The two doctrines of validity by pedigree and respect for law as such yield in combination an unstable conception of law as "an amoral datum" that has a kind of magical capacity to generate moral obligations. One easy way out for the positivist, and I think the only way, is to abandon the second doctrine and admit that there is no moral duty whatever to obey law simply because it is valid law. To support that startlingly radical proposition the positivist must cast his skeptical eye on the variously alleged grounds for "the moral obligation to obey the law as such," and soon he is likely to encounter the political theorist exploring the possible grounds for a perfectly general moral obligation to obey the democratic state and the moralist puzzled about the moral justifiability of civil disobedience.

The standard way of characterizing the individual citizen's moral problem concerning civil disobedience is as a conflict of reasons of basically different types. According to this conception, the question, Is it ever right to disobey a law, and if so, under what conditions? is exactly the same in form as the question(s), Is it ever right to break a promise, tell a lie, inflict pain on others (and so on), and if so, under what conditions? This approach to the problem assumes that there is (to use philosophical jargon that I do not altogether like) a "prima facie obligation" to obey the law that can in principle conflict with, override, or be overridden by "prima facie obligations" of other kinds. I would prefer to speak of "reasons for" and "reasons against," but since the term "prima facie obligation" has become fixed by a strong convention, it will be well to come to terms with it. So for the moment let us see what philosophers have meant by prima facie obligation, or PFO, as I shall abbreviate it.

In explaining what they mean by a PFO, some philosophers resort to an analogy with the idea of a vector of forces that is used in physics. The

---

[6] Lon L. Fuller, "Positivism and Fidelity to Law: A Reply to Professor Hart," *Harvard Law Review* 71 (1958): 630.

analogy is useful up to a point. We do feel "pulled in both ways," as we say, when we are in situations like that which Plato describes in the *Republic*, in which we have promised a neighbor to keep a weapon for him and return it when he requests and he then comes back in a furious homicidal rage against another party and demands that we return his property to him. Thinking no doubt of cases of this sort, Carl Cohen writes:

> One's ultimate or actual obligation in any morally complex situation will require the careful weighing of several, even many, *prima facie* obligations, some of which may conflict head-on with others. We may think of such *prima facie* obligations as components, or vectors, pushing us in different directions with differing degrees of force, the morally correct outcome of the set being our resultant obligation.[7]

Despite the intuitively familiar points of resemblance between PFOs and physical forces, this analogy is more misleading than helpful. In physics, a resultant force compounded out of component forces is always a kind of splitting of the difference, not always right down the middle of course, but a result determined in some measure by each of its components. When two forces act on a body, the resultant direction and velocity of that object will be a kind of "compromise." Its resultant direction, if the two forces are equal and at right angles to one another, will be at a 45° angle, splitting the difference between where it would have gone if only the one force were acting on it and where it would have gone if only the other force were acting on it. But in morals there is often no way of splitting the difference, in which case one must do the one duty or the other, rather than do a part of each. Plato's householder could hardly solve his problem by means of a compromise between the moral demand that he keep his promise to return another's lethal weapon and the moral demand that he protect a third party from harm. It would not do, for example, to substitute a less lethal weapon—say a somewhat brittle wooden club—for the original sword.

I think that we can avoid this difficulty and achieve greater clarity by thinking of PFOs and resultant obligations simply in terms of supporting and conclusive reasons. Then we can say that one's having promised to do an act *A* (say) is always a reason of direct relevance and at least some cogency in favor of doing *A* and one's promise not to do *B* is a reason against doing *B*, and in the absence of other reasons having a bearing on the situation, either would be a conclusive reason. Further, a PFO (general type of supporting reason) is not in every case a decisive reason, but it is always a relevant one and one that would be conclusive if no other relevant reason of greater strength applied to the situation. Thus if Jones has a PFO to do

---

[7] Carl Cohen, *Civil Disobedience: Conscience, Tactics, and the Law* (New York: Columbia University Press, 1971), p. 6.

A, then he has a moral reason to do *A* that is such that unless he has a moral reason *not* to do *A* that is at least as strong, then not doing *A* is wrong, and he has an actual obligation to do *A*.[8]

Philosophers have differed over the question of how many general kinds of PFOs there are and over which are basic and which are derivative. The following list of basic PFOs is, I think, representative and plausible, though I can make no stronger claim for it here:

1. The PFO of fidelity: to keep promises.
2. The PFO of veracity: to tell the truth (or better—not to tell lies).
3. The PFO of fair play: not to exploit, cheat, or "free load" on others.
4. The PFO of gratitude: to return favors.
5. The PFO of nonmaleficence: not to cause pain or suffering to others.
6. The PFO of beneficence: to help others in distress when this involves no great danger to oneself or third parties.
7. The PFO of reparation: to repair harms to others that are one's own fault.
8. The PFO not to kill others (except in self-defense).
9. The PFO not to deprive others of their property.
10. The PFO to oppose injustices when this involves no great cost to oneself.
11. The PFO to promote just institutions and to work toward their establishment, maintenance, and improvement.

Insofar as a given act is an instance of one of the above eleven kinds, that is, a moral reason in favor of doing it, and if it is not, at the same time, a negative instance of one of the other categories on the list, then it is a decisive reason. If it is a positive instance of one type and a negative instance of another, say a promise that can be kept only by telling a lie, then one's actual duty will be to perform the PFO that is the more stringent in the circumstances. That is all that a moralist can say in the abstract with any degree of certainty.

In addition to the list of eleven PFOs, is there also a PFO to obey the law? Is the fact that a contemplated act would be illegal a reason against doing so? Of course it might always be a prudential reason of some weight against doing it. You might get caught, and the risk is always a consideration to be weighed carefully by any reasonable person. But that is not what we are concerned about. We wish to know whether illegality is also a type of *moral reason*, a consideration that tends to bind us morally to refrain from the act and will ground an actual obligation to refrain if no other conflicting PFOs are pulling us even harder in the opposite direction. Philosophers have differed sharply over this question. Few are tempted these

[8] Compare M. B. E. Smith, "Is There a Prima Facie Obligation to Obey the Law?" *Yale Law Journal* 82 (1973): 950.

days to hold the view, so effectively demolished by Richard Wasserstrom,[9] that it can *never* be right to disobey a law, that "*X* is illegal" is always a decisive moral reason against doing *X*. But a growing number of philosophers hold the very opposite and surprisingly plausible view that "*X* is illegal" is no kind of reason at all, that there is not even a PFO to obey the law. (We do, of course, have a PFO not to do many of the things prohibited by law—not to kill, steal, and the like—but because these things are *mala in se*, not because they are illegal.) These philosophers usually argue that there is no sort of reason why anyone ought to obey a rotten rule created in a rotten system under an authoritarian regime or a thoroughly iniquitous constitution. Nazi rules against helping Jews were "valid laws" in Germany, all right, and duly enacted by Nazi legislatures. Their ruthless enforcement, moreover, gave every German citizen a prudential reason for obeying them. But the fact that helping Jews was illegal was itself morally irrelevant, neither here nor there in the moral universe, utterly beside the point. Surely, these philosophers conclude, not just *any* legal obligation in *any* legal system imposes a moral PFO, giving us a moral reason of any strength at all for obedience.

Philosophers on the other side usually grant the point and make a small strategic retreat. If there is a PFO to obey the law as such, they concede, it can only be in a reasonably just society, under a reasonably just constitution, with fair (presumably democratic) procedures for making and changing laws. But in such a state, they insist, the fact that *X* is illegal is always a moral reason, of some discernible weight at least, against doing *X*. But even that reasonably modified position no longer gains unanimous assent, and more and more philosophers, myself included, are coming to question it.

There is a dilemma for adherents of even the weakest version of the doctrines that there is a moral PFO to obey the law. (I refer to the version that restricts the PFO to valid laws in the citizen's own legal system when that system is democratic and by and large just.) Either this alleged PFO is one of the basic ones, on the same level as the eleven on our list, or it is derivative from some one or combination of them. If basic, it can be defended only by an appeal to self-evidence, for *ex hypothesi* there is no more basic ethical principle from which it follows. But whereas that kind of appeal is plausible in the eleven other cases (who could deny, for example, that "you promised" is always *a* reason, at the very least, for doing what was promised?), it seems much less so in this case. In any event when so many astute philosophers[10] are saying, "I don't see it," it certainly lacks argumentative

---

[9] Richard Wasserstrom, "The Obligation to Obey the Law," *UCLA Law Review* 10 (1963).

[10] For example, Rolf Sartorius, *Individual Conduct and Social Norms* (Belmont, Calif.: Wadsworth, 1975), chapter 6; A. John Simmons, *Moral Principles and Political Obligations*

force to rest one's case on the insistence that it is just obviously so. But if, on the other hand, the PFO to obey the law is derivative from one or more of the basic ones, one must be able to show how it is derived, and that is a notoriously difficult undertaking, not yet successfully done.[11]

Almost all of the basic PFOs on our list have been thought by one philosopher or another to be the ground, or part of the ground, for a derivative PFO to obey the law, but the most interesting attempts to derive such a PFO, and the most popular, invoke numbers 4 (gratitude), 1 (fidelity), 3 (fair play), and 10–11 (justice). Let us examine each of these attempts briefly but critically.

The argument from gratitude proceeds as follows. In general, by accepting benefits from others we incur "debts of gratitude." Many moralists derive the PFO to help one's parents from this basic one, and indeed Socrates, in Plato's *Crito*, likens his own relations to the Athenian state to that of a son to his parents and declines to resist even a fatally unjust application of its laws on that ground. We do accept the protection of the police, the armed forces, and the Public Health Service, and the benefits of the money system, the postal service, public schools, and so on; therefore we are said to have a debt of gratitude to the state and a PFO to obey its laws. Not to do so would be ungrateful.

What are we to make of this curious argument? In the first place, it should be observed that debts of gratitude have nothing to do with gratitude in the usual sense, which is a certain motive, attitude, or feeling. There can be no duty to have a particular feeling or to act from a certain motive, for the pinpoint control over our emotions that would be required by such a duty is beyond our powers of self-manipulation. Our only plausible duties are to do, or to omit doing, certain things (from whatever motive). A duty to repay services is less paradoxically called a "duty of reciprocation" than a duty of gratitude. Indeed, so separate are the ideas of reciprocation and gratitude that sometimes the former is taken as a sign of the absence of the latter, as was noted by St. Thomas Aquinas, who quotes with approval a passage from Seneca that "a person who wants to repay a gift too quickly with a gift in return is an unwilling debtor and an ungrateful person."[12] Nevertheless a duty of reciprocation is fully discharged by appro-

---

(Princeton, N.J.: Princeton University Press, 1979), chapter 8; Smith, "Prima Facie Obligation." I have found Simmons' brilliant new book especially useful.

[11] One early sketchy attempt was that of W. D. Ross, *The Right and the Good* (Oxford, 1930), pp. 27–28, who derived the PFO to obey the laws of one's country "partly (as Socrates contends in the *Crito*) from the duty of gratitude for the benefits one has received from it, partly from the implicit promise to obey which seems to be involved in permanent residence in a country whose laws we know we are *expected* to obey, and still more clearly involved when we ourselves invoke the protection of its law . . . and partly (if we are fortunate in our country) from the fact that its laws are potent instruments for the general good."

[12] As quoted by Josef Pieper, *Justice* (London, 1957), p. 107.

priate payment even when done in a grudging spirit of ungrateful resentment, and gratitude without suitable repayment, however commendable
for its own sake, cannot discharge a duty of reciprocation.

A stronger and more relevant point is also yielded by the example of the
gift. Unlike formal loans and contractual performances, a gift is not the
sort of thing that one has a duty to "repay." Gratitude may be appropriate
although it is not the sort of thing that can be exacted, but repayment is
not the sort of concept that has any application at all to the gift situation.
There can no more be a duty of reciprocation than a duty of gratitude to
return gratuitous gifts and favors. Suppose that the Joneses, obscure ac-
quaintances of yours, invite you to dinner, and you accept, to your later
regret. Do you have a PFO to reciprocate by inviting them to dinner?
Would you be blamably "ungrateful" if you did not? Would a cash payment
sent later through the mails be an acceptable mode of repayment? Suppose
that Jones is a rich man or the president of your university, someone who
entertains others constantly and lavishly and is more than occupied by his
own busy social schedule. Are you torn over your duty to reciprocate? Or,
to take examples of another kind, suppose that a young woman receives
flowers from an admirer, than candy, then dresses, then electrical appli-
ances, despite her continued efforts to discourage him. Finally she begins
to "doubt his motives." Is there even a trace of a moral reason here for
reciprocation? cooperation? obedience? Or suppose that a college teacher
gives a pretty coed a good grade when the student knows that her work is
poor. She might well wonder "What is he up to anyway?" but certainly not
"What should I do for him?" In the latter two cases not only is a duty of
reciprocation out of the question; it is also the case that one of the psychologically necessary conditions for the emergence of the feeling of gratitude
itself is absent, namely, the belief that the gratuitous gift or favor was offered from genuinely disinterested friendship or benevolence, with no "ulterior motive." In any event, even if we are grateful—let us suppose for a
good dinner given us by well-meaning but very boring persons who
wished only to please us—it does not follow that we have a moral PFO to
reciprocate, but at most that we may feel some trace of a desire or inclination to do so. (If only they were not so boring!)

The case for deriving a PFO to obey the laws of the state from a basic
PFO of "gratitude" collapses completely in the light of the above observations. If the argument is meant only to establish a ground for the feeling
of gratitude, then it needs to be supplemented by a showing that the state's
undoubted services and protections are genuine gifts rather than contractual performances and, further, that its motive was personal benevolence
or disinterested friendship (an enviable task); and even if there is a ground
for gratitude, there can be no duty to *feel* grateful; and even if there were
such a duty, it could not in turn ground a duty of reciprocation. Finally,

and most conclusively, even if there is some sort of duty repayment (which is most implausible), it could not take the form required by the argument, namely, faithful obedience to commands, for as M. B. E. Smith puts it, "The mere fact that a person has conferred benefits on me, even the most momentous benefits conferred from genuinely benevolent motives, doesn't establish his right to dictate all my behavior."[13] The benefits are no reason at all in support of *that* PFO. A fifty-year-old son may have numerous duties toward his eighty-year-old parents, but they will all be duties to help them, not to obey them. No matter how grateful he is to them for their past services, he can have no duty to let them determine, for example, at what hour he must come home at night or what foods he may eat.

Like any theory that has been defended by great philosophers in the past, the gratitude theory does have a grain of truth. There is a more plausible interpretation of something that can be called a duty of gratitude, and no doubt such a duty can yield, under very special circumstances, something like a PFO to comply with the laws of a state and even to perform certain positive services for it. If there is such a thing in ordinary interpersonal relations as a PFO of gratitude, it is not an obligation to reciprocate favor for favor, service for service, benefit for benefit, but rather an obligation to stand ready, in case one's benefactor should ever falter, to help him too. If a wealthy friend of his father gives a young person enough money to pay for his whole college education, he will appropriately feel grateful, especially if he believes that the gift was a genuine expression of benevolence or friendship without ulterior motive. But insofar as the payment was a genuine gift and not a loan, the young person will have no burdensome duty to repay a like sum during his postgraduate years. Presumably if the benefactor had intended to impose such a burden, he would have explicitly described his transfer of funds as a *loan*, not a gift. Suppose, however, that years later it comes to the attention of the younger man, now middle-aged and comfortable, that the elderly benefactor has come upon hard times, having lost all his money through unlucky investments, and now is suffering from bad health. Not to help him *now*, if he can, would indeed be ungrateful and a violation of a moral duty to reciprocate the old man's earlier favors. Similarly, an expatriate living happily abroad, although with warm feelings toward his native land and "gratitude" for having learned its language and culture and for having been shaped by its institutions, might feel morally impelled to come to the aid of his country in its time of dire need and pay taxes and bear arms in its defense. On the other hand, an Englishman at the start of the World War II or an Israeli at the outset of the Yom Kippur War who takes all of his goods and flees to Geneva or Cuernavaca would rightly be thought a morally derelict ingrate

[13] Smith, "Prima Facie Obligation," p. 952.

by his countrymen. In such cases one has a moral duty to come to the aid of one's country, a duty derived perhaps in part from having benefited from its laws and services in the past. But that is quite another thing than a general duty in good or hard times to obey each and every law or order.

The second way of deriving a moral PFO of obedience to law bases it on a deliberate undertaking of the citizen, a kind of formal promise to comply with laws, or at least a voluntary granting of one's consent to the law-maker's authority, which amounts to the same thing. Thus the PFO of obedience is like the obligation to discharge one's part of a bargain; the state provides its benefits *in exchange for which* the citizen provides his constant fidelity to law. (State benefits, on this view, are more like loans than gifts.) The argument can be stated simply: (1) a person can have no obligation to obey or support the state unless he has personally granted his consent to its authority, but once that consent is granted or promise made, a duty of obedience has been assumed; (2) we all have granted that consent; therefore, (3) we all have the standing duty (like all general duties, a PFO) to obey the law of the state.

The most doubtful part of the argument, of course, is its second premise. The reader might well claim that he (for one) never granted consent of the sort required by the argument. In fact, no representative of the state ever asked him to do so. His friend Angelo did so at the naturalization ceremony as part of a solemn oath with his hand on a Bible. But most native-born citizens never did anything of the kind. It will not do to say in reply to this that the reader's ancestors took the oath, either at the time of "the original contract" or at later naturalization proceedings, for there is no way to explain how a person can be bound morally by a promise made by another person at a time before he even came into existence.

A more plausible rejoinder than the "inherited obligation" ploy is that for which John Locke is famous: Of course the reader gave no explicit statement of consent; rather he granted a "tacit consent," not in language but in conduct from which the consent can be inferred. A. John Simmons has given a definitive refutation of this claim.[14] He points out first that there *is* a kind of behavior that can be called "tacit consent," but that it is not "unexpressed consent deduced from conduct," but rather "consent expressed in a certain way—by silence."[15] For an example he has us imagine a board meeting at which the chairman announces: "We will meet again next Thursday unless there are objections to that date. Does anyone have objections?" There is silence for one full minute, at the conclusion of which the chairman notes that all have agreed (consented) to his proposal. The

[14] A. John Simmons, "Tacit Consent and Political Obligation," *Philosophy and Public Affairs* 5 (1976).
[15] Ibid., p. 279.

reader will recognize this familiar notion of consent by silence but strenuously resist its application to his own case. How could anyone think that he consented to the authority of his government simply by being silent? No one in authority ever asked him if he consented. He was never presented with options and alternatives and asked to decide. He was no more aware that his silence on this question constituted consent than he is that his silence about network television scheduling constitutes an agreement to watch all the shows.

Simmons points out, however, that Locke surely did not mean by "tacit consent" the familiar notion of consent by silence. Rather Locke argued in two other ways, first, that our consent is implied by our acceptance of government benefits and, second, by our continued residence in the country of our citizenship. The odd thing about these closely interrelated arguments is that they imply that we can give our binding consent by accident, so to speak, unknowingly and unintentionally. Perhaps if I had known that I was assuming a lifelong obligation of fidelity I would at least have hesitated before accepting benefits. As it is, Locke puts me in the position that would be occupied by the lady in our earlier example if she learned belatedly that her acceptance of gifts from her suitor was a way of getting married and that he is now her husband come what may, for better or worse.

Elsewhere Locke writes that a sure sign of consent to governmental authority (whatever the consenter's actual intentions) is one's continued residence in a country. But in the absence of a clearly presented choice and a formal convention for indicating consent (like the board meeting described above), this too would be an "unknowing or unintentional consent," which is to say an absurdity. In modern nations at the present time, at least, there is no such general procedure; no genuine choice is ever made available to most of us. The reader might complain that he did not know that he was incurring a permanent obligation of obedience when he chose to settle down in his native land until he read Locke, and by then it was too late!

Perhaps it is possible in principle, however, although not presently the case, to design a political procedure that would make residence a sign of "tacit consent" to a country's laws. Simmons reminds us that Socrates in the *Crito* claimed that such formal procedures *were* available to every Athenian on attaining the "age of manhood." The Athenian state in effect told every young man that he could take all his property and "go wherever you wish with our blessing, if you do not like it here. Your silence will be taken as an acknowledgment of a lifelong obligation to obey our laws." Assuming that this was an accurate account of things in at least one ancient Greek city-state and that young Athenians were able to make a truly voluntary choice of political allegiance, we must now ask whether it is possible to design such a procedure for the modern state.

Surely the difficulties would be formidable. Perhaps it was not very difficult, economically or psychologically, for free Hellenic Greeks to change their residence from one city-state to another. All moves are disruptive, of course, but in total impact on the lives of the movers, a change from Athens to Corinth was probably no harder than a change from New York to California today. But now, the "option" for a twenty-one-year-old American youth to say good-bye to his family and friends, pack his bags, change his money, and board a jet plane for a new life in whatever alien land would deign to receive him is hardly a genuine "choice" at all. Simmons is hardly less scathing than David Hume had been in his eighteenth-century reply to Locke[16] when he (Simmons) writes that "our most precious 'possessions' are not movable property that can be put on the boat with one's books and TV set."[17] The legal opportunity to emigrate then hardly provides a procedure for voluntarily expressing one's consent by silence. Simmons' example of the opportunity at the board meeting to express an objection, freely and knowingly, by the easy and conventionally understood device of raising one's arm in response to a question bears little analogy to the forced and dangerous expedient of emigrating. The latter, Simmons tells us, is more like the case of the boss at the board meeting inviting all those who object to so signify by lopping off their right arms or implying by his manner that objection however expressed carries a high risk of demotion or firing.[18]

The third way of basing a PFO to obey the law is to derive it from the PFO of fair play. This argument was well formulated (and first named) in an influential article of John Rawls, which was later severely qualified and even renamed in Rawls' book.[19] A PFO of fair play comes into existence not only in sports and competitive games (as its name suggests) but also in a large variety of social settings. Its principal home, in fact, is in cooperative rather than competitive joint undertakings, in voluntary rule-structured associations like clubs, teams, partnerships, political parties, and the like, and in more informal joint enterprises, like voluntary clean-up or repair work among a group of friends who possess a car in common. Each person has his own share to do if all are to gain, but it is possible for a given person to cheat, not do his share, and thus take his benefit as "free"

[16] David Hume, "Of the Original Contract." First published in his *Essays Moral and Political* (1748).

[17] Simmons, *Moral Principles*, p. 99.

[18] Ibid.

[19] The earlier formulation is in John Rawls, "Legal Obligation and the Duty of Fair Play," in *Law and Philosophy*, ed. Sidney Hook (New York, 1964), pp. 3–18. Rawls' second thoughts are found in his *Theory of Justice*, pp. 342–49. In the book Rawls refers to "the principle of fairness" rather than "the principle of fair play," in part, apparently, to avoid the suggestion that all life is a game.

only because the others are doing their shares. The "free rider" does not "play fair." He may not harm anybody directly, but by cheating he exploits the others' cooperativeness to his own benefit. He "takes advantage of them," as we say. A paradigmatic example is not paying one's fare on a railroad train. The others pay in full confidence that everyone will, and the free rider takes advantage of that trust. So he gains at their expense. It is not that he harms them; that is not the gravamen of the grievance. Their share of the costs of the railroad (reflected in the owners' adjusted prices) may go up only a tiny fraction of a penny because of his nonpayment. But they have voluntarily foregone the benefits he got in expectation that he would forego them too. Their grievance is that he took advantage of them.

That complaint can just as well be expressed in the language of rights and duties. Adapting one of Simmons' examples, we can consider a community scheme to preserve water pressure during a dry spell by prohibiting the watering of lawns in the evening, although the facts are such that if as many as 5 percent of the homeowners watered their lawns, there would be no lowering of the pressure. Jones waters his lawn in the evening. He causes no harm to anyone because noncompliance has not passed the 5 percent threshold. Nevertheless, his neighbors are understandably indignant. They see that Jones profits *only because they forebear*. They cooperated and discharged their duties of fair play, and they had a right that Jones do so too.

Perhaps the most apt and familiar example is drawn from one of the largest of all the collective activities of our time, the cooperative movement of automobiles in all directions through a modern nation's highway system. Suppose that there is a restricted lane reserved for emergency vehicles on the right shoulder of a multilane road. You are creeping along bumper to bumper in heavy traffic, returning from a well-attended football game. You look in your rearview mirror and see a car pull into that forbidden lane and accelerate rapidly by the line of cars jammed in the permitted lanes. Generously you infer that there is some extreme emergency that has impelled this motorist to so desperate a course. But as he passes on your right you note that his car is packed with spirited revelers; there are pennants flying from all the windows, and lusty voices are singing the college fight song. The other motorists have stayed out of the restricted lane and because—only because—of their obedience, the disobedient motorist profits. He has exploited their good faith for his own benefit.

If a general PFO to obey the law can be derived from the basic PFO of fair play, then each individual citizen's duty of obedience is owed ultimately, not to the state, but to the other citizens, for it is essentially a duty not to take advantage of them even in "harmless" ways. There are indeed many examples of legal disobedience that does exploit unfairly the law-abidingness of others. Traffic infractions of course provide one class of examples. Income tax evasion provides another. But there are too many counterexamples for there to be a perfectly general PFO of obedience derived from the basic PFO of fair play. There are many types of cases where violating the law does not take advantage of anyone, and since the element of exploitation is not involved *necessarily* in every instance of law-breaking, "fair play" is by no means a perfect model. In those cases where exploitation of other citizens is involved (and indeed they are common), we have a PFO to obey the law not simply because it *is* the law, but rather because it would be unfair exploitation not to, just as in other cases, we may have a duty to obey the law, not because it is the law, but because it would harm someone, or break a promise to someone, or so on, not to.

Examples of nonexploitative law-breaking may not be typical instances of crimes in a democracy, but they are not so rare as to seem exotic. Most traffic violations either endanger or take advantage of others, but particular instances even of generally dangerous or exploitative types do neither— running a red light on empty streets late at night under perfect conditions of visibility, for example, or exceeding the speed limit on an empty stretch of highway when it is perfectly safe (except for the possibility of apprehension by a traffic cop) to do so. Whatever the reasons for avoiding such conduct, there is surely no one who can complain that he has been taken advantage of by it. Such law-breaking is neither harmful nor dangerous nor exploitative. What then could be the basis of a moral PFO to abstain from it? Then there are examples of so-called victimless crimes like smoking marijuana or cohabitation that abound in almost all penal codes. Not only do they not harm (or at least not *wrong*) anyone; they do not take advantage of anyone either. Surely the models of driving in a restricted lane and cheating on one's income tax do not apply to them.

Most deliberate law-breaking is obviously harmful to someone, namely, its victims. But even much wrongful law-breaking of that class cannot be thought of as exploitative of other parties who are *not* its victims. When *A* rapes *B* may all males complain that *A* took unfair advantage of male compliance with the rape law to benefit at all males' expense? When *B* murders her husband in a fit of wrathful jealousy, may all the other married people complain that she was able to get her way only because of their forebearance, that it is unfair to *them* that she acted on her wrath when they must repress theirs? Not very likely.

It is prima facie more plausible to claim that civil disobedience in the narrow sense (political protest) does invariably have the characteristic of unfair play and that exploitation is at least one of its inevitable moral costs even when it is justified on balance. If that is so, then there is always *some* reason against that kind of disobedience (a PFO to refrain from it) even when counterbalanced by reasons on the other side. When you sit in at the atomic energy site, for example, your fellow citizens might all be entitled to say, "You are able to violate the trespass laws to further your favorite moral cause *only* because we don't do the same every time we think we have a higher moral cause. If all our moral causes were promoted in your fashion, the costs to our democratic institutions, our public civility, and our domestic tranquility would be disastrous." This is often a quite proper thing to say to the rash civil disobedient whose political anger is more like self-righteousness than genuinely disinterested indignation. Civil disobedience is often *not* justified precisely on the ground that it is not fair play and is made possible only by the self-sacrificial forebearance of others. There is in fact a moral PFO of fair play, and when civil disobedience violates that PFO, it is usually unjustified. But some disobedience does not violate that PFO, and if it also does not violate any other basic and obvious PFO, there can be no grounds for calling it unjustified, except perhaps its contravention of an alleged PFO to obey the law as such. Civil disobedience in the narrow sense can be justified, as Rawls has insisted all along,[20] only when (1) it is done sincerely for a "higher moral cause," (2) when there are no other legal means available (when all democratic remedies have been exhausted), and (3) when civil disobedience is not yet so widespread as to be self-defeating and dangerous to the survival of mutually beneficial institutions. When it is done under these conditions, it retains its character as an unusual and extreme step and is not "exploitative" of anyone. To the question, What if everyone did it? the justified civil disobedient can answer that if everyone did it (where by "it" we mean disobedience that satisfies the above condition), the results would not be bad at all.

There is one further respect in which some law-breaking departs from the unfair play models, and this too has been emphasized by Rawls, especially in his book, in which he severely qualifies his earlier view of the importance of the fair play analogy. The benefits of government and the rule of law are not as equally distributed among the citizens of a modern industrial state as the benefits of traffic laws, for example, are distributed among motorists. So long as there is economic deprivation, social discrimination, and unequal access to powerful offices, society is not a "mutually advantageous" cooperative venture. If there is a PFO of obedience derived from the basic PFO of fair play, therefore, it could apply at most to the more favored members of society.

The final argument for a PFO of obedience to law derives it from what Rawls in his more mature work calls the "natural duty to uphold just institutions."[21] This argument has the advantage over his earlier reliance on "fair play" in that the basic PFO in question is one we *all* share, regardless of our position in society and the degree to which we share the benefits of

---

[20] *Theory of Justice*, pp. 371–77.
[21] Ibid., pp. 333–41.

common undertakings. Rawls begins by distinguishing technical senses of *obligation* and *duty* (terms that I have treated here, for reasons of convenience, as synonyms). Obligations are incurred only by one's own voluntary acts, for example, the obligations to keep one's promises, pay one's debts, and honor one's agreements. Duties typically attach to special stations, offices, or roles, whether or not we voluntarily occupy them; but our "natural duties" are those that everyone has, regardless of jobs or roles—for example, duties to be generally friendly, helpful to those in need, and not to be cruel. Among our other natural duties, Rawls reports, is a duty to work toward the establishment of just institutions and to strengthen and support them once they are established.

Rawls' account of these matters has much to recommend it. I think that there clearly is a "natural duty," in his sense, to uphold just institutions, and that it is one of the basic PFOs in our sense. Individual justice is much less likely to be done in general in the absence of strong and reliable just institutions that are constituted by clear and reasonable rules. I have in mind especially such political institutions and constitutive rules as the jury system, the universal franchise, free speech, majority rule in legislatures, and courts organized on the principle of due process. Insofar as one damages these institutional practices, one harms the cause of justice generally. That we are morally bound not to do such harm is as self-evident, I think, as that we are bound not to harm the cause of human happiness in general. Nevertheless, I doubt that a general PFO to obey valid laws can be derived from the basic PFO to support just institutions. Much law-breaking does damage or threaten just institutions, but equally certainly much law-breaking (including much unjustified law-breaking) has no damaging effect on them whatever—for example, running a red light at three in the morning, cohabiting, playing poker at home with friends (where this is illegal). These are actions that do not generate "disrespect for law," because they are unwitnessed or done in private. Perhaps many open and public acts of civil disobedience do damage just institutions, but there is no necessity that this be so. Rawls himself writes that civil disobedience, when it satisfies certain minimal conditions of reasonableness (including the circumstantial condition that such acts have not already become so common as to threaten to poison public discourse and lower standards of civility), actually functions as "a final device to maintain the stability of a just constitution,"[22] because it is an escape valve for pent-up indignations and is "disobedience to law within the framework of fidelity to law, although at the outer edge thereof."[23] Warfare against the state, covert subversion, disruption, violent intimidation, and the like do always carry the high risk of weakening just

[22] Ibid., p. 384.
[23] Ibid., p. 366.

institutions, but civil disobedience, paradoxically, can actually strengthen them.

There could be a derivative moral PFO to obey the law only if, of necessity, every individual instance of deliberate disobedience were a violation of some basic PFO, but that seems to be no more true of the PFO to uphold just institutions than of the PFOs of gratitude, promise-keeping, and fair play. The fact that an act would be illegal then, we may conclude, has no tendency whatever to make that act wrong. Why, in that case, does our conclusion seem, at first sight, so startling? That may be because in our legal system, as well as in many others that we can imagine, most of the actions that are legally prohibited also happen to be wrong on other grounds. The typical crimes of fraud and violence are wrong because they harm or endanger other people; they would be no less wrong if they were perfectly legal. Other prohibited acts, like driving in restricted lanes, are wrong even when harmless in the given case because they unfairly take advantage of the forebearance of others. If we knew that 90 percent of all illegal acts in our country are in similar ways wrong on the grounds independent of their illegality and all we knew of a given act is that it is illegal, then we would be entitled to infer, with a degree of confidence proportioned to the evidence, that the given act is wrong too. That is to say that illegal acts are "prima facie wrong" in a sense different from the one we have been considering, namely, that there is a *statistical presumption* that they are, in any given case, wrong. But that is not to say that it is their character as illegal that makes them wrong or contributes in any degree to their wrongness. Rather their illegality is a characteristic contingently linked to the other properties that truly make them wrong; so that its presence may be a more or less reliable index or clue to the presence of wrongness, not its ground or basis.

The conclusions of this chapter can now be stated tersely:

1 There is no general moral PFO to obey valid law, even in a democratic state with a just constitution.

2. The individual's moral problem in civil disobedience is not that of choosing between his higher moral cause and the PFO of obedience to law, but rather it is either

    a. no problem at all since his civil disobedience will not violate any PFOs but only break the law; or

    b. the problem of choosing between his higher moral cause and prudence (for example, personal safety); or

    c. the moral problem of choosing between conflicting PFOs, one that supports his loyalty to the higher moral cause and another basic PFO (such as the PFO of fair play or the PFO to support just institutions) that may in this particular case be in conflict with it.

In case c no *general* advice from a moral philosopher is possible except to weigh sensitively the two conflicting PFOs and act in accordance with the one that seems weightier in the present circumstances.

3. Legal positivists should drop their assumption that even bad laws deserve respect simply because they are laws and that they impose some small obligation, at least, of obedience. Then, having no more problem of reconciliation, they can hold to their primary contention that all properly enacted law is valid law.

4. The ancient quest for a perfectly general ground of political obligation can be abandoned.

Chapter Seven

THE MORAL AND LEGAL RESPONSIBILITY
OF THE BAD SAMARITAN

IN THE BIBLICAL PARABLE,[1] the good Samaritan was a person who came upon the victim of a violent crime, a total stranger to him, lying "half-dead" on the side of the road. Instead of passing by on the other side, as a priest and a Levite had done earlier, and thus staying "uninvolved," he bound up the stranger's wounds, transported him to an inn, prepaid the bill, and otherwise offered him aid and succor. We can speak, in contrast, of the "bad samaritan," referring to any person who is a stranger to a given endangered person and who, like the priest and the Levite in the biblical story, fails to come to that person's aid. More exactly, the bad samaritan is

(a) a stranger standing in no "special relationship" to the endangered party,

(b) who omits to do something—warn of unperceived peril, undertake rescue, seek aid, notify police, protect against further injury—for the endangered party,

(c) which he could have done without unreasonable cost or risk to himself or others,

(d) as a result of which the other party suffers harm, or an increased degree of harm,

(e) and for these reasons the omitter is "bad" (morally blameworthy).

Among the many questions for legal policy raised by the bad samaritan, the central one for our purposes is whether statutes may legitimately be enacted threatening him with criminal liability for his failure to prevent harm to others.

Among European nations, Portugal was the first to enact a bad samaritan criminal statute in the mid-nineteenth century. One hundred years later, a legal duty to undertake "easy rescue" had been recognized by the criminal codes of fifteen European nations.[2] In striking contrast, the En-

---

[1] Luke 10:25–27.

[2] Aleksander W. Rudzinski, "The Duty to Rescue: A Comparative Analysis," in *The Good Samaritan and the Law*, ed. J. Ratcliff (Garden City: Doubleday, 1966), p. 92. The countries listed are Portugal (1867), the Netherlands (1881), Italy (1889 and 1930), Norway (1902), Russia (1903–1917), Turkey (1926), Denmark (1930), Poland (1932), Germany (1935 and 1953), Rumania (1938), France (1941 and 1945), Hungary (1948 and 1961), Czechoslovakia (1950), Belgium (1961), and Switzerland (various cantons at various dates). Finland (1969) can be added to this list.

glish-speaking countries have remained apart from the European consensus. Their common law has never imposed liability either in tort or in criminal law for failures to rescue (except where there exist *special* duties to rescue, as, for example, those of a paid lifeguard toward the specific persons who bathe on his stretch of beach), and with few exceptions, the statutory law of Great Britain, the United States, Canada, and Australia has also treated the bad samaritan with grudging tolerance. By and large, it has left unpunished even harmful omissions of an immoral kind—malicious failures to warn a blind person of an open sewer hole, to lift the head of a sleeping drunk out of a puddle of water, to throw a rope from a bridge to a drowning swimmer, to rescue or even report the discovery of a small child wandering lost in a wood, and so on.

No doubt many legislatures in common law countries have declined to pass bad samaritan statutes for entirely practical reasons, including fear of administrative complications. With them I have no quarrel. I do find grave flaws, however, in various standard arguments presented by writers in the common law tradition that purport to show not simply that bad samaritan laws would be costly or inconvenient to administer, but that they are somehow morally illegitimate in principle. There are several arguments, or classes of arguments, but I shall limit my discussion here to three: the "enforced benevolence argument," the closely related "line-drawing argument," and the argument from the superior strength of negative to positive duties. I shall devote most of my attention to the enforced benevolence argument because it charges, in effect, that bad samaritan statutes can be justified *only* as an enforcement of morality or "coercion to virtue," not as a way of protecting prospective victims from violations of their rights.

THE ENFORCED BENEVOLENCE ARGUMENT

The first class of arguments identifies active aid as such with gratuitous benefit, a mistake (as it seems to me) that is made with remarkable frequency. It matters not to the writers who argue in this fashion that a given instance of active aid required hardly any effort by or danger to the actor, or that it was necessary to the very survival of the imperiled party. Insofar as it is active, these writers insist, it confers a mere gratuitous benefit, and therefore cannot have been required by duty, not even by *moral* duty. Thus, Jeffrie G. Murphy (to select one of many possible examples) writes:

> I can be highly morally lacking even in cases where I violate no one's rights. For example, I am sitting in a lounge chair next to a swimming pool. A child (not mine) is drowning in the pool a few inches from where I am sitting. I notice him and realize that all I would have to do to save him is put down my drink, reach down, grab him by the trunks, and pull him out (he is so light I

could do it with one hand without even getting out of my seat). If I do not save him I violate no rights (strangers do not have a right to be saved by me) but would still reveal myself as a piece of moral slime properly to be shunned by all decent people.[3]

These remarks are very puzzling to me, for the more natural view, I would think, is that the child in Murphy's example has a moral claim against the lounger, that in ignoring it the lounger violates the child's right to be saved, that the child's parents therefore not only have justification for reviling the lounger, for assigning him low moral grades, and for shunning him; they also have a legitimate personal *grievance* against him, on both their child's behalf and their own.

Murphy gives no arguments for his surprising interpretation of the drowning child example. But insofar as he fits into the tradition of writers with his view, his unstated assumptions are that apart from special moral relationships, our moral claim against others is only to be let alone, that is, not actively harmed; that any active help we get from others is a positive "benefit," and benefits, as opposed to nonharms, cannot be claimed against strangers as a matter of right. In Murphy's example, that which would have to be classified as "a mere benefit" is the child's very life!

Perhaps Murphy and others are misled by the fact that persons in desperate straits characteristically *implore* others for their help rather than claim or demand it, and, after rescue, express their gratitude and even offer rewards. These facts have independent explanations, however, that are quite compatible with a right to be assisted. A person is in no mood to be morally high and mighty and make righteous demands when he is drowning. Pleading for help is the natural animal response to imminent peril, as are warm appreciation and the impulse to reciprocate after the rescue. Rights are rarely in the forefront of attention through the typical salvation episode; they become more visible when they are infringed.

Another prominent philosopher, Lance K. Stell, purposes an analysis of the omissions in the biblical parable similar to that offered by Murphy of his own example of the drowning child. According to Stell, defenders of a right to be rescued have confused the moral requirements of justice with those of benevolence:

In the parable of the Good Samaritan: the injustice (violation of right) done to the man on the road to Jericho occurred at the hands of the thieves who beat, robbed, and left him for dead. The priest and the Levite who passed him by definitely did something immoral, but their immorality did not constitute a violation of the wounded man's *rights*. Their moral defect was to fail in kindness or benevolence. . . . Similarly, the wounded man did not have a right to

---

[3] Jeffrie G. Murphy, "Blackmail: A Preliminary Inquiry," *Monist* 63 (1980): 168 n. 6.

the Good Samaritan's aid. That aid reflected the true spirit of brotherly love—the disposition to respond with compassion to human need even though justice does not require it.[4]

In my defense of what I take to be the more natural account of the matter, I could concede to Stell that the moral defect that led the priest and the Levite to pass the victim by may well have been a failure in kindness, benevolence, compassion, and good will. But whatever character flaw explains their omission, it may yet be true that it was their duty that they failed to do and the victim's rights that were violated. If the recovered victim, months later, were to encounter the priest or Levite (having learned of their conduct toward him), he could indignantly voice a grievance against them, accusing them of having done him wrong. When wrongdoers knowingly violate the rights of others, their conduct, whether active or omissive, normally manifests the character flaw of injustice, but frequently such conduct is morally overdetermined, manifesting also a failure of sensitivity, sympathy, or benevolence. When the latter virtues are conspicuously missing, we may well choose to emphasize their absence in our subsequent account of the actor's wrongdoing. But it can remain true nonetheless that a victim's rights were violated, that a blamably cold-hearted person, precisely because of his lack of benevolence, has committed an injustice.

The biblical Samaritan, of course, was more than merely neighborly. He did his duty and then some. The victim would have had no complaint against him if he had done a good deal less. Rights tend to be rather minimal claims. But to have done nothing at all, in the manner of the priest and the Levite, would have been to fall well below the required minimum. As Judith Thomson has pointed out, there are minimally decent samaritans, good samaritans, very good samaritans, and splendid samaritans.[5] The biblical Samaritan was a splendid samaritan indeed. Justice required only that he be minimally decent. A surplus of benevolence prompted him to be more.

MISTAKEN VIEWS OF SAMARITAN INTERVENTIONS

Holding before our minds such examples of minimally decent samaritanism as that of Murphy's pool lounger had he pulled in the child, and the biblical Samaritan had he merely comforted the victim and reported his injuries to the authorities (or called an ambulance as would be required in our time), let us, in summary fashion, consider the overlapping descrip-

[4] Lance K. Stell, "Dueling and the Right to Life," *Ethics* 90 (1979): 12.
[5] Judith Thomson, "A Defense of Abortion," *Philosophy & Public Affairs* 1 (1971): 62–64.

tions that have been given of these actions by various writers (not always the same writers) in the common law tradition, namely: (1) as "mere" conferrals of benefits; (2) as gratuitous favors; (3) as fulfillments of the general imperfect duty to be charitable; (4) as performances of a specific duty toward *this* person, but one without a correlative right in the beneficiary; (5) as acts of supererogation. I think that all of these descriptions are mistaken accounts of minimally decent samaritan interventions, but perhaps the root mistake is the first one, in the application of the concept of benefiting.

Conferrals of Benefit

Speaking of an example similar to Murphy's pool lounger, James Barr Ames (writing in 1908) reports the orthodox Anglo-American view:

> however revolting the conduct of a man who declined to interfere, he was in no way responsible for the perilous situation; he did not increase the jeopardy; *he simply failed to confer a benefit upon a stranger.* As the law stands today, there would be no legal liability, either civilly or criminally, in . . . these cases. *The law does not compel active benevolence* between man and man. It is left to one's conscience whether [one] . . . shall be the good Samaritan or not.[6]

Whether or not *A*, the samaritan, intervenes to save *B*, the endangered party, in these cases, determines whether *B*'s interest remains as it was in the *status quo ante* (before the onset of his peril) or is disastrously set back. Yet Ames contends that the intervention positively benefits *B*, implying that it advances his interests to a condition superior to that of the *status quo ante*, so that *B* receives a kind of net windfall profit, all because of *A*'s munificent generosity. It is in this respect much as if *A* had walked up to a stranger on the street and handed him one hundred dollars!

Something has gone wrong here, and the cause must be the concept of benefiting someone, which evidently has more than one sense. The legal writers who have defended the common law seem often to use the term in a generic sense to refer to any and all ways of affecting another party's interest for the better: advancing it beyond its present condition, advancing it beyond its normal condition, preventing it from getting worse than it is

---

[6] James Barr Ames, "Law and Morals," *Harvard Law Review* 22 (1908), reprinted in *Good Samaritan and the Law*, p. 19; emphasis added. Ames here advocates changes of the traditional rule. A major source of the argument Ames criticizes is Lord Macaulay, who wrote in 1837: "It is indeed most highly desirable that men should not merely abstain from doing harm to their neighbors, but should render active service to their neighbors. In general, however, the penal law must content itself with keeping men from doing positive harm, and must leave to public opinion, and to the teachers of morality and religion, the office of furnishing men with motives for doing positive good" ("Notes on the Indian Penal Code," in *Works*, 8 vols. [New York: Longmans, Green, 1897], 7:497).

at the moment, preventing it from remaining worse than it normally is, and so on. These conceptions naturally invite use of the metaphors of the computational ledger and the business profit-loss curve plotted on graph paper, with various indicated starting points or "baselines" for comparison. To save a drowning person is indeed to "benefit" him in this generic sense, for it is to affect his interest in a favorable as opposed to an adverse or neutral way. It is to prevent his interest-curve from taking a sharp decline from the baseline of its normal condition as well as from the alternative measuring point of its immediately present condition.

The trouble with this generic usage is that it creates an especially tempting danger of equivocation. When it is so very obvious that the generic notion of "benefit" is applicable, it is easy to slide into one of the specific senses of "benefit" whose applicability is by no means evident. It does not follow from the fact that a rescuer affects the endangered party's interests favorably that he "benefits" him in the sense of elevating his interest-curve to a point on the graph *above* the baseline of his condition before he fell into the water. It is only the latter sense of "benefiting" that would support further description of the rescue as benevolent generosity, "active service," "positive good," and so on, or the effect on the rescued party as "profit," "gain," or "advantage." Benefiting another, in this latter sense, is often to go beyond duty in a manner approved by our moral ideals but not required by moral rules. The liberal advocate of a bad samaritan statute can agree that in this precise sense of "benefit," governmental coercion can never be used to force one person to benefit another. But he should insist that easy rescue of a drowning child is not a "mere benefiting" in this sense. It is a benefit only in the generic sense of affecting the child's interests favorably and specifically preventing a drastic decline in his fortunes from a normal baseline. That is quite another thing than conferring a windfall profit on him.

Gratuitous Favors

We have no duties to do favors or confer gifts on those to whom we stand in no special moral relationship. On the other hand, we are morally required to perform beneficial services for those to whom we have made promises, or to whom we are parents, children, spouses, immediate neighbors, nurses, guides, or protectors. On the view I am defending, a good swimmer on a bridge who watches a stranger drown in the water below has inflicted a harm, and a grievous one, by his omission, and this is so not only because unwanted death is the sort of thing we regard as a harm whatever its cause, but also because the victim has a right to the assistance of the stranger, and the stranger has a correlative duty to save him. Merely being a fellow human being is enough of a "relationship," on this view, to ground a duty to rescue when the threatened harm is that severe. On the contrary view, two mere strangers are not closely enough related for one party to have a duty to "benefit" the other (although it would be commendable to do so anyway), for in the absence of a special duty derived from job, role, or prior commitment, a successful rescue would be like a favor or a gift, and failing to help cannot be considered to be a way of harming.

How good a model is the gratuitous favor for the easy rescue situation? Consider a clear example of a failure to make a genuinely gratuitous rescue, the example of a condemned murderer whose last-minute appeal for clemency is denied by the governor. Here it is plausible to say that the governor merely "withheld a benefit" by his omission. The cause of the "harm" to the prisoner was his own crime and subsequent conviction, not any action or omission of the governor. At least part of the reason why this is so is that the governor had no duty to save the prisoner and the prisoner had no right to demand clemency. Clemency is something given freely, something "beyond duty," like a favor or a gift. This clear example provides us with a third specific sense of "benefit." One person benefits another (1) by restoring his interest to or maintaining it at a normal condition, or (2) by advancing his interests beyond a properly selected baseline (in this sense benefit is gain or profit), or (3) by any favorable effect on his interests (any generic benefit) that is gratuitous (like an act of grace or clemency).

Bestowing executive clemency *is* a good example of benefiting a person by preventing his interest-curve from sinking even lower. Withholding clemency in the same circumstances would not be to harm (further) the prisoner. These are precisely the two contentions held by my opponents about the easy rescues of drowning swimmers. The withholding of executive clemency can hardly be a model, however, for interpreting the bad samaritan's failure to make an easy rescue of another party from imminent and severe peril, although as we gradually change the examples to weaken the severity or probability of the threatened harm, or to increase the difficulty or danger of a rescue attempt, the model of the gratuity becomes more plausible.

When there is no duty to aid, for whatever reason, we use a different baseline for measuring benefits and harms in the first two senses. If the governor commutes the prisoner's death sentence, then since he had no duty to do so, we measure the prisoner's improved interest-condition from its state at the moment the governor's rescue is effected. By preventing the convict's condition from deteriorating from that point, *when he had no duty to do so*, the governor conferred on him a benefit in the second sense—a gain, profit, or advantage. If he had had a duty to commute the sentence, on the other hand, then the beneficial effect on the prisoner's interest-curve would be measured from some earlier "normal" point before death impended, and the governor's action would merely have restored the prisoner to his normal condition without any further profit or advantage. Similarly, the bystander's easy rescue of the drowning swimmer, given his prior duty to do so, does not advance the rescued party's condition beyond the normal baseline. Instead it simply restores the swimmer to his condition at that baseline. It is therefore not a "sheer gain"—not a net profit—for the imperiled party. When measured from the appropriate (duty-assigned) baseline, it is simply the prevention of a harm without a further gain.

Imperfect Duties

Some opponents of bad samaritan laws admit that there is a duty to aid those in peril, but interpret that duty as a mere "imperfect duty" in John Stuart Mill's sense. Mill, obviously taking charitable contributions as his model, defines "duties of imperfect obligation" as "those in which, though the act is obligatory, the particular occasions of performing it are left to our choice, as in the case of charity or beneficence, which we are indeed bound to practice, but not toward any definite person, nor at any prescribed time."[7] If there are more deserving needy people than I can help, and more worthy causes than I have funds to support, then a duty to be charitable can only require me to contribute a reasonable net amount, allocated as I see fit, among the eligible recipients. In the very nature of the case, some must do without help from me, deserving though they may be. It follows from their equal worthiness and my inadequate capacity to serve them all, that *none* of them has a right to my help, even though I have a duty to help as many of them as I can. In short, the reason why my duty is "imperfect," lacking determinate recipients with correlative claims against me, is entirely a logistic one, a problem of coordination that could be solved, if at all, by a cooperative scheme among similarly situated donors, defined by set rules. Nothing like this is involved in either Murphy's drowning child example or the parable of the good Samaritan, where the emergency is clear and present, an the aid can be given to one victim without being withheld from any other. There is no reason to think of the rescuer's duty as merely to select from among the equally needy those he can afford to help, for there is no other need so near and pressing as that which commands his attention and demands his help right now.

We encounter a more serious problem, however, when we modify Murphy's example by adding more imperiled parties. Suppose that there are *two* drowning babies in the pool, one twenty meters to the lounger's right and the other twenty meters to his left, and that the circumstances make it clear that the lounger, by taking a few steps in either direction, can easily

---

[7] John Stuart Mill, *Utilitarianism* (1957), p. 61.

scoop up one baby, but that there is insufficient time to rescue both. (We can suppose that the lounger is unable himself to swim or stay afloat in the water.) Now the lounger's duty begins to resemble the "imperfect duty" to contribute to charitable agencies. Since the lounger can save one but not both babies, neither baby, it will be said, can claim as a matter of right that *he* be the one who is saved. If the lounger is the same scoundrel as in Murphy's original example, he will be no more inclined to rescue one of two imperiled babies than he was to rescue the solitary baby, and he will let them *both* die. If he is philosophically clever, he will say in his own defense afterward, that while, of course, he deserves low moral grades for his heartlessness and for his failure to discharge a duty of imperfect obligation, nevertheless he violated no one's rights; no one was wronged; no one has a legitimate grievance against him. And for that reason (he will add) he cannot rightly be punished in the earlier example where he neglected only a single drowning child. To compound the paradox, the greater the number of hypothetical imperiled babies we throw into the fictitious pool, the more plausible will the lounger's case seem to become, that none of them had a right to his assistance!

These results are intolerably paradoxical in their own terms, but they are particularly unsettling to the liberal, for they seem to force him to embrace an inconsistent triad of propositions:

1. Criminal prohibitions are legitimate only when they protect individual rights, that is, there should be no victimless crimes.
2. Murphy's lounger in the two-or-more-drowning-baby cases should be criminally liable.
3. Murphy's lounger in those cases violated no one's rights.

I cannot escape this trap by giving up proposition 1, for that would be utterly to abandon either the liberalism that I have tried to defend in a number of publications, or else the analysis of harm as right-violating setback to interest, which I have also made repeated efforts to defend. Proposition 2 is hardly any easier to abandon. Since I would argue that the lounger should be criminally liable in the case where there is only one party in peril, I cannot, in all consistency, argue for his immunity when there are two or more in peril and it is easy for him to rescue one. The statute imposing that liability could have some legitimacy, I suppose, on the ground that it functions to diminish setbacks to interest, in this case to prevent the loss of salvageable human life, but that legitimacy would tend to be undermined by the bad samaritan's claim that his crime lacked a determinate victim since neither drowned child had a moral right against him to be saved (proposition 3). The reply to this claim must be that in fact at least one of the babies did have rights that were violated by the lounger's deliberate omission to act. Now the problem becomes that of giving a plausible account of those rights.

One possibility is to say that each child had a right against the lounger that he save as many of them as he could without unreasonable risk to himself. In this case that would be a right that each baby has that the lounger save one or another of them. It would follow that by failing to act at all, the lounger violated the rights of both babies, even though by hypothesis it would have been impossible to save one of them. A somewhat odd consequence of this view of the matter is that if the lounger had rescued one of the babies then he would have entirely fulfilled the moral right of the other, and his duty to the one baby would be entirely discharged by his rescue of the other.

Another interpretation is that each baby had a right, not to a rescue attempt from the lounger, but rather to equal consideration, and that by rescuing neither, the lounger violated that right. There are some difficulties with this view too. In giving neither imperiled party any consideration, the lounger treated them with perfect equality. Moreover, if one baby had been a boy and the other a girl, or one a black and the other a white, and a different hypothetical lounger, able to save only one but not both, chose on the basis of his bigoted racial or sexual preferences, it is not clear that the neglected party's rights would thereby be violated, especially if we add to the example that *this* pool lounger would have saved both had he been able to do so. It is part of the conception of a duty of imperfect obligation that the obligated party must save as many as he reasonably can, but that it be left up to his own free choice which ones are selected for rescue. In any case, the moral charge against our original lounger is not that he gave the babies unequal chances, but that he gave neither of them any chance at all. And for that reason, it might be thought that each of them has, equally, a grievance against him.

A final interpretation of the babies' violated rights does not conceive of them as rights that each held equally against the lounger. Rather, on this view we would say that only one of the babies was wronged by the lounger's omission, but that it is impossible to say which one. This view avoids the odd consequence of the joint-right theories that the lounger, had he rescued one baby, would thereby have fulfilled his obligation toward the other. Now we can say instead that had he rescued one baby he would have satisfied that baby's right against him without violating *or* fulfilling any right of the other baby, since the other baby is the one (we now know) who had no right against the lounger, and to whom the lounger had no duty. This third interpretation of the rights and duties of the parties in the two-baby case has some advantages, but like the others, it raises some daunting difficulties. One obvious drawback is that we cannot say who the bad samaritan's wronged victim is when the number who perished is greater than he could have saved, even though we can say that at least one of those who dies was indeed his victim.

In some ways, however, this "drawback" has the advantage of congruing with the way we think of the grievances of the unrescued when the numbers of those imperiled are vastly greater than the resources for rescuing them. When one thousand overboard passengers are imperiled, and only one can be saved (there is room for only one more in a tiny rescue craft), but the boatman chooses to rescue no one, the grievances of the one thousand (or their surviving loved ones) are greatly diluted. On the theory considered here, only one of the one thousand had a right against the boatman to be rescued, namely, the one the boatman would have selected had he been willing to rescue anyone at all, and, of course, we cannot know who that one is. But the odds are one thousand to one against its being any given one of those left to die. Mourning relatives can therefore believe only that there is one chance in a thousand that the boatman violated their relative's right to be saved, and modulate their resentment accordingly. The two sets of parents of the drowning babies, on the other hand, have a much stronger grievance. The chances that the lounger violated their child's right are 50-50. In either case the law could consistently charge the bad samaritan with something like "homicide by omission" on the grounds that the probability that the defendant violated the right to life of *someone or other*, on the facts given, is 100 percent, even though that person, in the formulation of the charge, would have to remain nameless.

The more serious flaw in this third account of the rights of the unrescued is that it appears to imply, in the two-baby cases, that only one child (we know not which) has a right to be saved by the lounger, even though there are no morally relevant factual differences between the drowning children or their circumstances. This result would appear to violate the rationality of right-ascriptions, in particular what is sometimes called the condition of "supervenience" that all ethical terms, properly employed, must satisfy.[8] Rights and other ethical predicates are said to be supervenient in the sense that their existence in a given case derives from other characteristics: we have the right *in virtue of the fact* that we have the other characteristics. It follows from supervenience that if we lacked the right-generating characteristic we should lack the right, and if we have exactly the same characteristics as some other person then we cannot differ from that person in respect to right-ownership. Without supervenience in this sense, the language of rights would be infected with arbitrariness.

My preference then is for some variant of the first kind of account, that which recognizes a claim against the undermanned rescuer in all the im-

---

[8] The term was introduced for this purpose by R. M. Hare in *The Language of Morals* (Oxford: Clarendon, 1952), p. 80.

periled parties. Corresponding to these claims, Murphy's lounger has only a duty of an "imperfect" kind—imperfect in still another way—that is to say that he is morally required only to do his best to save as many as he can. If he saves one, and the other drowns despite his best efforts, then he has not violated the other's right, for the drowning baby's only claim against him was that he save as many as he could, and that claim was honored. If he let them both die, he violated the rights of both babies by giving neither any chance at all.

Which one then was his victim? The answer, I should think, is that both babies had rights against him that he violated by his omission, but that his victim was the wronged party who would have survived but for that omission. Again, we cannot know who that party was, but it does not follow that this was a "victimless crime," because we *do* know that that victim was either baby *A* or baby *B*. There was definitely a victim then, even though he cannot be more definitely named. The victim, it should be emphasized, had no rights that the other drowning baby lacked. This solution does not violate supervenience. The two babies were equally wronged, but the victim was the one whose death was *the consequence* of the lounger's wrongful omission. The lounger committed homicide against one or another of the children by equally neglecting their rights against him. But given the unhappy circumstances and the lounger's limited opportunity, only one of the children dies as a result of his wrongdoing. That one should be quite sufficient, however, to convict him of homicide.

The lack of a determinate victim, however, makes tort liability (say for wrongful death) problematic. If it is impossible to say which baby is the victim, then there is no plaintiff with clear standing to bring civil suit. All who perished were wronged, but only the wronged party who was harmed as a result, the victim, can collect damages. Perhaps I should advocate some innovative tort policy that would permit a court to estimate the civil damages due the unknown victim(s) in cases where there were many more imperiled than could be saved, and permit claimants who can prove their rights were violated to divide that amount equally.

Suppose, for example, that one hundred passengers of a sinking ocean liner drown under conditions such that if the commander of the small rescue craft had properly done his duty, one and only one of these one hundred persons would have been saved. Suppose further that after considerable investigation of the lives and circumstances of the one hundred drowned individuals, the court estimates that the average person in the group suffered compensable damages of one million dollars. That figure in turn is our best guess of the amount for which the defendant would be liable if only that single plaintiff (whose identity we cannot know) who was the actual victim of the defendant's wrongful omission, had been granted standing to sue. The court, in employing an "innovative policy," then rules that all one hundred of the plaintiffs in the case, all of whom are now widows or widowers, split the one million dollars equally even though only one of them (we cannot know which) could have been a victim of the defendant's negligence, that is, the party he would have rescued had he done his duty. So the one million dollars is divided by one hundred, yielding ten thousand dollars as the sum owed by the defendant to each of the plaintiffs including the unknown victim who, unlike the others, was actually harmed as well as wronged. In this way, one might continue to oppose "victimless crimes" and advocate their exclusion from a penal code, while permitting what might be called "victimless torts" in cases of this kind.

Whatever difficulties may remain for this sketchy account of the rights violated in a total default of a duty of imperfect obligation, they are likely to be slight when compared to the moral paradoxes in the view of Murphy and Stell, that neither drowning baby has any right that is violated by the samaritan who fails to aid either of them when he could have rescued one safely and easily. I conclude, then, that when a person in a situation of scarce resources discharges his duty of imperfect obligation by saving some rather than others from among those equally eligible for his aid, he violates no one's rights, no matter how arbitrary his selection procedures. But when he violates his duty in that situation by giving aid to no one at all, then he violates the rights of at least some of the remainder. These wronged parties could have claimed in advance as a matter of right only that he attempt to rescue as many imperiled parties as he reasonably could, so that the wrongful omitter has equally violated that right in each of them. If any of them, through a posthumous spokesman, could establish in addition that he was harmed (killed) as a consequence, he would by that token have demonstrated that he was a *victim* of a wrongful omission, but typically that status cannot be demonstrated for a given party even when we know that someone or other must have been the victim.

Determinate Duties Without Correlative Rights

It is not entirely clear which of the two typical characteristics of imperfect duties Mill means to be the defining one: the lack of a determinate beneficiary or the lack of a correlated right-to-be-assisted in the beneficiary, or both. If the defining feature of imperfect duties is the lack of a particular assignable person at whom the duty can be said to be directed, then there can be perfect duties (with perfectly determinate recipients) which nevertheless cannot be claimed by the person at whom they are directed as his right. Some (but not all) duties toward the third-party beneficiaries of promises may fall into this category. There are also examples of saintly or heroic persons who think of themselves as having special duties derived from their personal ideals, or from their self-assigned vocation in life, or from God, that require them to do services for others much in excess of what they believe the others can demand as their right. We may dismiss such people as moralistic egotists, but we cannot convict them of a conceptual error. It is no contradiction to speak of a duty to help others that is not logically correlated with any right in the recipients to be assisted. Finally, I might mention as an example in this category the duties of noblesse oblige that were thought to be owed by nobles even to their unworthy underlings, simply because the duties attached to the station occupied by the nobles. Lords had duties to their servants under the feudal system that the servants could not rightly claim as their due.

It is possible, I suppose, for a philosopher to claim any or all of these duties as models for understanding the pool lounger's duty to rescue the drowning child, or the samaritan's duty to assist the battered victim of crime. It is possible for philosophers to claim anything at all. There is no conclusive way of refuting the claim that the drowning child and the battered victim have no moral right to be rescued correlative to the moral duty that others have to rescue them. There is a simple phenomenological test however, that all these models fail when we applied to the child and the victim. When we agree that the bystanders ought to offer assistance in these cases, indeed that they *must* offer assistance, do we also think that moral indignation on behalf of the recipient of the duty would be fitting if the bystander failed to do his duty, or would we just give the bystander low moral grades, adding that his flaws are no business of the person he declined to aid, nothing that person has a right to complain about? If A is pompous, vain, silly, dull-witted, or unimaginative, what is that to B, who is a mere stranger, a passive observer? B can make these adverse judgments about A and avoid his company, but can he claim as a personal grievance against A that A has these failings? Clearly not; and that is a sign that he has no right that A be a better person in these respects. That is A's business, not his. But the parents of the drowned child will feel understandably and plausibly aggrieved, and we can share their indignation vicariously with them. We would not acknowledge that their child's right was infringed if we thought of the bad samaritan's neglected duty as something like a duty of noblesse oblige. But clearly we cannot think of it that way; the persisting sense of grievance will not permit it.

Acts of Supererogation

The fifth version of the view I am attacking is the least plausible of all, and we need not spend much time on it, despite its surprising popularity.[9] That

---

[9] See, for example, Richard Epstein, "A Theory of Strict Liability," *Journal of Legal Studies* 2 (1973): 200.

is the view that the lounger and the samaritan, having no duty whatever to give assistance, perform "acts of supererogation," if they do. There are two common ways to interpret the concept of a supererogatory act, one quite specific, the other generic. In the specific sense, supererogatory acts tend to be harder than most acts required by duty. They are "above and beyond duty." Like the acts of saints and heroes, they are "meritorious, abnormally risky nonduties."[10] Minimally decent acts of easy rescue, by definition, are not supererogatory in this sense. There is nothing risky about calling an ambulance or yanking a small child out of the water. In the generic sense, a supererogatory act is an act "whose performance we praise but whose nonperformance we do not condemn."[11] But in that sense, easy rescues like that open to Murphy's pool lounger, fail to be supererogatory since even Murphy condemns their nonperformance.

MACAULAY'S OBJECTIONS TO BAD SAMARITAN STATUTES

There is no plausibility then in the view that a positive act of assistance *as such* is a "mere conferral of benefit" (either in the sense of profit or the sense of favor) or an act of generosity, charity, or supererogation. A more plausible argument concedes that the minimally decent samaritan acts required by the European statutes are moral duties correlated with the moral rights of endangered persons to be assisted, but insists that it is impossible in principle for the law to be formulated in such a way that these moral duties are enforced without at the same time requiring persons in other contexts to perform acts that *are* above and beyond their actual moral duties. There is, according to this argument, no nonarbitrary way of drawing and holding the line.

The classic statement of the line-drawing objection to bad samaritan statutes is that of Lord Thomas Macaulay, who discussed the question in the introductory notes he wrote in 1837 for the commission to revise the Indian penal code, of which he was a member.[12] Macaulay begins by asking to what extent omissions should be punishable when they produce the same consequences as positive acts that are punishable because of their harmfulness. His problem is to draw the line that separates the harmful omissions that are punishable from those that are not. He concludes by drawing the line where the Anglo-American law has always drawn it, in effect to immunize "samaritans," those persons in a position to help others

[10] See my "Supererogation and Rules," in *Doing and Deserving* (Princeton: Princeton University Press, 1970), p. 13.
[11] Henry Sidgwick, *Methods of Ethics*, 7th ed. (London: Macmillan, 1907), p. 219. Cf. Roderick Chisholm, "Supererogation and Offense: A Conceptual Scheme for Ethics," *Ratio* 5 (1963): 1.
[12] Macaulay, "Indian Penal Code," p. 497.

in distress to whom they stand in no "special relations." The following is one of Macaulay's examples:

> *A* omits to tell *Z* that a river is swollen so high that *Z* cannot safely attempt to ford it, and by this omission voluntarily causes *Z*'s death. This is murder if *A* is a person stationed by authority to warn travellers from attempting to ford the river. It is murder if *A* is a guide who had contracted to conduct *Z*. It is not murder if *A* is a person on whom *Z* has no other claim than that of humanity.[13]

Macaulay uses this example to illustrate his central contention that precise line-drawing, once we allowed criminal liability for samaritan omissions, would be impossible:

> It is true that none but a very depraved man would suffer another to be drowned when he might prevent it by a word. But if we punish such a man where are we to stop? How much exertion are we to require? Is a person to be a murderer if he does not go fifty yards through the sun of Bengal at noon in May in order to caution a traveller against a swollen river? Is he to be a murderer if he does not go a hundred yards?—if he does not go a mile?—if he does not go ten? What is the precise amount of trouble and inconvenience which he is to endure? The distinction between the guide who is bound to conduct the traveller as safely as he can, and a mere stranger, is a clear distinction. But the distinction between a stranger who will not give a halloo to save a man's life, and a stranger who will not run a mile to save a man's life, is very far from being equally clear.[14]

This example puts the advocate of bad samaritan statutes in a familiar kind of quandary. If it is reasonable to impose a duty to walk one step to warn the traveler, then surely it is reasonable to require two steps. The difference between two steps and one is so insignificant morally that it would be inconsistent to charge a bad samaritan with murder for failing to take one step, while letting another off for failing to take two. But the difference between two steps and three is equally insignificant, so it would be unreasonable to draw the line of duty at two steps. Similarly insignificant is the difference between three steps and four, or between 29 and 30, or between 999 and 1,000. So there will be no place to draw the line, the argument goes, that will not mark an arbitrary difference between those made liable and those exempted.

It is clear at this point that something has gone wrong with the argument. There may be no morally relevant difference between any two adjacent places on the spectrum, but there is a very clear difference between

---

[13] Ibid., p. 495.
[14] Ibid., pp. 496–97.

widely separated ones. It would be inconsistent to exempt one bad samaritan for failing to take two steps while convicting another for failure to take one, but there would be no inconsistency in convicting one for failure to take a half-dozen steps while exempting another for failure to run two kilometers. So the distinction between clearly good and clearly bad samaritans is not undermined.

One way of coping with Macaulay's quandary is to divide up the spectrum of hypothetical cases into three segments: (1) clear cases of opportunity to rescue with no unreasonable risk, cost, or inconvenience to the rescuer or others (including cases of no risk, cost, or inconvenience whatever); (2) clear cases of opportunity to rescue but only at unreasonable risk, cost, or inconvenience to the rescuer or others; and (3) everything in the vast no-man's land of uncertain and controversial cases in between the extremes. To err only on the side of caution, we would hold no one in the middle (uncertain) category liable. Then we could hold everyone liable who clearly deserves to be liable, while exempting all those who do not clearly deserve to be liable, both those who clearly deserve not to be liable, as well as those whose deserts are uncertain. Careful draftsmanship of statutes could leave it up to juries to decide where reasonable doubts begin. After all, the English tradition restricts jury findings of guilt to the stage before any reasonable doubts appear anyway, so there is no lack of precedent for using juries to determine such points. This solution to Macaulay's quandary has two very attractive merits. First, it allows for the ascription of criminal responsibility to some very bad samaritans who would escape altogether if Macaulay's test were used; and second, it avoids the absurdity of holding that there is no moral difference between widely separated points on the scale just because there is none between any two nearly adjacent ones. Murphy's lounger and others only slightly farther from the swimming pool deserve to be punished for not rescuing the child, whereas observers one hundred and two hundred meters away do not.

My proposed solution to Macaulay's problem then is to formulate bad samaritan statutes in relatively vague terms that allow juries the discretion to apply standards of reasonable danger, cost, and inconvenience. Elsewhere in the criminal law, juries have traditionally been assigned such responsibilities, for example, when they are charged with deciding whether an admitted killer pleading self-defense retreated as far as he reasonably could (ten steps? fifty meters? two kilometers?), and used deadly force only because it was reasonable in the circumstances to believe that lesser force would not protect him. Are not these judgments of reasonableness as much a matter of degree as judgments of "how far one should have to walk in the midday heat to save the life of another"?[15]

---

[15] Thomas Grey, *The Legal Enforcement of Morality* (1983), pp. 159–60.

As for the danger of uncontrolled prosecutorial discretion and its malicious use against decent but unheroic samaritans, I think the interpretation I have suggested of the unreasonable risk standard should be an adequate guard against the danger. Prosecutors have no motive for bringing charges against nonrescuers whom they know juries will not convict, and juries in nonrescue cases would be instructed to acquit defendants if they judge that the personal risks of rescue had reached the threshold—not of actual unreasonableness—but of the first germs of doubt about unreasonableness. Prosecutors could hope for convictions only in those cases where the reasonableness of the required effort's costs was uninfected by the slightest trace of uncertainty.[16]

Before leaving Macaulay, we should consider one of his favorite types of examples of nonpunishable omissions: failure to give money to starving beggars.[17] He was writing, of course, about India in 1835, and these examples were by no means as quaint as they may seem to us in a twentieth-century welfare state. In the India of Macaulay's time, a resident Englishman would encounter hordes of beggars on every street corner, and thousands of these would die every year of malnutrition or starvation. It was manifestly absurd to hold that each time a wealthy man encountered a beggar, he had a duty to rescue him by making a small contribution. Such rescues were not at all analogous to pulling drowning children out of the water and thus eliminating their peril once and for all; rather, the inevitable harm could only be forestalled. One way of looking at the contributions when they did occur was as beneficent gifts or favors beyond the call of

[16] In litigious twentieth-century America, one of the risks incurred by good samaritans (particularly physicians) is civil liability for negligence if they should somehow accidentally make things worse despite their good intentions. For that reason a criminal bad samaritan statute should create not only a duty to rescue but also a rescuer's immunity from civil suit except perhaps for gross negligence. Statutes that limit liability for unlucky rescue efforts are usually called "*good* Samaritan statutes" in the United States. Many states already exempt physicians in this way when they provide voluntary emergency care. The immunity is good policy when there is no legal duty to offer assistance; it is required by justice when there is such a duty.

[17] Macaulay's treatment of these cases is precisely parallel to his treatment of the river-fording case: "We are unable to see where . . . we can draw the line. If the rich man who refuses to save a beggar's life at the cost of a little copper is a murderer, is the poor man just one degree above beggary also to be a murderer if he omits to invite the beggar to partake of his hard-earned rice? Again, if the rich man is a murderer for refusing to save the beggar's life at the cost of a little copper, is he also to be a murderer if he refuses to save the beggar's life at the cost of a thousand rupees? . . . The distinction between a legal and an illegal omission is perhaps plain and intelligible; but the distinction between a large and a small sum of money is very far from being so, not to say that a sum which is small to one man is large to another" ("Indian Penal Code," p. 496). With the addition of the appropriate moral premise, Macaulay's argument can be converted into an argument for the modern welfare state financed by the graduated income tax.

both the donor's duty and the recipient's right. Perhaps a more plausible interpretation of them was as acts of charity discharging an imperfect obligation to give help to some, when help to all was impossible. In theory, it might be possible to require everyone, to a degree proportionate to his ability to pay, to contribute a fixed percentage of his income to some beggars or other, or to some charitable agencies or other, on pain of punishment, but the complexities of administration would be staggering. The problems would be too many even to mention here, but the most striking of them would be the coordination problem. Many beggars would still starve, since no one of them would have an enforceable right against any particular benefactor, and many might simply be overlooked in the confusion. Other recipients might collect from numerous sources, if only by lucky accident, while the most guileful of the mendicants might acquire fortunes. Any practical, fair-minded person would be opposed to such a system, but if such a person were also humane, he would desire instead some sort of scheme of coordination that would allow the starving as a class to be rescued by the wealthy as a class without unjust enrichments of the unworthy or unfair disproportions in the contributions exacted from the donors. A modern state's welfare system, with its maintenance of an income floor for indigents paid out of taxes from those able to pay, is just such a system. Now no one can plausibly be charged with failure to prevent a beggar's death by not making him a direct contribution, since agencies of the state will not permit the pauper to die in any case, and one can always plead in one's own defense that the state's money for this purpose comes from tax funds to which one has already contributed one's fair share. It may have seemed obvious to Macaulay that no unrelated samaritan has a duty to save a starving person's life by giving him money, but now we all have a general duty, enforced in a coordinated way, to support welfare with taxes, and the reasonableness of that duty is no longer seriously questioned.[18]

On the other hand, the random and unpredictable emergencies of life that require time and effort, rather than money, from chance passersby, are not obviated by state welfare systems. "Often an imminent peril cannot wait assistance from the appropriate social institutions. . . . Moreover, there are no unfairness problems in singling out a particular person to receive the aid [thus the rescuer's duty is "perfect" and determinate], and *easy* rescues do not unfairly burden the chance rescuer."[19] It is consistent, therefore, to defend a bad samaritan statute for the latter cases, while preferring

---

[18] The points in the paragraph are suggested by Grey, *Legal Enforcement*, and developed in a convincing way by Ernest J. Weinrib, "The Case for a Duty to Rescue," *Yale Law Journal* 90 (1980): 291–92.

[19] Ibid., p. 292.

a state system of income maintenance to handle the hungry mendicant cases.

NEGATIVE VERSUS POSITIVE DUTIES

A final argument against bad samaritan statutes rests on an alleged morally significant distinction between active doing and passive omitting reflected in many commonsense moral rules that impose much stricter "negative duties" *not* to inflict harm than corresponding "positive duties" to prevent harm, even when the degree of harm resulting, and the intentions and motivations of the actor, are the same in the two cases. Admittedly, where minimal effort is required to prevent harm, the moral duty to prevent it seems every bit as stringent as the negative duty not to inflict that same harm directly. Grey gives a typical example where the parity of positive and negative duties seems to hold: "*B* has a heart attack and reaches for the bottle of medicine that will save him. What difference does it make . . . if *A* pushes the bottle out of his reach or it is just out of his reach and *A* could easily give it to him, but does not?"[20] (assuming that motive, intention, and capacity are the same in the two cases). When more than minimal effort is required, however, then negative duties appear much stronger than corresponding positive ones, and indeed there may be no corresponding positive duties at all. There seems no doubt that in some cases, although not in all the cases bad samaritan statutes would cover, "we are under greater obligation to avoid taking a life than to save a life even though effort and motivation are constants,"[21] and that "we feel obligated to go to almost any length to avoid killing someone, but not under equally great obligation to save someone."[22] But if it is the certainty of an endangered party's death that is to be weighed against only a risk of harm to ourselves, and his gravely serious harm that is to be weighed against our mere effort, or inconvenience, or expense, however great, why should we not be obligated to go to "almost any length" to save him? After all, everything else being the same, we are obligated to endure almost any sacrifice in preference to killing him. Even though minimalist bad samaritan statutes can be justified independently of these questions, the questions cry out for our attention, if only because of the possibility they raise that juries should employ a much stricter test than I have suggested of the "unreasonableness" of the risk, cost, or inconvenience required by a rescue effort.

Tracing the superiority of negative over positive duties to the deeper distinctions on which that superiority is based is a complex matter, and

---

[20] Grey, *Legal Enforcement*, p. 158.

[21] Richard Trammel, "Saving Life and Taking Life," in *Killing and Letting Die*, ed. B. Steinbock (Englewood Cliffs, N.J.: Prentice-Hall, 1980), p. 167.

[22] Ibid.

only a light sketch is possible here. The underlying reason for the general superiority of the negative duties is that positive duties, if framed in the same unconditional terms ("Thou must save all of those in need that thou can"), would lead to unsolvable coordination problems. Moral duties, whether positive or negative, are derived from "moral rules" that, like all regulatory rules, are inherently social in scope and in function. Rules allocate shares of social responsibility to individuals. Their imposed requirements are the dues we pay for our membership in the collective community. They also assign persons to special jobs, roles, and offices defined by special duties or delegated tasks. Public morality is not simply a general name for the sum of all the autonomous private moralities; rather, it is essentially a way of coordinating private efforts for common goals. In some matters it makes no sense to determine what an individual's duty is in isolation from the public system of assigned shares and responsibilities. One does not determine each person's fair share without regard to similar assignments to all the others, and then hope that the results balance out. Rather each person's duty is determined in part by the nature and scope of the duties assigned to the others.

Assigning certain important negative duties can normally be made in a simple and unqualified way to each citizen without raising difficult coordination and motivational problems. A negative duty (e.g., the duty not to kill others) can be discharged completely, and the duty rarely costs us great effort or sacrifice. "It is a rare case when we must really exert ourselves to keep from killing a person."[23] Thus each of us is capable of assigning to himself the unqualified moral duty "Thou shalt not kill." On the other hand, we must in principle consult with our fellow citizens to determine a suitable rule, even a *moral* rule, governing our positive duty to rescue, because an individual duty to aid everyone who needs aid cannot be discharged completely. It would be unfair to those who attempt to do so on their own if others do not make similar efforts, and utterly chaotic if everyone tried, on his own, to discharge such a duty, independently of any known assignments of "shares" and special responsibilities.

It is true, therefore, that each has a duty to go to almost any length to avoid killing another, but not a parallel duty to go to almost any length to save others. But this moral truism can be very misleading. Part of the reason why I do not have a duty to maximize the harm-preventing I can achieve on my own, is that society collectively has preempted that duty and reassigned it in fair shares to private individuals. Collectively there is hardly any limit to how far we are prepared to go to prevent serious harms to individuals. Suppose a small child falls into a well. I am a mere bystander unrelated to the child's family, merely one of a crowd of frightened and

---

[23] Ibid., p. 168.

concerned citizens drawn to the scene. There is very little that can be required of me, beyond passive cooperation and noninterference. The actual rescue attempt will be made by individuals who have been assigned that responsibility by political authorities or specially related parties. They are the instruments of our combined social effort, and we all contribute (in theory) our own fair share of the costs. Collectively, we regard one child's life as a precious thing, almost beyond price, and no effort is spared to save it. But if each of us were charged simply and vaguely with the duty of doing the maximal amount of harm-preventing we possibly can, then there would be an uncoordinated mess. A system of such duties would be socially self-defeating, and full of inequities in the sharing of burdens as well as the receiving of needed assistance. Moreover, it would encourage officious intermeddling by the overzealous, among other forms of harmful blundering.

Each of us has a duty to call the fire department whenever we discover a fire. Beyond that we have no positive duty to fight the flames. That is the special responsibility of the skilled professionals we support with our funds. The reason why we have the duty to report the fire but not the duty to fight it is not just that there is minimal effort required in the one case and not in the other. It is rather that the very strict social duty of putting out fires is most effectively and equitably discharged if it is split up in advance through the sharing of burdens and the assigning of special tasks. Positive duties to rescue are every bit as serious and weighty as negative duties not to harm. Unlike the latter, however, they must be divided into parts, allocated in shares, and (often) executed by appropriate specialists. That way their full crushing weight does not fall equally on all shoulders in all cases, but is more efficiently and equitably borne by the community as a whole.

When all is said and done, however, there remains one class of positive duties to give assistance that cannot be discharged by institutional mechanisms and special assignments, namely, those cases of sudden and unanticipated peril to others that require immediate attention, and are such that a bystander can either make an "easy rescue" himself or else sound the alarm to notify those whose job it is to make difficult rescues. These positive duties, like corresponding negative ones, can be discharged completely and without exertion or risk. A sound system of social coordination would assign them to everyone. A citizen's duty to call the fire department, after all, is a vital part of our coordinated system of fire-fighting. Even samaritans can be required to do these social duties, for their cost is not burdensome, and the consequences of their omission can be disastrous.

Chapter Eight

IN DEFENSE OF MORAL RIGHTS: THEIR
BARE EXISTENCE

OUT OF A LARGE NUMBER of objections that philosophers have made to what I call "moral rights," I address only one in each of chapters 8–10 and attempt to rebut it, and thus in a sense come to the defense of moral rights. But there are many other objections that are frequently made that I cannot even consider in this limited space, and for all we know, some of them may be cogent, even decisive objections. So the theory of moral rights may yet be untenable even if everything I say in these three chapters is true. I do not claim to have proved that the theory is correct, or to have rebutted all the important objections to it. In each of the chapters I attempt to make only a small point, namely, that one kind of objection can be answered even if others cannot. That is a little point, to be sure, but in philosophy the so-called big points are often just such little points strung together.

FAMILIAR EXAMPLES

In Great Britain and the United States women manifestly have the right to vote. But there was a time when women did not have the right to vote in the United States, and even now women do not have the rights to vote in Kuwait and some other countries. These appear to be empirical judgments supported by the factual evidence. On the other hand, we are inclined to say that even in the United States of 1890, and even in Kuwait at present, women *really* had the right to vote, but that this right was wrongfully withheld from them by their legislators and constitution-makers. This second kind of judgment, which by now is familiar to us, is one that has raised philosophical problems. The existence of rights in this category is said to be prior to and independent of their enactment by legislatures, or their declarations, explicit or implicit, by constitution-makers. We need not and cannot confirm them, as in the first class of rights, by gathering empirical facts as evidence of their actual acknowledgment or enforcement in the political societies in question, because their existence is not said to depend in any way upon their recognition in those societies, but has some independent source that can establish them even where they are not generally valued or even wanted. In positing the existence of rights in this second class, we do not act as impartial social scientists describing the facts of actual practice for better or worse; rather we jump into the moral arena, and take a stand ourselves. All adult human beings, we might say, have a right to participate in the political decisions that govern their affairs, and of course, this holds for women too. Even where women as a class do not have a legal right to vote, they clearly have a moral right, derived from their humanity and the moral principle of equality, to vote along with men. The philosophical problem, not all of which I can address here, is to explain what such moral rights are and "where they come from," how we recognize them and resolve disagreements about their existence, and what practical consequence, if any, follows from their possession, especially when they are not given legal protection.

When we assert our own rights or the rights of others, very often the rights we affirm are of the sort I am calling "moral rights." An abundance of examples will illustrate how ordinary and familiar this category of rights is. In addition to Kuwaiti women's rights to vote, one can mention the right to breathe clean air claimed by enemies of tobacco smoking prior to any legal rules that might have been adopted to protect it; the right of a married couple to use contraceptives in the privacy of their own bedroom, first affirmed by the U.S. Supreme Court in *Griswold* v. *Connecticut*[1] decades after the practice had become both prevalent and illegal; the right of legally competent interracial couples voluntarily to get married even though the man and woman are of different races, a right first vindicated by the U.S. Supreme Court in *Loving* v. *Virginia*[2] in 1967; the right to organize into trade unions, claimed by British agricultural laborers before legal recognition was first forthcoming;[3] the right to picket peacefully that, until this century, was honored mainly in the breach; the right to know one's own medical prognosis ("Tell me the truth, Doctor," we say. "I have a right to know"); the child's right to a voice in family decisions, which is not and could not be a *legal* right;[4] a parent's right to be spoken to civilly by his or her children; a student's right to be graded without prejudice; a terminal patient's right (whatever legal rules or hospital codes may say about the matter) to the termination of treatment designed simply to keep him alive as long as possible; a young girl's right even among peoples whose traditional practice requires it of everyone, not to have a ceremonial cli-

---

[1] *Griswold* v. *Connecticut*, 381 U.S. 479 (1965).

[2] *Loving* v. *Virginia*, 388 U.S. 1 (1967).

[3] "A historian who said the British Agricultural laborer of 1810 had no right to organize in trade unions, would seem to be making a statement abut actual conditions which could be judged true or false as it accorded with the facts" (S. I. Benn and R. S. Peters, *Social Principles and the Democratic State* [London: Allen & Unwin, 1959], p. 92).

[4] The example is from R. B. Brandt, "The Concept of a Moral Right and Its Function," *Journal of Philosophy* (1983): 29.

toridectomy imposed on her as a precondition of the wedding ceremony;[5] the Indian widow's right, even before 1829 when the practice of suttee was banned throughout British India, not to immolate herself on her husband's funeral pyre, despite social, religious, and even political pressure to do so;[6] the right to the free exercise of one's religion that was systematically violated, for example, by the legal authorities of Iran in the case of the Baha'i religion, whose temples were destroyed and leaders executed; and finally the right to freedom from arbitrary arrests and incarceration, as in the standard Gestapo practice of raiding the homes of Jews and dissidents at 4:00 in the morning, pounding peremptorily on the door, and then carting away the terrified residents who were often never heard from again. Surely if we have any rights at all, we have rights not to be treated like that!

These examples are designed to show that moral rights are not some esoteric construction of otherworldly philosophers, but common parts of the conceptual apparatus of most if not all of us when we make moral and

---

[5] A special issue of *Time* (Fall 1990) describes the practice (p. 39)

a rite undergone by more than 80 million African women. Female circumcision—the mutilation of the external genital organs—is a centuries-old rite of passage, intended to ensure that young women become desirable wives [by eliminating a presumed motive to infidelity]. It frequently causes life-threatening blood loss and infection. It can also lead to painful intercourse, infertility and difficult childbirth. While often erroneously linked to Islamic scripture, it is not mandated by any religion and is practiced by people of many faiths in some two dozen black nations [as well as] Egypt and the Sudan. [It is the traditional practice of the lowly caste of Egyptian Arabs who collect the waste of the city of Cairo.] . . .

Midwives, village healers and elderly female relatives perform the ritual without anesthesia, using unsterilized razor blades. Parents look upon it favorably on the grounds that removing the clitoris purifies their daughters and deadens their interest in sexual pleasure. Ironically, the frigidity or infertility caused by the mutilation leads many husbands to shun their brides.

Doctors throughout Africa recognize the harmful effects of female circumcision but feel powerless to stop a practice so entrenched in custom and tradition. Many organizations are campaigning against it, and the new African Charter on the Rights of Children includes items condemning circumcision. Governments in Sudan and elsewhere have passed laws against it, but they are seldom enforced.

It will take education, not just laws, to halt what Africans view as a symbol of their culture. Asks Birhane Ras-Work, president of the Inter-African Committee on Traditional Practices: "How do you eradicate a tradition that is more powerful than a legal system?"

[6] "The practice of killing a favorite wife on her husband's grave has been found in many parts of the world . . . [among] the Thracians, the Scythians, the ancient Egyptians, the Scandinavians, the Chinese, and people of Oceana and Africa. Suttee was probably taken over by Hinduism from a more ancient source. Its stated purpose was to expiate the sins of both husband and wife and to ensure the couple's reunion beyond the grave, but it was encouraged by the low regard in which widows were held. . . . Isolated cases of voluntary suttee have occurred into the 20th century" (*The New Columbia Encyclopedia* [New York and London: Columbia University Press, 1975], p. 2662).

political judgments. One of the best definitions of moral rights in the present sense comes, ironically, from a philosopher who is an avowed skeptic about their existence. Raymond Frey defines a moral right as "a right which is not the product of community legislation or social practice, which persists even in the face of contrary legislation or practice, and which prescribes the boundary beyond which neither individuals nor the community may go in pursuit of their overall ends."[7]

Several further distinctions must now be made in order to clarify this definition. First of all, obviously, the categories of moral and legal rights overlap, so that a given moral right can also be a legal right if a rule calling for its recognition and enforcement has been duly enacted into law. The right of women to vote, long a moral right, has since 1920 also been in the United States a legal right. Second, a distinction must be drawn between moral rights in the sense I have been assigning to that term and moral rights in a much weaker sense, namely, the rights conferred on people by the rules of the conventional "morality"—or the "moral code" as we say— of their communities. These are the rights that Frey's definition attributes to "social practice" in contrast to genuinely moral rights that, coming from some objective and universal principles of morality, exist as independently of social practice as they do of legislative enactment. Conventional morality varies from group to group; we speak of bourgeois morality, "socialist morality," "Nazi morality" (which was an immoral morality indeed), Catholic morality, Eskimo morality, Hottentot morality, and the morality of the ancient Spartans or Babylonians. These various systems of norms for the most part contain many proscriptions and injunctions in common, but they also differ in some striking ways. Infanticide, for example, was permissible in Spartan and Hottentot morality; it is a dreadful sin in Catholic morality.

In contrast, what is sometimes called "true morality" is thought to be immune to such fluctuations, being at least to some degree "part of the nature of things," critical, rational, and correct. True morality, so understood, provides the standards and principles by which to judge the actual institutions of any given society, including its conventional morality—the rules and principles actually established in that society, for better or worse. Rights conferred by a universal true morality may also be a part of the conventional moralities of many societies, as the right not to be killed except in defense of self or others, or the right to have what was promised to one, are, for example. Furthermore, a moral right in the objective sense may be conferred by both a given code of conventional morality and a system of positive law, in which case it is a true moral right, a conventional

---

[7] R. G. Frey, *Interests and Rights. The Case Against Animals* (Oxford: Clarendon, 1980), p. 7.

moral right, and a legal right, all at once; or it may be unrecognized by both a country's conventional morality and its legal system, in which case it remains a true moral right anyway. This latter point is well illustrated, I think, by the Gestapo arrest, the right to the free exercise of religion in Iran, the right of Indian widows not to incinerate themselves, and the right of the daughters of the Cairo garbage collectors not to be subjected to sexual mutilations before marriage. Arguably, in each of these cases, critical morality confers a genuine moral right that is unrecognized, indeed explicitly denied, by both the conventional morality of the group and its legal system, insofar as it has one.

Third, there is a distinction between those moral rights that are exercisable even prior to legal recognition and those that cannot be exercised before being enacted into law. There is no way, for example, in which women can exercise their moral right to vote in a country where that right has not been given legal recognition, whereas one can exercise the moral right to picket peacefully before legal recognition, at least until the police arrive to haul one away. Better examples of exercisable moral rights are the right to practice one's religion (secretly) and the right to commit suicide in order to hurry a death that would otherwise be painful. This distinction is of no deep theoretical importance, but a fourth distinction, related to it, may be of greater interest. Women campaigning for the right to vote may say, "We demand our rights." This suggests that what they want is to be granted rights—legal rights—which they do not yet have, since in the example the only rights they have in respect to voting are moral rights, which being nonexercisable are not in themselves operative "voting rights." What good is it then to have nonexercisable moral rights? Are the women in the example merely demanding recognition of rights they already have when they demand their rights, like the followers of Martin Luther King who assumed that they already had certain constitutional rights whose benefits were being wrongfully withheld from them? King's followers were not asking for new rights but for enforcement of actual legal rights they were confident they already had. But in the women's case, valid laws on the books and "in effect" explicitly denied them what they were after.

The women's demand for their rights should be interpreted as a demand for new legal rights that they did not at the time possess. When they said that they "wanted their rights" they meant to put in a claim, based on their actual possession of a moral right, to be given the corresponding legal right. What they were asserting is that they had a right to be granted a right, a moral right against the state to be given a new legal right. The moral right functioned as the basis of their entitlement to the legal right analogous to the way in which a title establishes a claim to property. Without the moral right, the women could still have demanded the new legal right and fought for it effectively, but they could not have made claim to it as rightfully theirs, and could not have pushed that claim against the consciences of legislators. What the women wanted was not simply something that would be good to have, but something that they had coming anyway as their due, and this is an idea that the language of rights with its tone of urgency and righteousness is uniquely suited to convey.

Another word about terminology. Sometimes the term "natural right" means nothing more than "moral right" as we have defined it. In eighteenth-century terminology in particular, the natural was contrasted with the artificial. The natural is what is "there" to be discovered, quite apart from human design or construction, as opposed to that which owes its existence to human invention and design. If that is all we mean by "natural," then the terms "natural rights" and "moral right" are perfectly interchangeable. Natural rights are part of the nature of things to be discovered by human reason, whereas conventional and institutional rights, including legal ones, are the products of human draftsmanship and general compliance and acceptance. But sometimes the term "natural right" means more than critical moral right. In this further sense, a natural right is a moral right derived from "the nature of man," conferred on human beings as part of their original constitution, like their biological organs, bones, and muscles. And like their biological counterparts, natural rights in this conception are conferred by natural laws—the laws of our being. Here the idea of scientific laws reporting invariant regularities in experience and that of jural laws of the sort made by human legislatures, only here discovered not made, blend together to the irritation of many thinkers who would otherwise be sympathetic to the generic idea of a natural, that is, moral right. That is why I prefer the language of "moral rights" over the language of "natural rights," even when the terms are synonyms.[8]

Finally, we should distinguish between moral rights that some human beings have because of their special properties, offices, or relations to others—the special rights of children and the aged, of students, of criminal defendants, of promisees, and of citizens, and the more abstract rights said to belong to all human beings as such, simply by virtue of their humanity. The former group can be called special rights and the latter are commonly called "human rights." Both are equally moral rights, or natural rights in the generic sense, and both are frequently included in conventional moral codes and systems of jural law.

[8] Still another sense of "natural rights," usually left implicit, refers to rights based on natural *needs*, a conception that arouses the suspicions of some philosophers of libertarian persuasion. Other philosophers distrust the "natural rights" language because of the growing unpersuasiveness of the earlier idea of a "natural law" all of whose moral requirements ("natural duties") reduce to acting in accordance with one's own natural *inclinations*, and all of the defined sins reduced to acting contrary to the way we are actually inclined by our human natures to act.

ARE MORAL RIGHTS SUPERFLUOUS?

In the 1950s treatises and textbooks in moral philosophy were overwhelmingly concerned with our duties and what we ought generally to do (these were usually taken as equivalent). Typically, moral rights were addressed, in an appendix[9] or a late chapter,[10] as a kind of afterthought. Unlike duties, which were recognized as commonplace and foundational in the moral life, moral rights were suspect, and often thought to be mysterious or queer. The commonly heard question was "Where do they come from?" (We know where legal and other conventional rights "come from.") This difference is especially puzzling when one remembers that statements of rights are often logically connected to statements of duties. There are, to be sure, more consistent skeptics who have equally severe doubts about moral rights and moral duties, and indeed about all allegedly objective moral rules and principles. That kind of consistent skepticism poses a serious challenge to the theory of moral rights, if only because its doubts apply to both rights and duties. The more selective skepticism that singles out moral rights may be somewhat easier to cope with.

More commonly the token chapters on rights were dismissive in another way. Moral rights, instead of being queer or exotic, were thought to be commonplace, derivative, and trivial. To be sure, they are logically correlative with duties, but duties were the fundamental notion, and rights were merely an alternative way of speaking of other people's duties.[11] In theory, the moralist can say everything he needs to say in the language of duties (perhaps supplemented by talk of "values"); statements of rights were thought of as mere convenient short-hand ways of talking about duties and their logical consequences. Frey is a recent representative of this mode of dismissiveness. Rights-talk, on his view, is not merely derivative and secondary; it is in principle and in fact totally superfluous. "As far as I can see," he writes, "not even a practical advantage is gained by positing some moral right based upon agreed moral principles, since I, as a moral man implementing and following my principles, will behave the way you want

---

[9] W. D. Ross, *The Right and the Good* (Oxford: Clarendon, 1930), appendix 1, "Rights," pp. 48–55.

[10] Richard B. Brandt, *Ethical Theory* (Englewood Cliffs, N.J.: Prentice-Hall, 1959), chapter 17, pp. 433–54.

[11] Howard Warrender, for example, writes that "A 'right,' as the term is generally used in moral and political philosophy . . . is . . . a comprehensive description of the *duties* of other people toward oneself in some particular respect. . . . In this sense, the term 'right' has a rhetorical rather than a philosophical value. . . . The rights formula . . . is a loose, summarizing expression that would be useful in an argument where others are denying this right, or where longwindedness is to be avoided, or where its emotional and personal reference is to be emphasized, but as a vehicle of philosophical inquiry, it is insignificant" (*The Political Philosophy of Hobbes* [Oxford: Clarendon, 1957], p. 18).

me to even without [your having] the right."[12] Rights, in short, add nothing; they are dispensable entities with no further function than to confuse philosophers. If we list all the duties people have, then we need no further list of anybody's rights, for the universal discharge of duties would fully satisfy anything that might be claimed as a right.

The quick answer to Frey is that what one person's rights add to another person's duties is some measure of control by the right-holder over those duties.[13] He can release the other from his duty if he pleases, for example, thus exercising a kind of "moral power"[14] analogous to legal powers to bind or release. Moreover, the right-holder's right often provides the whole grounding for the other party's duty; it is for his sake that the other has his duty. If B has a right that A do (or omit doing) X for him, then B can claim X from A as his due. He is, morally speaking, in a position to say to A, "You owe me X as my due." Moreover, if A violates B's valid claim, B can voice a grievance against A, now being in a position to charge not only that "you acted wrongly," but also that "you wronged me" in so acting. If the wrongful act or omission of A's were a mere dereliction of his own duty instead of being also an infringement of B's right, then B would have no personal grievance, and A could reply to his complaint by saying, "What business is it of yours whether I perform my duties? That is a matter between me and my conscience, or between me and God. It is no proper concern of yours, so stay out of it." At the very least this reply is a misreading of the moral situation, and if it were correct, then B, having no claim, no grievance, no proper business or concern, no representation in the grounds of A's duty, and no control over the content of that duty, would have less dignity in the eyes of others, and, if he himself believed Frey's superfluity thesis, less respect for himself as a maker of moral claims against others, as a person whose own basic interests matter.[15]

If rights really seem superfluous to Frey, it may be because his "principles," which tell him in advance what he morally ought to do in every situation, themselves have respect for the rights of others already built into

[12] Frey, *Interests and Rights*, p. 12.

[13] Cf. H. L. A. Hart, "Bentham on Legal Rights," in *Oxford Essays in Jurisprudence* 2d Series, ed. A. W. B. Simpson (Oxford: Clarendon, 1973), especially pp. 179–80; and Carl Wellman, *A Theory of Rights* (Totowa, N.J.: Rowman & Allanheld, 1985), pp. 91–94.

[14] Wellman, *Theory of Rights*, pp. 42–51, 66–68, 147–57.

[15] The same kind of point can be made, *mutatis mutandis*, about respect for others. In the relevant sense of "self-respect," we respect ourselves when we think of ourselves as potential makers of claims in our own behalf. Similarly, to respect others is to think of them as potential makers of claims against us, and against other parties. It is useful for a rights-theorist to remind himself from time to time that rights-possession is attributed not only in the first-person singular, but in the first-person plural, and the second and third persons too. That reminder would save him and his readers from the mistake of taking rights to be essentially the contrivances of selfishness.

them. It is difficult to imagine how one could know what one ought to do (generally) without first determining what rights various persons are likely to have against one, and which of these rights are likely to be waived. There is, I think, considerable plausibility in the view that your rights have a moral priority over my duties, in the sense that the duties are derived from them rather than the other way round. It is because I have a claim-right not to be punched in the nose by you, for example, that you have a duty not to punch me in the nose. It does not seem to work the other way round. That is, it is not the case that my right not to be punched in the nose by you exists only because you have a prior duty not to punch people in the nose. My claim and your duty both derive from the interest that I have in the physical integrity of my nose. To make your duty basic and controlling is to misrepresent the way rights of this sort are grounded and to give no plausible grounding at all for your duty.

Consider, as an analogy to Frey's superfluity thesis, a blind man who is incapable of reading the "private property; stay out" signs along his path, but who has memorized a set of instructions on how to get to his destination: "one hundred steps straight ahead, two hundred to the right, three hundred to the left again," and so on. These instructions are at least partially analogous to Frey's "principles"; both are morally reliable directives that do not make references to rights. But in each case, part of the method for determining what the contents of the directives are is first to determine what rights various persons have against one. Once these rights are given their due, further explicit reference to them, supplementary to the principles they have generated, will be "superfluous."

Frey does not maintain that rights-claims are gibberish, communicating no sense. He generously concedes that right-talk is a somewhat confused way of focusing attention on the interests of the party or parties said to have the right, and of asserting the moral wrongness of harming those interests. These functions, he admits, can be forensically useful, provided no one is tempted to believe that there actually are such entities as moral rights.

"THERE OUGHT TO BE A LAW"

Frey's most interesting suggestion for preserving the intuitive meaningfulness of rights-talk puts him squarely in a tradition that goes back at least to Jeremy Bentham. One can get rid of the mysterious element in moral rights-talk, Frey suggests, by interpreting it as a confused and indirect way of referring to legal rights, which, being plain matters of fact, are not themselves mysterious. (Moral philosophers who assume that their subject matter is more mysterious than that of law have obviously never studied law with any seriousness.) I call this the "There ought to be a law" theory of moral rights, for it holds that the sentence "*A* has a moral right to do (have or be) *X*" is to be understood, insofar as it makes any sense at all, to be saying "*A ought* to have a *legal* right to *X*."

I agree that sometimes the "ought to be a law" analysis does seem to provide a sensible interpretation for moral rights-talk. It may, for example, be a plausible interpretation of the United Nations Declaration of Human Rights that the welfare rights it ascribes are proposed objects of legislative aspiration merely, in no sense existent and "in effect" everywhere *now*. If every human being has a moral right to "periodic holidays with pay," as the United Nations statement declares,[16] this can only mean that commercial and industrial organizations everywhere ought to put in place now plans to increase production to the point where universal employment is possible, and paid holidays are routinely affordable. Now, of course, the economic conditions of much of the world make the idea of mandated paid vacations a utopian dream, nothing that starving Ethiopian farmers, for example, are in a position to claim as their due, quite unlike the moral rights that Kuwaiti women have to vote in the national elections. The best analysis of the "periodic paid vacation" right, perhaps, is that it describes something that ought to be a legal or other conventional right when or if the time ever comes when the whole world can afford it.[17]

It may then be a reasonable interpretation of the welfare rights that manifestos assign so generously that they merely describe an arrangement of human affairs that is desirable and worth aiming at, but nothing yet existent as a true moral right at this instant. It is, however, quite unconvincing to say that the eventual fitness to be legal rights explains what we normally mean by the expression "moral rights," for this account cannot be reconciled with some familiar uses of the language of moral rights. It cannot plausibly explain what is meant, for example, by talks of persons exercising their moral rights before those rights were legally recognized, as in the case demonstrators arrested for illegal picketing, or religious worshipers conducting secret services in a country where they are persecuted. On the "there ought to be a law" model, what these people are "exercising" is no kind of actual right at all, but rather what ought to be a right, a kind of ideal right that they do not yet have and may never have, though they ought to. There is, in short, no actual right of any kind in these circum-

---

[16] The United Nations Universal Declaration of Human Rights (1948), article 24.

[17] Rights and duties are names of moral "positions." Sometimes a person is in a position to make a claim, but because of shortages or other incapacities, no one else is in the corresponding position to which the duty attaches. See the discussion of "manifesto rights" in my *Social Philosophy* (Englewood Cliffs, N.J.: Prentice-Hall, 1973), pp. 67, 110. We can say that when or if someone ever comes to occupy that position, then the claim of the other party, which is directed at the occupant(s) of that hitherto empty position, will generate a duty. The duty comes with the position, and is merely latent until the position is occupied.

stances to be exercised, but rather only a suitability to be a right, and how does one exercise a suitability? Moreover, when the state prevents one from doing what *would* be an exercise of the legal rights one ought to have, then on the "ought to be a law" theory, the state violates no right that one actually has at the time.

To be sure, many, even most, of the moral rights on our initial list of examples are also such that they ought to be legal rights. But that suitability is not what we mean when we call them moral rights. Their fitness to be legislated is something extra. The reason why we think that they ought to be legal rights is that we recoil at their violation now. The sexual mutilation of a young girl with unsterilized razor blades is a wrong to her. It is also true that it ought not to be permitted by law or by convention, but what we condemn here and now is not merely that the law does not prohibit it, but that it is done at all. The girl in our example would be wronged whether the act that wrongs her is legal or not, and *that* is why it ought not to be legal.

The Moral Right to Rebel

A second difficulty of the theory that a moral right is simply what ought to be a legal right is its apparent inability to provide a plausible account of what it could be to have a moral right to rebel against a tyrannical government. Since the right to revolt against established authority could not be a legal right conferred by the government in power, it could not very well be true that it ought to be so conferred. And yet it does make good sense to say, with Jefferson, that the right to rebel against tyranny is a genuine right that we all have *now* along with (or side by side with) our various legal rights.

The key premise in this simple valid argument, of course, is that the right to revolt cannot be made a legal right, not at least without serious, even insurmountable, practical difficulties. Independent arguments for the truth of this key premise have been made by various writers, of whom perhaps, the most typical was Joseph Story, the virtual founder of the Harvard Law School and U.S. Supreme Court justice during the turbulent 1840s. According to Robert Cover, Story, in his book *Commentaries on the Constitution*,

> hypothesizes a state of affairs in which the various departments of government instead of checking one another, "concur in a gross usurpation." He [Story] hypothesizes that the normal remedies would be unavailing should the oppressed group be a minority. In such a case, asserts Story [and now Cover quotes Story] "If there be any remedy at all . . . it is a remedy never provided for by human institutions. It is by resort to the ultimate right of all human

beings in extreme cases to resist oppression, and to apply force against ruinous injustice." The moral right was asserted here, [concludes Cover] side by side with denial of the possibility of institutional reflection of that right.[18]

The acts of "gross usurpation" that Story had in mind are acts of government officials contrary to law, violations of rules defining offices and limiting their powers, acts of corruption, bribery, and legally unwarranted coercion. When office-holders conspire to act improperly, and their crimes are covered up by their colleagues or vindicated by members of the judiciary, all of them parties to the conspiracy, then it is hard to imagine what further institutional remedy, beyond the definitions of the crimes actually committed, could become available. An institutional right to take to arms whenever one believes that rules have been violated to one's disadvantage would be chaotic. It is hard even to recognize a *moral* right, for example, to attack the nation's military forces in an attempt to overthrow the entire authority of government, in response to one particular set of abuses by corrupt officials.

The argument, however, does not have to involve "gross usurpation" in Story's sense, and in fact can make its point more clearly without it. Imagine then the following unlikely scenario. Suppose that a neofascist "Purple Shirt party" grows ever more powerful in an economically stricken United States. (A parallel example can be provided, of course, for the United Kingdom.) The central element in their program, let us imagine, is what they call "the final solution of the Ruritanian problem": all citizens of Ruritanian descent are to be rounded up and shipped to slave labor camps to be worked to death, or killed as part of some scientific experiment in the public interest. At first, there is no success in passing this program into laws, as all the state legislatures and the national Congress have non-Purple Shirt majorities, but after a number of years, as economic conditions worsen and citizens become more bitter and irrational, Purple Shirt majorities are established in all the legislatures, and the White House itself is occupied by a Purple Shirt president. Quickly the Purple Shirt program is enacted in the Congress and signed into law by the president. Ruritanian-Americans begin to be arrested, at first only in small numbers. One of them appeals to the highest court to overturn the legislation under which he has lost his liberty. The court decides, nine votes to nil, that the anti-Ruritanian legislation is unconstitutional, being in flagrant contradiction to most of the first fifteen amendments to the Constitution, including virtually the entire Bill of Rights. All Ruritanian prisoners are ordered released, and the laws under which they were captured pronounced null and void.

The peculiar characteristic of the Purple Shirt leadership, however, is their devotion to acquiring political power by means of democratic sup-

[18] Robert Cover, *Justice Accused: Antislavery and the Judicial Process* (New Haven and London: Yale University Press, 1975), p. 105.

port. They always resort to political persuasion by legitimate means. They are so confident of their political skills that they are able to maintain an untarnished record of respect for law and legitimacy, assuring that every move they make in the pursuit of political power is strictly in accordance with the laws of the land and the constitutionally specified rules of proper procedure. Accordingly, they introduce a bill to Congress, and simultaneously to the fifty state legislatures, to amend the U.S. Constitution. Article 5 of that document specifies how the Constitution is to be amended: two-thirds majorities are required in both houses of Congress and simple majorities in three-quarters of the state legislatures. So powerful have the Purple Shirts become that they have no trouble in finding the requisite votes. We can imagine then that the relevant prior amendments to the Constitution are themselves amended by ad hoc exceptive clauses excluding persons with at least three Ruritanian grandparents from their protection, or simply abrogated altogether. The Purple Shirts, having acted in accordance with proper procedures and respect for constitutional law at every step, are now free to implement their entire program. The original legislation is reintroduced, quickly passed, and signed into law. An appeal to the Supreme Court this time is promptly rejected by a unanimous vote. At this point the Ruritanians are all shipped to death camps; the Purple Shirt leadership goes to celebrate; the rest of us, confident of our moral position, prepare to go to war.

How could this military insurrection have been legitimized in advance by a legal rule conferring a right to rebel against tyranny? Even if it is coherent to grant a legal right to overturn by force a government that has committed no infractions, overt or covert, of legal rights—a tyrannical government of impeccable fidelity to proper procedure—could not the Purple Shirt legislative majorities in due time ratify the appointment of new Supreme Court justices known to be partial to the Purple Shirt program? Could not such a court, without conspiratorial "usurpation," find, after the fact, that the Purple Shirt government was not tyrannical within the meaning of the law? (If, instead, the would-be revolutionaries petition the court in advance to judge whether just cause for rebellion exists, how could the court decide affirmatively without joining the insurrection itself?) Returning to the problem of judicial judgment *after* a failed rebellion, is it possible to imagine that the losing side in a morally justified insurrection would be found by a magnanimous court of the very government that has just defeated them in a bloody civil war to be not guilty of treason or any other crime, that is, to have been legally justified in their failed insurrection? If it is inconceivable that this should happen, then what point would a "legal right to rebel" have? And yet, for all of that, I submit that there is a moral right to rebel against tyranny even though it would be pointless to attempt to write it into law in a "tyrannical democracy."

A stronger but less certain version of the argument might claim that a legal rule permitting rebellion against tyranny would be not only pointless but positively pernicious. It would surely be difficult to formulate such a right-conferring rule so as not to encourage misguided violence, and increase political instability generally. If we permit rebellion against tyranny, oppression, or injustice, how will we prevent people from rebelling over an inequitable tax law, or a particular instance of excessive criminal sentencing, or similar specific injustices? How could we possibly spell out the domain of the right in detail? How oppressive must oppression be to warrant rebellion? We could avoid these problems of legislative draftsmanship by producing a deliberately vague statement as a piece of "harmless rhetoric" of the sort characteristic of revolutionary manifestos, a spare moral tribute to an abstract idea. But this is just what Bentham hated, and with good reason: the idea that moral grievances automatically ground revolutionary violence. Bentham attributes to the Enlightenment revolutionaries who promoted the theory of natural rights the following attitude: "Whenever I find a man who will not let me put myself on a par with him in every respect [E.g. a nobleman or a rich man with unearned and undeserved advantages], it is right and proper and becoming that I should knock him down, if I have a mind to do so, and if that will not do, knock him on the head, and so forth."[19] It is a dangerous habit in mind indeed to shout, "To the barricades!" automatically whenever one encounters an injustice, whatever the extent, whatever the availability of a remedy, whatever the gravity of the evil. Rebellion is too costly a remedy for minor ills, and even abstract rhetorical tributes to morally justified rebellion included among a set of institutional rules probably do more harm than good.[20]

More Commonplace Examples

A final argument against the "ought to be a law" theory of moral rights might now seem anticlimactic. There is, however, an argument much

[19] Jeremy Bentham, "Conclusion" of *Anarchical Fallacies*, as quoted by Jeremy Waldron, *Nonsense upon Stilts: Bentham, Burke, and Marx on the Rights of Man* (London and New York: Methuen, 1987), p. 68.

[20] There are no doubt some harmless principles that escape these strictures. It may be salutary to be reminded from time to time by official state declarations that it is rightful to rebel against a government that is itself the product of a wrongful rebellion, and that it is justified even in law to use force to remove one who has himself unlawfully seized power, whether by military means or by electoral irregularities like forged ballots. When a supreme court in a democracy rules that election results were invalid, and a corrupt usurper refuses to give up his office or the support of the military that maintains him in office, then there would be a point in declaring or redeclaring the legality of an armed rebellion. But wrongful occupancy and refusal to relinquish office are the only examples of this kind that I can find, while there are many examples of principles that ought not to be included in a legal system either because of their incoherence, their pointlessness, or their mischievousness.

closer to everyday things than the imaginary "right to rebellion" scenarios we have been considering. The analysis of moral rights as properly legal rights cannot make sense out of many homely examples of moral rights on our list of familiar specimens. One might very well acknowledge, for example, a parent's right to be spoken to civilly by her children, and a student's right to be graded without prejudice by her teachers, while denying that those undoubted rights ought to be legal rights at all. At least these and similar moral rights, then, cannot plausibly be construed as mere ideally legal or properly legal rights. We think of them as rights against private parties, not necessarily against legislators,[21] and as rights that can be exercised, stood upon, waived, or infringed, quite apart from what the law might say about the matter.

But could not Frey, Bentham, et al. reply that these examples are cases of *conventional* moral rights only? They are resistant to the "ought to be legal" analysis, they might say, only because they already exist as part of the community's conventional moral code. Perhaps then a small modification in the "there ought to be a law" analysis is in order. Its defenders could retreat to the position that an assertion of moral right is a judgment that a given norm ought to be part of a conventional system of operative norms, either legal or merely conventional, for example, part of our prevailing moral code. Since the rights in question are already part of our conventional morality, to call them "moral rights" may simply be to judge that they ought to be maintained and strengthened as conventional rights. Their presence on our list of sample moral rights then can be accounted for by the amended theory.

A better example from our list then would be the right of a suffering terminal patient to active euthanasia from his willing doctor or friend. This right may not yet be part of our conventional code, but it is plausibly claimed to be a moral right by Yale Kamisar, for example, who proceeds to argue that it ought *not* to become a legal right because of the possibility of mistake and abuse.[22] One might, on the same grounds, argue that it ought

---

[21] A less common but equally effective example of an undoubted moral right not adequately analyzed in terms of the suitability to be a legal right *is* held against legislators. I refer to the moral right of American women before 1920 to vote. That moral right, we have seen, can be understood as the ground or title for a legal right that the women "had coming" as their due. But on the "There ought to be a law" theory, for a pre-1920 woman to say, "We have a moral right to the enactment of a legal right to vote" would amount to no more than "We ought to have a legal right to the enactment of a legal right to vote," an absurd redundancy. Since the statement to be analyzed made perfectly good sense, the analysis of that statement that converts it to nonsense must be mistaken.

[22] Yale Kamisar, "Euthanasia Legislation: Some Non-Religious Objections," in *Euthanasia and the Right to Death*, ed. A. B. Downing (London: Peter Owen, 1969), pp. 85–133. I attempt a reply to Kamisar in my paper, "On Deliberately Overlooking the Merits of the

not even be a conventional moral right. Yet it is arguably a critical moral right for all that.[23]

BENTHAM AND SUMNER ON MORAL RIGHTS

Bentham's use of the "There ought to be a law" gambit is somewhat different from that discussed so far. Unlike Frey, he does not argue "generously" that although ascriptions and claims of moral rights make no sense, people *seem* to be making sense when they ascribe or claim them, so what they must mean (or what perhaps they do mean) by "moral right" is simply "what ought to be a legal right," the latter notion making perfectly good sense. Rather Bentham argues in the opposite direction. If people mean by a moral right simply "What ought to be a legal right," they ought to say so. That would be unobjectionable.[24] But when they fall into the language of moral rights they inevitably are led to assume that what ought to be a legal right in our system of laws already is a right actually in force in some ghostly cosmic system of laws, parallel to but superior to our own, and this is both muddled and pernicious. "All such language is at any rate false . . . or at the best an improper and fallacious way of indicating what is true."[25] Bentham then concludes with characteristic rhetorical overkill: "Reasons for wishing there were such things as rights are not rights; a reason for wishing that a certain right were established is not that right; a want is not supply; hunger is not bread."[26]

To be sure, a reason for wishing to have a right is not the same thing as a right, but it taxes credulity to represent the couple cowering in bed as the Gestapo boots are pounding up their stairs as having no greater moral claim in that situation than a reason for wishing that they had a protective legal right! That is all the moral standing Bentham will allow them, all the content he will grudgingly concede to their moral right. At least Bentham understands, unlike the generous Frey, that what the genuine belief of

---

Case: An Unpromising Approach to the Right to Die," *Ratio Juris* 4 (July 1991). See below, pp. 268–69, and 272–76.

[23] Kamisar does not actually use the term "moral right," but he does clearly accept the view that some suffering terminal patients have an impressive moral case and apparently full moral justification for arranging their own deaths if there is someone to make the arrangements with. And in conversation with me he appeared to have no objection to speaking of moral rights in this connection.

[24] "If I say that a man has a natural right to [this] coat or [this] land—all that it can mean, if it mean anything and mean true, is that I am of opinion he ought to have a political right to it" (*The Works of Jeremy Bentham*, ed. John Bowring [Edinburgh: William Tate, 1843], 3:218).

[25] *Jeremy Bentham's Economic Writings*, ed. W. Stark (London: Allen & Unwin, 1952), 1:333.

[26] As quoted by Waldron, *Nonsense upon Stilts*, p. 37, from Bentham's *Anarchical Fallacies*. These remarks of Bentham's suggest an optative theory of moral rights: "I have a moral right to *X*" means "Would that this were a legal right!"

moral rights advocates, no matter how muddled or pernicious it might be, is that moral rights are actual rights, existent, and in effect, and not merely what ought to be contained in our legal or other conventional norms.

L. W. Sumner, in his recent excellent work on the theory of rights, sympathizes with Bentham's contempt for the muddled idea of a ghostly cosmic system of legal-like rules from which actual moral rights are derived. He tries to avoid that conception in his own account of moral rights, which I shall soon get to, but his accurate understanding of Bentham's motives is well expressed in the following passage:[27]

> Although a skeptical argument like Bentham's cannot show conclusively that the very idea of a natural [i.e., moral] right is incoherent, it would be strengthened if some alternative explanation could be given for the persistent belief in the existence of natural rights. Suppose that the legal system governing us has denied us some legal right which we believe we ought to have, and that we wish to make a case for being accorded that right. Since we believe that we ought to have the right then we believe that in an ideal system we would have it. It is then but a short and tempting step to claiming that an ideal legal system exists in which we *do* have the right, and then to saying that the right conferred on us by this ideal system constitutes our case for having the same right conferred on us by our *actual* system. The mechanism at work here is projection. As a corrective to the [moral] imperfections of the actual world we invent a [morally] perfect world in which individuals possess just those rights which, morally speaking, they ought to have, and then we treat this invention as though it were real.[28]

Positing moral rights then turns out to be an instance of wishful thinking, and that is what Bentham thinks explains the widespread and persistent belief in them.

How does Sumner manage to defend belief in the existence of moral rights without projecting his "wishes" into some ghostly cosmic system? He defines a moral right as "a morally justified conventional right."[29] "I have a moral right," he says, "just in case my possession of the corresponding conventional right is morally justified."[30] At times he suggests that a moral right is a species of a conventional right, so that I cannot have a moral right unless I already have the conventional right with the same content, that conventional right itself amounting to a moral right if its inclu-

---

[27] Paraphrasing Bentham, *Works* (1840), 2:501; 3:221.

[28] L. W. Sumner, *The Moral Foundation of Rights* (Oxford: Clarendon, 1987), p. 119.

[29] Ibid., p. 163. The primary application of the word "conventional" for Sumner is to the wide class of rules that are products of human design; or if not conscious design then mutual acceptance, recognition, efficacy, or enforcement. Some conventional rules are institutional rules. Some institutional rules are legal rules. All conventional rules, insofar as they confer rights, confer "conventional rights."

[30] For a more exact formulation, see ibid., p. 145.

sion in a conventional code or legal system is morally justified. But on the whole, I think that the best interpretation of his intentions is to say that a moral right is either an actual conventional right that is morally justified or what *it would be morally justified*, in the strongest sense, *to adopt as a conventional right* in case it is not a conventional right already. Either the conventional rule system in question already recognizes the moral right or it does not. "If it does," says Sumner, "then what must be justified is the continued recognition of the right. . . . If it does not, then what must be justified is altering the system so that it comes to recognize the right. . . . We may call each of these options—either maintaining an already existing conventional right or creating a new one—a social *policy*. A moral right exists when a policy of either sort is [morally] justified for the relevant rule system"[31]— usually a system of laws.

The major advantage Sumner claims for this analysis is that it explains what the moral credentials of a moral right are and why it has moral force, the answer being of course that it includes the requirement of moral justification. What is to be justified, however, is not a moral claim made by the right-holder in the face of some threatened infringement, but rather the social policy of introducing or maintaining a rule in a conventional system. This feature, Sumner contends, has the added advantage of making "no references to a ghostly realm of natural moral rules," since "the only rules referred to are conventional."[32]

Sumner's definition of "moral right" seems to be a more refined version of what I have called the "There ought to be a law" analysis. His version is stronger than most, in that it does not restrict the relevant class of justified conventional rules to legal rules. By virtue of this enlargement, his version of the theory preserves the possibility that some moral rights exist because it would be justified to maintain or introduce them into a system of conventional moral rules even though it would not be justified to include them as elements of a legal system. This move renders the theory immune to such counterexamples as the child's right to a voice in family decisions, a parent's right to be spoken to civilly, and so on. Moral rights of this class would not be justified as legal rights, but they might well be justified as rights conferred by conventional morality, and thus would qualify as genuine moral rights in Sumner's view.

Moreover, Sumner's analysis would please Bentham by its avoidance of any apparent commitment to a ghostly realm of legal-like rules. (I too share Bentham's ontological squeamishness in this matter.) The weakness of Sumner's account, however, lies in its failure to capture a central feature of moral rights, the fact that they are taken to be actual rights at the moment they are asserted, "in place," or "in effect," generating other people's moral

[31] Ibid., pp. 143–44.
[32] Ibid., p. 136.

duties, capable in many cases of being exercised, and in all cases capable of being either respected or violated. The indicative claim that I have a right to use contraceptives or to marry a woman of another race is not fully translated into any number of subjunctive claims that certain social policies would be justified. If it is a claim about justification at all, it is the straight-forward nonconjectural claim that interference or noncooperation with me in certain specifiable ways is not justified, that others have a real duty sub-ject to my control not to interfere in those ways.

It would appear then that an adequate definition of moral rights should satisfy at least two tests: (1) it should not be committed to a ghostly realm of legal-like rules ripped from their normal connection to actual legal insti-tutions, and (2) it should preserve the directness and matter-of-factness, the immediate nonsuppositional actuality of moral rights that is part of their normal conception. The way to do this, I submit, is to bypass an intermediate step in Sumner's derivation of moral rights. What is to be morally justified in Sumner's theory is a kind of legislative act of creating institutional or other conventional rules. I would substitute a simpler ac-count in which what is to be directly justified is not a hypothetical legisla-tive act or policy, but rather the claim of present moral right itself.

There are as many as six elements in Sumner's more complicated analy-sis:

1. The candidate for the status of moral right.
2. The rule purporting to confer that right.
3. A system of conventional rules requiring, permitting, or prohibiting certain kinds of conduct (e.g., a legal system or conventional moral code).
4. A legislative context: the actual circumstances in which the candidate rule would operate at the time at which it would be maintained or introduced into the system (i.e., right now). ("Moral rights which exist under some social conditions may fail to exist under others.") That is, they may acquire or lose their justifications, as historical circumstances change. This leads, Sumner says, to "a certain relativity in the concept of a moral right."[33]
5. An imagined act/policy of maintaining or introducing the candidate rule into the conventional rule system.
6. The correct principles of moral justification, whatever they may be (e.g., the principle of utility, a contractarian principle, the principle of autonomy, Tho-mist natural law theory, Kantian universalizability, Marxist historicism).

---

[33] Ibid., p. 147. This is a strong point in Sumner's theory that my own quite different theory should be required to accommodate. In a subsequent paper I hope to show how moral rights are derived and defended. Clearly, moral rights, however analyzed, must be understood as changing their content as the relevant historical circumstances change. I deny that moral rights, except in their most abstract formulations, are "eternal" or "immutable." Neither eter-nity nor immutability follow from their being *actual* as opposed to suppositional.

The candidate moral right turns out to be a genuine moral right if and only if the act/policy of maintaining or introducing it into the system of conventional rules is, in the actual present social circumstances, justified by the correct principles of moral justification, whichever they are.

The simpler account I propose would make reference to only two of the elements in Sumner's test: a statement of the purported moral right and the correct principles of moral justification, whichever they may be. On this simpler and more natural reconstruction, a purported moral right is a genuine moral right if and only if it is validated as such by correct moral principles. More precisely, it is a genuine moral right if and only if its truth follows from true premises, at least one of which is a moral principle. In a parallel way, a purported moral duty (like the duties not to act cruelly or deceitfully) is a genuine moral duty if it is certified as such by correct moral principles. If this simple derivation of duties is untroublesome, conjuring up no visions of a spooky cosmic legal system, why should not the correspondingly simple derivation of rights be equally untroublesome? The advantage of this simple form for a derivation of moral rights is that it explains how we can have moral rights in the same direct and immediate way we have moral duties, how the two come from the same source, and why they are called "moral" whether or not they are recognized by the conventional rule systems of particular communities. If a correct moral principle, conjoined with some factual premises, logically implies that I have a right to be free from arbitrary arrest and detention, then that right exists as a moral claim binding on public and/or private individuals.

THE GHOSTLY REALM

But where do the "correct moral principles" themselves come from if not from some ghostly realm? I cannot here attempt to give a complete meta-ethical grounding or even an identification of ultimate moral principles, but I can urge that they not be understood on the model of legal rules. They are not the legal-like statutes of some cosmic legal system, or some partial analogue of a legal system without its own charter or constitution, without its own offices and office-holders, without its own procedural requirements, without its own secondary rules for changing the primary ones, without its own legislature with its own store of sanctions, without the means to effective public promulgation, without its own trial courts and courts of appeal, and so on. This obscure conception is "spooky" because it posits a legal system that is not quite a real legal system like our earthly exemplars, the same perhaps in some quite essential respects as a legal system, but different in other equally essential respects.

Note that a "ghost" in folklore and fiction is the same as a human being in some respects—identifiable form and features—but totally different in other equally essential respects—no flesh and blood, no weight, no physical substance, no tangibility. For that reason "ghostly" is an apt term for a special cosmic legal system different in some essential respects from all mundane legal systems. Gilbert Ryle finds a similar use for the ghost analogy when he lampoons the Cartesian conception of the mind as "a ghost in the machine," a person conceived as essentially nonmaterial, but one whose function it is to pull the mechanical gears and levers, and connect or disconnect the electrical circuits of the body it operates. Yet the immaterial ghost is treated by the Cartesians as itself a kind of machine, a special *ghostly* machine that initiates bodily action by "flexing an occult nonmuscle," in Ryle's wonderful satirical phrase, in just the sort of way that causes the flexing of a nonoccult real muscle. A ghost among the gears is supposed to be essentially different from a material object and yet every property and function the Cartesians assign to it suggests that they understand it as if it were a special kind of material object—an occult nonmuscle-flexer. Similarly, we have a tendency to treat moral principles, which we normally distinguish in some ways from institutional rules, as if they were themselves the rules of an essentially institutional noninstitution (on analogy with the essentially mechanical nonmachines of the Cartesian philosophers).

The parallels between the so-called paramechanical hypothesis Ryle ascribes to Descartes and what we might call the "paralegal hypothesis" scorned by Bentham are striking. "The differences between the physical and the mental," says Ryle, "were . . . represented as differences inside the common framework of the categories of 'thing,' 'stuff,' 'attribute,' 'state,' 'process,' 'change,' 'cause, and effect' " so that minds were thought of, in Ryle's words, "rather like machines but also considerably different from them."[34] Similarly the differences between legal (or other institutional) rights and moral rights are represented as differences inside the common framework of the categories of "enactment," "adjudication," "amendment," "jurisdiction," "sanction," and so on, so that "moral rights," for example, are thought of as rather like legal (or other institutional) rights "but also considerably different," in fact essentially different, from them.

Again, Ryle comments, that

> the logical mould into which Descartes pressed his theory of the mind . . . was the self-same mould into which he and Galileo set their mechanics. Still unwittingly adhering to the grammar of mechanics, he tried to avert disaster by describing minds in what was merely an obverse vocabulary. The workings of minds had to be described by the mere negatives of the specific descriptions given to bodies; they are *not* in space, they are *not* motions, they are *not* modifications of matter, they are *not* accessible to public observation. Minds are

[34] Gilbert Ryle, *The Concept of Mind* (New York: Barnes & Noble, 1949), p. 20.

not bits of clockwork [concludes Ryle, satirically]; they are just bits of not-clockwork.[35]

In a quite parallel manner, some philosophers may have spoken of the moral as if it were both in essential contrast to the legal and yet set in the same logical mold. Still unwittingly adhering to the vocabulary of law, they try to avert disaster by describing morality in a merely obverse vocabulary. Moral rights are *not* enacted, *not* in force, *not* adjudicable, *not* amendable, *not* enforceable, and so on. Moral principles are not just standards applicable to legal rules; they are themselves spectral-legaloid rules of an essentially noninstitutional institution. No wonder Bentham was so scornful!

ELUDING THE GHOSTLY REALM

But there is no necessity that we think of moral principles in that way. Rather we should think of them as in essential contrast to legal rules of all kinds, both those of human institutions and those of their fancied celestial counterparts. Sumner joins Bentham in assuming that if we are to make room for the concept of an existing moral right actually "in place" now, but not part of any system of laws or other created rules, then we must invent a special spectral realm for it as its own home jurisdiction, so to speak. They look about them and see rights conferred by rules designed by human rule-makers to apply in clubs, churches, and corporations, in games and commercial transactions, in systems of civil and criminal positive law, even in the informal norms of conventional morality. When natural rights advocates claim that in addition to these institutional and other conventional rights, there are actually existent moral rights, their critics mistakenly infer that these rights too would have to attach to an institutional base, a special kind of institution to be sure, one not located anywhere in particular—well, *not exactly* an institution at all. And this quasi-institution becomes more "ghostly" the more one thinks about it.

It is interesting to note how the Bentham–Sumner argument turns the argument of the naive believer in moral rights on its head, and commits an equal and opposite mistake. The naive rights-believers, whose faith in moral rights, according to Bentham and Sumner, is a kind of wishful thinking, argue as follows:

1. There can be no rights except as attached to an institutional base, for example, to a legal system;
2. There *are* actual moral rights. Therefore—
3. There is an actually existing "ideal legal system" (albeit in a ghostly realm).

Bentham and Sumner, argue, on the other hand that

[35] Ibid., p. 19.

1. There can be no rights without an institutional base;
2. There is no institutional basis for "actual moral rights" (except in some "ghostly realm"—an idea that is confused and incoherent). Therefore—
3. So-called actual moral rights do not exist.

Both Bentham, as represented by Sumner, and their naive opponents thus share a common premise, namely, that there can be *no* rights without an institutional base for them, and this is the premise, I have been arguing, that is false. If I am right about that, one may logically elude both Bentham's case for rights-skepticism and the spooky realm to which his early opponents were reluctantly committed.

The truth of this matter was perhaps too simple for these authors (Bentham, Sumner) to notice. Ultimate moral principles, as both Bentham and Sumner agree, are rational principles, and reason neither has nor needs some special institutional home of its own.[36] When we affirm that some person has a moral right to something whatever the local institutions, positive laws, and established conventions may say, we are endorsing reasons, derived (as we think) from wider principles that are applicable in other contexts, in support of that person's claim. Those reasons themselves are addressed to the consciences of second and third parties, and place the right-holder in a moral position to assert her claims, whether she knows it or not. No mention of spooky institutions is required, only reference to broader principles providing cogent reasons in support of individual claims.

I cannot forbear from concluding this chapter with a kind of *tu quoque*. If Sumner's appeal to moral principles in justification of legislative acts and policies does not implicate him in the ghostly domain so scorned by Bentham, why should my appeal to such principles (possibly even the very principles) implicate my account? The only difference in our appeals to critical morality is that he invokes moral principles to justify legislative acts or policies toward maintaining and introducing conventional rules, whereas I invoke them to establish truth-claims on behalf of some statements of rights that have nothing necessarily to do with the rules of human institutions. I think we are both guiltless of the common error of reinterpreting essentially noninstitutional moral principles as if they were special-institutional rules. But my simpler account has the added advantage of preserving the direct and indicative character of rights-claims, which is assumed, at least in our time and in our culture, by moral common sense.

---

[36] But I do not advocate the image of reason as a homeless pauper or wandering vagabond. Needless to say, those images are misleading too.

Chapter Nine

IN DEFENSE OF MORAL RIGHTS: THEIR
SOCIAL IMPORTANCE

MANY PHILOSOPHERS who are skeptical about moral rights are less concerned to deny that moral rights exist than to doubt the value or importance they would have if they did (or if they do) exist. Some of these are "skeptical" in a stronger sense, not merely doubting or even denying that moral rights have positive value, but claiming that they actually have negative value on balance. These distinctions thus yield four new categories of moral rights skeptics: (1) those who deny that moral rights exist at all, but also deny that such rights would have positive value on balance if they did exist; (2) those who deny that moral rights exist at all, and also claim that that is a good thing because such rights would have disvalue on balance if they did exist; (3) those who concede that moral rights do exist but deny that they have the positive value that is often claimed for them; and (4) those who concede that moral rights do exist but regret that this is so, since they believe that the consequences of such rights tend to be more harmful than beneficial, hence of negative value on balance.

The fourth of these positions may seem paradoxical in its very formulation, for if a moral right, by definition, is one whose existence is not derived from any political enactment, and not subject to alteration by human volition, one that is discovered rather than invented or created, then to say that such a right exists and has disvalue seems to be to say that "true morality" (as opposed to any particular conventional morality) is inherently askew, and there is nothing whatever we can do about it, and *that* does have the sound of a paradox. I think the paradox can be avoided, however, if we interpret the fourth position as saying that the evil sometimes produced by appeals to moral rights is not a flaw in those rights themselves but in the way people tend to understand and exercise them. If the supporting argument for the fourth position, for example, is that possession of rights encourages a kind of self-righteous defense of selfishness, we might point out that this unhappily widespread phenomenon can better be ascribed to a deficiency in care for others and an insensitivity to their needs and feelings than to the possession of a valuable moral instrument (a right) that is, alas, subject to abuse, and dependent for its intended good effects on supplementary virtues that are not easily acquired.

Skepticism about moral rights is easy to come to by another route. Imag-

Drawing by William Steig © 1991 The New Yorker Magazine, Inc.

He Knows His Rights

ine a couple cowering in their bed awaiting an early morning peremptory knock of the Gestapo, as heavy-booted footsteps are heard outside their door. A legal right to due process would do them some good, but only if that right's correlative duty were reliably enforced. The legal right without enforcement would give them no protection. What good would it do them in that case to have a moral right? Such a possession would give them control over the moral duties of their persecutors, but what good would that moral power do them without physical power to back it up? With a moral right they would have the "satisfaction" of knowing that they were being wronged and not just suffering through their own fault or through the capricious occurrence of some natural accident. This would give them the opportunity to feel righteous and morally superior while they are whipped and clubbed. A moral right in these circumstances is like a "moral victory" (so-called) in a game that is hopelessly lost. Every honest supporter of moral rights, it seems to me, must concede this point to the skeptic. Even if moral rights are valuable commodities in general, they are not sufficient to reward their possessors to some degree in all circumstances. One can say in their behalf only that the world is better off generally for having them, that they do in many cases confer subtle benefits, but at most they are necessary not sufficient for one's overall good, and in no case are they guaranteed protections.

Moral Rights and Selfishness

Philosophical writers who doubt the value of moral rights, even as so qualified, can be divided, as we have noted, into two groups: those who charge
rights with having an actual disvalue, and those who reject the claims of
positive value that their defenders make for them. In the former group are
some (but not all) feminists, some (but not all) critical legal studies theo-
rists, and communitarians both of the left, following Karl Marx, and of the
right, following among others, Edmund Burke. Common to all these writers is the view that rights function to separate people rather than draw
them closer together in tighter communities, that rights are both an expression and a reinforcement of individual selfishness, and a threat to social
solidarity. Jeremy Waldron, after carefully interpreting Bentham, Burke,
and Marx, writes that "the great recurring theme in all three of these attacks
is that the rights of man embody as the be-all and end-all of politics a demand for the immediate and unqualified gratification of purely selfish individual desires. . . . For all of them, human life, to be bearable, involved a
substantial commitment to living together in community that is belied by
the abstract egoism of a theory of human rights."[1]

Assuredly, rights-claims are demands for things the claimant desires; if a
person does not want something, then why make claim to it? It hardly
follows, however, that the only desires any person ever has, and thus the
only desires whose satisfaction he ever lays claim to as a matter of right, are
"purely selfish" ones. In fact the desires protected by the most fundamental
moral rights, the human and civil rights mentioned in the leading manifestos, are precisely those most plausibly designated as natural, understandable, and *unselfish*. It is morally absurd to accuse the pre-teenage girl in an
African village of a purely selfish desire not to have her sex organ mutilated
as a precondition of eventual marriage (female circumcision), or to charge
the Indian widow with a purely selfish desire not to be burned alive on her
husband's funeral pyre (suttee), or to level similar charges against the suffering terminal patient for insisting that he be released from his painful
losing struggle, the Baha'i worshiper in Iran for attempting to practice his
religion, or the Gestapo victims for claiming a moral right to due process,
or second parties for judging with all of them that they do indeed have
such rights. Do such judgments, which can be made in the first, second, or
third person, singular or plural, really serve primarily to make people self-
ishly unconcerned about one another? The very opposite would seem to
be closer to the truth in these examples.

Perhaps some moral rights, property and contract rights in particular,
are instruments of and contributors to a kind of righteously callous self-

---

[1] Jeremy Waldron, *Nonsense upon Stilts: Bentham, Burke, and Marx on the Rights of Man*
(London and New York: Methuen, 1987), p. 44.

centeredness. Among the more prominent uses of such rights, after all, is their employment as counters in acquisitive commercial strategies, and we are all familiar with the sort of person who, although affluent himself, thinks that taxation for the support of the needy is a kind of theft—a violation of his sacred property rights. People to whom the words "mine" and "thine" come readily to the lips, and are frequently uttered with emphasis and passion, are hardly social paragons, contributing to the sense of community among the rest of us. But we must remember that those of us who would rather own some things in common, and in some contexts cooperate rather than compete, and to whom the words "we," "us," and "ours" come more readily to the lips than "mine" and "thine," will nevertheless treasure *our* rights and the possessions held in common that *we* have. A sense of community does not render rights obsolete; it just assigns some of them collectively to groups who then can assert them collectively against outsiders or against individual members who would harm the collective good. The group has a right not to have its facilities damaged or its treasury pillaged by anyone, and this right contributes to its general cohesiveness. It can hardly be the case, therefore, that all rights by their very nature serve to separate people.

Moreover, moral rights often resemble those legal rights that blend claims against others with what are called "powers." A power is a capacity under the rules to create, alter, or extinguish legal or moral relations (sometimes called "positions") both of oneself and of others. So, for example, my claim-right against you corresponds to your duty to me, but in addition I have the power of altering, suspending, or extinguishing your duty by choosing, for example, to waive my right and thus release you from your duty. In short, rights give us control over other parties' duties to us and (sometimes) over their duties to third parties. How we exercise this control is morally up to us, which is to say that we are morally at liberty to release or not release the other party from his duty as we see fit. There is no reason why we cannot exercise our power wisely, compassionately, or cooperatively if we choose. We do not have to demand our pound of flesh just because we have a right to it. So again we can see that rights, even if morally necessary, are by no means morally sufficient. Virtues of good judgment, sympathy, and considerateness are necessary also, if the rights are to be used constructively. These excellences of character are an essential part of morality too. But there is nothing in the very nature of a moral right that militates against the acquisition and cultivation of these gentler social virtues.

The main point in response to those who condemn moral rights as selfish and divisive, however, must rest on a specimen list of acknowledged moral rights of which the moral right to due process is perhaps prototypical. The German citizens made subject to Gestapo arrests, detention, torture, and death were up against the whole massive force of the totalitarian state, and condemned by a transformed community moral code and the explicit content of the state's enacted laws. The following entry appeared in Marie Vassilichev's *Berlin Diaries*: "On 26 August 1942 the dummy-reichstag had voted a law conferring on Hitler discretionary powers in the administration of justice. The preamble to the law read: 'At present in Germany there are no more rights but only duties. . . .' A few days later, in his weekly 'Das Reich,' Goebbels made clear what lay ahead: 'the bourgeois era with its false and misleading notion of humaneness is over.' "[2] It was evidently Goebbels' ideological conviction that a system that includes citizens' rights against the state is morally inferior to a system in which a united citizenry eagerly accept duties assigned by the state but never consider making any claims of their own against the state, or of supporting the claims made by any other person against the state. How admirable, chorused Nazi philosophers, what self-denying devotion to duty, how pure and uncorrupt! To those of us who react with repugnance and horror to this conception of social morality, it seems plain that when a community becomes highly cohesive and tightly organized, where togetherness prevails and dissent is muted, that is precisely when there is the greatest need for moral rights, their acknowledgment, and, where possible, their enforcement.

What does it mean after all for a person or her conduct to be selfish? A selfish person is not simply one who is devoted to the pursuit of her own ends. If that were true, then we could all be called selfish. In contrast, a genuinely selfish person is one who cares unduly or supremely for herself, whose conduct manifests an excessive concern for her own welfare, and who pursues her own comfort or advantage, in blamable disregard of or at the expense of others. It is grotesque to apply this word to victims of the Nazis or to the victims of the Argentine terror in the 1980s whose final desires and hopes were directed only to their own bare survival. Charging those who with trepidation and alarm point to what they call human rights violations against themselves or others with being selfish, socially dangerous persons, and citing their pliant conforming fellow citizens as moral exemplars, selflessly devoted to community values, is a transparent moral perversion. It is good that we have heard the last of it from the evil Nazis. Now it would be welcome if we could stop hearing similar perversities from respectable, well-intentioned intellectuals.

THE MORAL IMPOVERISHMENT THESIS

I turn now to the second group of those who doubt the importance that moral rights have or would have if there were any. These are philosophers

---

[2] Marie Vassilichev, *Berlin Diaries* (New York: Alfred A. Knopf, 1987), p. 78. I am indebted to Ruth Marcus for this reference.

who deny the case that others have made for the value of moral rights without going quite so far as to assert their actual disvalue. The proposition these philosophers deny is one I have defended, which we can call "the moral impoverishment thesis." I borrow this term from Richard Wasserstrom, who as a Justice Department attorney was a leader in the movement to implement the Civil Rights Acts of the 1960s in the Southern states. Wasserstrom found that there were some older blacks who had adapted so well to their assigned role under the old system as second-class citizens that they were wary of the equal status conferred on them by their newly declared constitutional rights. He states that "To observe what happens to any person who is required to adopt habits of obsequiousness, [and] deferential behavior in order to minimize the likelihood of physical abuse, arbitrary treatment, or economic destitution is to see graphically how important human rights are and what their denial can mean."[3] If this is what tends to happen to people when they have no legal rights and lack a belief or even a conception of their own moral rights, what would the consequences on human character be generally of a normative system that assigned no rights to anyone even though it did impose duties on people of a more privileged class to treat their inferiors decently? Wasserstrom replies that "Such a system would be a morally impoverished one. It would prevent persons from asserting those kinds of claims . . . which a system of rights makes possible."[4]

In my 1970 article "The Nature and Value of Rights,"[5] I tried to provide further content and support to Wasserstrom's moral impoverishment thesis. A good part of the argument is empirical; people who must live as

---

[3] Richard Wasserstrom, "Rights, Human Rights, and Racial Discrimination," *Journal of Philosophy* 61 (1964): 636. For an illustration of the sort of thing Wasserstrom may have meant, consider this World War I example from "Billie Dyer," by William Maxwell, in the *New Yorker*, May 15, 1989, p. 44:

> Camp Funston, in Kansas. It was the headquarters of the 92nd Division, which was made up exclusively of Negro troops—the Army was not integrated until thirty one years later by executive order of Harry Truman.
>
> At Camp Funston, a bulletin was read to all the soldiers of the 92nd Division: "The Division Commander has repeatedly urged that all colored members of his commands, and especially the officers and noncommissioned officers, should refrain from going where their presence will be resented. In spite of this injunction, one of the Sergeants of the Medical Department has recently . . . entered a theatre, as he undoubtedly had a legal right to do, and precipitated trouble by making it possible to allege race discrimination in the seat he was given. . . . Don't go where your presence is not desired."
>
> Is it possible for a white reader to imagine what it would be like for a black soldier to read this bulletin and *not* seethe with moral indignation? Is it possible that a black soldier could accept the claim that his rights end where the desires of others for his nonpresence, no matter how arbitrary or ill-founded, begin? To imagine such a person is to appreciate what Wasserstrom means by "moral impoverishment."

[4] Ibid.

[5] Joel Feinberg, "The Nature and Value of Rights," *Journal of Value Inquiry* 4 (1970).

slaves tend to become servile simply as a survival mechanism. The situation of rightless dependence on more powerful persons naturally breeds a servile character, imprinted with fear and characterized by obsequious flattery, flaunted obedience, submissive cringing, fawning, and meanness. The servile person is also likely to have a clever manipulative side; he turns his false humility off when he is with his own kind and will bully the less powerful. As C. S. Lewis put it, he is "alternately fawning and insolent."[6]

People who are confident of their own rights are less likely to develop servile characters. They are not forced to secure their needs by begging "favors" from masters who have no relational duties to them, on the one hand, or by stealing and cheating, or resorting to plain force on the other. To say they have moral rights is to say that morally they are in a position to *claim* what they want as their due, what they have coming, and what the other party is under a moral obligation *to them* (not merely regarding them) to provide. A claim is different from a mere demand like that of a gunman for your money or your life, and it is different from begging, imploring, or beseeching, for to claim is to invoke the authority of governing rules or principles by producing reasons certified by those principles as relevantly applicable and binding. The claimant has control over the claimee's duty that he activates by making the claim, but which he has the power to alter or even suspend as he wishes, just as he has the physical power to turn on or off a light by pushing a switch one way or the other. The right-holder has more dignity than a mere beggar who is not in a position to make claim to what he wants, or a highwayman who, in abandoning the moral posture altogether, forfeits, in large part, any claim he might have had to moral respect.

To respect a person is tantamount to respecting her rights, that is, to thinking of her as a prospective maker of weighty moral claims. If a person is thought to have no rights, not even the basic moral rights, she is by the same token thought to be unworthy of respect, and if she thinks of herself that way she can only cringe and beg, or cheat and steal, and will lack the virtue of self-respect, not to mention respect for others. No wonder that a whole human population without rights, lacking even the concept of a right, would be "morally impoverished."

A great many critics register their disagreement with this analysis. Most of them counter that a community that acknowledges moral duties of fairness and benevolence can dispense with rights. William Nelson, following Jan Narveson,[7] asks "Why does Feinberg think that people who do not regard themselves as possessors of rights but [do] regard others as having obligations and duties towards [regarding] them, will be unable to de-

---

[6] C. S. Lewis, *Studies in Words* (Cambridge: Cambridge University Press, 1961), p. 14.
[7] Jan Narveson, "Commentary on Feinberg," *Journal of Value Inquiry* 4 (1970).

mand that those others perform their duties and discharge their obligations? Why should they not be able to stand up, look . . . [the] other in the eye and complain just as loudly as anyone else when someone behaves toward them in a way which he was obligated not to behave?"[8]

Nelson anticipates my reply when on a later page he writes that "when Feinberg suggests that in morals someone who lacks rights is prevented from claiming or complaining he surely does not mean that he opens his mouth but no sound comes out." Exactly so. If *A* has a duty to treat his slave *B* decently, but *B* being a mere slave, has no right that *A* do his duty (or any other right against *A* for that matter), and *A* proceeds to violate his own duty by treating *B* cruelly, then *B* will be "able to demand" that *A* do his duty in the sense that if he opens his mouth to utter words of complaint, the intended sounds *will* come out, or if he merely speaks to remind his master, with the utmost tact, of his duties, (say) under a code of noblesse oblige, those sounds *will* come out. If he chooses incredibly to look his master in the eye and "complain loudly" that the master is neglecting his own duty, even those sounds will come out. But it is not a question of *B*'s physical abilities, his being able to utter certain sounds; it is a question not of what he *can* do, but of what he *may* do under the accepted rules that govern his conduct and *A*'s, and under those rules any claim he may make will be infirm; he will have no legal or moral power to affect his master's duties or his own; he will be able to complain but not entitled to complain; he will in a sense "have a complaint" but he will not have a genuine moral grievance; since he had no rights against *A*, he could not be wronged by *A*'s conduct but only hurt or harmed by it. If he tries to voice a grievance anyway, he is vulnerable—morally vulnerable—to *A*'s cogent reply: "What business is it of yours whether or not *I* perform *my* noble duties? The rules that govern our relations do not make me answerable to you." That reply does not exactly express respect for *B*, and under the rules, *B* is not worthy of respect since he has no rights. So adding to *B*'s moral repertoire a moral claim-right correlative with *A*'s moral duty to him, does make a moral difference.

Rights as Warrants of Appropriateness

A strategic digression. Philosophers have given thorough attention to moral rights to act, omit, possess, or be something or other, but they have neglected the widespread use of rights-idioms applied to states of mind like belief, feeling, attitude, and emotion. That surprising omission may be the consequence of taking legal models as the sole guides to the interpretation of rights-talk, for legal models like that of Hohfeld simply do not fit "the

---

[8] William Nelson, "On the Alleged Importance of Moral Rights," *Ratio* (1976): 150.

right to be certain," "the right to believe in the absence of evidence," "the right to feel proud," or (to come back to our primary concerns) "the right to feel aggrieved" or "morally indignant." The concept of a right in these contexts is to serve as a warrant of appropriateness. This kind of usage is sufficiently widespread to be standard and fixed, and cannot be dismissed as merely idiosyncratic, voguish, or slang. It is especially interesting in that it does not even superficially appear to rest on legal analogies. So the analysis of such terms will have to rely upon such words as "fitting," "suitable," and "appropriate," drawn from the nonlegal-like part of our moral vocabularies. Moreover, as we have seen, the account we have sketched of what it is to have a standard moral right to do, omit, possess, or be X, includes as one of *its* elements, a right in certain circumstances to feel indignant or aggrieved, which in turn, will have to be analyzed in terms drawn from the nonlegal-like sector of morality—from terms like "fitting," "seemly," and "appropriate." Two examples might be helpful here. The first is the old jazz lyric, "I've got a right to sing the blues." The second is the common situation in which one person gives expression to her fatigue at the end of a busy day, and the other replies reassuringly, "You've got a right to be tired."

What does it mean to say, "I've got a right to sing the blues"? It means that I am depressed, but more than that, I am understandably depressed, naturally depressed, depressed for just cause and good reason. I am not clinically depressed, or depressed for insufficient reason, or from illusory and neurotic causes. Objectively depressing things have happened to me. Even if I am not in fact depressed, I have an objective and natural warrant for depression. (My children have died; my wife has left me; I have lost my job.) It is only appropriate that I be depressed. I've got a *right* to sing the blues.

Much the same analysis applies to "You've got a right to feel tired." You have put in a long hard day, and fatigue is the natural consequence of that. It is not the weariness of ennui you feel; not a bodily expression of torpor or lassitude, but honest, well earned tiredness. ("Earned" in that usage is deviate or ironic. Benefits are the sorts of things that are earned. Here perhaps what are earned are "bragging rights": "What a lot of labor I expended today.") In any event, fatigue in this case is nothing mysterious, unnatural, inexplicable (in a normal way), or neurotic. And certainly the concept of irrational does not apply at all. Do not worry; your fatigue is appropriate. Its explanation gives warrant of that appropriateness. You've got a *right* to be tired.

Returning to the jazz lyric title, how would we analyze it if we understood it on a Hohfeldian legal model? Perhaps the jazz title refers to a claim-right, in which case it asserts that I am at liberty to be depressed if I choose to be (which sounds a little paradoxical already) *and* I am in a position to make claim to your noninterference, a claim that grounds your duty not to interfere. That is, you and all others have a duty to leave me alone in my depression. The analysis of what is meant, however, seems to undermine its truth, because it is not plausible to say that you violate my right by trying subtly to cheer me up and hurry my mending when my depression is understandable. Second, suppose the affirmed right is a mere bilateral liberty, and what the lyric says, therefore, is: I have no duty not to feel depressed just as I have no duty to be depressed. I can be either as I wish, or as I feel about it. Maybe there are "duties of reason," in this instance "a duty, if I am to be rational, to be depressed" (or, as the case may be, undepressed). But rationality does not appear to be the critical element here. The statement in the lyric title is not about what I am required or not required to do if I am to be rational, so much as about whether my feelings, which are not subject to my firm control in any event, are in a larger sense, appropriate in the circumstances. The third possibility is that the lyric claims a Hohfeldian power, in which case if the lyric speaks truly, it is possible for me to create a duty in you not to "interfere" with my feeling, or perhaps better, that you not make adverse critical judgments, voiced or not, about my feeling, for example, about its "irrationality" or "inappropriateness." Notice also that on this interpretation I also have the moral power to alter, weaken, or cancel your duty altogether, so that you become free after all to judge me adversely (as having irrational or inappropriate emotions). This is surely nonsense. Finally, the statement in the song title might claim an immunity, in which case I, the speaker, say to you that in respect to my blue mood, you have no power to alter my liberties, claim-rights, powers, or other immunities by anything you can do. This is more plausible, although a bit artificial.

Perhaps in the right to be tired example, the most fitting Hohfeldian gloss would be in terms of immunity. Your long labor gives you rightful immunity from certain kinds of criticism. It cannot be said of you that you are a weakling, or a lazy goof-off, or that you are feigning exhaustion to get out of doing the dishes. If you have a right to be tired, then none of these adverse judgments can be true or at least properly made. But this is not exactly like a Hohfeldian immunity. What is the correlative disability? What moral powers do others lack as a consequence of your immunity? There is no reference here to powers others do not have to change your moral position or relations. The "power" whose absence is affirmed is only the "power" (ability) to assert adverse critical judgments of a certain class and assert them properly or truly. But that is a big departure from a Hohfeldian power and a very weak analogy to it. The other Hohfeldian elements do even worse. Is your right to be tired a liberty? If so it means that you have no duty not to be tired, as well as no duty to be tired.[9] As if you

---

[9] There may be a related use, however. You are a soldier on guard duty, whose duty is to be wide awake and alert. But you have "a right to be fatigued," and fatigue makes alertness

had any choice in the matter! Is your right to be tired a claim-right? If so, I and others have a duty subject to your power—a duty to do what? To not interfere with your fatigue? To give or to withhold a cup of coffee? To offer a bed for the night? None of this coheres very well with what we understand by "a right to be tired," which, unlike typical moral and legal rights, does not affect the moral positions of others at all.

It does appear then that "appropriateness-rights" (as we can call them) are a quite distinct species of right, irreducible to rights in any of the Hohfeldian categories that classify ordinary moral and legal rights so well. What makes them relevant to the present discussion is the possibility, developed in the next section, that an appropriateness-right lies at the heart of our tacit criteria for determining whether a wrongdoer's misbehavior has violated another party's rights (in the more familiar legal-like sense). If the second party now has a right to feel aggrieved or indignant, in our estimation (or if another party has a "right" to have those feelings vicariously in his behalf), that is a sign that we believe that the misbehavior of the wrongdoer was more than just wrongful; rather we believe, on the basis of this test, that it specifically wronged the other party, who now can be considered its victim in the sense that requires not only harmed interests but violated rights.

In one way at least we can welcome the requirement that an appropriateness-right be involved in this way, for it obviates the danger of falling into an infinite regress of rights. It is often said that if one party's right is violated by a second party, then the first party is "entitled to complain." If this moral entitlement itself is understood as a moral right, how do we know when *it* is violated? The answer might seem to be that we apply the same test that we used in the case of the original right. If a party's right to complain has been violated then (we can be tempted to say) he has a new right to complain about the violation of his other right to complain, which in turn, had as its target the violation of the original right. In this way, it is possible to generate an infinite regress whose effect on our original analysis would be less than benign. But if the "right to complain" is a right in the quite different sense of "appropriate fit" between a wrongful action and a responsive feeling or attitude, the regress can be avoided. No sense can be given to violating a right to complain if that right consists merely in the appropriateness of an aggrieved response to another party's wrongdoing.

The philosopher who has made the most of the idea of being entitled to complain is Daniel Lyons,[10] some of whose insights are well worth borrowing. When we wish to distinguish between the party (*B*) who has a

---

impossible. That it was not inappropriate for you to be fatigued in the circumstances gives you an excuse for the inefficient performance of your duties.

[10] Daniel Lyons, " 'Entitled to Complain,' "*Analysis* (April 1966): 119–22.

legal right violated by another's (A's) behavior and the party (C) whose injury is only incidental—or to put the distinction in an equivalent way, between the party *to whom A*, had a duty, (B), and the party merely *regarding whom A* had that duty (C)—then we sometimes give "operational point" to the distinction by asking who has the right to sue, to enjoin, or to prosecute. The moral parallel to these legal operations, Lyons suggests, is some "special right to complain and feel aggrieved." Lyons is quite convincing in this contention, although I think he fails to appreciate how special this "special right" is, being not a moral analogue to a legal right, but a right in a totally different sense, consisting simply of the relation of appropriateness. Lyons' examples well illustrate his point.

> Consider this exchange: "You have no right to complain about welfare-cheats [said to a person who claims that his own rights have been violated by the cheaters]; you're on a pension yourself; you pay no taxes." "Nevertheless, since every welfare cheat discourages the community from giving legitimate pensioners their full due, my rights are involved—I do have a right to complain." Or this [example]: "Mother *you* have no right to be angry with Jim because he called off our wedding; I'm the one who was jilted." "Yes, but I spent a thousand dollars on the preparations."[11]

There are many examples, of course, as Lyons himself points out, of people feeling personally aggrieved and indignant, even when they are not entitled to those feelings: "For instance, the temperance people Mill mentions in *On Liberty* took other people's simple drunkenness as an offense directly against themselves. They undoubtedly felt this special indignation, but Mill would deny that they were entitled to it."[12] The disagreement between Mill and his opponents in the temperance movement was a substantive one, not merely a theoretical quarrel about the analysis of the concept of a right. Each side understood that aggrieved feelings are part of the test of whether a person genuinely believes that a right has been violated, but they disagreed in the case that divided them about whether such feelings were appropriate, a matter to be settled, if at all, by extensive moral argument.

The word "complain" that Lyons, following common usage, employs so frequently, could trap the unwary into the very regress from which appropriateness-rights were meant to protect them. Complaining appears to be a kind of linguistic *doing*, so that one can do that thing in response to a violation of one's right, unless prevented from doing so, in which case one can try to complain (act) in response to *that* constraint, and if further restrained, complain again, ad infinitum. But Lyons is not unwary. He dis-

[11] Ibid., p. 120.
[12] Ibid.

tinguishes complaining from protesting, interpreting the former as one kind of species of the latter, so what he can define complaining as "protesting, accompanied by a certain special kind or degree of aggrieved indignation." The "special kind" of feeling is the important thing, the complaining is merely giving it voice. One can have an appropriateness-right to the feeling, while either having or lacking the legal-like moral right to its expression at a given time or place, or in a given manner.

Despite the importance of the idea of an appropriateness-right there are some clear limits to its utility. It will be of little or no assistance in settling the question of whether a given wrongful action violated a right of some particular person or whether a duty had been owed to that person in the first place by the wrongdoer. After all, the feelings of grievance may themselves be inappropriate, in which case one has no "right" to them, and the reasons that settle the question of the appropriateness of the grievance feelings will be precisely those that will settle the substantive moral questions. *B* was a right-holder wronged by *A*'s conduct if and only if his feelings of grievance were warranted. Of that we can be sure. But the only way to show that the grievance was warranted is to show that *B* was a right-holder against *A*, and that *A* violated his right, a question more amenable to standard moral argument. So the point about appropriateness-rights offers no quick short-cut to a resolution of substantive disagreement, but only a circular trip around the problem.

Second, we should not look for more precision than is possible in the application of the grievance-feeling test even to the problem it is better suited to solve: that of determining whether a given person *believes* that he (or another) has had his rights violated. As an emotion, a sense of grievance (or indignation) is subject to different degrees of intensity, just as the moral grievance itself is subject to different degrees of seriousness, or moral gravity. But the emotional intensity is no reliable gauge for determining the degree of moral gravity, being itself the product of many factors in addition to moral judgment—irascibility, vulnerability, emotional volatility, bias, self-preference, and so on. If elements of that sort play too large a role in the production of grievance-feelings, those feelings may be, at least to some degree, mere animal anger, contempt, or hatred self-deceptively masquerading as moral indignation. We would be better advised to rest with the cautious position that some minimal threshold of grievance-feeling must be met if we are to ascribe to the aggrieved party any belief at all that his rights have been violated. It does not follow from this that the moral importance of the right believed to be violated is directly proportional to the intensity of the aggrieved party's anger.

Closely related to this point is the fact that our feelings of indignation are targeted at the persons we believe to have wronged us, not simply at their actions, so that the intensity of the feeling will vary more with such factors as our perception of the other party's motivation and intention, than with our appraisal of the importance of the right violated. Many of us will have little or no anger at all, raw or moralized, at the person who violates our rights inadvertently through clumsiness or absent-mindedness. "You should have watched what you were doing" may be the strongest moral denunciation we can muster, and even then we may prefer to say, "Forget it pal; it could have happened to anyone. Just pay for the repair job (or medical bill) and we can forget all about it." But if that is followed by an expressed unwillingness to pay compensation, indignation is sure to flower, and it will extend back to the original negligence (initially forgiven) as well as to the subsequent refusal to compensate. Then there will be no doubt that the victim believes he has been wronged.

There is one final set of complications in the idea of an appropriateness-right. Radical moralists and philosophers sometimes argue that some feelings or attitudes toward others are, in their very nature, never appropriate. It is understandable and natural perhaps (a philosopher might argue) that one experience envy at the good fortune (especially the undeserved good fortune) of another person, but envy is so corrosive of character, so unseemly in a person of moral dignity, that it is always inappropriate. So also, Nietzsche in a wonderfully subtle way has argued that pity is always inappropriate,[13] and Clarence Darrow has reached a similar judgment about vindictive anger.[14] I would not be surprised to learn that some radical moralist or other has in the same sweeping fashion denied the appropriateness of a sense of grievance and moral indignation at the mistreatment of one person (oneself or a third party) by another. If a sense of grievance is one of the conditions that must be satisfied if we are correctly to attribute to a person the belief that his or another's rights have been violated, and our hypothetical moralist denies that we ever have an appropriateness-right to such a feeling, it follows that the moralist denies that anyone ever has his rights violated, not because all who could violate those rights are too honorable to do so, but because there are no rights to be violated in the first place. That conclusion is so startlingly unwelcome that we might even take it to be the *reductio ad absurdum* of the premises from which it follows, in which case having what one believes to be a complaint, being morally indignant, having a sense of grievance against another for what he did to oneself, or a vicarious grievance for what he did to a third party—none of this is necessary, after all, for one to believe that one has had a right violated.

The best way to cope with this difficulty, I suspect, is to separate, somewhat more sharply than I have done, the emotional or affective element in the feeling that one has a grievance from the basic moral conviction that

---

[13] Friedrich Nietzsche, *The Will to Power*, trans. Walter Kaufmann and R. J. Hollingdale (New York: Vintage Books, 1968), Book 4, sections 365–68.

[14] Clarence Darrow, *Resist Not Evil* (Montclair, N.J.: Patterson Smith, 1973). First published in 1902.

one has been wronged and is entitled to protest in a self-confident and righteous manner. Moral indignation is moralized anger, that is, the anger that is a natural response to injury accompanied by the disposition to respond in a similar way to any similar wrong—"out of principle." But one could press one's rights or affirm the rights of others righteously, indeed "indignantly," with only a trace of genuine emotion. One could "feel" that one has a complaint without feeling angry at all, and one could voice a grievance in a matter of fact business-like way, with hardly a trace of emotion in one's consciousness, as when one confidently claims the compensation believed to be one's due from a merely negligent wrongdoer against whom one has no animus. When such an "innocent" tortfeasor absent-mindedly delays his payment of compensation, one may smile inwardly at the person's eccentricity, but voice one's grievance against him firmly nonetheless. The grievance is simply the claim that the other has wronged one, normally but not necessarily accompanied by "appropriate" anger. The belief that one has a complaint, that it would be morally appropriate, if one chooses, to *make* that complaint, is so essential to the belief that one's right was violated, that it almost defines that belief. And that remains true even if one's grievance ("complaint") is unaccompanied by a trace of the anger or resentment that some sensitive moralists would judge unseemly. Explaining rights-infractions in terms of "having a complaint" and its near synonyms makes a very small theoretical advance, but as I hope to show below, locates a factor (obvious though it might be) of crucial psychological significance for the right-holder.

THE "PHENOMENOLOGICAL TEST"

The moral impoverishment thesis, apart from explaining how some rights are valuable, has a further advantage of a practical kind: it provides us with a test for distinguishing cases where one party has a right against another from cases in which he merely stands to gain from the performance of the other's duty or from the other's supererogatory act of beneficence toward him. Let us consider two kinds of cases in which that distinction is unclear and controversial. In both of these examples, it is agreed that A ought to have helped B, that it would have been a good thing and indeed the morally right thing for A to have done, and maybe even A's duty to have done, but the question then arises after A's failure to do it: did his failure to assist B violate B's rights? The first example is the problem of third party beneficiaries of promises made to second parties. In one clear and uncontroversial example, a life insurance company (Alpha) promises Baker that if Baker pays the agreed upon premium, then upon his death an enriched sum will be paid to Charley, his designated beneficiary. Charley may not even know of the existence of this agreement. Still when Baker dies, Alpha is under an obligation to Charley to pay him the agreed sum, and Charley has a correlative right against Alpha that puts him in a position validly to claim that amount from Alpha, even though Alpha's original promise was not made to Charley, the beneficiary, but to Baker, the policy holder and promisee. If Alpha, the company, refuses to pay Charley, the third-party beneficiary, then clearly it will be violating Charley's right, for the money is owed to Charley even though the promise was made to Baker.

In contrast, suppose Alpha promises Baker to do something which, as it turns out, will incidentally benefit some total stranger, Carlos, and Carlos learns of the deal and eagerly looks forward to, even acts in reliance upon, his expected lucky windfall. Alpha then breaks his promise to Baker, thus incidentally ruining Carlos's hope of profit. In that case, clearly Carlos, the would-be third-party beneficiary of Alpha's promise to Baker, has not had his own rights violated since he did not have a personal right in the first place that Alpha keep his promise to Baker.

I am not interested now in deriving the grounds for the distinction between the two kinds of cases, although that seems an easy enough thing to do in these clear instances. Instead, I wish to propose what I call "a phenomenological test" for determining whether or not a person who believes that a benefit to one party was wrongfully withheld by another party is committed by his other judgments and moral responses to the further judgment that the unhelped party suffered a violation of his rights. It is not sufficient to generate that belief in a person to point out that she *already* believes that the one party was wrong not to behave in a way that would have been helpful, that she ought to have so behaved, indeed even that she had a duty to behave in that way. We can believe all that and still deny that the unhelped party had a right violated by the wrongdoer. How does one tell, if one is confused about the concept of a right, whether one holds the further belief that a right was violated? I suggest, combining the analysis adumbrated in my earlier articles with the interpretation suggested in the preceding section, that one does in fact hold that further moral belief if and only if one also believes the following:

1. Charley* could have appropriately claimed in advance the assistance from Alpha as his own due (by saying upon the fulfillment of the agreed conditions, "You owe me as my due . . ."). Therefore, Charley can appropriately press his claim with greater moral dignity than by mere begging or bullying, imploring or intimidating.

2. Charley can voice a grievance against Alpha afterward (if the promise is broken) by saying to him appropriately, "You wronged me by violating your agreement with Baker."

3. At any time during the life of the agreement Charley can release Alpha from his duty if Charley pleases, that is, he has the legal or moral power to control Alpha's duties in that way.

* Of course "Carlos" or any other proper name would serve as well as "Charley."

4. It is for Charley's sake that Alpha has the duty to act in the agreed upon way and not merely for some extraneous reason unrelated to Charley.
5. Whether or not Baker does his duty is Charley's "business," his proper moral concern.

If you believe that all five of these statements are true of a given transaction, then and only then do you believe that the third-party beneficiary in that transaction had a right to the benefit in question. These five statements do not provide a full and useful criterion for deciding whether Charley had a right; indeed they presuppose that substantive moral questions have all been settled. Instead they constitute a test of whether an outside judge is already committed by his other judgments and moral responses to that belief. And the interesting thing about this test for our present purposes is that several of the elements in it, particularly being in a position to make claims and afterward to voice grievances, are the grounds of the greater dignity and self-respect that are associated with the role of right-holder.

The other example is that of the notorious bad samaritan. Unlike the more celebrated good Samaritan of the New Testament, the bad samaritan lets an injured person, a stranger to him, lie where he fell on the street after being beaten and robbed, even though getting assistance for the battered victim would have cost him little more than minor inconvenience. Most, but not all, commentators on this matter agree that morality imposes a duty on the "samaritan" even though the injured party is a stranger, to assist him if he can, but there is great disagreement over whether the battered stranger has a right against the samaritan to his help. If you agree with the duty judgment but are not sure whether you hold the further right-judgment or not, I suggest that something like the five-part test proposed above will tell you whether you have that belief or not. If this test is inconclusive, it follows that you have no definite belief at all on the matter, and should apply the appropriate substantive criteria, whatever they are, to the facts to help you make up your mind. But if the test tells decisively one way or the other, it follows that you already have a belief on the question, entailed by your other moral beliefs, and you were confused about that only because of uncertainty about the meaning of the expression "a right."

I have argued elsewhere that the test shows that most of us, whatever we may say, do in fact believe that the crime victim had a right to the stranger's help. Suppose, first of all, that you were a friend or relative of the battered victim, yourself lying there with no life-threatening injuries of your own but with a serious disablement, say two broken legs. You ask the samaritan's assistance for your unconscious friend whose very life is endangered. When the stranger hesitates, you are surely in a position, morally speaking, to make claim to his assistance for your friend. "You can't just leave him there to die!" you might say. Clearly you are not in such a position, morally speaking, that you can only beg or implore the stranger for help; rather you and the friend you represent are in moral control over the other's duties, a role that confers much greater dignity on you than a belief that your friend's life had no value worthy of commanding even a stranger's respect.

Second, we can ask after the fact whether the stranger's failure to offer help is any business of the one neglected, whether it would be appropriate for him and his loved ones to feel, not just animal anger, but moral indignation against the nonfeasant stranger, and whether they are in a position to voice a genuine moral grievance against the stranger for his neglect of his acknowledged duty. When we agree that passing strangers ought to offer assistance in cases like this, indeed that they must offer assistance, I submit that most of us also think that moral indignation on behalf of the recipient of the duty would be fitting if the stranger failed to do his duty. The alternative is just to give the stranger low moral grades, adding that his flaws are no business of the person he declined to aid, nothing that person is entitled to complain about. There are examples, to be sure, where this sort of response *is* fitting. If some person, Abel, is pompous, vain, silly, dull-witted, or unimaginative, what is that to Baker, who is a mere stranger, a passive observer? Baker can make these adverse judgments about Abel and avoid his company, but can he claim as a personal grievance about Abel that Abel has these failings? Clearly not, and that is a sign that he has no right that Abel be a better person in those respects. That is Abel's business and not his. But the parents (say) of the battered victim in the samaritan case will feel understandably and plausibly aggrieved, and we can share that indignation vicariously with them. We would not acknowledge that their child's right was infringed if we thought of the bad samaritan's neglected duty as something like a duty of noblesse oblige (i.e., a duty with no correlative right in the beneficiary). But clearly we cannot think of it that way; the persistent sense of personal grievance will not permit it.[15]

RIGHTS, LOVE AND COMMUNITY

Armed with this analysis, we can now return to a charge against moral rights that we considered earlier, that they are in their very nature a threat to worthwhile community. The simplest models of worthwhile community are marriages, families, friendships, and simple partnerships. Confining his attention to marriages and families, Robert Young writes that "It is

---

[15] The preceding five sentences are taken from my "The Moral and Legal Responsibility of the Bad Samaritan," *Criminal Justice Ethics* 3/1 (1984): 64.

frequently where there has been a breakdown in the caring or loving relationships that hold between people that appeals to rights are made. When
loving relations break down and the caring for another's interest which is
morally proper goes by the board, people fall back on the auxiliary apparatus of rights. This is often understandable, but is not morally desirable
since it does nothing to mend the ruptured relations."[16] I have three quick
replies to this. I can concede the subordinate role of reciprocal rights-
claims in loving relationships. But having a right does not require one to
raise hell every time one perceives an infraction on the part of another. It
only "puts one in a position," morally speaking, to make claims or complaints. One can exercise those liberties and powers as one sees fit, and a
loving party will see fit to speak softly and gently, to forgive quickly, and
so on.

Second, loving relationships do break down, alas, and probably more
often than not, and when this happens rights-possession is not merely valuable; it is indispensable if one is to protect one's interests and preserve one's
self-respect. Moreover, there is a real moral value in respecting the other
person as a genuine maker of moral claims, even—Kant might say "especially"—in the absence of affection. But most important, rights are more
than a "fall-back auxiliary apparatus," for they are as necessary to love as
affection itself is, even during the period when affection flourishes. Part of
what is involved in caring for a person is a concern that she have those
things that she just happens to have a right to anyway—consideration for
special sensibilities and handicaps, fairness in the distribution of burdens
and labors, freedom from arbitrary hurts and embarrassments, and so on.
The rest of what is involved in caring is a concern that the loved one have
more than that minimum she could claim as a matter of right—unexpected
delights, unique tenderness, gifts, favors, symbolic gestures. Love may, in
this way, demand more than respect for rights, but it cannot survive with
less.[17]

[16] Robert Young, "Dispensing with Moral Rights," *Political Theory* 6 (1978): 68. See also
an astute recent article by Jeremy Waldron of which I was unaware when I wrote the original
paper on which this chapter is based. See his "When Justice Replaces Affection: The Need
for Rights," *Harvard Journal of Law & Public Policy* 11/3 (1988). In this paper Waldron works
out a kind of compromise between Kant and Hegel on the role of rights in marriage. Hegel's
view is similar to that of Robert Young. Waldron paraphrases it thus: "To stand on one's
rights is to distance oneself from those to whom the claim is made, it is to announce, so to
speak, an opening of hostilities; and it is to acknowledge that other warmer bonds of kinship,
affection and intimacy can no longer hold. To do this in a context where adversarial hostility
is inappropriate is a serious moral failing. As Hegel put it in an Addition to *The Philosophy of
Right*: 'To have no interest except in one's formal right may be pure obstinacy, often a fitting
accompaniment of a cold heart and restricted sympathies. It is uncultured people who insist
most on their rights, while noble minds look on other aspects of the thing' " (p. 628).

[17] One way to define "love" that does justice to its honorific associations is as a relation

Young quotes with approval a passage from Simone Weil meant to show how poorly rights serve a genuine community of reciprocally caring individuals. The very notion of a right, Weil claims, "has a commercial flavor, essentially evocative of legal claims and arguments. Rights are always asserted in a tone of contention; and when this tone is adopted it must rely upon force in the background or it will be laughed at."[18] A twofold reply can be made to these bold assertions. In the first place, it seems false that rights are always asserted in a tone of contention.[19] Rights, in fact, can be asserted coolly, automatically, with dignity and calm, or with embarrassment, regret, or even apology. Indeed they can be asserted without uttering words at all, as when a person makes claim to his coat by presenting his coat check token to the coat room attendant.[20]

---

between persons characterized by mutual affection *and* moral respect, among other things. For a striking and persuasive example of how affection without respect falls short of love, see Henrik Ibsen's play, *A Doll's House*. The benighted husband, Torvald Helmer, has genuine affection, of a sort, toward his young wife Nora. He predictably beams when he beholds her pretty face. He is even "proud of her," as a parent might be of a child or an owner of an art object. He is constantly petting her, as one might pet a cat or dog. Indeed, his favorite forms of address are the names of "cute" little animals ("Is that my little lark twittering out there?" "Is my little squirrel bustling about?"). Its bland conventionality aside, Helmer's affection may well be genuine. After all, we can be genuinely affectionate with animals (another class of playthings) too. But Helmer lacks all respect for his little pet, not only in the sense of esteem but also in the sense of recognition of the other as a potential maker of moral claims against one and against others. When she does finally make a claim against him, it is as if a mechanical doll had suddenly spoken. He just cannot take her seriously as a claimant, being unable even to conceive of her in that role.

This interpretation, I think, goes one step beyond that of Waldron, who writes, "To go back to the marriage example, I will suggest that there is a need for an array of formal and legalistic rights and duties, *not to constitute the affective bond* [as Kant almost seems to say] but to provide each person with secure knowledge of what she can count on in the unhappy event that there turns out to be no other basis for her dealings with her erstwhile partner in the relationship" (Waldron, "Need for Rights," p. 629). I would treat respect as closely tied to the idea of moral rights, and those rights as valuable not only for fallback security, but, as the object of moral respect, an essential constituent—not of "the affective bond" necessarily (if that means simply "affection")—but of the full bond of love. (Other elements are no doubt necessary too, like simple liking, for example.)

[18] Simone Weil, *The Need for Roots* (London, 1952), p. 18. The words quoted here are apparently a paraphrase of Weil's own words, quoted by Young ("Dispensing with Moral Rights," p. 68) from their author, Mierlys Owens, in "The Notion of Human Rights: A Reconsideration," *American Philosophical Quarterly* 6 (1969): 244.

[19] Even Carl Wellman appears (perhaps through inadvertent overstatement) to make this mistake. He writes, for example: "Claiming is striking a blow in a struggle to prevail over one's opposition" (A Theory of Rights [Totowa, N.J.: Rowman & Allanheld, 1985], p. 209).

[20] Having held this view for over twenty years, although perhaps having given it insufficient emphasis, I was quite astonished to read in Jeremy Waldron's *Nonsense Upon Stilts* (p. 196) that my theory is that "self-respect and human dignity really depend upon being in a position to make strident, querulous, adversarial claims *against* other people . . . that my ful-

An especially interesting example comes from a recent syndicated news-paper column by Zeke Wigglesworth, defending the quality of food service on international air flights by citing the many difficulties the airlines must surmount in order to serve hot meals at all. After an enumeration of these difficulties, he adds another one: "Then there is always some clod who tries to go to the washroom while the meals are being served, creating a traffic jam and demanding loudly that the stews [stewards or stewardesses] get the trolley out of the way."[21] I have on occasion played the role of the "clod" myself, and it is very embarrassing. The clod either forgets to stop in the restroom before boarding the plane or is so rushed he has no oppor-tunity. By the time he feels the call of nature, it is too late; the luncheon trolley already fills the aisle and there is no room to squeeze by.

Fortunately, there is a well understood moral convention governing sit-uations of this kind. The clod has the right of way, given that his natural need can be presumed to be more pressing, and the stewardesses must back their cart out of the way, thus delaying the service. (This suggests a new interpretation of "natural rights.") Both the stewardesses and the clod un-derstand that he has the right to proceed and they have the duty, under the convention, to get out of his way. But the clod need not assert his right by "demanding loudly" that the trolley be removed. Right-possession is not a license for vulgarity. He can assert his right without speaking at all, except for an embarrassed mumbled "sorry" as he passes the stewardesses. His right-assertion in that case would consist in his signaling his intention clearly, and his confident goal-directed strides toward the barrier, with the demeanor of a person who knows the rules and proceeds without hesita-tion, and with as much dignity as he can muster. Claiming in these circum-stances is simply exercising a legal-like, conventional moral "power," as if one were thereby pushing a button that creates—or "lights up"—the other parties' duties. This *can* be done apologetically, regretfully yet firmly.

RIGHTS AND POWERS

Weil's other point, in the passage quoted by Young, is about the impotence of rights-claims, even when "asserted in a tone of contention," if they are made in the face of superior physical force and thus are incapable of being enforced. In replying to it, I return full circle to the topic with which this chapter begins. If Salman Rushdie had been captured by the Iranians and presented to the Ayatollah, he could on that occasion have contentiously asserted his right of free expression, and righteously demanded to be re-leased. The Ayatollah was not known to laugh easily, but Weil refers in her

---

fillment, my freedom and self-realization depend on my muscular and self-assertive capacity to place limits on yours."

[21] Zeke Wigglesworth, Knight-Ridder Newspapers, April 16, 1989.

quote to the laugh of derision not the laugh of amusement, and Rushdie's situation would not have been very dignified if he had been dragged off by burly guards to be imprisoned. The truth is that rights may be necessary for respect and dignity but, except perhaps in the case of genuine heroes, they may not be sufficient. It also helps to have the rights recognized by the other party or even backed up by some physical or military force.

Moral rights, then, do not help much, or not at all, in the face of machine guns manned by the lackeys of powerful immoralists or other unimpressed antagonists, even from the point of view of moral dignity. But before one dismisses moral rights for that reason, consider the alternatives. The dissident couple seized in their home by the Gestapo have at least three options. They can affirm their moral rights calmly and firmly, thus triggering derision and cruelty; or they can abandon moral language to make idly heroic demands, as if *they* had the monopoly of force in the situation; or they might prostrate themselves and beg for mercy. Surely, the hopeless assertion of right is not any *less* consistent with dignity than its alternatives, although all three are hopelessly doomed. My analysis of rights as claims, in any case, implies only that the right-holder by virtue of his right is in a moral position to make claims against others, not necessarily that he is in a physical or political position to make claims without having his face kicked in. For this so-called moral advantage to be a genuine advantage it is necessary that those to whom rights-claims are made have some capacity of moral recognition and at least some minimal moral responsiveness. It is no wonder that Gandhi maintained his impressive moral dignity even in the teeth of superior force from his enemies in British India. The Nazis would have allowed him no moral dignity at all.

It is interesting that one of the most impressive of the proposed techniques for retaining dignity in the face of tyrannical power does not employ the concept of a moral right at all. The Stoic moralist Epictetus makes no claim that he or anyone else has moral rights of any kind. The only thing of value to him is his unsoiled excellence of character, or "virtue." Virtue, in turn, consists in doing one's duty, or rather in trying one's best to do one's duty, since actually succeeding in doing one's duty is sometimes beyond one's power. One's subjective duty, however, which is to try one's best to do one's objective duty, is *always* within one's power. The next step is to value, and consequently to desire, nothing but one's own moral excellence, and since *that* virtue is always possible to achieve, one can never be harmed or disappointed. Thus he says in his chapter of the *Discourses* entitled "Of the Right Treatment of Tyrants":

> When the tyrant says to anyone, "I will chain your leg," he who chiefly values his leg cries out for pity; he who chiefly values his own moral purpose says "If you imagine it for your interest, chain it."

— "What! Do you not care?"

— "No, I do not care."

— "I will show you that I am master."

— "You? How should *you*? Zeus has set me free. What! Do you think he would suffer his own son to be enslaved? You are master of my carcass; take it."

— "So that when you come into my presence you pay no attention to me?"

— "No, I pay attention only to myself; or if you will have me recognize you also, I will do it, but only as if you were a pot."[22]

Epictetus is a writer with no conception of himself as a right-holder or maker of moral claims against others. What matters to him, and all that matters to him, is his duty, and since no one and no thing can ever prevent him from doing that duty, the virtue that consists in fidelity to duty is always within his grasp. No tyrant can deprive him of *that* by preventing him, for example, from dying bravely rather than cravenly or theatrically.

Without question, there is a kind of dignity in the Stoic slave's defiance of the tyrant, although if he soon becomes a bloody corpse, his dignity does not last long. And the dignity is surely different, qualitatively different, from that of the righteous resister who thinks of himself as dying in defense of his rights or the rights of other parties rather than in discharge of his duty. The Stoic resists in a spirit of genuine indifference to whether he succeeds or fails. The important thing is that *he* do *his* duty not that any other fancied good is achieved thereby. There is something disturbingly make-believe about his mental disposition. His duty is to play well the part assigned to him, while aware all along that it is only a "part," only an occasion for virtue, nothing more. There can be a pretended compassion but never real compassion, for that would imply that there can be something other than one's own virtue that is worth genuinely caring about. If a closely related person—a spouse, a child, or a friend—suffers severe pain, says Epictetus, "do not disdain to accommodate yourself to him, and if need be, to groan with him. Take heed, however, not to groan inwardly too."[23]

Moral duty conceived in the Stoic fashion, unlike moral rights, purports to be a comprehensive and self-sufficiently valuable thing. Rights are important only when backed by power, whereas Epictetan duty is important even without power, even without genuine goals of any other kind, without success in one's projects, without victory in one's conflicts, without compassion, without love. It is not likely that Simone Weil, a woman of genuine warmth and courage, would prefer the exclusively duty-devoted Stoic conception to that of the human rights partisans. To respect rights

---

[22] Epictetus, *Discourses*, book 1, chapter 19—"Of the Right Treatment of Tyrants."

[23] Epictetus, *Enchiridion* 16.

after all is to respect all the aims and goals and interests that rights defend. To give one's total devotion to playing well one's part in a play in a spirit of indifference to real-life outcomes, on the other hand, is to detach one's behavior from anything else worth caring about, in a spirit of unbecoming moral egotism. Weil disdains rights in part because, unbacked by power, they cause tyrants to laugh derisively. The best answer to the problem of the immoral tyrant is not to crawl into a self-insulating shell of selfish "virtue," giving up all desires and cares but one all-consuming concern for one's own invulnerable goodness, but rather to leash real power to one's moral rights.

Moral powers, so-called, without back-up physical power will be impotent against physical force unrestrained by moral responsiveness. But before leaving this depressing topic, we should look at the idea of a "moral power" a little more closely. Moral and legal powers are not just alternative techniques—like nuclear power, hydroelectric power, psychological power, persuasive power, and political power—for producing the same kinds of effect within the physical world. Rather they provide ways of producing their own distinctive types of effect within their own distinctive realm—effects on people's moral positions, their duties, liberties, claims, immunities, liabilities, and further moral powers—and these distinctive effects are produced, not by some other kind of natural power, on a par with electric power or military power, but by rule-defined offices and statuses, offers, acceptances, transfers, acts of consent, and so on. Between two parties who are in some way potential competitors, yet have not rejected the whole moral game in favor of physical force, rights-claims, more than any of their alternatives, dispose the parties toward reasonableness. Carl Wellman makes this point well: "Claiming is an appeal to . . . the grounds of one's rights, and thus an appeal to reasons rather than to mere force."[24] In the case of moral rights of the sort listed at the start of this chapter, appeal is not made literally to titles, chits, receipts, warranties, and so on—these are *legal* or legal-like reasons—but to moral reasons, in Wellman's words, "statements that imply some moral conclusion."[25]

It is an important source of the value of moral rights then that—speaking very generally—they dispose people with opposed interests to be reasonable rather than arrogant and truculent. The more widely spread the respect for the general practice of rights-claiming, the less likely (or at least the less quickly) people are to resort to physical force. That is part of the full case for the importance of rights. That case is not undermined by the truism that general reasonableness will not impress the unreasonable.

There is a lamentable tendency among social philosophers to conclude

[24] Carl Wellman, *A Theory of Rights* (Totowa, N.J.: Rowman & Allanheld, 1985), p. 210.
[25] Ibid., p. 170.

that if something is not "*the* good" then it cannot even be *a* good; that if something is not self-sufficiently good, as Epictetan "virtue" claims to be, then it cannot be in its own right intrinsically good; that if something is not all by itself sufficient for human well-being, then it cannot be a necessary element of, or even an important contributor to, that well-being. To cite a familiar example, liberty without minimal health or wealth or opportunity does its possessor no good, as is commonly and correctly observed. Therefore (the argument goes) political liberty, conceived "negatively" as an absence of state coercion, is a counterfeit good and an unworthy goal. That these inferences are non-sequiturs is too obvious a point to dwell upon. Similarly, we can concede to Robert Young and Simone Weil that rights to autonomy and privacy, to free expression, to freedom from physical assault and from verbal incivility, to due process, to equal treatment, to free association, to free religious practice, and so on, will not compensate one for the lack of affection and loving care, or the absence of physical safety, but that shows only that moral rights are not enough for a good life, not that they are unnecessary or undesirable. (Actually what it shows is that a lot of other things are necessary too.) And the insufficiency of rights-possession as a defense against ruthless totalitarian oppression is a feature that rights share with every good thing, including affection and loving care. (Perhaps the Stoics' total and exclusive devotion to duty-based "virtue" is an exception, but it comes—as Weil, I suspect, would be the first to acknowledge—at unacceptable cost to one's humanity.) In the end, every form of goodness can be said to presuppose the protection of political and ultimately physical power. But that is not even the slightest reason for devaluing rights.

Chapter Ten

IN DEFENSE OF MORAL RIGHTS: THEIR CONSTITUTIONAL RELEVANCE

IF BY THE TERM "the founding fathers" we mean that group of patriots that prominently included the signers of the Declaration of Independence, then there should be little doubt that the founding fathers, or anyway most of them, believed that there *are* moral rights and that many, at least, of those moral rights are incorporated into the Constitution whether explicitly mentioned there or not. Shortly after Jefferson's famous phrase about our being endowed by our Creator with the "unalienable rights" to life, liberty, and the pursuit of happiness, there occurs the critical passage—that it is also a self-evident truth that "to secure these rights, Governments are instituted among Men." This clearly implies, or so it seems to me, that the crucial rights in question are taken to exist prior to and independently of government enactment, and that they are therefore what were frequently called "natural rights" in the eighteenth century, or "moral rights" in the sense I have given to that expression in chapters 8–10. Now if the protection of these moral rights is the purpose for which we have a government in the first place, it would be very strange indeed if the recognition and endorsement of those rights were not part of the basic law of that government. The very point of having a government—of founding a political state—is to secure these rights. How then could they fail to be a part of the legal framework of the government the founders constructed for that purpose?

The Constitution does mention a number of specific rights, many of which could be construed plausibly as incorporated moral rights: the exclusive right of authors and inventors to their respective writings and discoveries (article 1, section 8); specific rights in the sense of immunities, for example, to the suspension of writs of *habeas corpus*, to bills of attainder, and *ex post facto* laws (article 1, section 9); the famous First Amendment rights to the free exercise of religion, free speech, free press, and freedom of assembly; the right not to have soldiers quartered in one's house without one's consent; the right against unreasonable searches and seizures; the right to just compensation for property taken by the state; the rights against double jeopardy, excessive bail, cruel and unusual punishments, and involuntary servitude except as criminal punishment; the right to vote regardless of race or sex; and the famous Fourteenth Amendment rights to due process and equal protection, to name only some.

A few of these rights are claims-rights conferring control over other parties' duties; most, however, are immunity-rights rendering legally void certain types of government action and legislation. Some are held against private parties, but most are held against the state. Some are relatively precise and specific; some are quite abstract requiring considerable interpretation; some contain terms of the kind often called "essentially contested concepts," like "unreasonable," "due," "just," "excessive," and "cruel," requiring the interpreting judge to provide the appropriate standards for the application of these moral terms. Some of the mentioned rights could without difficulty apply in a state of nature prior to the establishment of civil society, but most are specifically claims against governments that would have no use before governments even existed. They could still be construed as moral rights, however, but conditional ones, rights that would hold against any government that might ever eventuate. As conditionally formulated in that way they could exist and be known before there was any point in asserting them, and thus validating reasons for the rights would not include references to the enactments of any government actually in existence.

The rights to life, liberty, and the pursuit of happiness are not names of still other specific rights that are included in the Constitution. Rather, they are category labels for classes into which a large miscellany of specific rights can be placed.[1] To say that all persons have rights in these categories does not tell us much about what these rights are. Moreover, the category labels themselves were obviously selected in part for their rhetorical impact and are extremely vague. The right to liberty, for one, is an excellent example of this vagueness. Most of our legal rights to liberty, including some that could be construed as also genuine moral rights, are conferred on us by particular statutes and precedents, these being permitted by the Constitution but not clearly required by it. Our legal rights not to be abducted or falsely imprisoned are examples. Most of the liberties conferred on us by the Constitution are indirect liberties derived from the Constitution's "nullification in advance" of any criminal prohibitions or other coercive restrictions that are contrary to our moral rights. These advance nullifications or legislative disabilities often take the verbal form "Congress shall make no law."

Not only are the category labels vague; they also tend to be somewhat arbitrary in the sense that they provide no guidance to the classification of a given right that seems fittingly includable in more categories than one. Almost every right, for example, seems to be a right to the pursuit of hap-

---

[1] See my *Social Philosophy* (Englewood Cliffs, N.J.: Prentice-Hall, 1973), pp. 70–71.

piness. And many rights protected by constitutionally valid criminal statutes can be interpreted as rights to liberty, for example, the rights to be
free from assault, battery, rape, even murder. (After all, when one loses
one's life, one loses one's liberty too.) Similarly, the constitutional rights
imposing limits on what the government can validly do to a citizen (freedom of religion, freedom of speech, freedom from unreasonable searches,
and so on) are virtually all classifiable as rights to liberty.

The final shortcoming of the traditional categories is that they are not
only uninformative, vague, and somewhat arbitrary; they are also slipshod
and perhaps incomplete. The urge to conceptual tidiness makes us want to
classify some clearly identifiable species of the rights to the pursuit of happiness as rights to property, and since property rights are often in apparent
conflict with the personal liberties of others (where your property begins,
my liberty of movement ends), some constitutional rights could better be
understood as belonging to the property category than as members of the
liberty grouping.

The reason for my interest here in the traditional taxonomy of moral
rights is that a newly posited generic rights-category has in recent years
generated a furious controversy that is not without its philosophical aspects. I refer of course to the "right of privacy," endorsed by the Supreme
Court in the famous case of *Griswold* v. *Connecticut*[2] in 1965, and applied
as a label for a hitherto unnamed set of generic moral rights that were said
to be tacitly incorporated into the Constitution. These rights, although
given a new name, are actually like the other specific rights in the Constitution, the First Amendment rights, for example, that protect private liberties to behave in a certain way by imposing legislative disabilities against
the valid creation of legal duties *not* to behave in those ways.

What was at issue in *Griswold* was the validity of a Connecticut statue
prohibiting the use "by any person" of contraceptives, and permitting any
doctor who counsels their use to be prosecuted and punished as if he were
the principal offender. To those justices in the majority who declared the
statute constitutionally void, the right of married couples to use contraceptives is as clear an example as one can find of a moral right—the kind of
right that governments are instituted among men to secure. Most of the
minority, on the other hand, presumably agreed with Justice Stewart that
the statute was "an uncommonly silly law," but found silliness to be no
ground for unconstitutionality in the absence of an explicit constitutional
declaration of a right to use contraceptives or of a right of a moral general
kind that would imply a right to use contraceptives.

Justice Douglas maintained that several explicit guarantees in the Bill of
Rights do imply or presuppose privacy rights, and in any case, said Justice

---

[2] *Griswold* v. *Connecticut*, 381 U.S. 479 (1965).

Goldberg, the Ninth Amendment declares that "The enumeration in the Constitution of certain rights shall not be construed to deny or disparage others retained by the people." The Ninth Amendment leaves open the question of whether the unenumerated privacy rights are retained by the people in virtue of their prevailing conventional moral code, or whether the rights in question are among those natural rights that governments are instituted among men to secure. The latter interpretation, however, has the founding fathers' general philosophical orientation behind it, and to most of us who find it morally outrageous that the state should presume to tell couples what they may and may not do in the privacy of their marital bedrooms, the defect of the law is not mere "silliness," but an arrogant invasion of rights, whatever the past or currently prevalent conventional morality may say.

It is by now commonplace among commentators that the constitutional right of privacy has been misleadingly named. The Connecticut statute invalidated by the *Griswold* decision was not constitutionally infirm because it restricted privacy in the usual sense of the term (a liberty to enjoy one's solitude unwitnessed, unintruded upon, even unknown about in certain ways). For even if, as Justice Douglas suggested, the Connecticut legislature replaced the objectionable statute with one that did not forbid the *use* of contraceptives, but only their manufacture and sale, thus giving the police no warrant in Douglas's words, to "search the sacred precincts of marital bedrooms for telltale signs of the use of contraceptives," and thereby protecting privacy in the usual sense, there still would be a violation of a very stringent moral right. Couples would still be deprived of the opportunity to use contraceptives if they choose, and this would importantly infringe their moral autonomy, for it would diminish their capacity to decide for themselves in what would otherwise be a zone of discretion, that of choices related to marital sexual intimacies and reproductive decisions. As many have suggested, the moral-hence-constitutional right in question would be better named "the right to autonomy" than "the right of privacy." As such, it is a category of rights to liberty distinguished from other rights to liberty by the content of the choices it protects, such pivotally central life decisions as those concerning the sexual intimacies, the home, the family, marriage, motherhood, procreation, and childbearing.[3] The list is open-ended, and could include other basic life decisions, and even, through classificatory overlapping, freedom of religion. To repeat, which category we place the moral right in is a matter of no importance. What *is* significant is that privacy rights, so called, are as vital to those who treasure them, even, as the rights to free speech, due process, and free exercise of religion—which after all, are parallel in their structure, being rights to lib-

---

[3] Warren Burger, *Paris Adult Theatre, I* v. *Slaton*, 413 U.S. 49, 65 (1973).

erty conferred in the form of immunities to governmental restriction in other vitally important areas of life.

A large number of commentators have criticized the Supreme Court's privacy decisions on one ground or another, but there is one line of attack in particular that rests on a deep skepticism about the existence of moral rights and is therefore worth discussing here briefly. I refer to the theory of constitutional interpretation sometimes called "originalism," sometimes "interpretivism," sometimes "value free constitutionalism." Whichever the name used, this theory received its definitive statement in the works of John Ely[4] and Robert Bork,[5] and numbers among its more influential advocates Chief Justice William Rehnquist[6] and former attorney general Edwin Meese.[7] Justice Sutherland defined the doctrine forcefully in a 1934 case when he declared that "The whole aim of construction as applied to a provision of the Constitution is . . . to ascertain and give effect to the intent of its framers and the people who adopted it."[8]

How would an originalist have decided the *Griswold* case? He would first scrutinize the black letter text of the Constitution to see whether the original framers or amenders expressed any strictures about the use of contraceptives. Following that easy inquiry, he would peruse the text again for any explicit reference to a more abstract right of unregulated sexual intimacy or reproductive options. Again, finding nothing explicit in the text, he would seek out language in the document (particularly in its provisions of various liberties and immunities) that could be interpreted as expressing the authors' and ratifiers' intention to create a right of sexual privacy, that is, discretionary freedom or autonomy in sexual matters not affecting third parties. Here he would ask himself what specific applications they were known to have in mind, which applications from among those they did not have in mind they would have been prepared to accept, or what their larger purposes were in choosing the language they used. The inquiry to this point would have been entirely factual—historical, empirical, and value-neutral—and its results would be entirely negative. No right to privacy; no remedy against the arbitrary interference of a silly statute; no sex without the risk of either pregnancy or arrest. This mode of interpretation "assumes that the doctrinal content of the Constitution was completely determined

---

[4] See especially his *Democracy and Distrust* (Cambridge, Mass.: Harvard University Press, 1980).

[5] See especially his "Neutral Principles and Some First Amendment Problems," *Indiana Law Journal* 47/1 (1971): 1–35.

[6] William Rehnquist, "The Nature of a Living Constitution," *Texas Law Review* 54 (1976): 693.

[7] Edwin Meese, "Constructing the Constitution," *UC Davis Law Review* 19 (1985): 22.

[8] *Home Building & Loan Association* v. *Blaisdell*, 290 U.S. 398, 453 (1934) (Sutherland, J., dissenting).

when it was adopted and that constitutional doctrines can be identified by a value-free factual study of the text or [its] 'original intent.' "⁹ When legislative disabilities cannot be located by this method, then of course there is no ground for overturning the corresponding legislation; it must stand as originally enacted by "the people's representatives," who are empowered to create any kind of law, however silly, that does not contravene the immunities declared explicitly in the Constitution.

Can a Supreme Court justice simply declare that there is a moral right to personal autonomy (one sense of privacy) in the predominantly self-regarding realm, and absent a compelling public interest weighing against it, that abstract right to autonomy entails a more concrete right to free choice in sexual and reproductive matters? The originalist replies that to do so would be to project the judge's own personal "value preference" into the Constitution where it is not otherwise to be found, and the Constitution itself gives courts no valid power to do that. Ely, who is not quite as restrictive of the Court's powers as Bork, when "left with the choice, in the exercise of judicial review, between [what he calls] 'the judge's own values,' and the values of the legislature . . . chooses the legislature's."¹⁰

Moreover, there are no moral rights anyway, and that which masquerades as such are really just the subjective preferences or "value choices," as Bork likes to put it, of the judge. In Bork's usage, as Lyons points out,¹¹ a "value choice" is not a value *judgment*; rather it is as personal and arbitrary as a raw wish, and is incapable in its very nature of being rationally supported. It follows that a judge's use of his own value preferences in interpreting the Constitution is partisan and "unprincipled," and that when two judges disagree about which rights governments are instituted among men to secure, there is no rational way to settle the dispute, and one opinion is as good as the other. Bork's value skepticism is apparently unlimited. The conscientious judge, therefore, in Bork's view, is restricted to the facts. He may implement the "values" (themselves mere "preferences") which he finds as matter of fact in the Constitution or in the authenticated intentions of its framers. But implementing the value preferences of others is not the same unprincipled activity as making a value choice of one's own. When the judge therefore is faced with a conflict between those of her own moral judgments (and even those judgments that regard moral rights as mere "value preferences") which she is so satisfied with that she wants to read them back into the Constitution, and those equally arbitrary and rationally indefensible value choices of a legislature as indicated in its express statu-

---

⁹ David Lyons, "Constitutional Interpretation and Original Meaning," *Social Philosophy and Policy* 4/1 (1986): 77.

¹⁰ Linda R. Hirshman, "Brönte, Bloom, and Bork: An Essay on the Moral Education of Judges," *University of Pennsylvania Law Review* 137/1 (1988): 182.

¹¹ Lyons, "Constitutional Interpretation," p. 97.

tory language or manifest intentions, she *must* choose those of the legislature, even those of the Connecticut legislature of the 1880s, all of whose members are long since dead.

The appellate judge who, like Bork, is a decent person, would in her private capacity, presumably condemn Connecticut's interference in marital birth control, but bravely do her higher judicial duty, recognizing her own moral judgment to be, like all moral judgments, a mere subjective preference, unsupportable by reason. Any other path to a decision would be "unprincipled," because it would be to take sides, without constitutional warrant, in a social conflict between a minority pressing its alleged rights and a majority whose value preferences are expressed in a valid statute. The satisfaction of a preference Bork calls a "gratification" or a "pleasure," so the "unprincipled" judge, as Bork calls him,[12] who arrogates the power of taking sides, will be choosing between the gratification married couples would derive from having their wishes for protection (which they may call "their rights") granted, over the gratification of outsiders who disapprove of what the other group wants, and would therefore take pleasure at restrictions of their liberty. The judge's preference for either one of these competing gratifications would be rationally indefensible, hence arbitrary, since there is no objective ground for preferring one to the other.[13]

Lyons has an even more telling example: "Prior to the Fourteenth Amendment, Bork would presumably respond to a suit seeking invalidation of the law banning Jews and Catholics from certain professions [by reiterating that] 'Where the Constitution does not embody the moral . . . choice, the judge has no basis other than his own values upon which to set aside the community judgment embodied in the statute.' . . . Bork's express reason for a judicial policy of 'restraint' is that all opposing positions, *including the rejection of bigotry*, are rationally indefensible, so that lacking [explicit] constitutional warrant, a judicial decision favoring one would be 'unprincipled' *just because* any 'preference' for one side or the other *could not* be 'principled.' "[14] Making the point forcefully in his own language of "gratifications," Bork concludes: "There is no principled way to decide that one man's gratifications are more deserving of respect that another's or that one form of gratification is more worthy than another."[15] This seems to imply that in Lyons' example, meant to apply to the period before there was an "equal protection of the law" clause in the U.S. Constitution, a Catholic's gratification at being a physician is not more worthy than a legislative majority's gratification at keeping her in her place. (In calling such comparisons of conflicting "gratifications" arbitrary, Bork goes even fur-

---

[12] Bork, "Neutral Principles," p. 3.
[13] Lyons, "Constitutional Interpretation," p. 98.
[14] Ibid., p. 98.
[15] Bork, "Neutral Principles," p. 10.

ther than Bentham whose theories his views otherwise resemble, for Bentham, as a utilitarian, believed in the objectivity of moral judgments, and would have the judge support the more extensive, intense, and durable "gratifications" in cases of conflict.)

I propose now to argue against Bork's originalism and in favor of its alternative, the theory of moral rights in the Constitution. The first argument is almost too easy. Many must have thought of it before, so perhaps there is a standard rejoinder to it that I have not encountered. As a matter of history there is little doubt that Jefferson was speaking for the vast majority of his colleagues, including those who were to become drafters, ratifiers, and amenders of the Constitution, when he declared that there are moral rights in the possession of the people for the securing of which governments are instituted among them. It would be absurd to posit such rights as part of the raison d'être of the state and yet deny that the basic legal structure of the state incorporates those rights. Therefore, the founding fathers, or most of them, as a matter of historical fact, believed that moral rights, whose existence was prior to and independent of their own deliberations and enactments, were part and parcel of the charter of the government they were designing. But according to originalism, the "original intent" of the founders is for us the source of constitutional law. So it follows that originalism itself is committed to the presence in the Constitution of rights that have a source independent of the intentions of the original drafters. Put in another way, it was the intention of the original framers that their own words and intentions not be the single key to subsequent judicial interpretation. Originalism thus is hoist with its own petard.[16]

The second argument is an ancient embarrassment for a *complete* ethical skepticism. The complete relativist about moral judgments would have to avoid making moral judgments of his own, whether about himself or oth-

---

[16] Petard is a French word derived from the verb *peter*, to break wind, from the related word for the expulsion of intestinal gas. This is a meaning it had originally in its Greek or Latin forms. In the fifteenth and sixteenth centuries the French military adopted this word for a metal or wooden case containing an explosive used to break down a door or a gate, or breach a wall, a kind of small bombshell. Later on it became a slang term for "a firecracker that explodes with a loud report." To be hoist with one's own petard, through analogical extension, came to mean "injured by one's own devices against others," as when the explosive goes off prematurely and a kind of backfire blows the soldier away, or when one is refuted by the application to one's own case of his argument for refuting others.

So I suggested in the text that this first argument makes the originalist hoist with *his* own petard. The "petard" in question is his doctrine that only the framers' intentions should guide constitutional interpretation. But *that* "petard" gets turned back on the originalists themselves, by a showing that the framers' clear intention was that subsequent courts, in interpreting their original intentions in specific clauses, give decisive weight to any natural rights that may be involved.

ers, whether about rights or duties. If he allowed himself, as Bork does for example, to make judgments about the duties of judges, he would have to subject those judgments to the same withering analysis he uses in criticizing the moral judgments ascribing rights and duties to parties in the conflicts between individuals and governments: they are mere subjective preferences, rationally indefensible, arbitrary, and so on. In that case Bork's own moral judgment would no sooner giveth than his theory would taketh away.

One might evade this traditional argument against moral skepticism by restricting the doctrine to statements of moral rights, thus exempting moral duties. Many moral duties, however, are linked logically to other parties' rights, and in many of these cases it seems at least as plausible to explain the duty as the consequence of the right as vice versa. Moral rights, like their institutional and legal counterparts, typically confer on their possessor "powers" to control the duties of other people, switching them on or off, for example, to facilitate the choices or protect the interests of the right-holder. It would seem arbitrary to concede that the duties exist in these cases but then assert that their beneficiaries lack all control over them, and cannot appropriately express personal grievances when they are left undischarged—in short, that the duties are objective facts while their associated rights are mere arbitrary "preferences" of the speaker.

Another part of the originalist argument, common to Bork, Ely, and many others, seems to me to commit a very subtle non sequitur. All of these writers claim at a certain point in the argument that for a judge to make a moral judgment is one and the same thing as her asserting her "own values" or her "own opinion." Ely describes the option of the judge in judicial review, when the Constitution is silent or unclear, as a choice between the values of the legislature and the judge's own values.[17] Speaking of *Roe* v. *Wade*, he goes so far as to say that "judges . . . occasionally impose their *personal* values"[18]—not just their values but their private personal ones, or their private beliefs or "opinions" about what is moral. Bork writes scornfully that his academic critics propose "that judges enforce good values or," he quickly adds, "the values that seem to the professor good,"[19] as if the values that *seem* good to someone or other could not, in the very nature of the case, actually *be* good.

The subtle fallacy in these formulations consists in an equivocal slide from the interpretation of an expression as a trivial truism to the interpretation of that statement as asserting a serious substantive point that the

---

[17] See Hirshman, "Brönte, Bloom, and Bork."

[18] Ely, *Democracy and Distrust*, pp. 2–3.

[19] Robert Bork, "Tradition and Morality in Constitutional Law," The Francis Boyer Lectures on Public Policy (Washington, D.C.: American Enterprise Institute for Public Policy Research, 1985), pp. 8–9.

reader is antecedently likely to consider false. One begins by assuming that when one is asked to make a judgment, one is being asked to express one's *own* opinion (who else's?), or what amounts to the same thing, the truth as *he* sees it. When a person makes a reasonable judgment about a matter independent of his own will or impression, it is *his* opinion after all, not someone else's, that he expresses. That is the truism: When I make a judgment it is my judgment that I make. The subtle equivocation begins when one qualifies the truism with the belittling words "*merely* one's own opinion," or "*simply* one's own belief," or "*solely* one's own judgment," as if the tautology that expressions of one's opinion *are* expressions of one's own opinion, necessarily implies that one's opinion is something merely subjective, unrelated to any matter of fact independent of itself that may, in the best cases, lend it credibility.

The slide continues and becomes more egregious when one moves from the tautology that when I express my opinion it is of course *my* opinion that I express to the conclusion that in all cases my opinion must be an opinion of a very special kind, a private or "personal opinion" peculiar to me and unsupported by any general or impersonal reasons that make no reference to me personally. When I say, for example, that broccoli tastes good, I express a "merely" personal opinion; when I say that broccoli is rich in vitamin C, I make claim to public and impersonal evidence. Surely, it does not follow from the tautology that when I express an opinion it is my opinion that I express, that every opinion I ever express is an opinion of the personal kind. In fact, nothing whatever of a substantive and controversial nature can follow from a mere tautology.

The mistake I have been trying to describe is often committed even more blatantly by people attempting to prove psychological egoism—the doctrine that all human motivation is selfish. The steps are well known.[20] The egoist begins with a truistic premise that he presents as if it were a self-evident substantive truth, namely, that "Every voluntary action is prompted by a motive of the actor's own." That is the premise that is analogous to "Every opinion a person expresses is his own opinion." The reason why the premise in the argument for egoism is true is that if a person's motive or intention in acting were not his own but rather that of someone else in control over him, we would not call the action *his*—that is, voluntarily his—in the first place. But then the slippage begins, as one slides from the truism that since I always act on my own motives, I am always seeking something for myself, a controversial substantive claim that seems contrary to experience; and from that one slides to "Every voluntary act is prompted not merely by the actor's own motives (as the truism says)

---

[20] See my "Psychological Egoism," in *Reason and Responsibility*, 7th ed., ed. Joel Feinberg (Belmont, Calif.: Wadsworth, 1988), pp. 498–99.

but also by a motive of a very special kind, namely, a selfish one." We have gone a long way without logical warrant from the truism with which we began. We do the same thing in the other case when we move from "an opinion of mine" to "an opinion of mine of a very special kind, namely, a so-called personal one."

By means of this logically illicit device, we can relativize everything. We can tell a scientist to appeal in support of his hypothesis only to reasons of a certain kind, say mathematical reasons, and then complain after the fact that he did not really appeal to mathematical truths but only to what he believed were mathematical truths; he "merely" expressed *his* opinion about what is mathematically true, and a "personal" opinion at that. Hence even judgments of mathematics are merely personal, private, subjective, and arbitrary. Alternatively, we can instruct a Supreme Court judge to admit only reasons of type R, say originalist reasons of the favored Ely–Bork kind, and then after the judge accepts our recommendation, we can complain that she is not really using originalist reasons at all, but *rather*, what is necessarily different, *what seem to her* to be originalist reasons, therefore her own private personal reasons instead of the objective factual reasons we wanted. Nobody can win *that* game.

When Bork writes that "In a constitutional democracy, the moral content of the law must be given by the morality of the framer or the legislator, never by the morality of the judge," he wants us to assume with him that any moral judgment made by the judge can only be his own private personal morality—"the morality of the judge"—and not the impersonal objective morality it may claim to be. Moreover, Bork wants us to transfer the self-evident truth of the tautologous premise to the very dubious tendentious conclusion, as if we had been asleep throughout the transition from the one to the other.

My final criticism of originalist arguments are directed exclusively to Bork who, in his Francis Boyer Lectures on Public Policy, used an opportunity to refine and amplify some of the views he expressed in the main source of his judicial philosophy, his influential *Indiana Law Journal* article on "Neutral Principles." In his lecture on "Tradition and Morality in Constitutional Law," Bork turns to what has been called, since Patrick Devlin's famous lecture, the problem of the "legal enforcement of morality." There in his confrontation with Millian liberalism, it is Bork himself, of all people, who accuses his opponents of moral relativism! The liberal position declares illegitimate all criminal statutes forbidding acts contrary to the community's morality except such acts as also cause harm to people other than the actor. So, for example, statutes forbidding homosexual relations between adults in private, even where such conduct is contrary to the prevailing moral conventions, may not legitimately be prohibited. Bork complains that this liberal principle (often called "the harm principle"[21]) would indefensibly restrict what a community, or its majority, "are entitled to regard as harms," since they may prevent physical injuries and economic losses but not what they think of as "moral harms." This in turn, he protests, amounts to "the privatization of morality," and "require[s] the law of the community to practice moral relativism."[22]

Let me respond to this remarkable criticism by asking you to imagine two citizens, Abel and Baker, and their respective like-minded subcommunities. Abel and Baker differ in some of their moral judgments about what is *really* moral and immoral, and consequently in their styles of life as determined by these judgments. Abel represents the moral judgments of the majority of the larger community, Baker those of a peaceful minority. Neither Abel nor Baker in this hypothetical example is a moral skeptic. Both believe that there is such a thing as moral truth, though each believes that *he*, not the other, is in possession of that truth. The government is not morally skeptical either. It believes that Abel and the majority live according to true moral judgments, whereas Baker's corresponding opinions are false. But the government also believes that some moral disagreements are extremely difficult to resolve even though they are amenable to reason, and that reasonable parties are sometimes found on both sides. In the case at issue, both sides are peaceful, and neither is likely to cause harm to anyone simply by putting its moral convictions into practice. The wisest policy, the government concludes, is one of toleration and noninterference. Bork at this point objects that the tolerant policy amounts to "the practice of ethical relativism," even though no party whatever in the story is a relativist or a subjectivist or a skeptic!

There is in fact something very odd in Bork's phrase about the law of a community forcing it to practice ethical relativism. It has something of the ring to my ears of an uncle guilty of "practicing" nepotism with his nephew. But it is more analogous to a school of epistemologists "practicing" phenomenalsim or epistemic realism. These "ism" words are the names of theories that have no logical bearing on practice, but only on philosophical understanding. Bork takes political toleration to be a sign of the tolerator's commitment to a non-practice-able metaethical theory, as if there could be no other reason for toleration than ethical skepticism. A genuine moral conviction, he suggests, logically requires the person whose conviction it is to attempt to impose it forcefully on others.

Moreover, the liberal principle, Bork claims, shows the liberal's true contempt for liberty because, while it entitles individuals to their moral beliefs,

---

[21] See my *Harm to Others* (New York: Oxford Universtiy Press, 1984).
[22] Bork, "Tradition and Morality," p. 3.

it does not empower them "to express those moral beliefs in law."[23] The latter argument strikes me as exceedingly strange, soliciting our sympathies, as it does, for the majority for having *its* freedom of expression so brutally suppressed, as if mere "expression" were all that is involved when a prohibition backed by criminal punishment is put into a criminal code! According to the liberals who would so callously interfere with the majority's right to express itself by threatening the minority with imprisonment, Bork tells us, "moral relativism is a constitutional demand."[24] I think this is the only time I have every encountered in print the argument that failure to punish minority dissenters violates the majority's right of free expression (by making it impossible for them to condemn the dissenters in a uniquely forcible way, that is, by rendering their conduct or opinions into punishable crimes), and further that judges who protect dissenters by invoking their moral rights are transforming moral relativism into "a constitutional demand." Again Bork seems to take "moral relativism" and "political toleration" to be logically intertwined, as if it were a sufficient reason for repression that the repressed opinions are false, and there are no other possible reasons for tolerating unpopular opinions than that one opinion is as good (true) as another.

The Court opinion Bork criticizes in his lecture is about what I think is properly called "vulgarity," and only misleadingly called "immorality." He quotes from the opinion of Justice Harlan in *Cohen* v. *California*[25] the oft-quoted sentence "One man's vulgarity is another's lyric." That sentence in the majority opinion makes the liberal claim that "The Constitution leaves the matter of taste and style . . . largely to the individual." The Court thereby reduces the entire questions of unorthodox style, Bork complains, to a matter of private preference.[26] Can this be the same Bork who asserted sixteen years earlier that judgments of moral rights are indeed mere expressions of personal preference?

As a liberal, I also disagree with Bork on the question of state regulation of taste, style, and manners. It may thus seem that both of us are inconsistent, each of us implying that one realm of morality is a matter of mere personal preference and another realm of morality a matter of objective judgment properly enforceable by law. There is nothing wrong with distinguishing the two realms, as we both agree, but from the point of view of common sense, Bork does it in such a way as to turn the truth upside down, for his view appears to be that the immorality of vulgarity is a matter of objective moral judgment enforceable by the state, whereas some seriously harmful conduct is condemned only as a matter of private preference.

[23] Ibid.
[24] Ibid.
[25] *Cohen* v. *California*, 408 U.S. 15 (1971).
[26] Ibid., p. 4.

On the other hand, the moral rights theory that I have been expounding maintains that Gestapo-style early morning arrests without due process violate moral rights; that prohibitions of contraceptives violate moral rights; that preventing a competent adult couple who love one another from marrying because one of them is of the wrong race is a violation of moral rights; whereas vulgarity in dress and manner is *not* a violation of moral rights unless it should somehow be seriously harmful to vital human interests in the manner of the rights-violations mentioned above—which seems unlikely. In a nutshell, Bork seems to hold that issues of human rights are matters of taste about which there is no disputing; whereas obvious matters of taste and style, on the other hand, are as issues of human rights are normally thought to be, questions for objective judgment and legal enforcement. There will not be many converts, I suspect, to that antipodean moral outlook.

In conclusion to this and the previous two chapters, I should like to recommend that people have more respect for their own considered moral judgments. Legal powers to make raids and arrests as they pleased were conferred on Gestapo agents by constitutionally valid German statutes and decrees, so they were not contrary to enacted law. Nor were they contrary to the thoroughly cowed or enchanted public opinion behind the new Nazi "morality." Yet who can deny that they were morally wrong anyway? Moreover, they were wrong because of the unconscionable harms imposed on their victims for no acceptable moral reasons. Identifying with the victims, we can intuitively apprehend and appreciate the moral claims they had against their oppressors, which were of course totally ignored, and on behalf of the victims we can, without shame or embarrassment, voice genuine moral grievances and feel genuine moral indignation. These are among the chief criteria for the application of the word "rights." So it follows not only that the Nazi actions were morally wrong, but that they violated moral rights and that is *why* they were morally wrong. The moral rights in turn did not stem from legal enactment and were in fact unrecognized and unprotected in both the governing legal and moral codes. Holding independently then of the accepted conventional rules, the rights were moral rights, and since they were moral rights held equally by all of us they were human rights.

To deny these truths is to deny the appropriateness of moral indignation, a moralized emotion expressing outrage not only to our feelings of human sympathy, but more centrally to our sense of fairness, and our respect for autonomy. Much the same could be said about a state's prohibition of the use of contraceptives, of interracial marriage, or of unfettered international travel, although the harms done in these examples fall short of the Nazi example. In all these cases the restrained victim of arbitrary legislation will insist that what he does in the area in question is *his* business, not the state's, not the public's, not his neighbor's, and not the legislature's. Some claimed moral rights, of course, are controversial, and others even spurious, but that should not prevent us in these paradigmatic cases from acknowledging the rights being claimed. Anyone can distinguish a genuinely believed judgment ascribing moral rights from a mere expression of an arbitrary wish or preference. Those who express their wishes and preferences in the language of moral rights cheapen that language and spread skepticism harmfully and unnecessarily. But it is equally harmful to trivialize our authentic rights-claims by regarding them as mere wishes. To deny the distinction between the two in that way is to break faith with some of our deepest convictions and to be untrue to what we really believe.

Chapter Eleven

AN UNPROMISING APPROACH TO THE "RIGHT TO DIE"

Erring on the Safe Side

There are many standard situations in life in which authorities are expected to make decisions based on the merits of the individual cases they are evaluating. In most of these situations we expect the decision-makers rigorously to exclude consideration of any grounds other than the merits of the case before them. We are not accustomed, for example, to having referees at athletic contests declare that even though the victory in the 100-meter dash would be awarded to Angelo if the referee considered the case entirely on its merits, he proposes instead to appeal to other relevant criteria independent of the merits of the case, and judge "all things considered" that *Mario* has won the race. And it would be unusual candor at the very least for an employer to award an important position to Paolo while conceding that the case for appointing Gianna based strictly on her fittingness for the job has greater merit. Nevertheless, the deliberate overruling of strictly internal considerations for the sake of normally irrelevant external ones, is a common practice in many legal and moral arguments. The controversy over the legalization of voluntary euthanasia is a good example.

In his influential 1958 article[1] Yale Kamisar seems to concede that when judged entirely on their merits there are instances of mercy killings by doctors or others that have full moral justification. I think Kamisar would agree that in cases of the kind he has in mind, the patient has a moral right to end his life, or lacking the ability for self-remedy, to have it ended for him by those who are willing and in a better position to do so. Kamisar even gives us a general account of the qualifying characteristics of the mercy killings he has in mind: The patient must in fact be "(1) presently incurable, (2) beyond the aid of any respite which may come along in his life expectancy, suffering (3) intolerable and (4) unmitigable pain and of a (5) fixed and (6) rational desire to die."[2]

Nevertheless, Kamisar opposes the legalization of euthanasia, resolutely arguing against proposals to transform the moral right to die into a legal

---

[1] Yale Kamisar, "Euthanasia Legislation: Some Non-Religious Objections," in *Euthanasia and the Right to Death*, ed. A. B. Downing (London: Peter Owen, 1969).

[2] Ibid., p. 87.

right to die by giving it legal recognition and enforcement. The reasons for his opposition have nothing to do with the merits of the cases he considers, but with the dangerous social consequences of giving any acts of killing legal certification. It would be better, he claims, to leave the law of homicide unchanged, bring murder charges against the family members, friends, and doctors who violate it, and then leave the fate of the mercy killers in the hands of sympathetic prosecutors, judges, and juries who will either refuse to indict, or else grant acquittals, suspended sentences, or reprieves, out of their recognition of the moral innocence of the criminal act. In that way, the "law on the books" will continue to testify to the community's profound and universal respect for human life, and serve to deter those who would kill for any reason, while "the law in action" would enable the bolder mercy killers to go unpunished for the crimes they undoubtedly committed, although from the highest and purest motives.

What considerations are powerful enough to outweigh the merits of individual cases of morally justified euthanasia? Kamisar lists them for us: weighed against the moral quality of some individual cases considered solely on their merits are the inevitable occurrences of mistakes and abuses in *other* cases. In effect, then, what Kamisar tells the suffering patient whose moral right to die is beyond question is: "If we change the law to permit *your* worthy case, then we will be legalizing other less worthy cases—patients who have been misdiagnosed, patients who might otherwise recover, patients who do not really want to accelerate their deaths despite earlier death requests made hypothetically, patients who are being manipulated by family members who see their life savings dwindle as the medical costs rise, and other instances of 'mistake' and 'abuse.' " What the blanket prohibition of homicide tells the responsible patient whose moral right to die is undoubted is that *he* may not do something that would be harmless or beneficial on balance because *others* cannot be trusted to do the same thing without causing grievous harm (unnecessary death).

Much the same kind of argument, it might be noted, was made in support of a blanket prohibition of alcoholic beverages in the United States in the 1920s. It is not an implausible argument on its face. Compulsive consumers of alcoholic beverages cause an enormous amount of harm to themselves and others, including (among many other examples) over 50 percent of the fatalities in motor car accidents. Many millions of us, on the other hand, are unaddicted social drinkers who imbibe for occasional relaxation and pleasure, and never to excess. We are responsible in the way we drink wine (say) with dinner, and we might well insist on our moral right to drink as we please. But the very law that permits that innocent activity in our case permits the not-so-innocent drinking of others who are certain to cause widespread death, mutilation, and heartbreak. Is it really asking too much of us to forego our nightly highballs so that others might be prevented from wreaking their havoc on the highways and their destruction of families elsewhere? Perhaps it is an unfair sacrifice to force on us, the argument concludes, but on balance, more harm by far is prevented by a blanket prohibition than by blanket permission, and if error in this difficult calculation is inevitable, it is better that we err on the safe side.

If there is a crucial disanalogy between this argument for the prohibition of wine and spirits and the argument of Kamisar for the continued prohibition of voluntary euthanasia, it is that the alcohol example is addressed to persons like us who are reluctant to give up some innocent pleasures, whereas the euthanasia argument is addressed to those, like Matthew Donnelly and the parents of Nancy Beth Cruzan, who are bent on escaping intolerable pain, in Donnelly's case, or pointless psychological suffering in the Cruzan case, and who might well wonder what it is in their horrible circumstances that can be described as erring on "the safe side."

Matthew Donnelly's experiences in his final days were "sadly typical" of a class of cancer victims, and seem to match closely the sort of case Kamisar had in mind when with admirable candor, he conceded that some patients might have a moral right to die. As James Rachels describes it,

> Skin cancer had riddled [his] tortured body. . . . A physicist, he had done research for the past thirty years on the use of X-rays. He has lost part of his jaw, his upper lip, his nose, and his left hand. Growths had been removed from his right arm and two fingers from his right hand. He was left blind, slowly deteriorating, and in agony of body and soul. The pain was constant; at its worst, he could be seen lying in bed with teeth clenched and beads of perspiration standing out on his forehead. Nothing could be done except continued surgery and analgesia. The physicians estimated that he had about a year to live.[3]

The "law on the books" commanded Donnelly not merely to sacrifice some harmless pleasures so that less responsible persons might not abuse theirs, as in the alcoholic prohibition example. Rather, it commanded him to forego his moral claim to a release from a full year's intolerable suffering. The argument that would overturn the merits of the individual case in the euthanasia example is to that extent at least, much weaker than its counterpart in the alcohol prohibition example. We have more reason, I think, to ban drinking wine with dinner than we do for prohibiting euthanasia in cases like that of Matthew Donnelly.[4]

The urgency of Donnelly's pain was missing in the case of Nancy Beth Cruzan, who was permanently incapable of experiencing pain—or anything else, for that matter. For several years Cruzan lay, at state expense, in a Missouri state hospital. As a consequence of a car accident, she suffered

---

[3] James Rachels, *The End of Life* (Oxford: Oxford University Press, 1986), p. 32.

[4] Rachels (ibid.) writes that "Mr. Donnelly begged his brother to shoot him, and he did."

virtual destruction of her cerebral cortex, leaving her irreversibly in a "persistent vegetative state," without cognitive function, permanently comatose, forever without consciousness.[5] It is impossible for me to understand how from her point of view this condition could possibly be preferable to death. Indeed, it is impossible to understand how, from the perspective of the person involved, this condition is distinguishable from death itself. Common sense would maintain that Cruzan was dead from the time her coma became irreversible. Legally, however, this judgment of common sense had no bearing on Cruzan's status. Despite the fact that her "cerebral cortical atrophy [was] irreversible, permanent, progressive, and ongoing,"[6] the brain stem continued to function, permitting various motor reflexes, maintaining body temperature, heartbeat, and breathing. She was unable to swallow food or water, so her body was kept going by a surgically implanted gastrostomy feeding and hydrating tube. Her parents, after six years of constant visits to the bedside of their unconscious daughter's body, sought a court order directing withdrawal of the feeding and watering tube. The Supreme Court of Missouri declined to issue this order. The parents then appealed to the U.S. Supreme Court, and their case became something of a *cause célèbre* in 1990.

If we assume that Nancy Cruzan, when alive, preferred that her body not be kept alive if she were ever to be in such circumstances, then the merit of her parents' case is clear. All of the judges agreed that American constitutional law gives every competent adult the right to refuse medical treatment, and that the feeding and hydrating techniques that were keeping Nancy Cruzan's body alive did constitute medical treatment. The issues became cloudy only when the Court considered the factual question of what Nancy's preferences actually were or would have been as to the continuance of this medical treatment. What little evidence was available to the Court—the verbal testimony of a close teenage friend—suggested that Nancy had a deep aversion to her body being kept alive in a persistent vegetative state. Thus, if the standard of evidence was that which is normally used in noncriminal cases, namely, a "preponderance of the evidence," the Court should have decided that the available evidence of Nancy's *not* wanting continuance being greater than the evidence that she would have preferred continuance, her consent to the feeding-hydrating tube could not be inferred. In other words, we had no evidence that she wanted to be kept alive, but *some* evidence, weak though it was, that she

---

[5] Ten days after I gave the original lecture on which this chapter is based, new testimony about Cruzan's preferences was presented to a Missouri court, which then was able to assess the *new* evidence as "clear and compelling." The court then approved the request that the feeding apparatus be removed, and Cruzan died a few days later.

[6] *Nancy Beth Cruzan, by Her Parents and Co-Guardian, Lester L. Cruzan et ux, Petitioners* v. *Director, Missouri Department of Health*, 110 S.Ct. 2841 (1990).

would prefer death. But the U.S. Supreme Court, backing the Missouri Supreme Court, argued that a higher standard of evidence is required in cases where the state's "interest in the protection and preservation of human life" is brought into play. The situation in the Cruzan case, as the Supreme Court saw it, involved a conflict between the state's "interest in preserving human life" and Nancy Cruzan's constitutional right to have her preference for discontinuance of medical treatment in such circumstances honored.

The main problem, of course, was that there is only scanty evidence of what Nancy's preference actually was. So, given the state interest in preserving life (as we shall see, a very strange notion indeed as interpreted in this case), the state has the right to require especially convincing evidence of the preference for death. And so Missouri required not just a preponderance of the evidence, or a probability barely greater than half, but rather that "evidence of the incompetent's wishes as to the withdrawal of treatment be *proved by clear and convincing evidence*."[7] The main issue before the U.S. Supreme Court was whether the Missouri Supreme Court had a right to substitute this higher standard of evidence. The highest Court ruled that it did have that right.

What the Court did, in effect, was to go beyond the probable facts that constituted the merits of the Cruzan case to an external value judgment that would determine, from the outside as it were, what the facts of the case were. That value judgment is the same as that underlying Kamisar's argument in euthanasia cases involving conscious, suffering patients, namely, that the Court's (skewed) allocation of the risk of error in our inferences to a person's preference is justified because it is more important *not* to terminate life support for someone who would wish it continued than to honor the wishes of someone (like Matthew Donnelly) who would not wish it continued. Like Kamisar, the majority of the Supreme Court is determined that if it must err, it err on the "safe side." But the comparative value judgment that they bring in from the outside to give shape to the facts of the case distorts those facts and, as I shall argue, misrepresents the case's actual merits.

THE ARGUMENT FROM ABUSABLE DISCRETION: HOW EUTHANASIA IS DIFFERENT

Before returning to the subject of euthanasia, it will be useful to consider one of the patterns of argument in other contexts that purports, often quite plausibly, to justify deciding cases on grounds other than what we can call their "internal merits." Consider, for example, the argument from abusable discretion. Suppose a legislature must decide what kind of night-time traf-

---

[7] *Cruzan by Cruzan* v. *Harmon*, 760 S.W. 2d, 408 (Mo banc 1488) at 415 (1988).

fic signal, if any, to install at an intersection that has been the site of many nocturnal accidents. The least expensive solution would be to leave drivers free to decide whether lighting and traffic conditions require a complete stop, or only a slow-down and careful perusal of the traffic in both directions. The two rival proposals are that the ordinary three-color alternating stoplight continue to operate all night long and the counterproposal that from midnight until 6:00 in the morning the three-color alternating signal be converted into a yellow blinker, which is only a cautionary warning signal not requiring a stop. Imagine that studies of accident rates at similar intersections elsewhere show that there are twenty deaths a year at intersections that have all-night yellow blinkers, and only ten deaths at the intersections that have ordinary three-color alternations day and night. The argument for the all-night operation of the standard three-color light then is that it will probably cut in half the death rate from accidents at that corner. The argument on the other side is that 99 percent of the drivers can be trusted to exercise careful discretion at this and other intersections, especially at night when traffic is very sparse and there are no obstructions to vision. It is not fair to this vast majority, so the argument goes, to inconvenience them by requiring them to stop, in total indifference to the merits of their own cases, just in order to deprive the tiny minority of untrustworthy drivers of a discretion they might abuse.

The riddle of abusable discretion does not arise where it is practical to design a system of licensing that will in fact judge each case on its merits, as, for example, one that licenses only exceptionally vulnerable and clearly capable and trustworthy persons to carry handguns. But a system that awards to some drivers a special license to go through red lights when they believe it is safe to do so would indeed be excessively difficult to administer. And when such special licenses are impossible, a form of ethical argument is often heard that strikes some people as highly paradoxical. A statute requiring the all-night operation of a normal stoplight is indeed justified, a motorist might admit, simply because it will save two or three human lives a year. "But," the motorist might continue, "I am a skilled and responsible driver quite capable of deciding on my own when conditions at that intersection require a stop. So I will feel quite justified on bright moonlit nights when no cars can be seen for a kilometer in either direction, in cautiously proceeding through a red light." And what if a traffic policeman gives him a ticket? "He too will be quite justified in giving me a ticket for my fully justified infraction of a fully justified statute." Only the justification of the driver's disobedience refers to the internal merits of his case. For the two other justifications, one political and one legal, this driver's case is not judged on its intrinsic merits. The decision to enact the statute was based on statistical studies of the behavior of *other* drivers (facts "external" to *this* driver's own conduct and disposition), and the wording of a statute that makes no allowance for the "internal" characteristics of this driver's situation that give his behavior its own justification. So much for judging each case on its merits!

As argument of similar form was frequently used by moderate drinkers in defense of their violations of the 1920s' alcohol prohibition law, a law they often conceded to be supported by good reasons. The prohibitory law appeared to have a morally legitimate aim, namely, reduction of the great harms caused by drunkards. But for people who had enjoyed their moderate drinking habits for decades and *knew* that they could be trusted to drink wine for dinner, or a highball at a party, without harmful consequences to others, it was natural to proceed in violation of a law they thought legitimate (for others) and to do so with clear consciences. This created a "market of innocents" and a business incentive for gangsters to sell in that market, with all the violent crime that led to the discrediting and eventually to the downfall, of Prohibition.

A law that grants terminal patients, their loved ones, or their physicians the legal authority to terminate lives, thereby confers discretion on those parties to decide their cases on the merits. If the situation is analogous to that in the traffic signal example, there will be some rare cases in which that discretion is abused. But the analogy is highly tenuous. What would count as "abuse" in the euthanasia case? What would be analogous to drunken or reckless driving in the other case? Again there is a danger of begging a central question in one kind of reply. One might say that the abuser of discretion is precisely he who uses it to choose death and not life, this being the kind of moral abuse that consists in giving priority to unworthy values like freedom from pain and personal autonomy. Whether is fact those values or the respect for human life are the most worthy ones is of course precisely the question at issue.

It is natural at this point to mention the defective analogy to capital punishment. There is an argument against the death penalty that is sometimes used as a model for arguing against the legalization of euthanasia. The arguments are superficially parallel in form: they both urge that the merits of the individual case be overlooked in order to prevent a greater evil, consisting of the inevitable occasional mistake. The resemblance of the two arguments, however, is only superficial. The crucial differences can best be appreciated by laying the two arguments side by side and comparing them.

The argument against permitting the death penalty. If we use the death penalty as our punishment for murder, then an occasional innocent person (maybe one in a thousand) by mistake or abuse[8] will be executed, and ex-

---

[8] See Charles L. Black, Jr., *Capital Punishment: The Inevitability of Caprice and Mistake* (New York: W. W. Norton, 1974).

ecution of course is irrevocable. This consequence is so evil that we are justified in overlooking the merits and demerits of individual cases, overlooking, that is to say, most prisoners' desert of death for what they have done. That would be to give these convicted murderers an undeserved benefit, a reprieve from the death penalty they deserve, but it is worth doing all the same, since they will still suffer life imprisonment with all its hardships (which they must deserve if they deserve the even greater evil of death), and they will not be turned loose to prey on other victims. (The loss in marginal deterrence would be very slight.) So the overall cost would not be great for securing a gain that is of supreme moral importance, namely, the prevention of an occasional serious and unjust mistake, the execution of an innocent person.

The parallel argument against honoring death requests from suffering terminal patients. If we legalize voluntary euthanasia, then an occasional salvageable, or not truly consenting patient (maybe as many as one in a hundred) will by mistake or abuse be killed or allowed to die. This consequence is so evil that we are justified in overlooking the merits of individual cases and turning down *all* death requests regardless of their merits, that is, regardless of the requester's desert of a cessation of suffering and shortening of the death process, both of which he takes to be benefits. This would be to confer not an undeserved benefit, but an undeserved harm, namely, the continuance of suffering and the extending of the death process. It is worth doing this, however, because the cost is not great [*sic*] to the terminal patients and their families,[9] and a great gain, the prevention of unnecessary killings, would be achieved.

In one respect the argument against euthanasia may actually be stronger than the argument against the death penalty. If the presumed incidence of unnecessary deaths in euthanasia cases would be ten times as great as in capital punishment cases, as we supposed in our formulation of the arguments above, then the antieuthanasia argument is strengthened proportionately. But that surmise is entirely arbitrary, lacking the necessary empirical support. Moreover, we must remember that prisoners who were entirely innocent of murder but falsely convicted anyway although they had nothing whatever to do with the crime are only a tiny percentage of those who do not deserve to be executed. There are those who did the deed they were accused of, but did it by mistake or accident, those who should have been convicted of manslaughter instead of murder, those who killed because they panicked in the face of threats from the victim although the imminence of harm required by the self-defense justification was missing, or who mistakenly believed they were being attacked with a knife during a scuffle. Perhaps all of these prisoners mistakenly convicted of murder are

[9] See Kamisar, "Euthanasia Legislation," p. 104.

in fact guilty of *something*, and deserve some punishment or other. But it would be a tragic and unjust mistake to inflict the penalty on them that is reserved for murder, the most serious crime of all, when in fact, although not in law, they are guilty of a lesser crime than that. When we add prisoners in this category to the presumably much rarer totally innocent bystanders who were arrested, prosecuted, and convicted by mistake, then the incidence of prisoners executed by mistake, it seems reasonable to suppose, would be at least as great as the number of patients mistakenly permitted to have the euthanasia they request.

But the most important point of disanalogy between the two arguments is the one that renders the argument against capital punishment much stronger than the parallel argument against euthanasia. Rejecting the death penalty on grounds external to the merits of the individual case confers an undeserved benefit on those who deserve to die for the sake of the suspected but unknown minority that do not deserve to die. It confers this windfall blessing at very small cost to any other interests. Rejecting euthanasia, on the other hand, confers undeserved harm on a majority of those terminal patients who request their own deaths. It thereby achieves a benefit to the small numbers of those whose requests are not genuine and those for whose disease a new cure will at the last minute be discovered (surely not a significant number), and those whose disease was curable all along. The argument must maintain, however, that this gain is achieved only at small cost, presumably the cost of frustrating the desires of suffering terminal patients to die—a value judgment so callous as to be utterly perverse. How, Matthew Donnelly might have asked, could a whole year of hopeless pain, intense and unremitting, be a "small cost"?

In summary, we have found in everyday reasoning that there are some prohibitory rules that are defended with argument even though their defenders acknowledge that their applications in some individual cases are harmful. Deliberately overlooking these bad results in some individual cases is said to be a price worth paying to secure the greater benefits of the absolute prohibition. Some of these everyday arguments can be quite rational and convincing. It *can* be a rational social policy to withhold from trustworthy individuals discretion to make their own decisions on the ground that the less trustworthy individuals who would also be given that discretion by the same general rule might abuse it with socially harmful results. This form of argument can be rational to the extent that techniques to separate those who can be trusted with discretion from those who cannot, say by licensing procedures, are difficult and impractical.

The important point for our present purposes is that even though they all can be convincing in some everyday contexts, none of these forms of argument are plausible models for the categorical restriction of voluntary euthanasia. The least implausible model is that presupposed in Kamisar's forceful argument for absolute prohibition. There may be no moral defect, Kamisar admits, in a given terminal patient's death request, when considered on the merits alone, and no reason internal to his case, for denying him the discretion to decide on his own whether his own life should continue. But if we grant discretion generally to all patients in similar circumstances, then some mistakes and abuses are bound to occur, and that would be an evil greater than the evil of denying the majority of patients the discretion their personal autonomy seems to require. So goes the argument from abusable discretion as applied to voluntary euthanasia. What separates the supporters form the critics of this argument is not a disagreement over the requirements of logic or over the empirical facts. It is a disagreement in value judgments—assessments of comparative costs or evils. Is it a greater evil that ten terminal patients suffering intolerable anguish be required to extend their hopeless existence against their clearly documented will than that one patient through medical mistake or the coercive influence of impatient relatives dies prematurely? The controversy over legalized voluntary euthanasia hinges on questions of this form.

COMPARATIVE EVILS AND NUMERICAL MUTIPLIERS

There is a comparative value judgment embedded in the Anglo-American criminal law, and traced by at least one writer to an Italian proverb,[10] which had wide currency in the eighteenth century and has been treated almost as a truism in Western nations ever since. In the pithy formulation of Sir William Blackstone, the maxim says that "It is better that ten guilty persons escape then that one innocent party suffer."[11] This use of numbers, of course, is a mere rhetorical device designed to make its message memorable. We cannot say with any degree of confidence that punishing the innocent is not only more unjust but exactly ten times more unjust than acquitting the guilty or that we are made to feel exactly ten times worse by the one kind of injustice than by the other. In fact, "we possess neither moral intuitions nor moral theories which could establish such a specific ratio."[12] The core message in the famous slogan then is simply that it tends to be more unjust (even) to punish the innocent than to acquit the guilty.

---

[10] B. Stevenson, ed., *The Macmillan Book of Proverbs* (New York: Macmillan, 1948), p. 1249. Jeffrey Reiman and Ernest van den Haag paraphrase the *Macmillan Book* account thus: "Thomas Fielding, *Proverbs of All Nations*, p. 59 (1824), citing an Italian proverb which is also a maxim of English law, [Fielding] says it originated in Italy, and that Dr. Paley was against it, while Blackstone and Romilly approved of it." The Reiman–Van den Haag discussion, "On the Common Saying that it is Better that Ten Guilty Persons Escape than that One Innocent Suffer" is found in *Social Philosophy and Policy* 7/2 (Spring 1990): 226–48.

[11] William Blackstone, *Commentaries on the Laws of England*, 21st ed. (1765) (London: Sweet, Maxwell, Stevens & Norton, 1844), book 4, chapter 27, p. 358.

[12] Reiman and Van den Haag, "Common Saying," p. 227.

This maxim of justice should probably be treated like other moral precepts, as deliberately but usefully vague.

Still there are two ways in which numbers might get involved when this ethical maxim is actually invoked in a real-life context. The first of these is well illustrated in the following series of examples:

> "One of two identical twins is witnessed committing cold-blooded murder. It is impossible for anyone but the twins to tell themselves apart, and each claims that he was elsewhere when the murder was committed. You must choose between executing both or acquitting both." Since you would choose the latter (wouldn't you?) you regard it as *worse* to punish an innocent person than to let a guilty one escape punishment. The example-giver might then increase the size of the suspect family. "Two of three identical triplets are witnessed committing cold-blooded murder (etc.). You must choose between executing all three or acquitting all three. Since you would still choose the latter (wouldn't you?), this implies even more strongly that you regard it as worse to punish an innocent person than to let a guilty one escape punishment."[13]

In principle, we could increase the size of the murderous group to ten or more, although we should soon have to find some nongenetic explanation for the indistinguishable features of the suspects.

Part of what these hypothetical examples show is that our so-called intuitions, which are so strong in the simple case of the identical twins, tend to weaken as the group of indistinguishable murder suspects grows larger. Part of the reason this is so, no doubt, is that we can no longer keep out of consideration the rights of unknown potential victims of this group of murderous rogues, and that weakens the focus of the example. No longer are we dealing with a comparison of two abstractions—ten acquittals of guilty persons versus one conviction of an innocent person. Now we have to add into our judgments a larger indeterminate number of potential innocent victims, and that so complicates the task for our intuitions that they can no longer give clear verdicts about the simple abstract moral problem with which we began. But we do learn something else of a useful nature from these examples, namely, that occasions for the making of comparative numerical judgments between evils (types of injustice) can and do arise, within limits, in ordinary life.

The second way in which numbers may become involved in our judgments of comparative evils occurs at the level of policy creation. When we want to decide which is the worse evil, the enforced deprivation of a moderate "social drinker's" glass of wine with dinner or the continuance of the drunkard's heavy and dangerous drinking opportunities, for the purpose of legislating wisely in this area of drug abuse, then we need to have some

---

[13] Ibid., p. 228.

accurate even though approximate sense of the relative numbers in the two groups. Once we get the numbers, our original question now assumes the more complex traditional formulation: which is the worse evil, x million unrestrained drunkards or the prohibition of the harmless drinking of y million "social drinkers"?

We have done enough, however, to set the stage for a consideration of the "abusable discretion" argument against legalized voluntary euthanasia. The question before us has at least two parts, one involving numbers and one involving values (or evils). Which is the greater evil, we might ask, a rule that permits authorities to end the lives each year of x,000 suffering or comatose terminal patients at the cost of y number of fatal mistakes, *or* a rule that categorically forbids the x,000 instances of voluntary euthanasia thus preventing the y number of mistaken killings? The evil caused by the first (permissive) rule is suffered by the y number of patients who because of diagnostic error, unanticipated development of new cures, or psychological pressures, die needlessly or against their real wills. The evil caused by the second (prohibitory) rule is at the expense of terminal patients who are suffering pain, severe discomfort, and the anguish of hopelessness, and those who are irreversibly comatose but whose voluntary preferences for death in these circumstances are known or inferable, and their friends and close relations. The prohibitory rule secures its benefits at the cost of pointless, emotionally wrenching, and expensive maintenance of cortically dead bodies, and the continuance of pain and suffering of x,000 terminal patients. Is it possible to defend some rough rule of thumb like the Blackstone formula that is used in the quite different context of guilt and punishment? Can we even hope to agree that x lives delivered from irreversible coma or intolerable pain is a greater good than the prevention of y deaths through mistakes? Or, put negatively, the y lives pointlessly ended is a greater evil than x lives pointlessly preserved in coma or pain?

The numbers do make a difference. Those who have had the universal nightmare, perhaps inspired in some cases by Edgar Allan Poe,[14] of being

---

[14] See for example, Poe's short stories "The Black Cat," "A Cask of Amontillado," and especially "The Fall of the House of Usher" in E. A. Poe, *Selected Writings*, ed. D. Galloway (Harmondsworth: Penguin Books). See also Michael Chrichton, *The Great Train Robbery* (New York: Alfred A. Knopf, 1975), pp. 191–94, from which I quote:

During the nineteenth century both in England and in the United States, there arose a peculiar preoccupation with the idea of premature burial . . . for the Victorians, premature burial was a genuine palpable fear.

Nor was this widespread fear a simply neurotic obsession . . . there was plenty of evidence . . . [that] premature burials did occur, and that such ghastly happenings were [often] only prevented by some fortuitous event . . . Victorians dealt with their uncertainty in two ways. The first was to delay interment for several days—a week was not uncommon—and await the unmistakable olfactory evidence . . .

The second method was technological; the Victorians contrived an elaborate series of

buried alive in their caskets can imagine few greater horrors. And who can doubt that in the long history of human burial customs this must actually have happened a few times? Maybe it still happens, say in one out of every fifty million burials, not because of the demonic madness of enemies but through the inevitability of careless mistakes. Even those of us who would rank accidental live burial at the top of a list of macabre evils, would require worse odds than one chance in fifty million for a justification of a statute forbidding burials, or even requiring long delays and reexaminations of the deceased. Incontrovertibly evil though it is, accidental premature burial is too rare and speculative a harm to have much weight in our policy decisions. If we thought its frequency were greater, say one in one million, we might consider tightening up our standards of care, even at the cost of considerable inconvenience and greater expense to many people, but surely not at the cost of extreme pain and suffering to many people, as in the voluntary euthanasia example.

Kamisar estimates that the number of victims of mistaken and unnecessary killing, if voluntary euthanasia were legalized, would be quite substantial, but his arguments for this estimate of numbers are not convincing, perhaps because he thinks that even small numbers of mistakes and abuses would be sufficient to discredit the euthanasia proposal, given the nature of the evil in those instances when compared with evils to those whose requests to die are turned down when euthanasia is kept illegal. In Blackstonian terms, I think that Kamisar believes that one life needlessly ended is a worse evil than ten lives needlessly and painfully extended.

Why does Kamisar think that under a system of voluntary euthanasia there would inevitably be, in his word, "appreciable"[15] mistake and abuse? Mistakes, he thinks, would arise primarily from mistaken diagnoses and prognoses, and the chance of last-minute medical discoveries. Exactly how frequently doctors diagnose curable illnesses to be fatal ones, and thus withhold treatments that would have been life-saving, I cannot say. But any sensible scheme of euthanasia would require multiple medical consul-

---

warning and signaling devices to enable a dead person to make known his resuscitation. A wealthy individual might be buried with a length of iron pipe connecting his casket to the ground above, and a trusted family servant would be required to remain at the cemetery, day and night, for a month or more, on the chance that the deceased would suddenly awake and begin to call for help. Persons buried above ground in family vaults were often placed in patented, spring-loading caskets, with a complex maze of wires attached to arms and legs, so that the slightest movement of the body would throw open the lid . . .

Most signaling devices were costly, and available only to the wealthy classes. Poor people adopted the simpler tactic of burying relatives with some implement—a crowbar or a shovel—on the vague assumption that if they revived, they could dig themselves out of their predicament.

[15] Kamisar, "Euthanasia Legislation," p. 105.

tations and other necessary ways of making sure, and despite the inevitability of some mistakes there are many more cases, like those of Matthew Donnelly and Nancy Beth Cruzan, that are perfectly clear. Why is not the incorrect judgment in clearly incurable cases that those cases might be misdiagnosed so far as we can know just as morally telling a mistake as the rarer misdiagnoses given so much emphasis by Kamisar?

As for last-minute medical discoveries, surely they cannot be the source of "appreciable" numbers of unnecessary killings. There is always a substantial delay between the discovery of a new medicine or a new surgical technique and its availability, and I suppose that awareness of the new possibility during that interval might in some cases revive hope and lead to postponement of mercy killing. In those cases the patient (or her guardian or proxy) and the physicians might keep the flickering hope alive as long as possible. In that way a sensible euthanasia scheme could accommodate the possibility of last-minute discoveries. But equally certainly there are other cases that are incorrigibly hopeless, or such that the slenderness of the chance of a last-minute discovery may not be worth the continued pain involved in the waiting. And in other cases there can be no chance whatever of a last-minute cure, since the last minute has already come and gone. Once a cerebral cortex has been destroyed, for example, there can be nothing, short of a literal miracle, that can restore the existence of the comatose person. One can quibble about numbers and probabilities, and even concede that the number of otherwise terminal patients who turn out to be salvageable because of last-minute discoveries is more than "tiny." The essential point from the moral point of view is that suspension of mercy killing for the vast majority of those who need and want it would be at least as serious a mistake as killing those who might have been saved, for all we know, by a last-minute discovery. Glanville Williams puts the point well: "Because of this risk for this tiny fraction of the total number of patients, patients who are dying in pain must be left to do so, year after year, against their entreaty to have it ended."[16]

Our traditional criminal law, Kamisar notes, does permit intentional killing in some circumstances, when it appears necessary, for example, to the defense of a threatened person or of third parties. And of course, mistakes in judging this "necessity" in individual cases are inevitable. Reasonable mistakes in self-defense or defense of others, Kamisar explains, "are the inevitable by-products of efforts to save one or more human lives."[17] But can we not, in a perfectly parallel way, consider reasonable mistakes in a legalized voluntary euthanasia scheme to be "the inevitable by-products"

[16] Glanville Williams, "Euthanasia Legislation: A Rejoinder to the Non-Religious Objections," in *Euthanasia and the Right to Death*, ed. A. B. Downing (London: Peter Owen, 1969), p. 142.

[17] Kamisar, "Euthanasia Legislation," p. 104.

of efforts to deliver human beings, at their own requests, from intolerable suffering, or from elaborate and expensive prolongations of a body's functioning in the permanent absence of any person to animate that body? Kamisar's answer is revealing: only the saving of human lives, he thinks, is a value great enough to justify the taking of a human life. "The need the euthanasiast advances . . . is a good deal less compelling. It is only to ease pain."[18]

This view of the matter, which would have astonished Matthew Donnelly and the parents of Nancy Cruzan, is readily expressible in a Blackstonian formula without any numbers in its comparative judgment. In respect to guilt and innocence, Voltaire writes of "the great principle that is better to run the risk of sparing the guilty than to condemn the innocent."[19] Here there is no mention of numbers, no comparison of ten guilty men with one innocent person, as in Blackstone's more rhetorical formula. Perhaps Voltaire intends (or should have intended) a ceteris paribus clause—numbers and other possibly relevant matters being equal—to disconnect and isolate the point he makes, while acknowledging that in real-life applications, matters are much more complex than his "great principle" would otherwise suggest, that numbers do count, and so do such externalities as the risk of further harm caused by the guilty who are "spared." Using Voltaire's maxim as a model for imitation we can attribute to Kamisar the view that it is better to run the risk that a patient, or her relatives and loved ones, will be made to suffer needlessly than to run the risk that a patient who requests euthanasia is not truly "terminal" or that his consent is not truly voluntary. Numbers aside, the maxim now says, when we compare one instance of needlessly taken life with one instance of needlessly extended life, considered in this abstract way, other things being equal, the former is always and necessarily a greater evil than the latter. That is, it is always a greater evil, other things being equal, to let someone die by mistake than to keep a person alive by mistake. This non-numerical formulation of Kamisar's view makes it into a more modest and therefore a more plausible claim. Nevertheless, in the concluding section of this chapter, after some efforts at clarification, I shall find reasons for rejecting it.

When the Value of Life Is Outweighed

It should be clear then that two kinds of mistake are possible in the voluntary euthanasia situation, that both have their costs and projected frequencies. One creates the danger that curable patients will needlessly be

---

[18] Ibid.
[19] Jean Francois Marie Arouet de Voltaire, "Zadig or Fate," in *Candide and Other Stories* (London: Dent & Sons, 1962), p. 20, as quoted by Reiman and Van den Haag, "Common Saying," p. 226.

killed or killed without their real consent; the other creates the danger that incurable terminal patients will have their sufferings pointlessly prolonged. It is the task of rule-makers to adopt the policy that will prevent the more serious mistakes, both in number and degree of evil, even at the cost of incurring inevitably the kind of mistake that exposes a smaller number to evils of lesser degree.

It will be my conclusion that one cannot say that one of the two kinds of mistake is in itself, isolated from other factors, always more serious than the other, and that ceteris paribus (degree of risk, numbers of affected people in each class, etc. being equal) that one kind of value (life), always is a weightier consideration than the other (cessation of suffering). Ordinarily we cannot get a pure ceteris paribus case, for there are always many variables in the euthanasia situation. In real life we compare real people who are always concrete and particular, and not mere abstract subjects for certain properties that interest us, and anyway, no two have exactly the same properties. When we compare Matthew Donnelly or Nancy Beth Cruzan, say, with another specific person who *can* be saved, although knowing it not, he demands euthanasia *now*, we must consider properties other than the minimal characteristics that define the classes we are comparing. We must consider how severe is the suffering, thus how great an evil it is in itself, how old the patients are, how complex, expensive, and likely to succeed any future discovered treatment would have to be, and so on.

Suppose we consider Donnelly who, let us imagine, is being asked to forego euthanasia because the rule permitting it will also enable a second patient to forego the soon-to-be-discovered last-minute treatment that can cure him. In a concrete example like this, we would have a hard time ignoring such traits as the comparative ages, the life expectancies with and without treatment, the degree of vigorous activity that in the best outcome will be possible. We do not in this case deal with people as if they were personifications of abstractions like Suffering and Potential Salvageability. The degrees of comparative value and evil in our options will always be more complicated than that, since every patient must have some specific age, physical condition, and general prospect. Can we in good conscience impose another year of unremitting pain on Donnelly in order to protect a general rule that would permit a seventy-year-old Alzheimer patient to be ready for a last-minute cure, when he will have a six-month life expectancy and an enfeebled bodily condition even if the possible last-minute "cure" eventuates?

My thesis is that in the abstract, or as close as we can get to it, it is misleading to judge either kind of consideration to be always more serious than the other, ceteris paribus, or that one type of mistake is always and necessarily more serious, ceteris paribus, than the other. Kamisar, on the other hand, implies that there is a categorical difference between the two types of mistakes, so that the one category in its entirety must always have priority. Considered "in themselves," in abstraction, ceteris paribus, he seems to say, we should always prefer the value in one category (life) over that in the other (surcease of hopeless suffering). On my view, in contrast, if we are forced to play the "whole category" game at all, we would have to conclude that the two categories of mistake are of equal seriousness.

It would be better, however, if we avoided this kind of judgment altogether. We might be tempted to say that the two kinds of mistakes *can* be compared in the abstract and that they are always of equal seriousness. But that is the wrong point, a conclusion as paradoxical as Kamisar's. It is *not* that the comparison between the two value categories can be made and always results in a tie. Rather the comparison cannot be made at all. The disagreement between Kamisar and me, as I have been reconstructing it, is not that he says, "Ceteris paribus, death is always worse," and I say, "Ceteris paribus, the two evils are always equal," but rather that he says the former, and I deny what he affirms. I assert nothing parallel to his affirmation, but simply deny that any such sweeping judgment can be made, either that death or suffering is always worse than the other "in itself, other things being equal."

In fact, "other things" (if we should ever reach agreement about which "other things" are relevant) hardly ever are equal, and even if, *mirabile dictu*, they are equal in a given case, the resultant value judgment would make no sense. To say that other things being equal death is a worse evil than suffering (or vice versa) is not to say something like: "Other things being equal an intense pain is a worse evil than a moderate one." In respect to intensity, duration, extent, and so on, pains are the sorts of things that can meaningfully be compared. But death and suffering lack relevant dimensions in which comparisons are possible. Units of time (days, hours) may be applied to both, but the relevant temporal measure for death is not the duration of the death itself, which of course is infinite, but rather how many days one might have been expected to live had a preventable death not occurred when it did. That is not the same temporal dimension in which we measure the duration of sufferings (How long do they last from start to finish?). In this and other relevant respects, then, death and suffering are simple incommensurables. It is easy enough to speak of "death in the abstract" or "suffering in the abstract," but real people do not live in the abstract.

Suppose we must compare the mistakenly permitted death of an eighty-five-year-old who is thereby deprived of an additional six months of sickly life with the mistakenly prolonged sufferings of Matthew Donnelly. Here it would seem that the suffering in one person is a worse evil than death in the other, or so at any rate we might judge if we were forced to judge. In contrast, the mistakenly permitted death of a twenty-year-old deprived of fifty years of vigorous life is probably a worse evil then the mistaken pro-longation of the suffering for one day of another person. What if an enemy of mercy killing declared that the young person deprived of fifty years of life has suffered a worse evil than any amount or degree of "mere" suffering in anyone? It is unlikely, I think, that he could maintain confidence in that judgment in the face of the hypothetical example of a person forced against her will to remain alive through fifty years of intense suffering. Identifying the one evil as belonging in the "death" category and the other in the "suf-fering" category only introduces the problem; it by no means settles it.

I am satisfied to let the Donnelly and Cruzan cases speak for themselves as examples of values that *can*, in a fully concrete context, outweigh life. That will enable me in the space that is left to deflate the value of "life preservation" as interpreted by various opponents of legalized voluntary euthanasia, especially the present U.S. Supreme Court. In this concluding section then, I shall concentrate, as it happens, on the pronouncements of the Court about the value of life in the case of Nancy Beth Cruzan.

Why is it that the enemies of voluntary euthanasia attribute so great a value to "life as such" that it is supposed to outweigh even the evil of suf-fering whenever they conflict? Justice Rehnquist in his majority opinion in the Cruzan case admitted that U.S. constitutional law[20] grants a right to all competent adults to refuse medical treatment if they wish. But this pri-vate "interest" in liberty must be balanced, Rehnquist declared, against rel-evant state interests. Chief among the latter is the state's interest in "the protection and preservation of human life." I am not sure how to explain this sense of "interest," but it would not be far off the mark to substitute for it "legitimate governmental concern." Sometimes the state interest in the protection and preservation of human life overrides the liberty interest of an individual in making his own decisions whether or not to accept a given medical treatment. Rehnquist's example of this is a Massachusetts case in 1905 in which the Court favored the state's interest in preventing epidemic disease over an individual's liberty interest in declining an un-wanted smallpox vaccination.[21] So even though "The forcible injection of medication into a nonconsenting person's body represents a substantial interference with that person's liberty,"[22] the state must give due weight to its function as protector of human life, even to the point sometimes of nullifying a citizen's constitutional right to liberty.

It is easy enough to understand why a court would legally compel a vaccination to help prevent the spread of a lethal disease, but how does this

[20] The primary source is the "Due Process" clause of the Fourteenth Amendment: "nor shall any state deprive any person of life, liberty, or property, without due process of law." The key word in the application of this clause to medical treatment is "liberty."

[21] Rehnquist cites *Jacobson* v. *Massachusetts*, 197 U.S. 11, 24–30 (1905).

[22] Quoted by Rehnquist from *Washington* v. *Harper*, 110 S. Ct. 1028 (1990).

example serve to explain the state's interest in keeping Nancy Cruzan's mutilated body alive long after Nancy's person had vanished forever from it? Preservation of the functioning body of a departed person does no one any good. Not Nancy, because she never knew the difference, being permanently and irreversibly unconscious. Not the state of Missouri, which paid costs of approximately $100,000 a year. Not Nancy's parents for whom the unnatural preservation of the body of their beloved daughter was a ghoulish torture.

There remains of course the interest of Nancy as she was before she suffered her accident. Let us suppose for a moment that it was her firm and informed preference to be let die in case she should ever be rendered irreversibly comatose in an accident. This in fact was what she did prefer, according to the testimony of her friend and former roommate. If that is true, then keeping Nancy's body going while she was comatose was not in the interest of Nancy as she was before her accident. I think we can speak of interests surviving the death of the person whose interests they were, as a kind of useful fiction. If I have an interest while alive that my estate go to my wife after I die, but then after I die my widow is cheated out of her inheritance by a conspiracy between my lawyer and my accountant, not only my widow's interest but the interest of my own in her security, which I was promoting before I died, is also set back. In deciding how to redistribute whichever of my widow's assets come to hand, the authorities might say such a thing as: "It is the testator's interests alone that should determine what is to be done." And this might be said quite intelligibly even though I, the testator, am now dead. In any event, on the assumption that Nancy Cruzan preferred before her accident that nutrition and hydration be withheld if she should ever become irreversibly comatose, it follows that it was not in her interest (not in the interest she had when she was capable of having any interests) that her body be kept alive.

Now consider the other possibility, that Nancy did *not* have an informed preference for the discontinuance of medical sustenance after the onset of permanent coma. On this assumption either she was indifferent, never having even considered the matter perhaps, or she had a firm and informed preference that her living body be sustained. If she was indifferent, then it cannot be the case that her preaccident interest would be set back by discontinuing her support. But if she preferred continuance, then it would appear that discontinuance would violate her preaccident interest. But what kind of interest could it be that would be based on such a preference? It could not be an interest in having *her life* continued, for *ex hypothesi* nothing that happens ever made any difference to her. If she had been asked whether she would prefer death or permanent unconsciousness, she could not possibly have expressed a rational choice, because from her own subjective point of view, there was not one iota of difference between death and permanent unconsciousness. From the perspective of the person whose life is at issue there is only a choice between permanent unconsciousness on the one hand and permanent unconsciousness on the other. On either alternative, there is no possibility of strivings, aversions, projects, goals, attachments, plans, actions, perceptions—the necessary components of a *human* life, as opposed to the "life," if we may use the word in that way, of a mere biological organism.

There remains a further possibility. A person in Nancy's position might conceivably think of her body as her own property and accordingly dictate what is to be done with it after she ceases to be. She might make a provision in her will that if she should become irreversibly comatose, her body should be kept alive so that it could be a useful test of the safety of new medications, thus sparing some poor animal that sacrificial role, or so that it could be an organ bank for keeping spare bodily parts in good working order until they can be transplanted, and the like. We can even imagine a time in the distant future when the state would claim to have an interest in that sort of resource, and overrule the claim that a body is the private property of the person who died to be disposed of as she pleases, so that the state could seize all "living corpses" for medical purposes. For the present, however, it makes sense to say that a person has an interest and a right in the disposition of her future vital remains, even though the organism that was once her body is still alive. But it does not follow from a person's donation of her living body to a recipient that the recipient has a duty to accept it or use it according to its previous owner's desires. The state of Missouri, stuck with the heavy financial costs, might well have said—if only the law permitted it—"Thanks, but no thanks." The situation, it seems to me, is much like a person willing his 1953 Chevrolet to the state to be preserved in a well-lit automotive show room in perpetuity. After all, the car was the testator's property to dispose of as he wished. But even if he had also willed an adequate amount of money to cover costs, the state could feel justified in turning it down as not worth the bother. Indeed, when one realizes what an irreversible vegetative state is, one wonders why it would ever be in the interest of the state to preserve a body in that condition, unless it be through lingering doubts about the medical diagnosis. At any rate, no state interest remotely analogous to the interest in preventing epidemic can be imagined for keeping an unoccupied body alive.

Two types of mistake might be made in the treatment of patients in a persistent vegetative state, one of them very infrequent, the other very insignificant whenever it does occur. The infrequent mistake would be misdiagnosis—the expectation that the coma is irreversible when in fact it is not. In this age of high-tech X-ray instruments, however, a cerebral cortex can be known to be both functionally incapacitated and progressively deteriorating, so that only a negligently superficial examination could lead to the mistaken prognosis. Physicians being human, of course, are fallible, and there will always be the possibility of error, but mistakes of this kind will not occur in significant numbers.

The other kind of mistake would be one of misattribution to the patient of a preference about the disposition of her living body. If she wants discontinuance of nutrition and care and does not get it, then that is a serious error, if not for her interests, for the interests of her parents, close relations, and friends, not to mention the bill-paying taxpayers. If, however, she prefers to have her body preserved in the manner of transferred property, just as if it were some handsome machine or art object, at the state's expense, and this genuine preference is misinterpreted or otherwise not honored, then *that* mistake is not a serious one. In short the risk of mistaken killing in cases of this kind is not in itself a very grave danger, partly because the purely medical mistake that could lead to the killing would not be made in significant numbers, and the mistaken attribution to the patient of a prior preference for death would not in itself be a very great evil.

The majority of the U.S. Supreme Court, however, found the danger of a mistaken withdrawal of life-sustaining treatment from Cruzan a more serious evil than the danger of a mistake in the opposite direction, mainly because death is irrevocable and mistaken killings are therefore uncorrectable. The official summary of the Court's decision encapsulates the argument exactly:

> The clear and convincing evidence standard . . . serves as a social judgment about how the risk of error should be distributed between the litigants. Missouri may place the increased risk of erroneous decision on those seeking to terminate life-saving treatment. An erroneous decision not to terminate results in the maintenance of the *status quo* with at least the potential that a wrong decision will eventually be corrected or its impact mitigated by an event such as an advance in medical science or the patient's unexpected death. However, an erroneous decision to withdraw such treatment is not subject of correction.[23]

To this argument from the irrevocability of mistaken decisions to kill, Justice Brennan in his dissenting opinion makes the clear and obvious rejoinder: "From the point of view of the patient, an erroneous decision *in either direction* is irrevocable."[24] She is nonexistent in either case, but her remains are on display permanently in the one case, but decently removed from view on the other.

> An erroneous decision to terminate artificial nutrition and hydration, to be sure, will lead to failure of that last remnant of physiological life, the brain-

[23] *Cruzan* v. *Director, Missouri Department of Health*, at 2844.
[24] Ibid. at 2873.

stem, and result in complete brain death. An erroneous decision *not* to terminate the life-support however, robs a patient of the very qualities protected by
the right to avoid unwanted medical treatment. His own degraded existence
is perpetuated; his family's suffering is protracted; the memory he leaves behind becomes more and more distorted.[25]

Brennan correctly points out that there is no state interest in the preservation of merely biological life without consciousness, and hence that there
can be no more a legitimate governmental function to maintain such "life"
than there is to preserve some giant plant or vegetable. A life "completely
abstracted from the interest of the person living that life"[26] can have no
special value the state is committed to protect—nothing like the public
health that can be threatened by an epidemic disease.

Of course Matthew Donnelly in *his* last days, was in no way like a vegetable. Vegetables do not suffer pain and despair. But given the incurability
of his condition, Donnelly's life was even less worth preserving, against his
manifest will, than Nancy Cruzan's against the presumed preference she
might have had before her accident. There was no point at all in keeping
Nancy Cruzan's body alive, but no more possibility of harm to Nancy in
doing so. The case for granting Donnelly his passionately requested relief,
however, was stronger than that. We owe deliverance to the likes of Donnelly and we cruelly wrong such people by withholding it from them. Letting them suffer unnecessarily is not to err on the "safe side." In life's difficult closing games there is often no safe side to err on; delay and inaction
can be as serious a mistake as hasty or premature action. In that case we
had better do whatever we can to let suffering patients determine their own
course.

In summary, we have seen that most of the arguments against the legalization of voluntary euthanasia (or in favor of creating legal impediment to
it) are indirect arguments. They do not argue that individual cases judged
internally, that is, on their own merits, do not warrant euthanasia. Indeed,
some of these arguments candidly concede that judged on the merits, many
individual cases do deserve euthanasia. Rather, these arguments favor deliberately overlooking the merits of individual cases, and cite extraneous
considerations in favor of a blanket prohibition. The most plausible of
these arguments is the argument from abusable discretion, which maintains that if legally competent individuals are granted the discretion to decide on their own whether in certain circumstances to continue or to terminate life-sustaining treatment, the inevitability of honest mistakes and
not-so-honest abuses will create evils that outweigh the evils of sustaining

---

[25] Ibid.
[26] Ibid. at 2870.

the comatose and the pain-wracked against their presumed wills. Convincing as the argument from abusable discretion may be in some contexts (e.g., traffic control) it fails in its application to the euthanasia situation, because it cannot be shown that the likely number of mistakenly killed individuals would constitute a greater evil than the likely number of mistakenly sustained individuals. The philosophical problem of voluntary euthanasia is in large part a matter of comparing real risks. The enemy of voluntary euthanasia errs in minimizing the evils of human suffering and overrating the value of merely biological life in the absence of a human person, or in the presence of a human person whose sufferings are too severe for him to have a human life, even though his heart beats on.

Chapter Twelve

SEVEN MODES OF REASONING THAT CAN JUSTIFY OVERLOOKING THE MERITS OF THE INDIVIDUAL CASE—WHEN THE FACTS ARE RIGHT

THE PREVIOUS CHAPTER examined, briefly in one instance but in detail in the other, two modes of reasoning in practical ethics that, when applied to the problem of legalizing voluntary euthanasia, appear at first sight to warrant a categorical rejection of legalization, even in individual cases where it seems warranted "on the merits." Major attention in that chapter was paid to what I called "the argument from abusable discretion," and its parallel employment in arguments for the exceptionless prohibition of alcohol and for requiring traffic signals even at "safe intersections" at "safe times." Less but I hope sufficient attention was given to another pattern of reasoning often used in the capital punishment debate when it is claimed that mistaken execution of the innocent is a much graver injustice, other things being equal, than mistaken nonexecution of the truly guilty. That argument too might entitle us to overlook the "merits" (demerits!) of a convicted heinous murderer in order to avoid in other cases, the occasional execution of a mistakenly convicted innocent person. I showed considerable respect for both of these modes of reasoning (even so far as endorsing the argument against the death penalty), but I claimed that the euthanasia problem has special features that render less than compelling the application to *it* of arguments of that form.

In this supplementary chapter, I extend the inquiry of the previous chapter to cover five other types of reasoning that warrant our respect in general, and especially in contexts where they yield clear and compelling arguments, but again I argue that their applications to the euthanasia problem are unconvincing. I do not consider any of the standard textbook examples of moral problems stemming from the conflict between "act-utilitarianism" and individual rights. Rather, I restrict my attention to the problem of constructing general rule-governed practices, and the temptation that we face as "moral legislators" in deciding whether to adopt a rule that would have us overlook the merits of some individual cases.

FORMING VALUABLE HABITS

The third pattern of argument (after the two discussed in the previous chapter) applies to rules only in a private, not a public sense. The problem it typically generates is for us in our capacities as private individuals responsible for our own behavior, not hypothetical legislators with the power to impose public rules on others. Typically, the problem it addresses is whether I ought to adopt "as a rule" a habit of action that will apply even to areas of my conduct where it has no direct utility, and whether I should willingly act in accordance with the habit even in cases where such conduct would have no observable "merit" or point, except that of strengthening the habit itself.

It is a useful driving habit always to signal a turn, even on those not infrequent occasions when one can see that no other cars need to know of your intention to turn as, for example, when you are in your own driveway about to turn into your garage and there are clearly no other cars on your property, or when you are already in a lane marked (say) "right turn only." If your attention is called to the unnecessary character of your automatic actions in those particular circumstances, you will understand how taking the trouble to signal in those cases might seem silly, but nonetheless defend the rationality of your acts by demonstrating what an important contribution to your safety in the long run is made by having a habit that is so rigid and automatic. It is comforting to know that your automatic pilot will never fail in those other cases where it is really needed.

This example, however, does not provide a model for the euthanasia case, which is much closer to being utterly singular and nonrepeatable. Matthew Donnelly and Nancy Cruzan (see chapter 11) need never worry about forming "the habit of being killed" when they consent explicitly (in his case) or hypothetically (in hers) to mercy killing. After all, we have only one life each. The argument from useful habit formation, however, might be applied more plausibly not to suffering or comatose patients but to those whom they (or their anguished family members) might implore to release them. It is possible that for some doctors or nurses, similar cases might arise over and over. By refusing to accede to the requests for euthanasia each time they are made, even in individual cases where the request is clearly well founded, the medical practitioner may strengthen her habit of responding in similar ways in future cases. By ignoring the merits even of the most clearly well-founded cases, she may (so the argument goes) strengthen her respect for the sanctity of human life, a habitual response that will serve her well generally. But this argument in an important way begs the question. A defender of euthanasia can point out that if the medical provider's decision in the individual case is wrong when considered entirely on its own merits—if, for example, she declines to rescue Donnelly—then she will simply strengthen her disposition to decide similar cases in the future wrongly. She will strengthen her respect for human life at the cost of her sympathy with human suffering and her respect for personal autonomy. If bodily life as such—mere maintenance of vital signs—is a more important value than alleviating suffering and respecting autonomy, then the argument has some plausibility, but that is the very point at issue, and cannot be assumed in the argument for itself. Moreover, in the turn-signaling example, the only cost of the acquisition and reinforcement of a valuable habit is some minor "silliness" and redundancy. In the euthanasia example, the physician's habit comes at the expense of the patients or their loved ones, clearly greater cost than occasional pointless repetitiveness.

INSUFFICIENT VOLUNTARINESS

Another way of interpreting the abuse of discretion, which was neglected in the previous chapter, is to think of discretion exercised in a fashion that falls short of an ideal perfect voluntariness—choices made while drunk or wracked with pain, for example. One is not truly exercising one's discretion, the argument goes, when one makes a serious choice in such a condition, and it is an abuse of discretion to treat an expression of choice as if it were the speaker's own, not that of an alien condition impeding the clarity of his vision, and not representing his true values at all. Yale Kamisar makes much of this point when he mocks advocates of voluntary euthanasia for the suffering patient as requiring that the choice be honored "only if the victim is both sane and crazed by pain"[1]—not to mention drugs. Drugs and pain deprive the patient of the calm clear-headedness he needs for rational deliberation, the argument goes, so it would be to abuse the patient's discretion if we accepted his choice as genuinely his own under those conditions.

I think that there is a subtle mistake in this argument. What should be required is not that an extremely important choice should meet some exalted standard of ideal voluntariness, but only that it be as voluntary as possible in the circumstances. Kamisar's analysis would seem to imply that a badly beaten boxer, glassy-eyed but still on his feet, who has "taken enough" and wants to quit, does not deserve to have his choice honored. The referee and the boxer's handler might reply with apparent cogency that the boxer is suffering such a painful battering from his opponent that his

---

[1] Yale Kamisar, "Euthanasia Legislation: Some Non-Religious Objections," in *Euthanasia and the Right to Death*, ed. A. B. Downing (London: Peter Owen, 1969), p. 93. Kamisar attributes the quoted remark to one Dr. Frohman in the latter's "Vexing Problems in Forensic Medicine: A Physician's View," *New York University Law Review* 31 (1956): 1215, 1222.

decision to quit cannot be clear-headed enough to be voluntary.[2] Similarly, persons with headaches should not be permitted to choose to take a couple of standard aspirin pills until their pain has worn off.[3] In fact, varying standards of voluntariness are normally tailored to fit the special circumstances of the decision-maker, and what is required is only that the decision be voluntary enough, that is, sufficiently voluntary to accord with *any* reasonable purpose.

Some writers, for example, argue that options offered to inmates in prison can never be exercised voluntarily enough for a given prisoner's consent to be treated as valid, because given the restrictive environment of prisons, coercive pressure must always be affecting his choices. If we offer a reduced sentence to an eager prisoner on condition that he "voluntarily" consent to be a subject in a possibly dangerous medical experiment, then obviously his choice, given that he hates prison, will be severely deficient in voluntariness. But if we tailor our standard to the context the decision-maker actually is in, and to its desirability (suppose that he deserves his imprisonment), it might turn out that his choice to be an experimental subject is *voluntary enough* to do him justice, indeed as voluntary perhaps as it possibly could be in his restrictive but justified circumstances. It would be less voluntary if he were kept uninformed about the risks, or if he was retarded, or if he was bullied and threatened by the guards, and so on. But it could be that none of these factors that generally reduce voluntariness are present, in which case the prisoner's choice might be as voluntary as it can be, given that he is in a prison. And given his settled preferences, that might be voluntary enough. Similarly, the "pain-crazed" patient's reiterated request for life termination, while a long way short of a general ideal of voluntariness, might be voluntary enough in his intolerable and unmitigable circumstances.

STATISTICAL DISCRIMINATION

One kind of ground that is often proposed for deliberately overlooking the merits of particular persons in the assignment of advantages and disadvantages is that the person is a member of a clearly defined class of people who have a statistical property of a relevant sort, whether or not the individual in question has that property himself. Thus, since women on the whole live longer than men, retirement annuity companies often pay greater monthly benefits to retired men than to retired women, even though it is patently false that *every* retired woman lives longer than *every* retired man. Similarly, since male drivers under twenty-five years of age cause more car

---

[2] See generally Joel Feinberg, *Harm to Self* (New York: Oxford University Press, 1986), chapters 20, 26, 27.

[3] Ibid., pp. 117, 123, 341–43.

accidents than females of comparable age, insurance companies charge higher premiums to men in that age group. Similar arguments, despite some strong protests, have recently carried the day in the United States for withholding legal drinking privileges from people in the eighteen to twenty-one age group even though the members of this group have full rights and responsibilities of citizenship in various other respects. They are mature enough to be conscripted, to vote, to pay taxes, to get married and to have babies, yet in respect to having a cocktail before dinner, they are treated by the rest of adult society as children. On the other side of the argument, the case for the exclusion of this entire group from legal drinking privileges rests on incontrovertible evidence that we can thereby reduce substantially the number of deaths and serious injuries from car accidents.

The moral objection to statistical discrimination is that it unfairly sweeps the innocent and the harmless along with the guilty and the dangerous. This is precisely what prejudice is: a kind of unfairness that is literally "prejudging," that is, attributing a property to an individual person, and acting accordingly, in the absence of any direct evidence that he has that property, but only the very indirect evidence that other persons who share some resemblance (e.g., in age, gender, race, or ethnic group) to that person have it. Sometimes persons disagree over the propriety of statistical discrimination. When it is the price some people must unfairly pay in order to save hundreds of lives, there seems to be a case for tolerating the acknowledged injustice. But in most circumstances the moral cost of injustice is unredeemed by any great harms it might plausibly be said to prevent. Suppose, for example, that a statistical survey discloses a significantly higher percentage of alcohol abuse among American Indians, Irish, and Russians than in other ethnic groups. Imagine further that statistical projections show that a likely saving of one hundred lives a year could be achieved by withdrawing legal permission to drink from just these persons. The indignation that would greet such discriminatory legislation would be boundless.[4]

The statistical discrimination in these hypothetical examples, despite its effectiveness in reducing harm, is obviously illegitimate, and the reason is clear. The correlation between statistical class membership and a specified type of behavior in these examples does not connect the behavior to any causally relevant factor in each member of the class. That a given person is a member of the statistically dangerous class is a ground for suspecting that he might have a characteristic that is causally connected with danger, but the class membership itself is not that property. We would not be justified in inferring a causal connection between being an American Indian or be-

---

[4] See Joel Feinberg, *Harm to Others* (New York: Oxford University Press, 1984), pp. 199–202.

ing Irish or being Russian and being prone to drunkenness, even if it were discovered that there is a genetic basis for alcoholism and that the responsible genes are found more commonly in these groups than in others. If a laboratory test could be devised for determining the presence of these genes, then there would be no obvious unfairness in excluding from the drinking privilege all who have the genetic propensity to dangerous drunkenness, regardless of which ethnic group they happen to belong to. As a general rule of thumb, whenever a legislature is tempted to withhold licenses on the basis of statistical correlations between group membership and danger-proneness, it should first make every reasonable effort to establish a genuine causal connection between the danger-proneness and some trait that is relative common in the group, and then legislate directly against that trait, no matter which group it is found in. Only when such efforts at separation fail should statistical discrimination even be thought to be an option, and even when it is a possible option, its attractions as a harm-reducer will in all but extreme cases be outweighed by its glaring unfairness.

What has all this to do with the right to die? The answer is: very little. Even if we decide that the prevention of a handful of unnecessary deaths is more important than the injustice done to those who as individuals have a moral right to choose death, we could hardly argue for that conclusion by any helpful analogy to statistical discrimination. If we consider the class of hospitalized terminal patients as analogous to an ethnic group with a large incidence of alcoholism, or an age group with a large incidence of automobile accidents, we will find no such "flag properties" characteristic of that group. There is no statistical evidence, for example, that serious accident and disease victims have any suspicious statistical properties, much less an established greater propensity to mistakes and abuses, than the general population, that could conceivably justify us in depriving every member of the class of the power to determine his own course. The class in question is a randomly miscellaneous aggregate of persons lacking even a statistical property that would signal a greater than average tendency to be involved in mistakes and abuses.

THRESHOLD ARGUMENTS

There are some acts that are harmless in themselves, but are such that if everyone did them then the results would be disastrous. Moreover, it is often said, if we let one person do an act of this kind, then there will be no nonarbitrary reason not to permit everyone else to do it. So it follows that either (1) we enforce a blanket prohibition of the act in question, or (2) we tolerate arbitrariness or favoritism in our assignment of licenses to the small number who will be permitted, or (3) we have a blanket permission, in which case the results will be "disastrous." It would seem then that the least evil of the alternatives is to enact a blanket prohibition, thus overlooking the claims of some people to exceptional treatment. A standard example is a city ordinance forbidding persons from walking on the grass in a public park on the ground that while the first one hundred or so persons to create their own shortcut path across the lawn can do so without harming the blades of grass they trample on, a number greater than that would approach the threshold of harm at which point blades of grass are crushed and killed. Why not license one hundred people only then, or to play it safe, even a smaller number like seventy or eighty persons to take a shortcut across the lawn? The answer usually given is that selecting the lucky seventy could not help being arbitrary or favoritistic. To be sure, there are not relevant objective criteria for determining who is to be allowed to walk on the grass analogous to special danger or vulnerability, and specially tested competence and trustworthiness, which are the criteria for determining who may carry handguns. So there is a sense in which selective licensing would have to be "arbitrary." There are acceptable though not always practical ways, however, of exploiting that arbitrariness. Licenses could be sold or auctioned, or simply distributed randomly through a lottery, in order to avoid favoritism.

The cruder threshold arguments for blanket prohibitions are subject to still further criticism. To the question "What would happen if everyone did it?" the answer often is "Not everyone will want to do it even if everyone is permitted to do it." The relevant question is "What would happen if everyone *in a position to gain* by doing it actually did it?" Sometimes if we permit everyone in this smaller group to do something that is in their interest to do, the results will not be harmful at all, much less "disastrous." There may, for example, be only twenty people who see any advantage in straying from the paved sidewalks in the park.

As I have written elsewhere,[5] however, the problem need not be that simple. The legislator must consider not only how many people would refrain from doing certain actions if those actions were legally permitted, but also *why* they would refrain. As we have seen, some types of behavior are socially harmful if generally done, socially innocuous if done by only a few, yet such that not many would want to engage in them, or find it in their interests to do so, even if they were permitted. There is no justification for the prohibition of such conduct. But there is another category, important but easily overlooked. The types of behavior in this second group are harmful if widely done, harmless if done only by a few and in almost everyone's interest to do; yet even if permitted these acts would not be done by enough people to reach the thresholds of harm, because many

[5] Ibid., pp. 226–27.

or most people would refrain out of moral scruples or civic spirit from doing what they know is in their interest. It would be to take advantage of these honorable souls to permit others to do what is harmless only because of *their* conscientious forbearance.

Threshold arguments, in any event, seem to be very poor models for the voluntary euthanasia problem. What is the feared harm to the rest of us if those suffering terminal patients who wish deliverance are allowed to die? At what numbers do such hurried deaths reach the threshold of that harm? If everyone in relevantly similar circumstances were also treated the same way (allowed to die), in what way would the results be disastrous for the rest of us? Glanville Williams, with another argumentative purpose in mind, has presented a hypothetical example of circumstances that make a threshold argument relevant, and its contrast to the actual circumstances in which hospital patients make death requests shows how unavailing the "threshold" analogy is as a reason for neglecting the merits of individual cases and creating instead a blanket prohibition of voluntary euthanasia. Williams calls his hypothetical example a "parable."

> In the state of Ruritania many people live a life of poverty and misery. They would be glad to emigrate to happier lands, but the law of Ruritania bans all emigration. The reason for this law is that the authorities are afraid that if it were relaxed, there would be too many people seeking to emigrate, and pop-ulation would be decimated.
>
> A Senator . . . wants to see some change in this law, but he is aware of the power of traditional opinion, and so seeks to [make] his proposal modest . . . [and full of safeguards against abuse]. According to the proposal, every per-son, before being allowed to emigrate, must fill out a questionnaire in which he states his income, his prospects, and so on; he must satisfy the authorities that he is living at a near starvation level.[6]

What if every Ruritanian were allowed to emigrate? That would clearly bring the entire (remaining) country over the threshold of harm to the brink of catastrophe. What if every Ruritanian in a position to gain by emigrating and desirous of doing so, were permitted to leave? That too might bring the remainder over the threshold of harm. What if the actual numbers of those applying to depart fall just short of the threshold but only because a substantial number of those standing to gain by departing do not apply because of self-sacrificing patriotic concern for the welfare of the country? In that case permitting the others to go would be to exploit the virtue of some of the remainder, and that would be an injustice. What

---

[6] Glanville Williams, "Euthanasia Legislation: A Rejoinder to the Non-Religious Objec-tions," in *Euthanasia and the Right to Die*, ed. A. B. Downing (London: Peter Owen, 1969), pp. 137–38.

if the Ruritanian government realizes that the number of those wishing to emigrate is sufficient to bring the country over the threshold of harm, and therefore establishes a quota of those who may leave, and a series of objective tests to assure that those in greatest need and those whose loss would least harm Ruritania, and *only* those, be allowed in the quota? That would be to avoid arbitrary and favoritistic selection.

In some ways Williams' analogy seems close to the euthanasia situation. Quite obviously, emigration is analogous to death. But in relevant ways the situations are quite different. In particular, threshold and quota arguments apply quite clearly in the emigration case, but not at all in the euthanasia situation. To the question what would happen if everyone in a position to gain (or cease to suffer) by means of euthanasia and who was genuinely desirous of doing so were legally entitled to have their lives ended, a complaisant answer could be given. There would be no threatened decimation of the population, indeed no appreciable movement toward the threshold of any accumulative social harm. People who would die soon anyway are allowed to do so slightly prematurely; all that is different is that a few months of intense pain and suffering are avoided—hardly a situation in which the conditions of social or economic harm accumulate with each new case in a steady march toward the threshold of harm.

SLIPPERY SLOPE ARGUMENTS

This common denomination refers to arguments of two quite distinct types, one logical, the other empirical. The logical argument maintains that the position under attack logically commits its advocate to another position that he does *not* advocate, and indeed which he may find antecedently unacceptable or repugnant. Thus if Alberto argues that all policy issues in a democratic state should be settled by a majority vote of parliament, Luigi may point out to Alberto that his position implies, indeed *logically requires*, the further position that it should be left up to the parliament to decide whom a person may be permitted to marry, a logical consequence that may fill Alberto with horror and cause him to withdraw or qualify his original position. Strictly speaking, the logical version of the slippery slope argument is a *reductio ad absurdum*—a demonstration that one's opponent is logically committed to a further position that even he will agree is unacceptable. Logical necessity is the slipperiest of all slopes. Once one sets foot on it, one is pushed by the force of logic alone irresistibly to the bottom of the slide.

In contrast, the arguments in the second broad slippery slope category rest on empirical generalizations rather than logical necessity, and are accordingly much more modest. The empirical arguments are of two sorts. The first may be called "falling domino" arguments, and the second, arguments from "the thin edge of the wedge." In the former type we are to think of the dominoes as already in place, on a stage already set. The fall of domino A is not particularly regrettable considered in itself ("on its own merits"), but it will knock down domino B, which unfortunately just happens to be in its path. But that is no tragedy in itself except that B is so located that when it falls it will knock over C, and so on until domino N falls, and that would be an evil considered entirely in its own right. In short, the fall of A initiates a causal sequence leading indirectly through intermediate steps to the relatively remote final result, which in turn is something generally agreed to be repugnant. Conservatives employ this kind of argument when they condemn measures that advance a welfare state on the ground that they lead to "creeping socialism." Liberals employ it when they argue against government censorship of pure pornography that it will lead step by step (domino by domino), as it has in the past, to censorship of serious literature with sexual themes. How good an argument of this form is depends upon how the dominoes are in fact arranged, and that is a matter that calls for empirical investigation.

The wedge argument shares this empirical character with the domino argument. Its claim, however, is not that the stage is already set either by design or chance, with the dominoes already in place for their multiple tumble, but rather that the policy under attack in the argument, however innocent its immediate goals may appear at first sight, will create, if only as a side effect, improved opportunities for subsequent independent steps, perhaps by independent agents, toward an ulterior goal that is unacceptable. "You say that you only want A," says the user of this argument to his opponent, "but once you win A and have your foot (or the thin edge of your wedge) in the door, you (or perhaps someone else with a different political program) will be better able to promote B, and having won B either they or others will have a better chance to gain C, and so on, down the bumpy road (to remix the metaphors!) to repugnant N." This slope is bumpy instead of slippery. Each step is distinct and new, and is meant to be achieved by employment of the improved opportunities created by the earlier steps. Each stage in the process is an intermediate political battle over one proposal, waged on the road to something else, and bringing the ultimate goal, something the speaker dreads and fears, that much closer. The wedge argument, when its factual premises are true, can be rationally legitimate, just like the other forms of the slippery slope argument. Furthermore, since it has no objection to first step A when considered on its merits alone, but deliberately overlooks those merits for the sake of what it takes to be offsetting evils located elsewhere and later in time, it falls into the class of arguments we have been considering in this chapter.

But how good are slippery slope arguments when deployed against permitting voluntary euthanasia of suffering terminal patients like Matthew

Donnelly or irreversibly comatose "living corpses" like Nancy Beth Cruzan? In this application the slippery slope arguments in all three forms fare poorly. The *reductio* argument, in all the forms in which it has been leveled against the legalization of voluntary euthanasia, is an especially dismal failure. If one explicitly restricts one's advocacy to *voluntary* euthanasia, then one can hardly be vulnerable to the charge that one's advocated position logically entails involuntary euthanasia, much less the Nazi pogroms of noneuthanasian murders. The latter charge is made superficially plausible to the unwary, in virtue of the historical fact that the Nazi used the word "euthanasia" in the very name of their programs of mass extermination of the physically handicapped, the mentally retarded, the racially "impure," and in the end of all whose existence created social or political problems for them. They were of course exploiting the laudatory associations of the word "euthanasia," which could then be used as a euphemistic cover for their evil activities. "Euthanasia" in the beginning meant merciful deliverance of hopeless sufferers at their requests and for *their* sakes, not over their protests and for the sake of the political convenience of others. One can hardly argue against recent advocates of voluntary euthanasia that the position they support logically entails their approval of the mass extermination of "undesirables"! There is no logic in that.

The fallen domino argument escapes that absurdity. Its claim is that the dominoes are so arranged that once a particular legislature legalizes voluntary euthanasia, then inevitably political pressures will mount for the legalization of nonvoluntary euthanasia, for example, of extremely impaired and pain-ridden newborn infants, or of hopelessly incompetent ("insane") adults, which will in due time be legalized, softening up public opinion for *involuntary* euthanasia (i.e., the killing of those who are capable of giving their voluntary consent, but refuse to do so), encouraging politicians to move in that direction, and so on. All these claims could be true, it should be emphasized, even though contrary to the intentions of the person who advocates *only* voluntary euthanasia. He may simply be unaware of the unfortunate way the dominoes happen to be situated relative to one another. Whether the argument is a good one depends on how the dominoes are in fact situated, and that is a complicated empirical question about which no one can pronounce with dogmatic confidence. But at least a look at the mere surface of things does not suggest the concealed presence underneath of all these ominous potentialities. And in any case, if there is a powerful independent moral case for the legalization of voluntary euthanasia, one would think that the burden would be on its opponents to show that the dominoes are lined up in order, and that the fall of those that are likely to topple would be a bad thing. The independent moral case is obvious enough. It derives from the virtue of compassion, the obligation to prevent suffering, and respect for the principle of self-determination.

The wedge version of the slippery slope argument has its own complications, but in the end, it is no stronger than the domino version. In many cases, the advocate of legalized voluntary euthanasia, being a humanitarian especially sensitive to suffering in others, will also, as an independent matter, support nonvoluntary euthanasia, say in newborn infants with congenital diseases, or with impairments incurred in pregnancy or delivery—exposed spinal cord, incurable incontinence, chronic pain, blindness, and brief life expectancy (all of these together). He will seem vulnerable to the charge that "Because of the existence of many persons like you, it is wrong to legalize voluntary euthanasia for the likes of Matthew Donnelly and Nancy Cruzan. Once you get your wedge inserted in this way, it will encourage you, and improve your opportunity to legalize euthanasia for hopelessly suffering infants, and who knows where the process will stop? Baby-killing generally will follow, then killing of retarded adults, and so on." But the psychological attitudes (sympathy and respect) that lead one to advocate euthanasia for the intensely suffering hopelessly doomed, whether competent or not, would not lead anyone to advocate "baby-killing generally" or the killing of the retarded, any more than humanitarianism slides naturally or inevitably into Nazi cruelty. The danger is imaginary, or at the very least needs empirical corroboration. As for the step from voluntary euthanasia to the killing, at parental request, of hopelessly doomed infants, that is a natural movement. But this concession should not leave the opponent of euthanasia jubilant for long. His humanitarian opponent might well respond to this application of the wedge argument as C. M. Cornford did "when he said that the wedge argument means this: that you should not act justly today, for fear that you may be asked to act still more justly tomorrow."[7]

In summary, we have found in everyday reasoning that there are some exceptionless negative resolutions, prohibitory rules, and principled denials that are defended with argument even though their defenders acknowledge that their applications in some individual cases are silly, unfortunate, or harmful. Deliberately overlooking these bad results in some individual cases is said to be a price worth paying to secure the greater benefits of the absolute prohibition. Some of these everyday arguments can be quite rational and convincing. It is rational to cultivate certain useful habits even to the point of rigidity, and even at the cost of making automatic responses in particular situations, responses that are silly and unnecessary considered in their own right, for example. Similarly, it *can* be a rational social policy to withhold from trustworthy individuals discretion to make their own decisions on the ground that the less trustworthy individuals who would also be given that discretion by the same general rule might abuse it with

---

[7] C. M. Cornford, as quoted by Glanville Williams, ibid., p. 143.

socially harmful results. This form of argument, which would have us tolerate restrictions that are pointless in some individual cases, can be rational to the extent that techniques to separate those who can be trusted with discretion from those who cannot, say by licensing procedures, are difficult and impractical. Even statistical discrimination, which treats individuals as bearers of statistical properties, rather than judging each on his own individual merits or demerits, can sometimes be justified although in many contexts it is strikingly unfair.

Opponents of capital punishment (as I mentioned in the previous chapter) often argue that even though in most individual cases we can be confident that the convicted prisoner really is guilty and really does deserve to die, we should nevertheless deliberately overlook the evidence in these individual cases and choose instead a general rule forbidding the death penalty across the board on the ground that mistakes inevitably occur, and that when they do, the injustice of punishing an innocent person is so odious that it is worth forebearing to execute hundreds of criminals who deserve death in order to avoid executing one who does not. That argument too can be convincing, even though it treats individual cases with a predetermined rigidity.

Threshold arguments for universal prohibitions of those actions that lead to accumulations of conditions approaching the threshold of harm often tend to be unconvincing in everyday situations, especially when the accumulations will not reach that threshold if only a licensed few perform the actions in question, and this privileged minority can be licensed without objectionable arbitrariness or favoritism. When these conditions cannot be satisfied, however, then threshold arguments lose their cogency, and the rule-maker can say to the person who is restricted that he may not do actions that in his case would be harmless enough, because if everyone who wishes to do the same were also permitted to do so, the results would be socially harmful. This too is a form of everyday argument for neglecting to judge individual cases "on the merits." But cogent as it may be elsewhere, it is a total failure in the euthanasia context.

Finally there are the three versions of the slippery slope argument, all of which *can* be compelling when the requirements of logical necessitation are properly recognized, or when the empirical facts are as maintained and the dominoes are situated in the appropriate fashion, and when the next stop down the slope would be an evil rather than a good. Slippery slope arguments are frequently abused, but there is no necessity that this be the case. In any event, they are sometimes valid, and they make clear examples of arguments for rigid policies that justify deliberately overlooking the merits of individual cases in applying some general inhibition or restriction.

The important point for our present purposes, however, is that even though they can be convincing in some everyday contexts, none of these forms of argument are plausible models for the categorical restriction of voluntary euthanasia. The consequences of preventing a person from achieving deliverance from pain in a given case, for example, are much worse than the silliness of redundancy of rigid habit application. The undeserved treatment justified by the argument against capital punishment is an undeserved benefit for those convicted murderers who deserve to die, not the undeserved harsh treatment of the suffering terminal patient, so the former can hardly be a model for the latter. Statistical discrimination may be justified in some contexts, but it hardly applies to those who are terminally ill, since they constitute a random aggregate about which no relevant statistical inferences may be made. Threshold arguments are plausible when applied to the harms caused to a country by the massive and uncontrolled emigration of its citizens, but nothing like that sort of accumulation to the threshold of social harm can be found in the euthanasia situation.

Chapter Thirteen

ABSURD SELF-FULFILLMENT

A RECENT AUTHOR adds a twist to the ancient legend of Sisyphus, who was condemned by the gods to perpetual life spent pushing a large rock to the top of a hill from which it fell down the other side, once more to be pushed to the top, and so on forever. "Let us suppose," writes Richard Taylor, "that the gods, while condemning Sisyphus to the fate just described, at the same time, as an afterthought, waxed perversely merciful by implanting in him a strange and irrational impulse, namely a compulsive impulse to roll stones . . . e.g. through implanting some substance that has this effect on his character and drives."[1] Such a modification would be merciful but also "perverse," Taylor maintains, "because from our point of view there is clearly no reason why anyone should have a persistent and insatiable desire to do something as pointless as that."[2]

Taylor's remodeled Sisyphus, meaningless as his activities may seem to us, at least can find his rock-pushing career *fulfilling*. Insofar as a powerful disposition to push rocks has been built into him, he is only doing what he is inclined by his nature to do when he pushes the rock, just as a dog fulfills his nature by chasing a rabbit, or a bird by building a nest. One can criticize Taylor, however, for his apparent confusion of self-fulfillment (doing what it is in one's nature to do) with compulsion. In Taylor's revision of the legend, a substance in Sisyphus's blood forces him to "want" to push stones, just as repeated injections of heroin into the veins of an unwilling prisoner would impose an addiction to heroin on him and make him "want" his subsequent fixes. The causal mechanism employed by the gods, however, need not be that crude, and we can imagine that they remake Sisyphus's nature in a more thoroughgoing way so that the disposition to push large objects, stemming from a reconstructed complex of glands and nerves and basic drives, becomes an integral part of Sisyphus's self rather than an alien element restraining him. Let us add a twist to Taylor's twist then, and have the gods provide Sisyphus with a new nature rather than imposing an addiction on his old one. We can think of a rock-pushing Sisyphus as no more "addicted" to his characteristic activities than we are to walking upright or to speaking a language. Our new Sisyphus's activities, furthermore, are self-fulfilling, not simply because they satisfy his de-

[1] Richard Taylor, *Good and Evil* (London: Macmillan, 1970), p. 259.
[2] Ibid.

sires, nor simply because they involve his own willful acquiescence, but rather because they express some basic genetic disposition of his nature.

Taylor does not use the word "absurd" in describing Sisyphus's peculiar activities, but a whole tradition, one of whose most prominent recent members was Albert Camus,[3] finds that term eminently appropriate. The words Taylor uses are "meaningless," "pointless," and "endless." Perhaps endless repetitive cycles of pointless labor with no apparent purpose or result is only one species of absurdity, or perhaps pointlessness is only one among several grounds for judging an activity to be absurd. (The closely related but distinct characteristic of futility through purposeful but self-defeating actions may be another.) In either case, pointlessness and generic absurdity are not identical notions. But few would deny the synthetic judgment that there *is* an absurdity in pointless labors that will plainly come to nothing. Taylor isolates this absurdity by contrasting it with both painfulness and loneliness. It is not because Sisyphus's labors are arduous and body-bruising that they are absurd, for we can imagine that his rock is small and his labors undemanding. They would be no less pointless, and therefore no less absurd for that. Moreover, as Taylor suggests, we could give Sisyphus some partners so that the rock-moving activities are conducted by teams of two or more persons. That would reduce the loneliness of the enterprise but not its silliness. The essential absurdity of pointless activity is captured in a non-Sisyphean example that Taylor himself provides: "Two groups of prisoners, one of them engaged in digging a prodigious hole in the ground that is no sooner finished than it is filled in again by the other group, the latter then digging a new hole that is at once filled in by the first group and so on endlessly."[4]

Many philosophers have said that insofar as human existence is absurd, there is a ground for certain negative attitudes—suicidal despair, detached cynicism, philosophical pessimism, Camus' haughty scorn or existential defiance. Other philosophers, addressing a somewhat different datum, have said that insofar as a given human life is self-fulfilled it is a good life, and provides a reason for certain positive attitudes toward the human condition—hope, satisfaction, acceptance, or reconciliation. Often the "optimists" say that some lives, at least, are completely fulfilled and most lives fulfilled to some degree or other. There is no antecedent necessity that they all be fulfilled or that they all be unfulfilled; it all depends on skill or luck. "Pessimists," on the other hand, claim that all lives are necessarily absurd (meaningless, pointless, futile), so their view is more sweeping. In any event, "absurdity" and "self-fulfillment" are quite different notions so that

---

[3] The various essays in which Camus gives his most thorough account of absurdity have been translated into English by Justin O'Brien and published in one volume under the title *The Myth of Sisyphus and Other Essays* (New York: Random House, 1955).

[4] Taylor, *Good and Evil*, p. 258.

optimists and pessimists are not even talking about the same thing. Taylor suggests, quite plausibly, that life might be *both* absurd and at its best, sometimes, self-fulfilling. What are we to make of that combination of truths? What are the consequences for optimism and pessimism? What general attitudes are appropriate if it is accepted? These questions call for closer examination of the concepts of "absurdity" and "self-fulfillment" and how they might fit together, and some comments on the question of how we can judge the rational appropriateness of cosmic attitudes.

ABSURDITY IN INDIVIDUAL LIVES

We should attend to the undeniable examples of absurdity *in* life before raising the subject of the absurdity *of* life. Since some elements in any life are absurd, we can focus our attention on these familiar occurrences and inquire what it is we are saying about them when we judge them to be absurd. Thomas Nagel provides some useful instances of absurd events that, since they are easy to respond to playfully, are irresistibly comic: "Someone gives a complicated speech in support of a motion that has already been passed; a notorious criminal is made president of a major philanthropic foundation; you declare your love over the telephone to a recorded announcement; as you are knighted your pants fall down."[5] Some of Nagel's examples are human actions that can be criticized as reasonable or unreasonable in relation to the actor's presumed motives and ends. Others are mere happenings leading directly to states of affairs that themselves can be thought of as irrational relative to some larger presumed purposes: The image of a great statesman or scientist standing bare-legged with his trousers around his ankles as the queen tries to award him his knighthood conflicts irrationally with the presumed purpose of the ceremony, which in part is to create a dignified and moving spectacle. *If* the pants-dropping incident had been deliberately chosen it would have been subject to the charge of irrationality, since it could have been anticipated to produce results that would defeat the larger purposes for which it was chosen. In this indirect way, even mere occurrences and unchosen states of affairs can be judged "irrational," and sometimes irrational to the point of absurdity. In addition to doings, activities, careers and lives, mere happenings and states of affairs, we also judge beliefs, hypotheses, convictions, desires, purposes, and even people to be absurd, and usually we can explain what this means in a fairly straightforward way by substituting the word "irrational" and locating the absurdity in question on a map of the various species of irrationality. On other occasions, as in the fallen pants example, a mere occurrence is related indirectly to irrationality by the showing that *if* it were

[5] Thomas Nagel, "The Absurd," *Journal of Philosophy* 68 (1971): 718.

thought, contrary to fact, to be somebody's deliberate doing, that doing would be patently irrational.

The paradigmatic type of irrationality is false or unwarranted belief. When something analogous to flagrant falsity or manifestly fallacious argument is a defect of such nonbeliefs as desires, purposes, instrumentalities, actions, and states of affairs, then they too can be characterized as irrational or unreasonable, although the word "absurd" seems to fit them more comfortably. *Websters Collegiate Dictionary* tells us that when the intensifier *ab* was added to the Latin word *surdus* (dull, deaf, insensible), the result was a Latin word translatable as "not to be heard from," and the derivative English word meaning "laughingly inconsistent with what is judged as true or reasonable." "Falsehood" and "invalidity," then, are not quite enough to explain absurdity. The absurd is what is *palpably* untrue or unreasonable, outlandishly and preposterously so, literally "unheard of" or not to be entertained. One element, then, that the various sorts of absurd things have in common is their extreme irrationality, whether that be the apparently knowing assertion of manifestly false propositions, or the apparently voluntary making of manifestly unreasonable decisions, or the apparently eager living of a manifestly pointless life.

A second element in all absurdity is implicit in the first, but deserves to be clearly stated on its own. Where there is absurdity there are always two things clashing or in disharmony, distinguishable entities that conflict with one another. This element is referred to variously as the "divorce,"[6] disparity, discrepancy, disproportion, or incongruity between discordant objects. In general, things that do not fit together—means discrepant with ends, premises incongruous with conclusions, ideals disharmonious with practice, pretensions in conflict with realities—are found wherever there is absurdity. But having located the absurdity, we may attribute it either to the relation of disharmony itself, or exclusively to one, or to the other, of the discordant objects.

In some cases we adopt the point of view of the standard and "laugh down" at the incongruous object, as when we delight in the undignified fall of the pompously powerful. In other cases we take the opposite viewpoint, that of the comically discrepant object itself, and we laugh at the standard, as, for example, when we laugh at cute children masquerading as adults, or in a quite different example, we laugh at a risqué story and thus have some fun with the sexual conventions violated in the tale. Perhaps not all funny things are absurd, and surely not all absurd things are funny, but discordance is an element common to many comic and absurd things.

Another form of disparity is described in Nagel's astute account of ab-

---

[6] Camus, *Myth of Sisyphus*, p. 22.

surdity,[7] namely, the clash or disharmony between various perspectives from which we form attitudes and make judgments. There is an unavoidable discrepancy between the natural subjective way of viewing ourselves— as precious in our own eyes, full of genuinely important projects, whole universes in ourselves, persons who "live only once" and have to make the most of the time allotted us—and various hypothetical judgments made from a more universal perspective: we are mere specks, or drops in the ocean, or one of the teeming hive, absolutely inessential to the grand scheme of things, no more lovable in ourselves than are any of the zillions of individual insects whose infinitesimally transitory lives are equally as unimportant in the long run as our own. Our subjective point of view is an expression of the "seriousness" with which all living beings must view their situations, a necessary expression of our biological natures. But the broader perspectives that yield a different and conflicting picture are available to any being with imagination and modest conceptual development. Judged from these perspectives, the human expenditures of effort and emotion in the pursuit of "important goals" are just so many posturings, and we mortals are absurd figures who strut and fret our hour upon the stage. The absurdity in the human condition, Nagel tells us, consists in a special kind of conspicuous discrepancy, that between unavoidable pretension or aspiration, on the one hand, and reality as perceived from a truer perspective on the other.

Not all of Nagel's examples of absurdity within human lives are equally plausible models for the alleged absurdity of human life as such. Applied to Sisyphus, at any rate, and to some actual Sisyphean lives, Nagel's "conspicuous discrepancy between pretension or aspiration and reality" seems less strikingly relevant than Taylor's conception of absurdity as ultimate futility and pointlessness. Careful reconsideration, however, will reveal that Taylor's "futility or pointlessness of activity" and Nagel's "discrepancy of perspectives for viewing oneself," while irreducibly distinct types of absurdity, are nonetheless equally proper examples of the absurd genus. Taylor's type of absurdity applies more naturally to the Sisyphean model for the human condition, but Nagel's conception provides another model of its own, equally challenging as a picture of the absurdity of human life as a whole, and equally familiar, as a recent *New Yorker* cartoon shows. Two small figures, recognizable as a well-dressed middle-class couple, are on the patio of their suburban home, while above them a full moon and vast panoply of stars glimmer and sparkle. The discrepancy between the human beings' inevitably extravagant sense of self-importance and their actual tiny role in the whole picture is indicated by the little man's comment to his

---

[7] Nagel, "Absurd," pp. 716–27. See also his *The View from Nowhere* (New York: Oxford University Press, 1986), pp. 208–32.

little wife: "Why, no! Why should I feel small? I've just been put in charge of the whole Eastern region."[8]

Nagel's kind of absurdity is not necessarily involved in the Sisyphus story, but if it is added to the pointless labor that *is* involved, it adds a whole new dimension of absurdity to that already present. Moreover, Sisyphus's labors might be motivated by a genuinely sensible purpose, and thus be unabsurd in Taylor's sense, yet absurd anyway in a sense closer to Nagel's. Imagine, for example, that the gods have sentenced Sisyphus only to climb a large mountain and plant a small flag on the top. As soon as he succeeds in doing that, his penalty has been paid once and for all. It takes Sisyphus years (or centuries) to climb the mountain but then he finds that he has forgotten the flag. He returns to the base, recovers the flag, and spends another millennium or so climbing a peak only to discover that he is on the wrong mountain. And so on *ad infinitum*. Sisyphus's labors would not be pointless in that case since they would have a sensible aim, but how genuinely absurd his constant mistakes would be whether committed in pursuit of a purpose or not! Or suppose that the gods in the original legend had not only assigned Sisyphus his endless self-defeating labor, but had also required him, before each trip to the summit, to write "I am a bad boy" one hundred times on his rock. What an absurd comedown for the proud and once mighty Sisyphus! Now his labors are doubly absurd, both pointless and conflicting with his natural self-importance.

Moreover, to further accentuate the difference between Taylor's and Nagel's criteria, it can be noted that the traditional Sisyphus, before we began tampering with the legend, was *not* absurd by Nagel's criterion. He had no illusions or false pretensions, and his resigned "aspiration," although pointless, was perfectly realistic. If his plight, therefore, is to be taken as a model for the absurdity of the whole human enterprise, we shall have to expand Nagel's account of absurdity to include examples from within human life of the sort Taylor emphasized, for instance, the prisoners' digging and filling in of holes, or the ordering of intricately ornate wedding cakes and consuming of them before they are even wrapped, or in general giving with one hand and taking away with the other[9] contrary to all reason. Taylor's and Nagel's conceptions of absurdity, however, do share a generic

---

[8] Cartoon by Handelsman, *New Yorker*, July 6, 1981, p. 34.

[9] Or first taking away and then giving, as in the unfunny example of absurdity from the Civil War: "Lincoln and Brooks lingered at the cot of a wounded soldier who held with a weak white hand a tract given him by a well-dressed lady performing good works that morning. The soldier read the title of the tract and then began laughing. Lincoln noticed that the lady of good works was still nearby, and told the soldier that undoubtedly the lady meant well. 'It is hardly fair of you to laugh at her gift.' The soldier gave Lincoln something to remember. 'Mr. President, how can I help laughing a little? She has given me a tract on the "Sin of Dancing," and both my legs are shot off' " (Carl Sandburg, *Abraham Lincoln: The War Years* [New York: Harcourt, Brace, 1926], 2:293).

character. They are two distinct species of absurdity but both can be subsumed, in their separate ways, under the "discrepancy" rubric. The discrepancy in Taylor's case is that between the kind of labor that is normally thought to be sheer drudgery and a purpose inadequate to justify it or to provide it with any reason whatsoever. Ultimately, pointlessness is a kind of discrepancy, or massive disproportion, between means and ends. It must also be said, in fairness to Nagel, that his conception of absurdity *can* be applied to some Sisyphean individuals. If in fact some of us are quite similar to Sisyphus, but we pretend to be otherwise, then we are absurd in Nagel's sense too.

A careful perusal of absurd elements within individual human lives will disclose still other models of absurdity in addition to Taylor's "pointlessness" and Nagel's "unrealistic pretension and aspiration," and these additional types of absurdity can also be treated as species of discrepancy, conflict, or disproportion. We must first follow up our earlier suggestion by distinguishing pointlessness from futility. A pointless action or activity is one that has no intelligible purpose the achievement of which gives it value and explanation ("point" or "meaning"). Moreover, it is not the kind of activity that carries its own reward quite independently of any further purpose, but rather the sort of activity we normally think of as sheer drudgery (like rock-pushing). Since it does not possess value in itself, but rather, if anything, a kind of negative value, and it has no envisaged consequences for the sake of which it is undertaken, it is utterly valueless, or worse. A totally pointless activity will not only lack a conscious objective beyond itself; it will also lack any unforeseen actual consequences that could confer value back on it by a kind of fluke.

Some activities have a point, but are very little less absurd than totally pointless activities since their conscious objective is manifestly incapable of justifying the drudgery that is meant to achieve it. The intrinsic disvalue of the activity is an exorbitant (hence irrational) price to pay for so trivial a reward. Sisyphus's labors would not be totally pointless if his whole motive was to receive a piece of candy from the gods every century or so. His endless labors would hardly be any less absurd in that case, and the absurdity in question would be a manifest disproportion between means and end. Following W. D. Joske, we can call this species of absurdity *triviality*.[10] Obviously burdensome activities that are absurdly trivial are

---

[10] W. D. Joske, "Philosophy and the Meaning of Life," *Australasian Journal of Philosophy* 52 (August 1974): 93–104. Joske gives an example of a whole individual life that could seem absurd because trivial in this sense. "We find ourselves bewildered by the school master in Guthrie Wilson's novel, *The Incorruptibles*, who devotes his life to parsing and analyzing every sentence of *Paradise Lost*." A contrasting example of a life that is absurd because futile would be one devoted full-time to an attempt to square the circle.

not much less absurd than burdensome activities that are wholly point-less.

Futile activities (still another species of absurdity) do have a point, and a reasonably proportionate one, but nonetheless are absurd because they are manifestly inefficacious means to the achievement of their nontrivial goals. If they had a chance to achieve the worthy objective that motivates them, they would not be absurd, but it is evident to us, the observers, or even in the worst case to the actors themselves, that continued participation in the intrinsically valueless activity will be fruitless, hence futile. The reasons for the absurd activity's instrumental inefficacy can be various. In the simplest cases, nature itself stands in the way and success is rendered impossible by laws of nature, as with efforts to high-jump ten feet off the ground, or by contingent individual incapacities, as when a dog repeatedly chases sea gulls on a beach with the presumed intention of catching one of them, but continually fails because of its lack of speed and other requisite physical skills, but never gives up making its absurd efforts. The most in-teresting class of futile activities, however, are those in which the instru-mental inefficacies are the result of the self-defeating character of the actor's own techniques and strategies, especially when flagrant and manifest to any observer. The tale is told of a workman who opens his lunch pail every noon, examines his sandwiches, and comments; "Ugh, tuna fish again." Finally, after weeks of witnessing this ritual, a fellow worker asks, "Why don't you have your wife make you some other kind of sandwich?" to which the first worker replies, "Oh, I'm not married. I make my own lunches." The worker's constant failure could be charged to poor memory or some other cognitive failure, but to the observer who thinks of it as absurd, it is as if the actor deliberately takes steps every day to frustrate his own purposess.

In summary, purposeful activities can be placed on a spectrum of ab-surdity. At the one extreme are intrinsically worthless activities that are engaged in even though they have no vindicating purpose beyond them-selves. These activities are totally pointless. Then come burdensome or dis-liked activities engaged in only because they are expected to produce some minor advantage for which the instrumental labors are massively dispro-portionate. These are absuredly trivial activities. They too constitute a whole section of the spectrum, becoming less and less absurd as their achieved goals reduce the disproportion of their means. Then come the inherently burdensome activities that do have a clearly vindicating purpose but are ill-designed to achieve them. These are absurdly futile activities when it would be plainly evident to an observer that they are hopelessly inefficacious. If there is a chance of success, the activity may be reasonable, hence unabsurd, even though in fact the vindicating objective is never achieved. To these absurdities, explained in term of means-ends disproportions, we must add Nagel's favorite types of absurdity, which are explained in terms of other poor fits, especially the failure of pretensions and aspirations to fit objective facts. In short, an absurd element within an individual life can fall within five or more categories. It can be pointless, trivial (instrumentally disporportionate), futile, unrealistically pretentious, or otherwise incongruous or a "poor fit," like actions that presuppose false or logically inconsistent beliefs.

THE ALLEGED ABSURDITY OF HUMAN LIFE AS SUCH: SOME PHILOSOPHICAL INDICTMENTS

Taylor, Camus, and Nagel, each in his own way and each making his own special qualifications, looks with favor on the judgment that there is absurdity in the human condition as such. It will be useful here to discuss critically some of the reasons given by these philosophers. We can begin with Taylor who finds all human activity to be as pointless (in the long run) as that of Sisyphus. He uses the words "meaningless" and "pointless" instead of "absurd," and as we have seen, means by them "endless repetitive activity that comes to nothing." The endlessness, no doubt, is not essential to the meaninglessness. If Sisyphus pushed his rock continuously for four score and ten years only, before being mercifully killed by the gods, Taylor could and would judge his finite career as a rock-mover to be absurd, just as he judges the finite lives of men and mice to be absurd.

Meaninglessness for Taylor is mitigated but not cancelled by achievement, because achievements do not last. Some achievements, for example *Hamlet*, Beethoven's *Fifth Symphony*, and the Notre Dame cathedral, last longer than others, and might therefore qualify as less absurd than the transient and trivial triumphs in which most of us take what pride we can. But from any sufficiently broad point of view, long compared with the span of human lives or even the lives of nations and planets, but infinitely narrower than the perspective *sub specie aeternitatis*, the difference beween the durability of Notre Dame and that of a pioneer's log cabin is utterly insignificant. All of our goals, Taylor says, are of "transitory significance," and "having gained one of them we immediately set forth for the next as if that one had never been, with this next one being essentially more of the same."[11] Unlike Sisyphus, however, most of us beget children and pass on our values, our modest achievements, and fresh opportunities to them. That fact does not impress Taylor, who replies that "Each man's life thus resembles one of Sisyphus's climbs to the summit of his hill and each day of it one of his steps; the difference is that whereas Sisyphus himself returns

[11] Taylor, *Good and Evil*, p. 262.

to push the stone up again, we leave this to our children."[12] The enterprise is thus collective, but it still comes to nothing in the end.

What could human existence conceivably be like if it were to escape this absurdity? This is a crucial question that all philosophical pessimists must answer if their sweeping judgments of universal absurdity are to be fully intelligible. For unless we know what contrasting situation is being ruled out we cannot be sure what a given assertion is "including in." Unless we know what *would* count as nonabsurdity, if there were such a thing, we have nothing to contrast absurdity with. If all conceivable universes are equally and necessarily absurd on their face, so that one cannot even describe what nonabsurd existence would be like, it is not very informative, to put it mildly, to affirm that this our actual universe is absurd. It is a test of the intelligiblity of a philosophical doctrine that it succeed in ruling out some contrasting state of affairs.

Taylor's doctrine fortunately seems to pass the test, more or less. He has us imagine that Sisyphus is permitted to push an assortment of stones to the top of his hill and combine them there into a beautiful and enduring temple. This would be to escape absurdity, Taylor says at first, for "activity . . . has a meaning if it has some significant culmination, some more or less lasting end that can be considered to have been the direction and purpose of the activity."[13] But soon he changes his mind. He does not wish to make meaningfulness a matter of "more or less," for then he would have to admit that some human activities and lives are to some degree, at least, meaningful, and comparisons of the relative meaningfulness of various individual lives would at least make sense. But that would be to vindicate rather than to destroy common sense on this question, and Taylor, his sights set high, quickly withdraws his concession by requiring that the temple must endure—not simply be "more or less lasting"—"adding beauty to the world for the remainder of time."[14] When we look at a meaningless life like that of the legendary Sisyphus or that of a drug-addicted teenage suicide, and compare it with one of the relatively meaningful human lives suggested by common sense, say that of Jefferson or Shakespeare, the differences at first are striking. But "if we look at them from a distance" (say from a point in time one hundred million years from now) they "are in outline the same and convey to the mind the same image"—pointless labor and emotion coming to nothing.[15] It is the temporal distance that make the difference. The view from remote distances in time reveals things as they truly are, whereas the detailed close-up picture is distorted and illusory.

Taylor makes another hypothetical supposition. Let us suppose that af-

[12] Ibid., p. 263.
[13] Ibid., p. 260.
[14] Ibid., p. 263.
[15] Ibid., p. 264.

ter a finite period of intense labor Sisyphus finishes a gloriously beautiful temple, and then is allowed by the gods to rest on his laurels and spend the rest of eternal time in admiring contemplation of his significant achievement. Now at last we seem to have an unchallengeable conception of non-absurd existence, but Taylor quickly dashes our hopes. Eternal rest, he rightly claims, would be "infinite boredom," and that too would become in due time a kind of pointlessness or absurdity. Unfortunately, he does not consider other possibilities that would save his doctrine of universal absurdity from vacuity. For example, Sisyphus could be allowed to die after a brief rest period but before his proud satisfaction turns to boredom, while his temple is preserved forever by the gods, or Sisyphus could be permitted to live forever, alternating creative activity with replenishing periods of rest, while the gods guarantee the permanence of his achievements. I suspect that Taylor, like Bernard Williams,[16] would find even the latter arrangement no escape from infinite boredom, so that his final view, if he had finished his argument, would be that *almost* any conceivable form of life would be absurd, either because it fails to produce permanently lasting achievements or because it leads to boredom. The qualifier "almost" serves to give meaningful contrast to Taylor's absurdism since the remaining conception of nonabsurd existence rules out a relevant contrast (merciful death with the assurance of everlasting preservation of achievements).

Permanent preservation of personal achievement is not, however, a plausible requirement for nonabsurd meaningfulness. Indeed, there is something absurd in the idea that the gods would clutter up the universe to all eternity with modest monuments to everyone's best deeds. And if only Shakespearian and Beethovian triumphs are preserved, then by Taylor's standards, life becomes absurd for all the rest of us.

According to Camus, human beings necessarily crave a certain kind of cosmic order, significant culminations of their efforts, and a kind of transparent rational intelligibility in the world of experince. But the world has no such order; it works to destroy the point of whatever temporary achievements it permits; and it is in its central core alien, dense, and irrational. Hence the inevitable confrontation and the inevitable absurdity.

Camus seems to know exactly what he wants from the world. He believes also that the world, by its very nature, cannot provide him with what

---

[16] Bernard Williams, "The Makropoulos Case: Reflections on the Tedium of Immortality," in *Problems of the Self* (Cambridge: Cambridge University Press, 1973), pp. 82–100. Jonathan Glover replies to Williams: "But I am not convinced that someone with a fairly constant character *need* eventually become intolerably bored, so long as [he] can watch the world continue to unfold and go on asking new questions and thinking, and so long as there are other people to share their feelings and thoughts with. Given the company of the right people, I would be glad of the chance to sample a few million years and see how it went" (*Causing Death and Saving Lives* [Harmondsworth: Penguin, 1977], p. 57).

he wants, and that he, by his very nature, cannot modify or relinquish those wants, hopeless though they be. There is therefore a "divorce" in the nature of things, an ineradicable discrepancy between human nature and the rest of nature, and it is this irreconcilable clash that generates the absurdity of the human condition. He wants a universe that cares about him personally, a world that he can identify with instead of feeling alienated from, a world that can heal the deep sense of loneliness all sensitive beings experience when they encounter nature as an "other." Most of all, he cannot help wanting to live forever, although as a rational being he knows that death is inevitable. His unmodifiable yet unsatisfiable desires are more then mere wants; they are natural *needs*. "The absurd is born of this confrontation between human need and the unreasonable silence of the world."[17]

Camus eloquently describes the feeling of absurdity evoked in him by forests and oceans ("At the heart of all natural beauty lies something inhuman"), and by bustling human marketplaces. Always at its core is a vital yearning that he knows has no hope of satisfaction, yet no possibility of being extinguished. "At any street corner the feeling of absurdity can strike any person in the face."[18] One reliable evoker of that feeling is what Camus calls the "collapse of the stage setting." Individual lives proceed according to their fixed rhythms, and then suddenly "one day the 'why' arises and . . . [a] weariness tinged with amazement."[19] The feeling to which Camus here refers is one, I dare say, that almost all of us have experienced at one time or another, but for pessimistic philosophers it is more than a feeling, in that it contains the materials for an argument for human absurdity. I first remember experiencing the feeling and toying with the argument while observing crowds of shoppers in a supermarket. (Since then, I have come to call it the "supermarket regress.") Suddenly the stage setting collapsed, and the shoppers' life patterns seemed to make no more sense than the hole-digging in Taylor's example of the prisoners. Why are all those people standing in line before the cash registers? In order to purchase food. Why do they purchase food? In order to stay alive and healthy. Why do they wish to stay alive and healthy? So that they can work at their jobs. Why do they want to work? To earn money. Why do they want to earn money? So that they can purchase food. And so on, around the circle, over and over, with no "significant culmination" in sight. Vindicating purpose and meaning are constantly put off to another stage that never comes, and the whole round of activity looks more like a meaningless ritual-dance than something coherent and self-justifying.

As an argument for inevitable absurdity, the supermarket regress is only

---

[17] Camus, *Myth of Sisyphus*, p. 21.
[18] Ibid., p. 9.
[19] Ibid., p. 10.

as strong as its premises. One presupposition of the argument in particular is weak, namely, the assumption that no human activity is ever valuable in *itself*, but that vindicating value is always postponed until some future consequence arrives, which in turn can never be valuable in itself but only valuable as a means to something else that cannot be valuable in itself, and so on, forever. This paradox is not an accurate picture of all human activity, striking as it may seem when it naturally suggests itself to an observer of crowds of human animals mechanically pursuing their ritualized goals. In fact, the impossibility of intrinsically valuable activity is itself an illusion produced by what Moritz Schlick in a remarkable essay[20] called "the tyranny of purpose."

There is another kind of insight, also natural and common, that can lead one too hastily to interpret human activity as absurd. Altogether unlike Camus, we can think of ourselves as part and parcel of nature, one biological species among many others. Then we can examine the life cycles of the lesser species and come to appreciate their absurd character, here responding not to apparent circularity as in the human case, but to a value regress proper, in which justifying purposes are put off forever. Various insects,[21] amphibians, and fish, for example, seem to have no ultimate purpose of their own but to stay alive long enough to reproduce, so that their progeny can also stay alive long enough to reproduce, and so on forever, as if simply keeping a species in existence were an end in itself with no further purpose needed. This has seemed to many human observers to be the very model of absurdity, an utterly pointless existence.

The absurdity is accentuated in the case of species like the salmon, whose members struggle and strive heroically, swimming against the currents, battered against rocks, plundered by predators, until the survivors reach the headwaters of their native streams, tattered, torn, and dying. Even then the ordeal is not over, for the males at least must fight off their own intraspecies competitors for an opportunity to entice females to lay eggs, to fertilize them, and only then to die. What is the point of all this effort? Simply to produce another generation of tiny salmon to start all over again, feeding and growing as they head down river toward the ocean, then after a time in salt water, heading back upstream amid the many dangers and against all odds, to reproduce and die. The whole process has no apparent point except its own further continuance. To some human observers that natural cycle is a kind of collective effort to discharge a task that makes no more sense than that assigned as punishment to the solitary Sisyphus. The human life style is perhaps less fixed and rigid, and surely more varied, but

[20] Moritz Schlick, "On the Meaning of Life," in *Philosophical Papers* (Dordrecht: Reidel, 1979), 2:112–28.

[21] See Taylor's illustration of the New Zealand Cave Glowworm (*Good and Evil*, pp. 261–62).

insofar as it resembles that of the insects, toads, and fish, it is equally self-contained and pointless.

The best response to this argument is that it projects human needs and sensibilities into other species. The human observer simply does not have the salmon's point of view. A well-bred salmon will love the life of a salmon, which after all, is the only life it can know. The life cycle for it may seem to be its own point, with no further purpose, no further achievement external to it, needed to establish its rational credentials. To insist that without permanently preserved achievements and lasting monuments, the life of a salmon is absurd, is a piece of parochial prejudice on the part of human beings.

Both the supermarket circle and the biological regress purport to show that human life is pointless because justification for any of its parts or phases is indefinitely postponed, never coming to a final resting place. We choose to do A only because it will lead to B, which we desire only because of its conducibility to C, which we value only as a means to D, and so on. In the biological regress argument the chain of justification proceeds in a straight line, so to speak, never coming to an end. It therefore fails to show how any component human activity can truly have a point beyond itself. In the supermarket version of the argument the chain does not proceed endlessly and infinitely only because it closes a circle at some point going round and round indefinitely, starting over again at regular intervals without ever having justified anything. Nagel thinks of these arguments as "standard" attempts to demonstrate absurdity, and although he is sympathetic to their motives and conclusions, he regards them as failures. Part of his ground for rejecting the arguments from circular and linear regression is factual. Some individual acts within life, he says, have a point even if the general statement of (say) the supermarket regression is correct. "Chains of justification come repeatedly to an end within life, and whether the process as a whole can be justified has no bearing on the finality of the end points. No further justification is needed to make it reasonable to take aspirin for a headache, attend an exhibit of the work of a painter one admires, or stop a child from putting his hand on a hot stove. No larger context or further purpose is needed to prevent these acts from being pointless."[22]

Nagel's three examples of actions with a genuine point beyond themselves make a heterogeneous lot, but the aspirin and hot stove examples, at least, convincing as they are, do not substantially weaken the force of the supermarket circular regress. One can think of human life as an endlessly circular quest for a vindicating point that is never to be found, even though some individual acts in the generally pointless pursuit do have *their* points. It is possible after all to hold *both* that there is a point in taking aspirin and

[22] Nagel, "Absurd," p. 724.

in keeping infantile hands off hot stoves *and* that in the main course of human life the activities that preoccupy us are inevitably absurd, forming an inescapable circle of activities each of which lacks a justifying point. It is not that aspirins are absurd, only that their use is not part of the central pattern that *is* absurd.

It is difficult to offer a sympathetic ear to Camus' other complaints, although one must acknowledge that he does know how to capture a mood that circumstances can induce in any of us, and that circumstances might understandably produce regularly in some of us. What Camus refers to as "needs," for example, that one live forever, or that we can have a full and perspicuous understanding of all the phenomena of nature that science struggles with piecemeal, are for others—indeed for most others—quite dispensable wants that can be relinquished or modified as the evidence suggests, without cost to one's integrity.

What sort of response does Camus recommend to what he takes to be the absurdity of human life? Suicide, he says, would be a pointless gesture. Self-deception is the common way out. But embracing consoling myths is inconsistent with one's integrity. There is in fact no way of reconciling the cravings inherent in our nature, as he sees it, with the uncompromising denials of the alien cosmos. The existentialist hero acknowledges his inherent absurdity without wincing; he cherishes his consciousness of it, keeping it forever alive as the evidence of his integrity. He has no hope that things could be different, but lives to the hilt and dies well, like a blind person who cannot relinquish his desire to see though he knows the desire is hopeless.[23] In his defiance of what is necessary, he claims to achieve his integrity, and in his revolt his happiness. If Camus were a Columbia River salmon, he would lead the way over the rocks and up the rapids and be the first to fertilize new eggs, but he would never for a moment abandon his conviction that the whole enterprise is absurd, and his stubborn scorn would enable him to feel quite good about himself. If only a fish could be like a man!

Before leaving Camus, it is interesting to note his suggestion of how absurdity might relate to self-fulfillment. If it is in my nature as a human being—ineluctably—to crave unity, intelligibility, and immortality, then according to Camus my absurdity consists in the "divorce" between my nature and the large world of which it is a part, which defeats rather than fulfills it. It is in my nature then, quite absurdly, to be out of harmony with the universe. Camus' prescription that I defiantly embrace this absurdity and live to the hilt, amounts to a recommendation that I attempt to fulfill that nature, absurd as it is, and be defiant of the uncooperative universe. One can interpret Camus as recommending *as a means to full self-fulfillment*

---

[23] Camus, *Myth of Sisyphus*, p. 91.

that I be intensely and continuously conscious of my absurdity, that is, of the clash between larger nature and my nature. The beginnings of a paradox can be found in this conception: Can it be "fulfilling" to fulfill a nature in conflict with itself? Can one find one's fulfillment in frustration, one's triumph in defeat?

The absurdity of the human condition, according to the third theory, that of Nagel, derives from the clash of perspectives from which we can view ourselves: that of purposeful actors living out our lives and that of disinterested spectators of the very lives we earnestly live. Only human beings are capable of viewing themselves from a detached and impersonal perspective and making judgments from that viewpoint of their own insignificance. When we do view ourselves in that detached way, then the ordinary way of regarding our lives, which we cannot help but adopt if we are to pursue our lives at all, seems absurd to us. A mouse also regards his own life in the same serious everyday way that humans do, but since "he lacks the capacities for self-consciousness and self-transcendence that would enable him to see that he is only a mouse,"[24] he is not absurd. Human beings can diminish (but probably not eliminate) the absurdity of their own lives by allowing their individual animal natures to drift and respond to impulse, in short by becoming as much like mice as possible, but this would involve "considerable dissociative cost."[25]

Nagel is confusing when he talks as if he is making judgments about the absurdity of others' lives when he is only explaining the way in which those lives might come to *seem* absurd, either to those persons themselves or to a sensitive observer. Thus when he talks about possible "escapes" from absurdity and admits that a mindless life spent drifting with impulse is less absurd than more characteristically human lives despite its dissociative cost, he is using "absurd" to mean "seems absurd," much as psychoanalysts often equate "guilt" and "feelings of guilt." The life of a mouse *is* absurd when we look at it from an imaginatively extended perspective that the mouse itself cannot achieve. When Nagel denies the mouse's absurdity on the ground that *it* has no transcendental consciousness, he explains why the mouse's life cannot *seem* absurd to it. But the mouse's life can still seem absurd to *us*, and really be absurd nonetheless. Nagel, in short, at least in much of his discussion, takes the essential discrepancy in an absurd life to be a relation between two components of the being whose life it is—his natural and inevitable seriousness, and his awareness from a higher perspective of his own insignificance. But one could lack that kind of discrepancy, as mice do, and enjoy a more unified consciousness that in turn is discrepant with an external reality, the unaccommodating and alien uni-

[24] Nagel, "Absurd," p. 718.
[25] Ibid., p. 726.

verse. Nagel employs the latter conception of absurdity too when he speaks of the clash between subjective pretension and objective reality, and that is the notion that is used by Taylor and Camus when they make judgments of real, not merely apparent, absurdity.

The distinction between really being and only seeming absurd quickly suggests another, that between absurdity as a property of one's situation, and absurdity as a flaw in one's outlook or self-assessment—put tersely, between *absurd predicaments* and *absurd persons*. It does not follow, of course, from the fact that a person is in an absurd predicament that she is an absurd person, for she may have redeeming insights into, and attitudes toward her situation that put her beyond criticism or mockery. The human predicament that we all share is absurd according to Taylor because achievements do not last and there is thus a necessary and objective discrepancy between effort and outcome. It is absurd according to Camus because the universe is resistant to our inherent craving for order and intelligibility, and there is thus an ineradicable disharmony between our needs and the world's indifference. The human predicament is absurd according to Nagel because of the irresolvable clash between the importance we attach to our lives and the essential dubitability of all schemes of justification for that importance. All three writers agree that the absurdity of our human predicament is not a matter of "more or less" and not a matter that could be different from what it is. It is otherwise with the absurdity of persons. Some people are obviously more absurd than others in that there is a greater clash between their beliefs and their evidence, their mean and their ends, or their pretensions and their real characters and situations.

A person is also absurd—and this is the interesting point—when there is a radical discrepancy between her assessment of her situation and the actual nature of that situation. If one is really in an absurd predicament, if, for example, all of one's labors are bound to come to nothing in the end whatever one chooses to do about it, and one stubbornly denies that absurdity, adopting inappropriate attitudes and embracing vain hopes, then one becomes more than a little absurd oneself. Thus Sisyphus escapes personal absurdity by correctly appraising the absurdity of his predicament, realistically abandoning hope, and cooly proceeding with his labors in an existentialist spirit of "Let's get on with it,"[26] thus maintaining a kind of dignity and self-respect. But Sisyphus would surely be absurd if, like Don Quixote, he talked himself into believing that his labors had an intrinsic worth and importance and were essential to the maintenance of the world order. Indeed we could imagine a number of possible Sisyphuses varying in their degree of personal absurdity or unabsurdity as their beliefs, assess-

[26] This is the final line of Jean-Paul Sartre's play, *No Exit* (*Huis Clos*), translated by Stewart Gilbert (New York: Alfred A. Knopf, 1946).

ments, attitudes, and pretensions vary in their degrees of fittingness to their predicament. The situation of all these hypothetical Sisyphuses, however, is the same and as thoroughly absurd as a situation can be, for whatever any Sisyphus chooses to do about it, he must engage in endless repetitive cycles of pointless and unproductive labor.

How can a person be unabsurd if his life as a whole is unavoidably absurd? Some self-attitudes do not further anyone's escape from absurdity, and in the case of the person whose situation itself is absurd and whose projects and enterprises are pointless, they positively accentuate the personal absurdity of their possessor. Vanity, excessive pride or shame, pompous self-importance, even well-grounded self-esteem if taken too seriously, are absurd in a person whose situation guarantees the pointlessness or futility of his activities. Think of Shelley's Ozymandias, for example, who built a monument for posterity directing his descendants to "Look on my works, ye Mighty, and despair!" A tick of cosmic time later only "Two vast and trunkless legs of stone / stand in the desert . . . Near them, on the sand / Half sunk, a shattered visage lies."[27] How absurd was Old Ozymandias, self-declared "King of kings"! Almost equally absurd would be the towering self-regard of an eminent physicist for having won (and deserved) the Nobel Prize. Think of his proud medal found on some desert of the next millennium by beings whose school-children have a far more advanced understanding of physics than he did. A little bit of genuine humility, perhaps, is a virtue of anyone in any situation, but for a person in an absurd situation it is essential if the absurdity of his predicament is not to rub off on his character.

We can now venture some tentative conclusions. We can conclude first of all that there are elements properly characterized as absurd in every life. Moreover, some whole lives are predominately absurd, those, for example, spent largely in sheer drudgery to no further point, or those whose overriding pursuits were rendered futile by uncooperative circumstances or self-defeating strategies. Further arguments, however, to the conclusion that human life as such—and therefore each and every human life necessarily—is absurd are not convincing. Taylor and probably Camus (though he is less clear) are impressed by what they take to be the pointlessness (meaninglessness) of the human condition, a conclusion supported also by the arguments from the supermarket circle and the biological regress, but these arguments, because of confusions about the concept of pointlessness, are at best inconclusive. When we are speaking of activities *within* human life we characterize them as pointless when they are, first of all, apparently without worth for their own sakes, when, for example, they appear to be sheer drudgery, like pushing rocks and digging holes. If a given instance

[27] Percy Bysshe Shelley, *Ozymandias*, lines 2–4, 11, 12.

of sheer drudgery then appears to have no further point beyond itself that would confer instrumental value and intelligibility upon it, then and only then do we call it pointless. For an activity to be utterly without point or meaning then is first of all for it to have no value in its own right, and only then, for it to have no further purpose the achievement of which explains and justifies it. The supermarket circle and biological regress concentrate on showing that vindicating purposes never get wholly realized, but this would establish pointlessness only if all activities, human or animal, were sheer drudgery, without value in themselves. Some activities carry their own point within themselves, and for that reason, whatever their envisioned or actual consequences they are not "pointless." An adult salmon who has grown to maximum size and strength in the ocean, and is ready to begin his dangerous dash upstream to mating waters, is about to savor salmon existence in its purity, the salmon equivalent of "living to the hilt." "This is what being a salmon is all about," he might declare joyously. He will get battered about in the process, but if he could reason he might well conclude that the risk of injuries is justified by the inherent rewards, and like an adolescent football player preparing for his first game, he would be alive with anticipatory excitement.

Taylor asserts that human lives are absurd in the sense of having no point, but restricts the notion of a "point" to a state of affairs subsequent in time whose achievement confers instrumental value back on the life that created it, or at least is intended to do so whether successful or not. But there might be no such "point" outside of or after a person's life, yet nevertheless his life might have its own point—indeed it might *be* its own point. A fulfilled life may be absurd (pointless in Taylor's sense), yet not truly pointless because fulfillment *is* its point. This second kind of "point" looks backward in time, and exists because it fits some anticipatory condition, like an antecedent disposition. Actions producing the first kind of "point," in contrast, look forward to a time beyond their own termination, and to the production of lasting achievement. There is little point in that sense to the salmon's heroics, but they might yet escape absurdity if they discharge a fundamental native disposition of salmon nature—as they clearly do.

THE CONCEPT OF SELF-FULFILLMENT

There are various technical concepts of self-fulfillment associated with the writings of such philosophers as Plato, Aristotle, Rousseau, and Hegel, whose histories go back to the earliest beginnings of Western philosophy and are equally venerable in Eastern thought. There also seem to be one or more notions of self-fulfillment, perhaps less clearly conceived and articulable, that are part of ordinary thought, as, for example, when people say that one kind of life, or one kind of marriage, hobby, or career, is preferred because it is more fulfilling.

In applying the ordinary concept of self-fulfillment, people seem, on different occasions, to use as many as four different models for their understanding. On the first model, fulfillment is simply the answering to *any* anticipatory condition, whether one's own or another's—promises, hopes, expectations, desires, requirements, or whatever. The second is "filling up, being made full." The third is the opposite of the second, namely, emptying, unwinding, discharging, untying—draining one's cup of life to the dregs. Each of these familiar models comes with its own metaphors to guide (or obscure) the understanding. It is the fourth model, however, that of "doing what comes naturally," that purports to be more "philosophical," and is the more important one for our present purposes. This model restricts itself to the basic dispositions of one's "nature," and where these differ or conflict, to the "higher" or "better" ones. Moreover, fulfillment on this model is not merely a discharging, but also a maturing and perfecting of our basic dispositions. Finally, fulfillment so interpreted is often said to be a "realizing of one's potential," where the word "potential" refers not only to one's basic natural proclivities to engage in activities of certain kinds, but also to one's natural capacities to acquire skills and talents, to exercise those abilities effectively, and thus to produce achievements. Insofar as one fails to "realize one's potential," one's life is thought, on this as well as the third model, to be "wasted."

This understanding of self-fulfillment is much too abstract to be useful, and the main challenge to the philosophers, from Aristotle on, who have tried to incorporate it, has been to give it specificity. Almost anything one does can be said to fulfill a prior disposition to act in precisely that way in circumstances of that kind, or to implant or strengthen the habit of acting that way in the future. Thus almost any action can be said to discharge a natural tendency, to be a doing of what it is in one's nature to do. Philosophers who have fashioned a technical concept of self-fulfillment from the vaguer everyday notion have for the most part assigned it a crucial role in the definition of "the good for man." For that reason, most of them have begun the task of specification by ruling out as self-fulfilling, actions that violate objective standards of morality or that are radically defective in other ways. If a man has the bad habit, acquired and reinforced over a lifetime, of stealing purses, then a given act of stealing a purse, even though it fulfills one of the basic dispositions of his (evil) character, cannot be allowed to count as self-fulfilling. The same kind of fiat has excluded evil actions that discharge native propensities, for example, the angry tirades or physical assaults of a person who is irascible, hotheaded, or aggressive "by nature." Such arbitrary exclusions do not shock common sense, but there does seem to be at least as much warrant in ordinary conceptions for saying that it may be a bad thing that certain kinds of self be fulfilled, but that the discharging of basic "evil" dispositions remains fulfillment, and properly so called, anyway.

Some philosophers in the grand tradition have also excluded from their conception of self-fulfillment, activities that fulfill dispositions peculiar to individual persons, so as to give special importance to activities that fulfill those dispositions that define our common human nature. The phrase "a person's nature" is of course ambiguous. It may refer to the nature he shares with all and only human beings, his "generic nature" as it were, the nature that makes him classifiable as the kind of being he is, or it may refer to the nature that belongs uniquely to him, his "individual nature," the character that distinguishes him from all other individuals of his kind. My generic nature includes my disposition to walk upright and to speak a language,[28] among other things. It is part of *my* individual nature, on the other hand, to be interested in philosophy, to be punctual at meetings, to be slow at mathematics, and to be irritable when very tired or hungry. Some of the traits that characterize me but not everybody else are not thought to be part of my individual nature because they are weak and tentative habits rather than governing propensities, or because they are trivial (like my habit of scratching my head when deliberating). My individual nature is partly acquired; my generic nature is derived entirely from heredity. I come into existence with it already "loaded and cocked."

Those philosophers of fulfillment who attach special significance to our generic natures tend to draw heavily on biological as well as mechanical metaphors. In a fulfilled life our preprogrammed potentialities "unfold" like the petals of a rose, each in its time, until the plant is fully flowered and "flourishing." Then there follows an equally natural, gradual withering and expiring, and the life of one plant, at least, has been fulfilled. Another plant, much like the first, is caught in a frost and nipped in the bud, never to achieve its "own good" as determined by its natural latencies—the very paradigm of a tragic waste. John Stuart Mill refers to qualities that are "the distinctive endowment" not of the individual in question but of a human being as such: "the human faculties of perception, judgment, discriminative feeling, mental activity, even moral preference,"[29] these understood as

---

[28] There have been feral children who have permanently lost their ability to learn a language and children born without legs who never acquire the ability to walk. But insofar as these persons are human beings, they are born with the innate *capacity* to acquire the dispositions and skills involved in walking and talking even though circumstances prevent that capacity from being realized. The capacities in question are often conditional ones: all human children have the capacity to learn a language, which is activated between the ages of two and twelve only, and only if they are made part of a language-speaking community during those years. That conditional capacity to acquire the dispositions and skills involved in language use is common to all human beings.

[29] John Stuart Mill, *On Liberty* (Oxford: Blackwell, 1946), p. 51.

standing to human nature in the same relation as that in which unfolding and flourishing stand to the nature of a rose.

I believe it is a mistake, however (and not one committed in common thought), to exclude individual natures from one's conception of self-fulfillment. If we are told by philosophical sages to act always so as to unfold our generic human natures, we have not been given very clear directions at all. Any number of alternative lives might equally well fulfill one's generic nature, yet some might seem much more "fulfilling," in a perfectly ordinary and intelligible sense, than others. William James makes the point well:

> I am often confronted by the necessity of standing by one of my empirical selves and relinquishing the rest. Not that I would not, if I could, be both handsome and fat and well dressed, and a great athlete, and make a million a year, be a wit, a *bon vivant*, and a lady-killer, as well as philosopher, a philanthropist, statesman, warrior, and African explorer, as well as a "tone-poet" and saint. But the thing is simply impossible. The millionaire's work would run counter to the saint's; the *bon vivant* and the philanthropist would trip each other up; the philosopher and the lady-killer could not well keep house in the same tenement of clay. Such different characters may conceivably at the outset of life be alike possible to a man. But to make any one of them actual, the rest must more or less be suppressed.[30]

All James' possible careers might equally well fulfill his human nature, just as all the variously colored unfoldings of roses might equally well fulfill a rose's generic nature, but a rose cannot pick its own individual character, whereas a man has some choice. Since some of James' lives (presumably the philosophical one, to begin with) would be more fulfilling than others, it must be his individual nature qua William James that makes that so. The point would be even clearer if James had listed among the possibilities, "anchorite monk," "operatic *basso profundo*," "brain surgeon," and "drill sergeant." Some of these careers obviously accord more closely than others with *anyone's* native aptitudes, inherited temperament, and natural inclinations. How does one choose among them if one is seeking fulfillment? By "knowing oneself," of course, but not simply by knowing well the defining traits of *any* human being. To be sure, making the choice itself is a characteristically human act and calls into play all of the generic human traits of Mill's list—perception, discrimination, insight, and the like—but to exercise those traits effectively and well, and thus unfold one's generic human nature, one must first know one's individual character as so far formed, and make the decision that best fits it. Mill's final and favorite metaphor, indeed, is that of a life fitting an individual nature in the way a

---

[30] William James, *Psychology* (New York: Henry Holt, 1893), 1:309; as quoted in Lucius Garvin, *A Modern Introduction to Ethics* (Boston: Houghton-Mifflin, 1953), p. 333.

shoe fits a foot: "A man cannot get a coat or a pair of boots to fit him unless they are either made to his measure or he has a whole warehouseful to choose from; and is it easier to fit him with a life than with a coat.[?]"[31]

Some of a person's individual nature is native, for example, much of what we call aptitudes, temperamental dispositions, and physical strength. A fulfilling life therefore is one that "fits" these native endowments. But we make our own natures as we grow older, building on the native base. We begin, partly because of our inherited proclivities and talents, to develop tastes, habits, interests, and values. We cultivate the skills that grow naturally out of our aptitudes, and as we get better at them we enjoy them more and exercise them further so that they get better still, while we are inclined to neglect the tasks for which our skills are inadequate, and those abilities wither and decay on the vine.[32] The careers we then select as workers, players, and lovers, should be those that fit our well-formed individual natures, at least insofar as each stage in the emergence of the self grew naturally out of its predecessor in the direction of our native bent.

Emphasis should be given to the further point that fulfillment of one's generic and individual natures are interconnected and interdependent. The passages in *On Liberty* in which Mill urges fulfillment of the "distinctive endowment" of generic humanity occur, ironically, in a chapter entitled "Individuality as One of the Elements of Well-Being," and nowhere in that chapter can Mill discuss individuality for long without bringing in human nature and vice versa. His view clearly is that it is essential to the generic nature of human beings that each think and decide for himself rather than blindly follow all the rest, so that in cultivating the capacities that human beings share in common, each individual will at the same time be promoting his own distinctive individuality. If I pick a career that fits my individual nature instead of blindly drifting with custom or passively acceding to the choices of another, then I have exercised my generic nature as a thinker and chooser, at the same time that I have promoted the fulfillment of my individual nature as a person with a unique profile of interests and aptitudes.

Useful as it may be for some purposes the distinction between generic and individual natures is vague and ragged about the edges, a point we can

[31] Mill, *On Liberty*, p. 60.

[32] John Rawls calls the statement of this psychological tendency "the Aristotelian Principle" and states it as follows: "Other things being equal, human beings enjoy the exercise of their realized capacities (their innate or trained abilities), and this enjoyment increases the more the capacity is realized, or the greater its complexity. The intuitive idea here is that human beings take more pleasure in doing something as they become more proficient at it, and of two activities they do equally well, they prefer the one calling for a larger repertoire of more intricate and subtle discriminations." Rawls cites the preference among good players for chess over checkers and among good mathematicians for algebra over arithmetic (*A Theory of Justice* [Cambridge, Mass.: Harvard University Press, 1971], p. 426).

appreciate by returning to the plight of Taylor's Sisyphus. Depending on the extent to which the gods had to tamper with him, he has either had a new individual nature grafted on to his basic human nature, or else a new (hence nonhuman) generic nature installed in him. If we say the former, then we must think of his infinite rock-pushing proclivities as merely personal eccentricities, only contingently unshared by other persons who share his human nature. If we say the latter, then the individual nature of Sisyphus and his generic nature coincide, since he is now one of a kind, the sole member of his new species. A rock-pushing instinct that is so specific would be such a departure from what we normally think of as human nature, so totally unshared by any other humans that perhaps there would be a point in saying that Sisyphus has a new generic nature, humanoid but not human, and that he is now the only member of the biological species *Homo sapiens geopetris*—sapient rock-pusher. Still more plausible, perhaps, we might think of the new Sisyphus as a borderline case for our old classifications. Unless we hold to the discredited doctrine of fixed species, we can simply declare that there is no uniquely correct answer to the question of whether Sisyphus' generic nature has been changed, and that considerations of convenience and tidiness are as relevant to its resolution as are any questions of fact.

Moreover, when we consider thoughtfully the whole range of hypothetical Sisyphuses from which we might draw in order to flesh out Taylor's example, we are struck with how very vague the notion of a "nature" is, whether generic or individual. What is in Sisyphus's nature (or the nature of anyone else) is very much like what is in his (cluttered) closet or in his grab bag, including everything from aptitudes and interests to addictive compulsions. Think of all the variations on Taylor's theme: the gods might have implanted in Sisyphus an *appetite* for stone-pushing that makes regular and frequent demands on him, like hunger or the "sex urge" in others, and corresponding in its cycles to the time it takes to push a rock of standard size up Sisyphus' assigned mountain and then return again to the bottom of the hill. "Ye gods!" he might exclaim after each round of labors, "how I hunger for a nice big rock to push," and the accommodating deities always have one ready for him, like the next ball up in a pinball machine. Or the gods might have designed for him a peculiar talent for rock-pushing much like others' talents for piano-playing, tennis, or chess. The new Sisyphus starts all over as a perpetual youth, and from the start he is a veritable prodigy at rock-pushing. He comes to enjoy exercising his skills, and makes ever-new challenges for himself. He pushes the rock right-handed, then left-handed, then no-handed, then blindfolded, then does two at a time, then juggles three in the air all the way to the summit, eager to return for another rock so that he can break his record, or equal it next time while dancing a Grecian jig. Or the gods do their job by implanting an instinct for rock-pushing so that Sisyphus goes about his chores without giving them so much as a thought (except in rare reflective moments and then only to shrug his shoulders and get on with it). His work is as natural and unremarkable to him as having a language or standing upright is to us, or building a dam to a beaver, or peeling a banana to a chimpanzee. Or (perhaps more plausibly) the gods implant a drive or more general proclivity of which stone-pushing is only one of numerous possible fulfillments. If there were only opportunity to do so, Sisyphus would find it equally in his nature to push wooden logs, or plastic bags, or iron bars, or to pull lift, carry, and throw objects, or to push them while swimming against a current, or to pile, hook, or nail them on to one another as in construction work, and the like. But pushing rocks up a mountain will do as well as any of the other activities as fulfillments of his drive to move and manipulate physical objects and he can be grateful to the gods for that. Or, the gods can use Taylor's own suggested method, and give Sisyphus (say) a shot in the arm after each trip so that he will feel a "compulsive impulse" to push the rock up once more in order to get relief in the form of another addicting shot. This technique would keep the gods busier than the others, but they could let some internal gland, timed to secrete the essential substance into Sisyphus's bloodstream at appropriate intervals, do the work for them. There is something especially ingenious in this last scheme, for the "shot" given at the base of the hill creates the impulse to push the rock up the hill and also the addictive need, when its first effect wears off, to be renewed by another shot, and so on, ad infinitum.

If the gods' gift to Sisyphus is merely an appetite to push rocks he may yet fail to find self-fulfillment on balance in an indefinitely extended lifetime of rock-pushing, just as one of us might fail to be fulfilled in a life that gives us all the food we need, but nothing else. Sisyphus will have the periodic satisfactions of regular appetite satiation, and that is certainly some benefit to him, but the deepest yearnings of his nature will nevertheless be forever denied. Much the same can be said of his condition if the gods simply addict him chemically to a substance that creates a rock-pushing itch, or if they implant in him an extrahuman instinct to push rocks that fails to dovetail or integrate with the human instincts he must continue to maintain if he is to preserve his identity with his earlier self. The model that makes talk of Sisyphean self-fulfillment most plausible is probably that in which the gods impart to him talents for rock-moving that he can forever after exercise and glory in. So endowed, he can find self-fulfillment through his developed virtuosity, in the same way others find fulfillment in lives of skilled cello-playing or cabinet-making.

No conception of self-fulfillment will make much sense unless it allows that fulfillment is a matter of degree. We begin life with a large number of potential careers some of which fit our native bent more closely than others but any of which, if pursued through a lifetime, would lead to substantial fulfillment, so that the pursuit of no *one* of them is indispensable to a fulfilled life. Imagine a warm and loving woman who is superbly equipped by her nature to be a parent, and has thought of herself throughout her girlhood as a potential mother. She marries and then discovers that she is barren. Had she not been infertile she would have achieved fulfillment in a long lifetime of nearly full-time motherhood. Is it now impossible for her to be fulfilled in a life without children? Clearly not, for the very traits that make her "superbly equipped" to be a mother will make her more than a little qualified for dozens of other roles, and a fulfilled life could stem from any one of these, from social work to school-teaching,[33] or even from a career based on independent specific aptitudes like poetry or basket-weaving. She may be disappointed that her chief ambition is squelched and her regrets may last a lifetime, but disappointment and fulfillment can coexist with little friction, as they do to some degree in most human lives. Thus, we each have within us a number of distinct individual possibilities, several (at least) of which would be sufficient for (a degree of) fulfillment, but no one of which is necessary. But the most fulfilling ones are those that best fit one's latent talents, interests, and initial bent and with one's evolving self-ideal (as opposed simply to one's conscious desires or formulated ambitions).

Some fulfilled human lives are relatively monochromatic, having a single dominant theme; others are diversely colored, having a harmonious orchestration of themes with equal voices. All of them approach fulfillment insofar as they fill their natural allotment of years with vigorous activity. They need not be "successful," or "triumphant," or even contented on balance in order to be fulfilled, provided they are long lifetimes full of struggles and strivings, achievements and noble failures, contentments and frustrations, friendships and enmities, exertions and relaxations, seriousness and playfulness through all the programmed stages of growth and decay. Most important of all, a fulfilled human life will be a life of planning, designing, making order out of confusion and system out of randomness, a life of building, repairing, rebuilding, creating, pursuing goals, and solving

---

[33] Aptitudes and basic dispositions differ in an important way from ordinary desires, plans, and ambitions. The latter characteristically tend to be more precise and determinate than the former, and therefore less flexible and easy to "fulfill." Many ambitions are for some relatively specific object and when that object does not come into existence the ambition is denied. General interests, talents, and drives, however, can typically find substitute objects that do equally well. If one has a highly developed mechanical aptitude, for example, one can employ it equally well as an airplane or an automobile mechanic, as well as a carpenter or a plumber, or in a hundred other callings. One's ambition to be an automobile mechanic, on the other hand, is squelched once and for all, by the denial of opportunity to enter that particular field. For this reason, fulfillment is, on the whole, less difficult to achieve than successful ambition or "satisfaction."

problems. It is in the generic nature of the human animal to address the future, change its course, make the best of the situation. If one's house falls down, if one's cities are in rubble, if disaster comes and goes, the human inclination is to start all over again, rebuilding from scratch. There is no "fulfillment" in resignation and despair.

Sisyphus does seem very human after all, then, when he reshoulders his burden and starts back up his hill. But insofar as his situation is rigidly fixed by the gods, allowing him no discretion to select means, design strategies, and solve problems on his own, his life does not fulfill the governing human propensities. If he can fulfill his nature without these discretionary activities, then he has really assumed the nature of a different species.

In all the variations on the Sisyphus myth that we have spun thus far, the gods have assigned a very specific job to Sisyphus that requires no particular judgment or ingenuity on his part to be performed well. They have imposed a duty on him rather than assigning a responsibility.[34] He has a rote job to perform over and over, a mulish task for a mulish fellow, and his is not to reason why or how, but only to get on with it. Suppose, however, that the gods assign to Sisyphus an endless series of rather complex engineering problems and leave it up to him to solve them. Somehow rocks must be moved to mountain tops and there can be no excuses for failure. "Get it up there somehow," they say. "The methods are up to you. Feel free to experiment and invent. Keep a record of your intermediate successes and failures and be prepared to give us an accounting of the costs. You may hire your own assistants and within certain well-defined limits you have authority to give them commands, so long as you are prepared to answer for the consequences of their work. Now good luck to you." If Sisyphus's subsequent labors are fulfilling, they will be so in a characteristically human way. His individual nature will be fulfilled by a life (endless and pointless though it may be) that fits his native bent and employs his inherited talents and dispositions to the fullest, as well as fitting his more specific individual tendencies, for example, a special fascination (perhaps also a gift of the gods) with rocks.

WHY DOES SELF-FULFILLMENT MATTER?

Why should it "matter" that a person is unfulfilled if, despite his stunted and dwarfed self, the product perhaps of alienating work and other "unfit-

---

[34] The distinction between duty and responsibility is well made by J. Roland Pennock in "The Problem of Responsibility," *Nomos III: Responsibility*, ed. C. J. Friedrich (New York: Atherton, 1960), p. 13: 'We normally reserve [the word "responsibility"] for cases where the performance of duty requires discernment and choice. We might well say to a child, 'It is your responsibility to take care of your room', but we would not be likely to say, 'It is your responsibility to do as you are told'."

ting" circumstances, he finds a steady diet of satisfactions in delusory occupations, escapist literature, drugs, drink, and television? Why should it
"matter," to turn the question around, that a person finds fulfillment when
his life looks as absurd from a longer perspective as the life of a shellfish
appears to us?

Think first of what a substantially unfulfilled life involves. A person
comes into existence with a set of governing dispositions that sets him off
with others as a being of a certain kind. For twenty years he grows and
matures, enlarging and perfecting his inherited propensities so that he becomes utterly unique, with a profile of talents and individual traits that, as
a group, distinguish him from every other being who has ever existed, and
constitute his individual nature. Perhaps he is capable of seeing, from time
to time, that this "nature" of his is more than a little absurd. What he does
best and most, let us imagine, is play chess and ping-pong and socialize
with others who share those interests. He takes those pursuits more seriously than anything else in his life. But he knows that they are, after all,
only games, of no cosmic significance whatever, and certainly of no interest
to the indifferent universe, to posterity, to history, or to any of the other
abstract tribunals by which humans in their more magniloquent moods are
wont to measure significance. And yet, absurd as it is, it is *his* nature, and
the only one he has, so somehow he must make the best of it and seek his
own good in pursuit of its dominant talents. Whose nature could he try to
fulfill, after all, but his own? Where else can his own good conceivably be
found? It was not up to him to choose his own nature, for that would
presuppose that the choosing self already had a nature of its own determining its choice. But given the nature with which he finds himself indissolu-
bly identified for better or worse, he must follow the path discovered in it
and identify his good with the goals toward which his nature is already
inclined.

Now suppose that he makes a mess of it through imprudence, frivolity,
or recklessness; or imagine that the world withdraws its opportunities; or
that lightning strikes and leaves him critically incapacitated for the realization of his potential. That leaves him still the pleasure of his diminished
consciousness, his soma pills and television programs, his comic books and
crossword puzzles, but his deepest nature will forever remain unfulfilled.
Now we think of that nature, with all of its elaborate neurochemical equip-
ment underlying its distinctive drives and talents and forming its uniquely
complex character, as largely unused, wasted, all for naught. All wound up,
it can never discharge or wind down again. In contrast, the life of fulfillment strikes us as one that comes into being prone and equipped to do its
thing, and then uses itself up doing that thing, without waste, blockage, or
friction.

When any nature is left unfulfilled it is likely to strike us as a bad thing, an objectively regrettable fact. Perhaps we would withdraw or modify that judgment when we come to appreciate how absurd that nature's preoccupations really were. But from the point of view of the self whose nature it is, nonfulfillment is more than a bad or regrettable thing to be graded down in some negative but modifiable "value judgment." It may or may not be all those things in some final balancing-up, all things considered. But from the point of view of the individual involved, nonfulfillment marks the collapse of his whole universe, the denial once and for all of his own good. There is a world of difference in the use of the word "good" as a predicate of evaluation, and its use in the venerable phrase of the philosophers—"one's own good." My good is something peculiarly mine, as determined by my nature alone, and particularly by its most powerful trends and currents. Anything else that is good for me (or in my interest) is good because it contributes to my good, the fulfillment of my strongest stable tendencies. One can judge or evaluate that good from some other standpoint, employing some other standard, and the resultant judgment may use the words "good," "bad," or "indifferent." It may not be a good thing that my good be achieved or that it be achieved in a given way, or at a given cost. But it is logically irrelevant to the question of *what my good is* whether my good is itself "good" when judged from an external position. My nonfulfillment may not be a "bad thing on balance" in another's judgment or even in my own. My nonfulfillment may not be "objectively regrettable" or tragic. But my nonfulfillment cannot be *my good* even if it is from all other measuring points, a good thing.

It is perhaps not quite self-evident that my good consists in fulfillment. A hedonist might hold out for the position that my good consists in a balance of pleasant over unpleasant experiences while denying that the basic disposition of my nature is to seek pleasure, thus denying that pleasant experiences as such are fulfilling. I cannot refute such a heroic (and lonely) philosopher. But I would like to urge against the philosopher who is overly impressed with the fact of human absurdity, that if my good is fulfillment, it must be fulfillment of *my* nature and not of something else. That my nature is eccentric, absurd, laughable, trivial, cosmically insignificant, is neither here nor there. Such as it is, it is my nature for better or worse. The self whose good is at issue is the self I am and not some other self that I might have been. If I had had any choice in the matter I might have preferred to come into existence with the nature (that is the potential) of William James, John F. Kennedy, or Michael Jordan, but I cannot spend all my days lamenting that the only nature whose fulfillment constitutes my good is my own!

The prerequisite to self-fulfillment is a certain amount of clear-eyed, nondeluded self-love. A moment ago I spoke of one's own nature "such as it is," "for better or worse." These phrases recall the wedding ceremony and its conception of marital love as loyalty and devotion without condition or reservation. Totally unconditional devotion may be too much to ask from any lover, but within wide limits, various kinds of human love of others have a largely unconditional character. Gregory Vlastos describes parental love, for example, in a way that makes it quite familiar: "Constancy of affection in the face of variations of merit is one of the surest tests of whether a parent does love a child."[35] Judgments of merit have nothing to do with love so construed. A child's failures, even moral failures, may disappoint his parents' hopes without weakening their loyalty or affection in the slightest. A parent may admire one child more than another, or like (in the sense of "enjoy") one more than another, as well as judge one higher than the other, but it is a necessary condition of parental love that, short of limiting extremes, it not fluctuate with these responses to merit.

The love that any stable person has toward himself will be similarly constant and independent of perceived merits and demerits. I may (realistically) assign myself very low grades for physique, intellect, talent, even character—indeed I may ascribe deficiencies even to my individual nature itself—while still remaining steadfastly loyal and affectionate to myself. Aristotle was right on target when he said that a wise man ought to have exactly that degree of self-esteem that is dictated by the facts, neither more nor less. But self-esteem is not self-love. I have self-love for myself when I accept my nature as given, without apology or regret, even as I work, within the limits it imposes, for self-improvement. We have been through a lot together, my self and I, sharing everything alike, and as long as I have supported him, he has never let me down. I have scolded him, but never cursed his nature. He is flawed all right, and deeply so, but when the warts show, I smile, fondly and indulgently. His blunders are just what one would expect from anyone with his nature. One cannot come to hate a being with whom one has been so very intimate. Indeed, I would not know how to begin to cope with another self after all my years of dependency, "for better or worse," on this one. In this way self-identity can be conceived as a kind of arranged marriage (I did not select the self that was to be me) that in a stable person ripens into true love, but in an unstable one sours into rancor and self-destruction. And the truest expression of one's self-love is devotion toward one's own good, which is the fulfillment of one's own (who else's?) nature—absurd as that may be.

THE CRITIQUE OF COSMIC ATTITUDES

Some lives are manifestly and incontrovertibly absurd. Lives spent moving metaphoric rocks back and forth to no further end and lives spent tangling

[35] Gregory Vlastos, "Justice and Equality," in *Social Justice*, ed. Richard B. Brandt (Englewood Cliffs, N.J.: Prentice-Hall, 1962), p. 44.

with metaphoric windmills are cases in point. Other lives are full of achievement and design. In these lives, intermediate goals lend meaning to the pursuits that are instrumental to their achievement, and they in turn are given a point by the more ultimate goals they subserve. No goal is *the* ultimate one, however, for the most general ends are themselves means to a great variety of other ends, all tied together in an intricate and harmonious web of purpose. There may be no purpose to the whole web except its service to its own component parts, but each constituent has a place and a vindicating significance to the person whose life it is. Such a life is, relatively speaking, not absurd. There is no doubt an important practical point in distinguishing human lives in terms of their degree of absurdity, even in highlighting and emphasizing the distinctions. (Marx's doctrine of alienation is an example of the social utility of making such distinctions.) As we have seen, however, philosophers have found reason to claim that there is a kind of cosmic absurdity inherent in the human condition as such. As we stand back and look at ourselves from an extended temporal position, the distinction between absurd and nonabsurd lives begins to fade into insignificance, and finally vanishes altogether.

We also make useful distinctions between relatively fulfilled and unfulfilled selves, or fulfilling and unfulfilling lives. However we interpret "fulfillment"—as the development of one's chief aptitudes into genuine talents in a life that gives them scope, or an unfolding of all basic tendencies and inclinations, or an active realization of the universally human propensities to plan, design, make order—there are wide differences among persons in the degree of fulfillment they achieve. Some lives are wasted; some are partially wasted and partially fulfilled; others are nearly totally fulfilled. Unlike the contrast between absurd and nonabsurd lives, these distinctions seem to be time-resistant. If Hubert Humphrey's life was fulfilling to him, that is a fact like any other, and it never ceases to be true that it was a fact. From any temporal distance from which it can be observed at all it will continue to appear to be a fact (though a diminishingly interesting or important one).

Consider a human life that is near-totally fulfilled, yet from a quite accessible imaginary vantage point is apparently absurd. Insofar as the person in question is fulfilled, he ought to "feel good" about his life, and rejoice that he has achieved his good. Suppose that he realizes then how futile it all was, "coming to nothing in the end." What would be the appropriate attitude in that event to hold toward his life? Unchanged pride and satisfaction? Bitterness and despair? Haughty existential scorn? We can call such responsive attitudes taken toward one's whole life and by implication toward the whole human condition, "cosmic attitudes." One of the traditional tasks of philosophy (and what philosophy is entirely about in the minds of innocent persons unacquainted with the academic discipline of that name) is to perform a kind of literary criticism of cosmic attitudes. It used to be the custom for philosophers not only to describe the universe in its more general aspects but to recommend cosmic attitudes toward the world as so described.

I welcome the suggestion of Nagel that the appropriate responsive attitude toward human lives that are both absurd and fulfilled is *irony*,[36] and I shall conclude by elaborating that suggestion somewhat beyond the bare recommendation that Nagel offers.

None of the familiar senses of irony in language or in objective occurrences seem to make any sense out of the advice that we respond to absurdity with irony. What Nagel has in mind clearly is another sense in which irony is a kind of outlook on events, namely, "an attitude of detached awareness of incongruity."[37] This is a state of mind halfway between seriousness and playfulness. It may even seem to the person involved that he is both very serious and playful at the same time. The tension between these opposed elements pulling in their opposite ways creates at least temporarily a kind of mental equilibrium not unlike that of the boy in Lincoln's story who was "too scared to laugh and too big to cry," except that the boy squirms with discomfort whereas irony is on balance an *appreciative* attitude.[38] One appreciates the perceived incongruity much as one does in humor, where the sudden unexpected perception of incongruity produces laughter. Here the appreciation is more deliberate and intellectual. The situation is too unpleasant in some way—sad, threatening, disappointing—to permit the relaxed playfulness of spirit prerequisite to the comic response. There *is* a kind of bittersweet pleasure in it, but not the pleasure of amusement. The situation is surely not seen as funny, although perhaps it would be if only one could achieve a still more detached outlook on it. One contemplates a situation with irony when one looks the facts in the eye and responds in an appreciative way to their incongruous aspects as such. Irony is quite different from despair-cum-tears, scornful defiance-cum-anger, and amusement-cum-laughter. It is pleasant enough to be expressed characteristically in a smile, but a somewhat tired smile, with a

[36] Nagel, "Absurd," p. 707: "If *sub specie aeternitatis* there is no reason to believe that anything matters, then that doesn't matter either, and we can approach our absurd lives with irony instead of heroism or despair."

[37] *Webster's New Collegiate Dictionary* (1976), based on *Webster's Third New International Dictionary of the English Language*. Of the five English dictionaries I consulted, only this newest one contained any definition of irony as an attitude. Is that because this sense is relatively new or because dictionary-makers have heretofore overlooked it?

[38] "The President takes the result of the New York election [a defeat for his party] philosophically, and will doubtless profit by the lesson. When Colonel Forney inquired of him how he felt he replied: 'Somewhat like the boy in Kentucky who stubbed his toe while running to see his sweetheart. The boy said he was too big to cry, and far too badly hurt to laugh' " (*Frank Leslie's Illustrated Weekly*, November 22, 1862).

touch both of gentleness and mischievousness in it, as befitting the expression of a tempered pleasure.

In one of the most moving scenes of the twenty-seven-part BBC documentary film on the First World War, a group of British reinforcements is shown marching toward the front. We know that they are cannon fodder marching to their own slaughter, and they know it too. They are foot-sore and bone-weary, and splattered with mud, and a steady rain is falling. The song they sing as they march is not a rousing anthem like "La Marseillaise" or "Rule, Britannia!," not a cocky fight song like "Over There," not a jolly drinking song like "Waltzing Matilda," not a sentimental ballad, hymn of lamentation, or mournful dirge. Instead they sing to the stirring tune of "Auld Lang Syne" the famous nonsense verse they created for the occasion:

> We're here because we're here
> Because we're here because we're here;
> We're here because we're here
> Because we're here because we're here . . .

The observer of the film feels a sudden pang and finds himself near tears, but quickly he perceives the absurdity in the lyrics and responds appreciatively to it, just as the troops, by selecting those words, are responding to the perceived absurdity in their situation. The sensitive observer sees how fitting the ironic response of the soldiers is (and how dreadfully false any of its standard alternatives would have been) and himself takes a quiet sad pleasure in it. The soldiers were in an inescapably absurd predicament, without hope, and only by their unflinching acceptance of the absurdity of their situation are they saved from absurdity themselves. For us, the unseen audience, there is an inspiration in their example that makes the scene noble.

I do not mean to suggest for a moment that the march of the doomed soldiers is an apt metaphor for the whole of human life. The soldiers' brief lives were tragically wasted. If they had been specially bred military animals they might have found both a personal and biological fulfillment in their peculiar demises, but they were ordinary humans whose bizarre and untimely deaths climaxed their undeveloped and unfinished lives. In contrast, many individuals do achieve fulfillment in long, active, creative lives. These lives are more than just "worthwhile"; they represent to those who lead them the achievement of the only condition that can plausibly be deemed "their good." So philosophical "pessimism," the view of Schopenhauer and others that *no* life can *possibly* be worth living given the absurdity of the human condition, must be rejected. Its logical contrary, that cosmic optimism that holds that all human lives necessarily are, or always can be, good and worthwhile, must also be rejected, in favor of the commonsense view that fulfillment requires luck, and luck is not always good in a world that contains violent passions, accidents, disease, and war.

In this chapter, however, I have tried not only to sketch a conception of the good life and the bad but also to recommend an appropriate attitude toward the human condition generally. Imagine a person who both through his own virtues and good luck has led a maximally fulfilling life into his final declining years. He has realized his highest individual potential in a career that perfectly fit his inherited temperamental proclivities. His talents and virtues have unfolded steadily in a life that gave them limitless opportunity for exercise, and he has similarly perfected his generic human powers of discrimination, sympathy, and judgment in a life full of intermeshing purposes and goals. All of this is a source of rich satisfaction to him, until in the philosophical autumn of his days, he chances upon the legend of Sisyphus, the commentary of Camus, and the essays of Taylor and Nagel. In a flash he sees the vanity of all his pursuits, the total permeability of his achievements by time, the lack of any long-term rationale for his purposes, in a word the absurdity of his (otherwise good) life. At first he will feel a keen twinge. But unless he be misled by the sophistries of the philosophical pessimists who confuse the empty ideal of long-term coherence with the Good for Man, he will soon recover. And then will come a dawning bittersweet appreciation of the cosmic incongruities first called to his attention by the philosophers. The thought that there should be a modest kind of joke at the heart of human existence begins to please (if not quite tickle) him. Now he can die not with a whine or a snarl, but with an ironic smile.

Chapter Fourteen

THE ABSURD AND THE COMIC:
WHY DOES SOME INCONGRUITY PLEASE?

GIVEN THAT SOME PHILOSOPHERS respond to certain forms of perceived absurdity with negative emotions ranging from conceptual discomfort to suicidal despair, it is a somewhat surprising fact that absurdity has been put by others to a variety of positive uses. Some consumers of the arts have developed an actual preference for absurdities. The incongruous meetings and absurd juxtapositions of images in the better surrealistic paintings allow them to be riveting in a quite distinctive way, and move the emotions in a manner that is easier to appreciate than to understand. In the repertoire of "the theater of the absurd" are plays in which the essential absurdity of human beings, portrayed as dupes and clowns in an alien and inscrutable universe, is positively celebrated. And many people have a taste for those absurd incongruities that are, for all their lunacy—indeed precisely because of their lunacy—delightfully comic.

Some effort therefore should be made to explain how incongruity—utterly absurd incongruity—can please. In particular we should examine the conceptual relation between the absurd and the comic, not with the aim of providing yet another account of the essential features of *all* humor (there may be some funny things that do not exploit absurd incongruities), but rather to cast light on the uses of absurdity, one of which surely is to provide comic amusement.

Some philosophers following Hobbes have taken the basic object of laughter in funny experience to be the "sudden glory arising from [the] conception of some eminency in ourselves, by comparison with the infirmity of others or with our own formerly."[1] A stranger slips on a banana peel and suffers an undignified pratfall. We observers experience a "sudden glory" as we sense the contrast between his misfortunate and our own impunity. Other writers find the basis of funny experiences to be the sense of relief from restraint that comes from the release of pent-up nervous energy. Others hold out that the true common denominator in all funny situations is the amusement caused by the perception of incongruity. We need not consider here which of these three standard theories, if any, is the correct

[1] Thomas Hobbes, *Human Nature*, chapters 8, 13, in *English Works*, ed. Sir William Molesworth (London: Bohn, 1840), volume 4.

one, or whether they all have a piece of a more complex truth, as it is now customary to say. I wish only to point out that two of the three standard theories need invent no further theory to explain why we take pleasure in the element they invoke to explain what the comic is. There is no further room for the question why sudden glory in the perception of one's own superiority should please one. There is no mystery there. Neither is anyone naturally puzzled that release from restraint should be enjoyable. But why should the awareness of strikingly incongruous elements in our experience, simply as such, tickle us so? Why should absurdity not play its more familiar role, and darkly turn our thoughts toward pointlessness, futility, baseless pretension, and suicide?

Whatever else may also be funny, there is no doubt that one of the most prominent classes of objects of our laughter is the ludicrously absurd. Since not all incongruities, not even all absurd incongruities, are funny, however, a full philosophical theory should explain what makes some incongruity comic and some not, and also why it is that we should take such pleasure in the incongruous when we do find it funny—why the sudden perception of absurdity in a situation can trigger the biological laugh reflex and produce pleasure in the laughing person. No philosophical theory that I know of has done this job satisfactorily, perhaps partly because clear-headed philosophers who have focused on the concept of absurdity are few and far between. But of those many more numerous philosophers of the comic, the theory of Max Eastman[2] seems to me to provide the most useful starting point.

We find nothing comic, Eastman reminds us, unless we are at least in a moderately playful mood. Sisyphus will find nothing remotely amusing in the absurdity of his situation if he is (as Camus would have him be) dead serious about it. An outsider, on the other hand, can find amusement in another's plight in proportion to the absurdity he finds in it, if he detaches the absurdity, so to speak, from the serious elements in the situation, and responds to it playfully. Some of the most exquisite comedy is directed at patently absurd reasonings and ludicrously incongruous situations, but only when we can take them playfully, only, that is, when distracting anxieties, fears, and such emotions as anger, sorrow, compassion, and indignation, have been "paid off" and sent on a holiday. In short, an element of absurdity in an unhappy situation is itself a comic element in that situation no matter how unhappy the whole complex of which it is an element, but that is only to say that *if* we could isolate that element, abstract it from its surrounding context, and focus narrowly on it in a wholly playful spirit, we would find it amusing. Why even that should be the case, no theorist has fully explained.

---

[2] Max Eastman, *Enjoyment of Laughter* (New York: Simon & Schuster, 1936).

Writers who have discussed this subject have traditionally employed the word "incongruity" chiefly, reserving the term "absurdity" for a special species of incongruity of derivative interest. Often they have been imprecise in their definitions of "incongruity" and consequently quite promiscuous in their acceptance of examples of incongruity. John Morreall, for example, defines "incongruity" in one place as "a conflict between some mental input and the framework into which that input is received,"[3] and then proceeds to explore examples of surprised expectations as models of incongruity. But not just anything that is unexpected, not just anything whose occurrence (like an unseasonable hot spell) is improbable, is by that fact alone an incongruity. I may have expected my daughter when the telephone rang, but when the call turns out to be from my son instead, I would register mild surprise but hardly by speaking, impressively, of an "incongruity" in my experience. There are so many kinds of "conflict" in the world that a broad definition of incongruity in terms of (unspecified) conflict would lead us to find incongruities everywhere. We would seem to swim in "incongruity." Still, unless the incongruities are uncommon enough to be treated as exceptional, they will not stand out as deviations from norms of a distinctively interesting kind. Somehow, if incongruities are no longer outnumbered decisively by garden-variety regularities and congruences, they lose something essential to their conception. I once took the two-year-old son of some friends on a walk through his neighborhood. He had just learned, more or less, the concept of broken and he spoke the word over and over again as he pointed to almost everything, a snapped twig on the sidewalk, a white spot of bird dropping on the curb, a loose bumper, a scratched fender on a parked car. The world for him was a thoroughly "broken place" and he reveled in its manifest imperfections.

Morreall gives us an example of an absurdity: Roentgen's accidental discovery of X-rays when he noticed to his surprise that a screen glowed when the cathode rays were discharging. "Here was a phenomenon Roentgen did not expect, and which he had no way of explaining."[4] But what Roentgen discovered was not an incongruity in the sense that it conflicted with what was known. Rather it was simply a new datum that Roentgen found surprising. What he just noticed should not be called an incongruity just because he was surprised to discover it. The more striking incongruity perhaps is that between the importance of the discovery and the lack of effort and understanding that led to making it.

Two objects are incongruous when taken together if one does not match, or fit, or measure up to the other (where the latter is a standard),

[3] John Morreall, "Funny Ha-Ha, Funny Strange, and Other Reactions to Incongruity," in *The Philosophy of Laughter and Humor*, ed. J. Morreall (Albany: State University of New York Press, 1987), p. 190.
[4] Ibid., p. 192.

or when one is discrepant with the other, or discordant, or anomalous, or disproportionate. In principle, there is hardly any limit on the type of objects that may stand in the relation of incongruence with one another, but the following list contains some of the more interesting varieties: efforts may be disproportionate to results; objects and actions may fail to satisfy relevant standards of appropriateness; appearance may fail to match—and may even distort or conceal—truth, as pretense may conflict with reality and ambition with capacity; expectations may lead to extreme disappointment; instrumentalities may be inadequate to achieve goals, or hypotheses to constitute explanations; concepts may clash with the objects subsumed under them. D. H. Munro might as well be speaking of incongruity in general when he defines what he calls "the inappropriate" as "the linking of disparates, the collision of different mental spheres, the obtrusion into one context of what belongs in another."[5]

So far, what we have said of the incongruous we could also say of the absurd. It is important to note, however, that the absurd and the incongruous are not identical and interchangeable. The absurd is a species of the incongruous but not all incongruities, even when abstracted from their serious contexts and responded to playfully, are absurd. Residents of Arizona could hardly imagine a more incongruous sight than that which greeted them after an unprecedented Christmas Eve snowfall in 1987: the usual assortment of cactus plants—saguaros, prickly pears, yucca, cholla, and all—covered with snow! Surely that was an incongruous juxtaposition, but there was no point in calling it "absurd," and no one did. Clashing colors, say a shocking pink blouse with electric orange skirt, are incongruous, but again there is no tendency to judge them "absurd." What further feature then must an incongruity possess in order properly to be described as absurd?

The primary difference between absurdity and other incongruity is that absurdity somehow reflects on *reason*, applying paradigmatically to that which seems patently unreasonable or rationally unintelligible. The concept obviously does not apply therefore to snow on cactuses, or to clashing colors, or to ordinary mild surprises. Moreover, the absurd seems to differ in degree from other irrationalities, being that which is extravagantly, wondrously, or incomprehensibly irrational, a description that would not apply to garden-variety mistakes, false but plausible beliefs ("near misses"), or simple misunderstandings. Absurdity is irrationality with a flair.

It is tempting at this point to declare that it is the absurdity of an incongruity that makes it comical (when it *is* comical), and not just its generic nature as incongruous. After all, such incongruities as cacophonous or dis-

[5] D. H. Monro, *Argument of Laughter* (Notre Dame, Ind.: University of Notre Dame Press, 1963), p. 235. I have profited from this useful book.

sonant noises, clashing colors, and snow-covered cactuses are neither absurd nor funny. We must, however, be very careful here. These examples of unfunny and nonabsurd incongruities also have other attention-directing characteristics that may interfere with the isolating of their component incongruities, and prevent their comic character from being properly noticed and naturally appreciated. Snow on cactuses is strikingly beautiful, and the beauty absorbs our attention and distracts from our notice of incongruity. Similarly, clashing colors and dissonant chords evoke negative responses. As long as we are reacting to perceived ugliness or painful impact on the senses, we will be distracted from the notice of incongruity that would otherwise, in splendid abstraction, seem funny.

How else can we explain the common reaction of amusements at perceptual incongruities that do not implicate the standards of rationality, the sight, for example, perhaps from behind, of a very tall and thin person walking with a very short and dumpy companion?[6] It happens all the time, and seldom fails to bring an amused smile to the face of an observer. Another example, attributed by Eastman to the 1930s radio comedian, Abe Martin, is the observation that there is no sight more amusing than that of a full beard over a sheet in bed.[7] Morreall imagines that he would laugh at the unexpected sight of a large orange pumpkin in his bath tub.[8] There is no affront to reason in these examples, but also no striking beauty or ugliness, no sensuous discomfort, or other distraction. When we can focus easily on the incongruity without the distraction, we seem (at least in a significant number of examples) to be naturally amused. Why that should be remains a mystery, and one that will remain perplexing even after the less mysterious comic appeal of the absurd has been explained.

Examples of nonabsurd incongruities when they amuse us at all (and there are many that fail altogether, at least at first sight, to amuse) characteristically evoke amused smiles. Genuine absurdities, on the other hand, can seem much more profoundly comic, and even when not profound can evoke snorts, chortles, and belly laughs. Other absurdity is not particularly funny, but nevertheless pleases us in a noncomic way precisely because it is absurd. We have before us then a number of categories: (1) nonabsurd incongruity that fails to amuse because it is striking in some other way, for example, beautiful, ugly, or painful (snow-covered cactuses, clashing colors); (2) nonabsurd incongruity that tickles the mind precisely because of its incongruous juxtapositions even without absurdity, and typically evokes the smile of appreciative but mild amusement (e.g., at the appear-

---

[6] See James Sully, *Essay on Laughter* (London: Longmans, Green, 1903), who uses this as a standard instance of comic incongruity.

[7] Eastman, *Laughter*, p. 49.

[8] Herbert Spencer, "A New Theory of Laughter," in *The Philosophy of Laughter and Humor*, ed. John Morreall (Albany: State University of New York Press, 1987), p. 130.

ance of Mutt and Jeff); (3) funny absurdity that delights the mind, paradoxically, by making no sense itself at all (e.g., a shaggy dog story or an
Irish bull) or by showing up something else as pointless, futile, disproportionate, baselessly pretentious, or otherwise ridiculous; and (4) absurdity
that is not funny, but nevertheless pleases us in a valuable noncomic way
precisely because it is absurd.

Examples now follow of the third and fourth categories. Category 3 is
easy and prototypical. Funny absurdity is a familiar and substantial subclass
of humor (some have claimed it is the *only* class of humor). One absurdly
funny situation that rarely fails to draw a laugh is that in which an inept
person tries to tell a funny story but fails, thus evincing in a ridiculous way
his own futility and ineptitude. The disparity between goal or expectation,
on the one hand, and inadequate or unsuccessful efforts, on the other, is so
manifest in the failed attempt, that it produces laughter as a kind of afterthought. This is especially likely when there is an embarrassed silence followed by an acknowledging remark from the speaker than breaks the tension, for example, "That was a joke." To be effective, shaggy dog stories
require long, drawn-out tellings, so they often fail in the comic way just
described. But when they succeed they are the clearest examples of the
sheer comic delight that utter irrationality can produce in us, especially
when it catches us by surprise.

> A man enters an elegant bakery shop on Fifth Avenue and makes a special
> order, with down payments, of a multitier frosted cake baked in the shape of
> the letter S. The skeptical baker complains that the ordered cake is too big,
> and that its awkward shape will require that a specially made tin plate be or-
> dered, at considerable cost. "Don't worry," says the customer, "I'm in no
> hurry, and I don't care about the expense." A week later on the appointed day,
> he returns to pick up the cake, but he is disappointed at what he finds. The S
> is a script S. He had failed to mention that he wanted a capital S. The following
> week he returns again, but once more changes his order. Now he wants a
> German gothic S. It takes a month to make and bake that cake, but alas, it is
> an italic S—all wrong. But the customer's patience is inexhaustible. He gladly
> pays the expenses of a German medieval historian to consult on the exact shape
> of the gothic S, and a new tinsmith to make the mold. Further difficulties in
> producing the exact shade of pink frosting lead to further delays and false
> starts, but six months after the original order was made a satisfactory cake is
> produced. The customer, beside himself with delight, writes a check for
> $23,479.21. The equally delighted store owner thanks him warmly and asks,
> "Can you transport it yourself or should I box it here and have it delivered to
> your address?" "Oh, don't bother wrapping it," says the customer, "I'll eat it
> here."

To be maximally effective, endless complications should be introduced,
and the telling should take at least ten full minutes, so that the surprise

ending can drive home the self-defeating pointlessness of the cake-eater's conduct, which itself produces delight and amazement in the listener.

Irish bulls are a lesser comic form but they provide another example of the delight caused to us when we are in a playful mood, and someone appears to defy logic (the ultimate undefiable authority) by affirming something extravagantly irrational (usually logically contradictory). The mayor of Dublin some fifty years ago complained that "Things have come to a fine pass, when little children, not yet old enough to walk nor talk, go running through the streets of Dublin, blaspheming their Maker." We smile not at some incongruous image but rather at an image that it is logically impossible to form, and the sheer irrationality of the description fills us with delight.

The other subclass of the third category of incongruity, in which the story is not itself senseless but shows up the false pretenses or senselessness of something else outside the story, is illustrated by Herbert Spencer's account in his theory of humor of an imaginary occurrence. We can call it "the story of Spencer's goat":

> You are seated in a theatre, absorbed in the progress of an interesting drama. Some climax has been reached which has aroused your sympathies—say, a reconciliation between the hero and heroine, after a long and painful misunderstanding. . . . And now while you are contemplating the reconciliation with a pleasurable sympathy, there appears from behind the scenes a tame kid, which, having stared round at the audience, walks up to the lovers and sniffs at them. You cannot help joining in the roar which greets this contretemps.[9]

Spencer's primary concern is to explain the psychological mechanism of laughter rather than to account for the impression that the perceived event itself is funny, and he does that well enough in terms of the release of tension through the discharge via alternative channels of accumulated "nervous energy." Not all release of tension, however, even when accompanied by laughter, involves any sense of the comic. We laugh after escaping danger; we laugh from sheer delight at good news; we laugh from embarrassment, and from a dozen other causes, only one of which is the perception that some event is funny. What is it then, we might ask, that made the caprine contretemps comic? The full answer is no doubt complex, but a key element surely is the deflation of the sense of seriousness and importance, both of the fictitious affairs depicted in the drama and (especially) of the audience's absorption in them. Suddenly the goat arrives, representing a kind of reality principle, natural and unpretentious, going about sniffing, chewing, and evacuating, and making the contrivances of the human beings seem phony and their vaunted rationality oppressive.

---

[9] Herbert Spencer, "The Physiology of Laughter," from his *Essays on Education* (London: Dent, 1911). Reprinted in Morreall, *Philosophy*, p. 106.

The escape of diverted nervous energy through alternative channels may explain the resultant burst of laughter, but the unexpected perception of human absurdity explains why the object of the laughter seemed funny. I have seen similar effects at baseball and football games in huge stadiums when suddenly a stray sea gull interrupts the action by strutting about the outfield utterly unconcerned with the events intently observed by fifty thousand spectators. Players and umpires surrender some of their dignity to chase it away, but it returns seeming even more dignified and disdainful, to resume the "important" search for worms in the grass. The game, which until that point had seemed so structured and rational, seems, during one comic interlude, to be ridiculous.

Comic absurdity commonly occurs, although this is not its only pattern, when two things come into sharp contrast and one of them is, at least for the moment, made to look ridiculous in comparison with the other. The humor in the cases of Spencer's goat and the wayward sea gull leads us to laugh on the part of rationality, with its unexpected animal exemplars, at the affairs of human beings, suddenly and temporarily perceived in contrast as ridiculous. In other cases, we allow ourselves, like naughty children, to defy the authority of reason, and to laugh in (protective playfulness) at majestic rationality itself. Typically, it is not clear, when irrational behavior strikes us as funny, which of the contrasting elements we are laughing *with* and which we are laughing *at*. (*Don Quixote* remains ambiguous in this respect, which is a source of its fascination.) Sometimes our identifications switch back and forth between the standard and the deviating behavior, or else rest impartially at a point between them, exulting in the sheer incongruity. (Since one of the contrasting elements is the standard of rationality itself, this incongruity is also absurd.) These comic situations are the most absurd, and to many of us perhaps the most funny.

One of the early talking films was a short comedy of Stan Laurel and Oliver Hardy. These two veteran film comedians played the role of door to door salesmen. They begin their day's work by parking their car in front of the first house on the block, and with bouncy optimism carry the goods to the door, primp themselves, and ring the door bell. The door is opened by their first, and as it turns out last, customer of the day, an irascible Scot in full regalia, and with a rich Scottish brogue. After a brief exchange the householder slams the door in the salesmen's faces. Crestfallen, Laurel and Hardy return to their car, then rally their spirits, and go back for another try. Slowly the crescendo of escalating hostility builds up. This time Hardy puts his foot in the door. When the Scot slams it again, it causes great pain to Hardy, and also unhinges the door to the Scotsman's rage. The Scot turns his fury next on to the salesmen's car, injuring his own foot by kicking the tires. After Laurel and Hardy remove the unhinged house door and slam it to the ground, the Scot begins dismantling the car. In one scene the "customer" is shown busily at work removing first the fenders and then the hood, while the salesmen in the background are removing his window shutters preparatory to smashing the glass. By now the action has speeded up, and the movements of the actors resemble that of mechanical dolls in speeded-up films, busily engaged in the utterly mad task of destroying one another's property long after their initial grievances have been forgotten. Could anything be more irrational? Perhaps I was in a peculiarly risible mood when I saw the film, but as the excitement mounted on the screen, I was bent over in paroxysms of laughter. It was the funniest thing I had ever seen.

But this is the way the world could end. Opposing armies might be un-leashed against one another so as to protect the national honor of their countries. A military impasse could then be reached, at which point the saturation bombing of civilian centers is undertaken by one side. In retali-ation the other side drops a demonstration nuclear bomb, incidentally (perhaps inadvertently—who knows? who cares?) killing one hundred mil-lion people. Instantly a retaliatory raid of massive proportions is launched, and the mad dance of unreason, so comical when looked at playfully in abstraction from its costs, reels on to its wild climax, the death of all civili-zation. The funny element in this tale, the extravagant disproportion be-tween ends and means and the self-defeating pointlessness of everyone's conduct, is precisely that which Laurel and Hardy treated in costless ab-straction in their film and made us laugh uproariously at. Why is unreason so funny? Do we dare take irrationality unseriously?

The fourth category distinguished earlier is unfunny absurdity that pleases in some other—noncomic—way precisely because it is absurd. The first example of this is the famous short story of O. Henry about the im-poverished married couple who wished to buy each other Christmas pres-ents. The husband sells his most valuable possession, his watch, in order to buy a handsome comb for his wife's hair. Independently, the wife sells her beautiful hair to buy a chain for her husband's cherished watch. All this ingenuity and devotion comes to nothing in the end. Worse than that, it comes to a net loss for both parties, who now have, in effect, traded prized possessions for useless objects. What an absurd result! If it had all been the work of one person ineffectively pursuing his own interest, it would be a tale of utter self-defeating irrationality. Insofar as it is *as if* the work of one irrational planner, the narrative is a story of absurdity. It is a charming tale that gives the reader great pleasure, as she savors the irony in "the neat symmetry by which the two acts of self-sacrifice cancel each other out."[10] For all of that, the story is not the slightest bit funny, and the reader whose response is to guffaw at the ironic twist at the end, has probably identified

---

[10] Munro, *Argument of Laughter*, p. 37.

too sentimentally with the fictitious couple and succumbed to a kind of hysteria on their behalf. That would be almost as inappropriate a response as laughter at the plight of poor Oedipus, whose luck was no better.

A different but similarly ironic example is the film *The Treasure of the Sierra Madre*, which is about a trio of adventurers who undergo almost Sisyphean travails, dangers, conflicts, and betrayals to find a fortune by gold-prospecting in a remote mountainous area. Having triumphed over every challenge, the surviving prospector, played by Walter Huston, discovers that bandits, repelled in their efforts to steal his burros, have emptied the pouches carried by the burros, and—in their ignorance—thereby spilled the gold dust into the winds, to be scattered irrecoverably. Immediately appreciative of the irony, although deeply and desperately disappointed, Huston can only laugh at the absurdity of this result of his life's labors. He does not weep; he laughs, at first a chuckle, then a roar, then a torrent of head-tossing hysteria. There is nothing funny in that moving and memorable scene. The audience, more detached from the painful loss than the fictitious character could possibly be, will be moved in a distinctive way by the perceived ironic absurdity. The loss is so moving and the character's sad plight so riveting that the playfulness requisite for comic amusement will be impossible. In this event the absurdity stirs its own distinctive emotion; humor is blocked but grief is mitigated by the vivid and independently valued perception of the absurdity.

The final example of the fourth category is entirely different. In one of his most famous cartoons for the *New Yorker*,[11] Charles Addams created a memorable scene of a downhill skier proceeding on his way while behind him his two ski tracks diverge, one going on each side of a large pine tree that had been in his path. In the foreground a stationary skier is looking back over his shoulder observing the scene with a look of blank astonishment on his face. It is a simple drawing but one that is complex in its effects. The impossibility divergent ski tracks introduce a jarring element of incongruity into the pleasant winter scene, and of course the incongruity is an absurd one since what has apparently happened *could not possibly have happened*. It would be irrational to believe that the skier passed over the fifty-foot pine tree so that the whole tree came between his legs, or that he collided with the tree, bending it almost to the ground as he passed over it so that it sprung back elastically immediately thereafter, or that either the skier or the tree or both became intangible ghosts for the moment so that they could pass right through one another without impact. All of these things are impossible, yet the evidence of our senses suggests that one of them *must* have happened!

The drawing is fascinating to ponder and pleasantly absorbing to con-

[11] *New Yorker*, 1940.

template, yet if I am not mistaken, it is not particularly funny. There may be some intermixed elements of the comic in the cartoon, but they do not explain the drawing's primary appeal, which lies in its ingenious exhibition of absurdity to be treasured for its own sake. The comic elements in the cartoon are probably best explained by the role of the other figure in the drawing, the astonished observer. We often find it funny to observe the confusion in the face of a person who has been made the butt of a practical joke. We can see that the person's belief system has come into head-on collision with some new experiences that do not fit in. To say that the new experiences are "discordant," "anomalous," or "disproportionate" is to understate the matter. The observer's mind is flooded with incongruity that he knows not how to process. His mental states are not merely incongruent, they are contradictory, and that is absurd!

The cartoon is more complicated, however. We are in the picture too, and the joke is equally on us. The observer's confusion fails to be all that amusing when we ourselves focus on the puzzle that generated it. If we knew in advance what magical manipulation had misled the puzzled observer, we could laugh at the incongruous linking of disparates in *his* mind. But as far as we know, there is no explanation of that sort to be found, and we are equally "victims" of the joke and that is not so funny.

Nonetheless, the situation is pleasing to us in a predominately unfunny way. Part of our pleasure may be simply the admiration we feel for the imagination and ingenuity of the cartoonist. Unless we are overcome with envy, it is always pleasant to appreciate masterful technique for its own sake, and indeed that is an element in our appreciation of art generally that is difficult to disentangle from our genuinely aesthetic response to the art object or music itself. If we found nothing in the cartoon itself to enjoy, however, except grounds for admiring the skill of the cartoonist, we could have no coherent conception of what the skill is. We admire the artist because of the value we attach to what he has produced. Our appreciation of that end product then cannot be merely a reflection of our admiration for the skills that produced it.

It would not be surprising to discover that purely theoretical absurdity is generally not so funny as practical absurdity. We laugh at self-defeating action, disproportionate means, pointless activities, transparent futilities, and the like. These are ways of behaving that violate the rules of practical reason. Believing against the evidence, even having contradictory beliefs, are instances of believing (not acting) contrary to the rules of theoretical reason. We do not invest energy in them. Beliefs are not goals or targets of aspiration. We do not commonly strive to achieve them or make them part of our conception of well-being. Our practical choices, on the other hand, determine more directly how we are to live. They are in a deeper way voluntary, and linked to our strivings. We produce more "nervous energy" (as

Spencer called it) in connection with them, and when that energy is diverted by absurd obtrusions it seeks release in laughter.

We have considered enough examples now to see that absurdity as such, when it can be playfully detached from the experience of which it is a part, whether it be repugnant to theoretical or practical reason or both, and whether it is mixed with elements of admiration for an artist's wit or not, can be amusing, and that even when amusement is not its consequence, it can please an observer in other ways. I can only make speculative suggestions of how that can be so. One clue comes from the contrast between absurdity, which violates standards of rationality, and nonabsurd incongruities resulting from the violation of standards of other kinds. Violations of standards of dignity and decorum, for example, may or may not be absurd, though they are always incongruous (if only with the standards they violate), and frequently funny. Indeed, these actions can be funny even when not absurd, as when a dignified dandy slips and is forced to tumble through a series of graceless and awkward gyrations to keep his balance. This class of things can overlap with the absurd, and be all the more funny for it, as when the pompously dignified person through a slip of the tongue utters a spoonerism—as the Rev. Mr. Spooner himself did when he announced from his Oxford pulpit that the following week the congregation would be visited by "our queer dean," and remained unaware that he did not say "our dear Queen" as he had intended. It is possible for the comic response in humor of this class to be directed at the standard itself (this is often mischievous or "naughty") or at the person who deviated from it, or as we have seen, first at one then at the other. The same can be said of comic deviations from standards of conventional propriety of other kinds.

Violations of standards of morality, however, insofar as they involve cheating, fraud, violence, pain, and suffering, are not likely to be funny. In some unusual cases we might laugh (although indignation is the more typical response) from the point of view of the standard against the scoundrel, and interpret the malefactor's deviation from the standard to be in some way laughably absurd. But insofar at least as we accept the moral standard in question, we never laugh from the point of view of the violator against *it*. Immorality is not a laughing matter.

Sometimes deviations from standards of rationality cause laughter directed at the absurd deviator. Inadvertent Irish bulls are one case in point. Legend has it that Yogi Berra, when told by his dinner party host that it was now only sixty minutes before game time, and the stadium in Baltimore was one hundred miles away, replied complacently, "Don't worry; I'll drive 90 all the way." Another time, speaking of a restaurant suggested by a friend, Berra remarked, "Oh, nobody goes there any more; it's too crowded."

On other occasions, and this perhaps is what most needs explaining, we actually dare laugh at reason itself, and glory in the absurdity that comes from its violation. We laugh slyly and mischievously sometimes, but at others more whole-heartedly, at what we understand to be violations of the canons of theoretical reasoning in matters of belief and affirmation, or the standards of practical reasonableness in matters of behavior. Violation of the rules of theoretical reasoning amuse us, as we have seen, in the case of Irish bulls (logical errors), mathematical errors (the Berra story), physical impossibilities (the properly comic elements in the predominately unfunny Addams cartoon), grossly inadequate explanations, and monumental irrelevancies. An example of the inadequate explanation category is the story of the prideful mouse. A lion moves through the jungle intercepting lesser creatures and terrorizing them by roaring mightily and saying, "I'm so big and strong, why are you so weak and puny?" One by one, deer, dogs, zebras, and giraffes flee in mortal fear. Then the lion encounters the mouse. "I'm so big and strong, why are you so weak and puny?" he roars. Whereupon the mouse stands up on his hind feet and replies, "*I've* been sick."

The best example I know of the monumental irrelevancy is from a scene in Charles Dickens' *Little Dorritt*.

> The major characteristics discoverable by the stranger in Mr. F's Aunt were extreme severity and grim taciturnity, sometimes interrupted by a propensity to offer remarks in a deep warning voice, which being totally uncalled for by anybody, and traceable to no association of ideas, confounded and terrified the mind. Mr. F's Aunt may have thrown in these observations on some system of her own, and it may have been ingenious, or even subtle: but the key to it was wanted.
>
> The nearly-served and well cooked dinner . . . began with some soup, some fried soles . . . and a dish of potatoes. The conversation still turned [on the subject of] the receipt of rents. Mr. F's Aunt, after regarding the company for ten minutes with a malevolent gaze, delivered the following fearful remark:
>
> "When we lived at Henley, Barnes's gander was stole by tinkers."
>
> Mr. Pancks courageously nodded his head and said "All right, ma'am."[12]

As we have seen, affronts to rationality are likely to be more deeply comic when the rules of *practical* reason are violated, because we characteristically make our greatest investment of hopes, purposes, energies, and fears in the practical realm, the world of potential activity being the one in which we most consciously live and breathe. Violations of practical reason can amaze and delight us, as we have seen, in cases where actors use disproportionately great or small means to their ends, in cases of utterly point-

[12] Charles Dickens, *Little Dorritt* (Harmonsdsworth, Middlesex: Penguin Books, 1967), p. 199.

less activity (as it turns out in the end) as in the shaggy S-cake story, in cases of the exposure of groundless pretension (Spencer's goat), and in examples of transparent futility, as in the Laurel and Hardy microcosmic analogue of irreversible destructive madness. Our identities fluctuate back and forth in these examples, sometimes, for instance, leading us to laugh in an Olympian way at the follies of Laurel and Hardy, sometimes shifting impishly to the other side where, free from real-world costs, we are able to frolic in unrestrained lunacy with those madcap nitwits, before shifting finally to a kind of neutral ground where our comic focus is on the relation of nonconformity to reason itself, which we find ourselves (temporarily of course) relishing for its own sake.

The best clue to the nature of absurd humor may be found, I suspect, in the nature of play and the attitude of playfulness. There are some things the small child must not—dare not—do. She must not defy her parents or other adult authorities delegated by them; she must not strike, kick, bite, or scratch her parents, or for that matter anyone else; she must obey certain elementary rules of prudence, keeping her hands out of fires and not running in front of moving cars, and the like. These and similar requirements can be seen from the child's point of view to be burdensome constraints, and nothing brings greater delight to the child than to be suddenly released from them. That might lead to serious consequences in the real world, harm to self and others. But in her playful imagination, with squeals and giggles, the child might pound daddy in the chest, challenge his authority by shouting "No!" in response to every parental affirmation or imperative, then squealing in mischievous merriment and fleeing from (playfully fancied) parental retribution. In a way, the rules of practical (and of course theoretical) reason are the ultimate authorities, destined eventually to replace the authority of the parents, and to remain forever immune to serious (nonplayful) challenge. How delightful it is then when we can for an interval "suspend our disbelief" and glory in an ultimate liberation even from these rules and restrictions![13]

---

[13] G. K. Chesterton's description of Lewis Carroll captures the nostalgic quality of childhood playfulness of which Carroll was the master evoker, and its appeal to the permanent child in most adults:

We know what Lewis Carroll was in daily life: he was a singularly serious and conventional don, universally respected, but very much of a pedant and something of a philistine. Thus his strange double life in earth and dreamland emphasizes the idea that lies at the back of nonsense—the idea of *escape*, of escape into a world where things are not fixed horribly in an eternal appropriateness, where apples grow on pear trees, and any odd man you meet may have three legs. Lewis Carroll, living one life in which he would have thundered morally against anyone who walked on the wrong plot of grass, and another life in which he would cheerfully call the sun green and the moon blue, was by his very divided nature, his own foot on both worlds, a perfect type of the position of modern nonsense. His wonderland is a country populated by insane mathematicians. We

Irrational conduct in real life usually has bad consequences for someone or another. (Is that a tautology?) We will always have difficulty therefore in pulling out the grossly irrational element and responding to it playfully. But in fiction and free-wheeling imagination we can focus on absurdity as such, without any difficult psychological exertions or self-manipulations, and when we do we can experience once more the same emancipation as we once found in childish play, the same defiant embracing of the ridiculous, the same effort to escape as when we once struggled squirming and giggling, against our recapture by reality. In one's imaginary identifications one can let oneself go entirely and smash the Scotsman's windows and the salesmen's car. Here is ultimate liberty at no cost. The world does not come to an end. Nor is any real car dismantled or doors torn off hinges. We are laughing at reason now, in a way the ultimate impiety in a rational being.[14]

Of course, in real life we cannot often extract the ridiculous from a mad situation and focus our response playfully on it; there are usually too many dreadfully serious matters inextricably connected with it. The carefree context of childhood no longer exists. But in our adult imaginations we can abstract the absurdity, embrace it, and glory in it. The striking contrast between our impiety and the impersonal authority of reason (which is what absurdity is) tickles us into laughter.

We would do well to remind ourselves in conclusion that while it is often impossible totally to detach the absurdity from the serious elements in a situation, we can often partially succeed in doing so, in which case we often respond to it with an attitude part way between seriousness and playfulness, or even an attitude that is serious and playful both at once. This response, in turn, when it has certain other qualifying characteristics, is sometimes called irony, itself an appreciative but impure reaction to the incongruous aspects of a situation. But an account of this subtle attitude, and the range of circumstances that evoke and warrant it, must await another time and place.

---

feel the whole is an escape into a world of masquerade; we feel that if we could pierce their disguises, we might discover that Humpty Dumpty and the March Hare were Professors and Doctors of Divinity enjoying a mental holiday. (G. K. Chesterton, *The Defendant* [London: R. B. Johnson, 1901], pp. 44–45.)

[14] This remark puts me in sharp disagreement with George Santayana, who wrote that while absurd incongruities when they capture us by surprise can be momentarily pleasing (as in the manner of "a jack-in-the-box popping from nowhere into our plodding thoughts") nevertheless leave "an undertone of disgust" or "a certain aftertaste of foolishness." That is because "man, being a rational animal, can like absurdity no better than he can like hunger or cold." See George Santayana, *The Sense of Beauty* (New York: Scribner's, 1896), pp. 245–58. Reprinted in Morreall, *Philosophy*, p. 92. I think that Santayana underestimates the persistence of the playful child in the adult "rational animal."